NYĀYA THEORY OF KNOWLEDGE

NVĀYA THEORY OF KNOWLEDGE

By

S.C. CHATTERJEE

BHARATIYA KALA PRAKASHAN

Delhi : : (India)

Revised Edition : 2018

Published by
BHARATIYA KALA PRAKASHAN
3421-A, IInd Floor, Narang Colony,
Tri Nagar, Delhi-110035
Ph. : 27393083
Web : www.bkpbooks.com
E-mail : sales.bkpbooks@gmail.com

NVĀYA THEORY OF KNOWLEDGE

ISBN : 978-81-8090-146-1

Printed by :
G.S. Offset, Delhi

CONTENTS

Chapter III

Chapter IV

II. PERCEPTION AS A METHOD OF KNOWLEDGE (*PRATYAKṢA-PRAMĀṆA*)

Chapter V

Chapter VI

Chapter VII

Chapter VIII

Chapter IX

III. THEORY OF INFERENCE (*ANUMĀNA-PRAMĀṆA*)

Chapter X

Chapter XVIII

Chapter XIX

PREFACE

The history of Indian Philosophy is a record of many different forms and types of philosophical thought. There is hardly any system in the history of Western Philosophy which has not its parallel in one or other of the systems of Indian philosophy. But of the Indian systems, the Vedānta has received the greatest attention and it has sometimes passed as the only Indian system worth the name. This is but natural. The Vedānta with its sublime idealism has an irresistible appeal to the moral and religious nature of man. It has been, and will ever remain, a stronghold of spiritualism in life and philosophy. It is like one of "the great living wells, which keep the freshness of the eternal, and at which man must rest, get his breath, refresh himself." "The paragon of all monistic systems," says William James, "is the Vedānta philosophy of Hindustan." Although we have not such a sublime monism in the Nyāya, yet its contribution to philosophy is not really inferior in any way. In fact, the other systems—the Vedānta not excepted—have been greatly influenced by its logical and dialectical technicalities. In their later developments all the systems consider the Naiyāyika as the most powerful opponent and try to satisfy his objections. The understanding of their arguments and theories presupposes, therefore, the knowledge of the Nyāya.

As a system of a realism, the Nyāya deserves special study to show that Idealism was not the only philosophical creed of ancient India. Then, as a system which contains a thorough refutation of the other schools, it should be studied before one accepts the validity of other views, if only to ascertain how far those views can satisfy the acid test of the Nyāya criticisms and deserve to be accepted. But above all, as a thorough going realistic view of the universe, it supplies an important Eastern parallel to the triumphant modern

Realism of the West, and contains the anticipations as well as possible alternatives of many contemporary realistic theories. The importance of the Nyāya is, therefore, as great for the correct understanding of ancient Indian philosophy, as for the evaluation of modern Western Philosophy.

The theory of knowledge is the most important part—in fact, the very foundation of the Nyāya system. This book is an attempt to give a complete account of the Nyāya theory of knowledge. It is a study of the Nyāya theory of knowledge in comparison with the rival theories of other systems, Indian and Western, and a critical estimation of its worth. Though theories of knowledge of the Vedānta and other schools have been partially studied in this way by some, there has as yet been no such systematic, critical and comparative treatment of the Nyāya epistemology. The importance of such a study of Indian realistic theories of knowledge can scarcely be overrated in this modern age of Realism.

The scope of the book is limited to the history of the Nyāya philosophy beginning with the *Nyāya-Ṣūtra* of Gautama and ending with the syncretic works of Annaṁ Bhaṭṭa, Viśvanātha and others. It does not, however, concern itself directly with the historical development of the Nyāya. There are ample evidences to show that Nyāya as an art of reasoning is much older that the *Nyāya-Sūtra*. We find references to such an art under the names of *Nyāya* and *vākovākya* in some of the early Upaniṣads like the *Chāndogya* (vii. 1.2) and the *Subāla* (ii). It is counted among the *upāṅgas* or subsidiary parts of the Veda (*vide Caraṇavyūha*, ii; *Nyāya-Sūtra-Vṛtti* 1.1.1). It is mentioned under the names of *ānvīkṣikī* and *tarkaśāstra* in some of the oldest chapters of the *Mahābhārata* (*vide sabhā, anuśāsana* and *śānti parvas*). We need not multiply such references. Those here given show that the Nyāya as an art or science of reasoning existed in India long before the time of Gautama, the author of the *Nyāya-Sūtra*. As a matter of fact, it has been admitted by Vātsyāyana, Uddyotakara, Jayanta Bhaṭṭa and others that Gautama was not so much the founder of the Nyāya as its chief exponent who first gave an elaborate and systematic account of an already existing branch of knowledge, called *nyāya*, in the form of *sūtras* or aphorisms. It is in these *sūtras* that the Nyāya was developed into a realistic philosophy on a logical basis. What was so long mere logic or an art of debate became a theory of the knowledge of reality. It is for this reason that the present work is based on the *Nyāya-Sūtra* and its main commentaries.

So far as the account of the ancient Nyāya is concerned, my sources of information are mainly the *Nyāya-Sūtra, Nyāya-Bhāṣya, Nyāyavārttika Nyāyavārttikatāparyaṭīkā, Tātparyapariśuddhi, Nyāyamañjarī* and *Nyāyasūtravṛtti*. In my account of the modern and syncretist schools of the Nyāya, I have mainly made use of Gaṅgeśa's *Tattvacintāmaṇi* with the commentary of Mathurānātha, Jagadīsa's *Tarkāmṛta,* Annaṁ Bhaṭṭa's *Tarkasaṁgraha* and *Dīpikā*, Varadarāja's *Tarkikarakṣā*, Keśava Miśra's *Tarkabhāṣā* and Viśvanātha's *Kārikāvalī* with *Siddhāntamuktāvalī* and *Dinakarī.* I have also consulted several English expositions of Indian philosophy, like Dr. Jhā's *Nyāya Philosophy of Gautama*, Sir B. N. Seal's *Positive Sciences of the Ancient Hindus*, Sir S. Radhakrishnan's *Indian Philosophy*, Dr. D.M. Datta's *Six Ways of Knowing,* Professor Keith's *Indian Logic and Atomism*, Dr. S.N. Dasgupta's *History of Indian Philosophy,* and MM. Kuppusvāmī śāstrī's *A Primer of Indian Logic.* My indebtedness to these and other works has been indicated by footnotes in the proper places.

The method of exposition adopted in the book is comparative and critical. I have always tried to explain and develop the ideas and theories of Indian philosophy in terms of the corresponding ideas and concepts of Western Philosophy. The great danger of this is the tendency to read, consciously or unconsciously, Western ideas into Indian philosophy. I have taken all possible care to guard against the imposition of foreign ideas on the genuine thoughts and concepts of Indian philosophy. As a general rule, the different parts of the Nyāya theory of knowledge have been first explained and compared with those of the other systems of Indian philosophy. For the sake of completeness, the Indian theories have sometimes been elaborated in such details as to give one the impression of prolixity. I have then undertaken a discussion of the Indian views from the standpoint of Western philosophy. No attempt has been made to affiliate the Indian views with parallel views in Western philosophy. Such an attempt cannot surely do justice to the originality and individuality of Indian thought. While bringing out the points of agreement between Indian and Western philosophy, their difference and distinction have not been ignored and passed over. I have not been able to support or justify the Indian theories on all points. It has been found necessary to modify them in some places and supplement them in the light of Western philosophy. At the same time, I have duly emphasised the special contributions of Indian philosophy towards the solution of the problems of knowledge discussed in Western philosophy.

In conclusion, I take this opportunity to express my gratitude first to the late lamented Professor Henry Stephen, of revered memory, who by his life and teaching made the study of Western philosophy popular among Indian students and infused into my youthful mind the spirit of an intensive philosophical study. I have also to acknowledge my indebtedness to Sir B.N. Seal, who was a versatile genius and an eminent authority in Indian and Western philosophy, and from whom I received great inspiration and valuable guidance in the early days of my researches in Indian philosophy. I have to express further my deep sense of gratitude to Professor K.C. Bhattacharya, a profound thinker and astute metaphysician, who for some time held the George V Chair of Philosophy in the Calcutta University. It was my proud privilege to sit at his feet, and discuss and clear up some of the abstruse problems of logic and philosophy treated in this book. I have to acknowledge with thanks the great help I have received from MM. Pandit Sītārām śāstri, of the Calcutta University, while studying some original works of the Nyāya philosophy.

I have to express further my most grateful thanks to the great savant, Sir S. Radhakrishnan, George V Professor of Philosophy, Calcutta University, and Spalding Professor of Eastern Religions and Ethics, Oxford University, for the constant encouragement, help and guidance I have received from him in completing this work. My thanks are also due to my esteemed friend and talented writer, Dr. D.M. Datta of the Patna College, for reading considerable parts of the manuscript and for making valuable suggestions.

Author

ABBREVIATIONS

BP.	...	Bhāṣāpariccheda (Nirnaya Sagar edn.).
NB.	...	Nyāya-Bhāṣya.
NBT.	...	Nyāyabinduṭīkā (Bibliotheca Indica edn.).
NK.	...	Nyāyakandalī (Vizianagram edn.).
NL.	...	Nyāyalīlāvatī (Nirnaya Sagar edn.).
NM.	...	Nyāyamañjarī (Vizianagram edn.).
NS.	...	Nyāya-Sūtra.
NSV.	...	Nyāyasūtravṛtti.
NV.	...	Nyāyavārttika (Chowkhamba edn.).
NVT.	...	Nyāyavārttikatāparyaṭīkā (Do.).
NVTP.	...	Nyāyavārttikatāparyapariśuddhi (Bib. Ind. edn.).
PS.	...	Padārthadharmasaṁgraha (Chowkhamba edn.).
SC.	...	Siddhāntacandrikā (Nirnaya Sargar edn.).
SD.	...	Śāstradīpikā (Do.).
SM.	...	Siddhāntamuktāvalī (Do.).
SS.	...	Sārasaṁgraha (Benares edn.).
TB.	...	Tarkabhāṣā (Poona edn.).
TC.	...	Tattvacintāmaṇi (Bibliotheca Indica edn.).
TD.	...	Tattvadīpikā (Calcutta edn.)
TK.	...	Tarkakaumudī (Nirnaya Sagar edn.).
TKD.	...	Tattvakaumudī (Calcutta edn.).

TM.	...	Tarkāmṛta (Do.).
TR.	...	Tārkikarakṣā (Benares edn.).
TS.	...	Tarkasaṁgraha (Calcutta edn.).
TTS.	...	Tattvārthādhigama-Sūtra (Bib. Jain edn.).
VB.	...	Vyāsa-Bhāṣya.
VP.	...	Vedāntaparibhāṣā (Calcutta edn.)
VS.	...	Vaiśeṣika-Sūtra (Chowkhamba edn.).

INTRODUCTION

The Nyāya philosophy is primarily concerned with the conditions of valid thought and the means of acquiring a true knowledge of objects. Nyāya as a science lays down the rules and methods that are essentially necessary for a clear and precise understanding of all the materials of our knowledge as these are derived from observation and authority. With this end in view, the science of Nyāya deals with all the processes and methods that are involved, either directly or indirectly, in the right and consistent knowledge of reality. That this is so appears clearly from the common use of the word *ānvīkṣikī* as a synonym for the *Nyāyaśāstra*. The name *ānvīkṣikī* means the science of the processes and methods of a reasoned and systematic knowledge of objects, supervening on a vague understanding of them on the basis of mere perception and uncriticised testimony. In other words, it is the science of an analytic and reflective knowledge of objects in continuation of and as an advance on the unreflective general knowledge in which we are more receptive than critical. It is the mediated knowledge of the contents of faith, feeling and intuition. Accordingly, Nyāya (literally meaning methodical study) may be described as the science of the methods and conditions of valid thought and true knowledge of objects. In a narrow sense, however, *nyāya* is taken to mean the syllogistic type of inference, consisting of five propositions called its members or constituents.[1]

It should, however, be remarked here that the epistemological problem as to the methods and conditions of valid knowledge is

1. Pratijñādipañcakasamudāyatvaṁ nyāyatvam, *Dīdhiti* on TC., II, Chapter on Nyāya and Avayava.

neither the sole nor the ultimate concern of the Nyāya philosophy. Its ultimate end, like that of the other systems of Indian philosophy, is liberation, which is the *summum bonum* of our life. This highest good is conceived by the Nyāya as a state of pure existence which is free from both pleasure and pain. For the attainment of the highest end of our life, a true knowledge of objects is the sure and indispensable means. Hence, it is that the problem of knowledge finds an important place in the Nyāya philosophy.

But an enquiry into the conditions of valid thought and the methods of valid knowledge presupposes an account of the nature and forms of cognition or knowledge in general. It requires us also to consider the nature and method of valid knowledge in general and the nature and test of truth or validity in particular. Hence the preliminary questions that arise in the Nyāya theory of knowledge are: What is cognition or knowledge as such? What are its different forms? What is valid knowledge? What is meant by a method of valid knowledge in general? What do we mean by truth or validity? What is the test of truth, the measure of true knowledge, the standard of validity? What are the constituents or factors of valid knowledge?

It is a matter of historical interest to note here that, among other things, the problems of knowledge in general and those of the methods of valid knowledge in particular were brought home to the Naiyāyikas by the Buddhists and other sceptical thinkers of ancient India in the course of their scathing criticism of the realistic philosophy of Gautama.[1] They set at naught almost the whole of the Nyāya philosophy as an edifice built on sand. The Nyāya teaches that the highest good is attainable only through the highest

1. This is clear from the opening verse of Uddyotakara's *Nyāyavārttika* in which it is stated that the object of the *Vārttika* is to remove the misconceptions of the critics of Gautama's teaching even though it was well explained by the great commentator Vātsyāyana. In explaining this verse Vācaspati mentions the name of Dignāga, the great Buddhist logician, as one of the hard critics of Gautama's philosophy. In the *Nyāyavārttikatātparyaṭīkā* he has given a clear account of some of the difficulties raised by the Buddhists in connection with the question of *pramāṇa*.

knowledge. But the theory of knowledge in it is a vicious circle. It take upon itself the futile task of Kant's first Critique where he examines reason in order to prove the validity of thought and reason. "If it is the business of Kant in his *Critique of Pure Reason* to show how mathematics is possible, whose business is it to show how the *Critique of Pure Reason* itself is possible?"[1] With regard to the Nyāya theory of knowledge a similar question is asked by the Bauddha critics. It is pointed out by them that a criticism of knowledge must be made by the instrument under criticism and thereby presupposes the very thing in question. Thus the validity of knowledge is made to rest on the validity of the methods of knowledge. To maintain that our knowledge is true we must prove that it is really so, that it is derived from a valid method of knowledge which always gives us true knowledge and never leads to a false result. But, then, how are we to know the validity of that method of knowledge? From the nature of the case, the task is an impossible intellectual feat.

With regard to the knowledge of validity there are two possible alternatives. The validity of knowledge may be cognised by itself, *i.e.* be self-cognised. Or, the validity of one knowledge may be cognised by some other knowledge. The first alternative that knowledge cognises its own validity is inadmissible. Knowledge, according to the Nyāya, cognises objects that are distinct from and outside of itself. It cannot turn back on itself and cognise its own existence, far less its own validity. Hence, no knowledge can be the test of its own truth. The second alternative, that the validity of any knowledge is tested by some other knowledge, is not less objectionable. The second knowledge can at best cognise the first as an object to itself, *i.e.* as a particular existent. It cannot go beyond its object, namely, the first knowledge, and see if it truly corresponds with its own object. An act of knowledge having another for its object cognises the mere existence of the other as a cognitive fact. It cannot know the further fact of its truth or falsity. Moreover, of the two cases of knowledge, the second, which knows the first, is

1. *The New Realism,* p. 61.

as helpless as the first in the matter of its own validity. It cannot *ex hypothesi*, be the evidence of its own validity. Hence, so long as the validity of the second knowledge is not proved, it cannot be taken to validate any other knowledge. It cannot be said that the second has self-evident validity, so that we do not want any proof of it. This means that one knowledge, of which the validity is self-evident, is the evidence for the validity of another. But if the truth of one knowledge can be self-evident, why not that of another? Hence, if the second knowledge has self-evident validity, there is nothing to prevent the first from having the same sort of self-evidence. As a matter of fact, however, all knowledge has validity only in so far as it is tested and proved by independent grounds. Truth cannot, therefore, be self-evident in any knowledge. If, by such arguments, the validity of knowledge itself is made incomprehensible, there can be no possibility of assuring ourselves of the validity of the methods of knowledge, such as perception, inference and the rest. The value and accuracy of a method of knowledge are to be known from the validity of the knowledge derived from it. It follows from this that if the validity of knowledge is unknowable, that of its method is far more unknowable.[1] Hence, we are involved in a vicious circle; the validity of knowledge depends on the validity of the method of acquiring such knowledge, while the validity of the methods is to be tested by the knowledge derived from them. As Hobhouse puts the matter: "Our methods create and test our knowledge, while it is only attained knowledge that can test them."[2] It is the contention of the Bauddha critics that the Nyāya theory of knowledge is involved in such circular reasoning in the attempt to prove the validity of knowledge. This contention, if admitted, renders the Nyāya philosophy utterly worthless. It becomes a hopeless attempt to realise the highest good by means of the highest knowledge which is impossible.

It was with the object of meeting the difficulties raised by its critics that the old Nyāya entered on a critical study of the problems

1. *Cf.* NVT., pp. 4-5.
2. Hobhouse, *Theory of Knowledge*, p. 487.

of knowledge in its relation to reality. After Vātsyāyana's first elaborate exposition of Gautama's *Nyāya-Sūtra*, his worthy successors had to defend the Nyāya against renewed attacks. They discussed both the logical and metaphysical problems more fully and also many other questions of general philosophical interest. The result is a fully developed and complete system of philosophy.[1]

The modern school of the Nyāya, beginning with Gaṅgeśa, attempts to give greater precision to the thoughts of the old school. It lays almost exclusive emphasis on its theory of knowledge. The forms and concepts invented by it give the Nyāya the appearance of a symbolic logic. The old theory of knowledge is a criticism of thought as related to the real world of things. It is more empirical and practical, and it tries to discover the relations between reals. The modern theory becomes more formal or conceptual. It tries to find out the relations of meanings and concepts. It develops into a formal logic of relations between concepts and their determinants. The old Nyāya gives us what may be called philosophical logic, while the modern Nyāya is formal logic and dialectic.

The Syncretist school develops the Nyāya further by incorporating the Vaiśeṣika theory within it. The categories of the Vaiśeṣika become a part of the objects of knowledge (*prameya*) in the Nyāya. But this synthesis of the Nyāya and the Vaiśeṣika does not ignore their differences with regard to the theory of knowledge. One is as severe as the other in its criticism of the opposed logical theories.

The Nyāya theory of knowledge is the cumulative body of the logical studies and their results in the different schools of the Nyāya. It may be said to have three aspects: the psychological, the logical and the philosophical. The first is concerned with the descriptive analysis of the facts of knowledge. The second is interested especially in the criticism of the forms and methods of knowledge. The third is an attempt to determine the final validity of knowledge

1. An account of the controversy between the Naiyāyikas and the Bauddha logicians is given in Dr. S.C. Vidyābhūṣaṇa's *History of Indian Logic*, Bk. II, Ch. II.

as an understanding of reality. These aspects of the Nyāya epistemology, however, are not to be found in abstract separation from one another. In the next chapter we shall have to discuss the mainly psychological question as to the nature and forms of knowledge.

I. METHOD OF VALID KNOWLEDGE (*PRAMĀṆA*)

Chapter I

Nature and Forms of Knowledge

1. Definition of Knowledge (*Buddhi*)

If we take knowledge in its widest sense to mean any way of cognising objects, then valid knowledge will be a special form of cognition (*buddhi*). All cognitions are not valid knowledge. Hence in order to understand the nature of the method of valid knowledge (*pramāṇa*), we have to consider first the nature and different forms of cognition or knowledge (*jñāna*) as such.

In the Nyāya-Vaiśeṣika philosophy cognition (*buddhi*) is taken to mean the same thing as apprehension (*upalabdhi*), knowledge (*jñāna*) and cognisance (*pratyaya*).[1] Hence, we say that knowledge means awareness or apprehension of objects. It includes all cognitions that have a more or less determinate objective reference. The object of apprehension may be a thing or a quality, an act or an emotion, the existent as well as the non-existent. But in every case in which there is knowledge there must be something that stands out as the object of knowledge. Knowledge consists simply in the manifestation (*prakāśa*) of objects.[2] All things are made manifest or revealed to us when they become objects of knowledge. Further, knowledge is said to be the property of illumination or manifestation that belongs to the self. Without this luminous light of knowledge we lose the ground of all rational practice and intelligent activity. It is on the basis of knowledge of some kind that all living beings deal with other objects of the surrounding world. Hence knowledge (*buddhi*) is regarded as the ground of what may be called the

1. *Buddhirupalabdhirjñānamityanarthāntaram*, NS., 1.1.15.
Buddhirupalabdhirjñānaṁ pratyaya iti paryāyāḥ, NK., p. 171.
2. *Arthaprakāśo buddhiḥ*, TK., p. 6.

behaviour or conduct of a living being. A living creature behaves differently in relation to different objects because it somehow knows them to be different. Then we are told more definitely that knowledge is that kind of awareness which is meant when, by introspection, one says 'I am knowing'.[1] This means that knowledge is intellection as distinguished from affection and volition. Something different is meant by the phrase 'I am knowing,' from what is meant by saying 'I am desiring or willing or doing something, or simply being pleased or displeased with it.' Although knowledge is distinguishable, it is not separable, from feeling and volition. In knowledge the knower does not passively allow himself to be impressed by external objects and end by having mental copies of those objects. According to the Nyāya, the self is not a mere aggregate or series of conscious phenomena, which is only acted on and determined by sense-impressions, but has no power to react on and determine them. This materialistic and sensationalist theory of the self is rejected by the Nyāya. On the other hand, it conceives the self as a conscious agent which receives impressions of sense, knows external objects through them and acts upon things according to its subjective purposes. Knowledge is a cognitive fact by which we have an apprehension or understanding of objects. But it is bound up with certain affective elements, namely, the feelings of pleasure and displeasure, according as the known objects are pleasurable or painful. Through such feelings knowledge leads to certain conations, *viz.* desire, aversion and volition in the form of an exertion (*samīhā*) to obtain pleasurable objects and avoid painful ones.[2]

Hence, knowledge may be said to be a cognitive phenomenon which is generally connected with conation through the mediation of feeling. In any particular act of knowledge of an object, there is a feeling of being pleased or displeased with it and an active attitude of desire or aversion which may lead to certain overt movements towards or away from the object. The Nyāya, however, does not

1. TS. and TD., p. 32.
2. NB., 1.1.1-2.

go so far as to say that knowledge is at once a phase of cognition, feeling and conation. In cognising an object we may also cognise its pleasurable or painful character and also become conscious of certain tendencies in relation to it. But the actual feelings of pleasure and pain or the conative processes of desire, etc., take us beyond cognition. Knowledge is not a phase of feeling or the will, although it may be generally connected with them. It has a distinctive and self-sufficient character of its own and should not be reduced to feeling or volition.

With regard to the essential nature of knowledge we may ask: Is knowledge a substance or an attribute? Is it a mode or an activity? According to the Nyāya, knowledge is an attribute of the self. It is not a substance, since it cannot be the stuff or the constitutive cause of anything, nor is it the permanent substratum of certain recognised and variant properties. The Sāṅkhya and the Yoga systems look upon cognition as a substantive mode or modification (*vṛtti*) of the material principle called *buddhi*, as it reflects the light or consciousness of the self in it. This, the Naiyāyika contends, is unintelligible. We cannot understand how the self's consciousness, which is immaterial and intangible, can be reflected on any material substratum. We should not speak of any reflection, but rather say that knowledge or consciousness belongs naturally to *buddhi* itself. But this will commit us to the absurd hypothesis of two selves or subjects for any case of knowledge. In truth, however, there is but one conscious subject for all cognitions in one person.[1]

It is generally believed that knowledge is neither a mode nor a substance but a kind of activity or function (*kriyā*). The Bauddha and the Mīmāṁsā systems agree in describing knowledge as an activity, a transitive process.[2] The Nyāya, however, emphatically repudiates the conception of knowledge as an activity. Jayanta in his *Nyāyamañjarī* (p. 20) traces the act theory of knowledge to a grammatical prejudice, a confusion between knowledge as

1. NB. NVT. NSV. and NM. on NS., 1.1.15. See also NS., 3,2,1, ff.
2. Jñānakriyā hi sakarmikā, *Sāstradīpikā*, p. 56. *Cf.* also *Nyāyabinduṭikā*, Ch. 1.

manifestation and the verb, 'to know' as denoting an action. When we hear the expressions 'I know,' 'I cognise,' etc., we are apt to be misled into the belief that knowledge or cognition is an activity or process. But this only shows how in philosophy we may be deceived by the vague expressions of ordinary language.

Knowledge, although it is not an activity of any kind, is still a transient phenomenon as it appears from the three tenses of the verb 'to know.' It is a dated event which is to be regarded as a quality and so can be perceived like physical qualities. Just as physical qualities are perceived by their special sense organs, so knowledge is perceived by the internal sense called *manas*.[1] But knowledge cannot be the quality of any material substance, since, unlike that, it does not admit of external perception. Physical properties are perceived by the external senses, but knowledge is not so perceived. Being thus fundamentally different from all physical qualities, knowledge is to be regarded as the property of an immaterial substance called soul. Still, knowledge is not an essential attribute of the soul. The soul has acquired this property in its bodily setting, *i.e.* in relation to a body. To the Advaita Vedānta, knowledge or consciousness is just the self, the very stuff of it. For the Nyāya, knowledge appears as the result of a relation between the soul and the body, which in themselves are not knowledge. But when it does appear, it has to exist as an attribute inhering in the soul substance.

Knowledge, as an attribute of the self, is always directed to objects. It always refers beyond itself, *i.e.* to objects outside of and different from itself. Knowledge is never self-manifested.[2] The capacity of self-manifestation in knowledge is, according to the Nyāya, a mere hypothesis of the Sāṅkhya-Vedānta and the Prābhākara Mīmāṁsā. Cognition cannot cognise itself. It can grasp, not itself, but an 'other.' Knowledge is not indeed, like the will, a way of acting on other objects, only it refers or points to something else. We shall have to consider later the question as to how

1. NM., p. 496; TB., p. 18.

2. *Vijñānamanātmasaṁvedanam*, NVT., p. 4.

knowledge can be known. The direction towards an object is what has been called 'international inexistence' by Brentano and Meinong. They take it as a character common to all psychical phenomena.[1] The Nyāya, however, limits it to cognition and denies to cognition the capacity of being directed to itself, *i.e.*, being self-cognised.

From what has been said it will appear that knowledge is conceived by the Nyāya in a very wide sense. In Western philosophy thought or consciousness, as a cognitive fact, has sometimes been regarded as an essential attribute of the mind and a pervasive character of all mental phenomena.[2] The Nyāya, however, does not pass over the distinction between thought (*jñāna*), on the one hand, and feeling, including pleasure and pain, desire and aversion, and will, on the other. Under knowledge it brings together all cognitive facts, like sensation, perception, inference, memory, doubt, dream, illusion and the like. In this sense the *buddhi* of the Nyāya corresponds to cognition which, placed by the side of feeling and will, gives us the tripartite division of mental phenomena in the traditional school of Western psychology. It stands, as Alexander also has said, "for all kinds of apprehension of objects, whether sensation, or thought, or memory, or imagination, or any other."[3]

So far the Nyāya view of knowledge seems to be just and comprehensive. But, then, a more fundamental problem is raised. It is the ontological problem of the status of knowledge as a fact or reality. Is knowledge a quality, or a relation, or an activity?

First, we have the act theory that knowledge is an activity. It is not difficult to see what induced some philosophers to accept this view of knowledge. There can be no knowledge unless the mind responds to the influences of the surrounding world. At any moment of inattention or absent-mindedness we do not perceive sounds or know things other than those in which we are engrossed, although the sounds or things may be acting on our senses. If there is to be

---

1. Vide Russell, *The Analysis of Mind*, pp. 14 f.
2. *Cf.* Descartes's distinction of *res extensa* and *res cogitans*.
3. *Cf. Space, Time and Deity*, Vol. II, p. 82.

knowledge, the mind must react to the actions of other things on it. Knowledge is not a reflection of objects on the mind which receives them passively like a mirror or reflector. It is a process in which the mind actively reaches out to objects and illuminates them. Hence knowledge must be a kind of activity, rather it is a mental activity.

The act theory of knowledge has been accepted by various schools of philosophy. In Indian philosophy, the Bauddha and the Mīmāṁsā systems uphold it. For the former, to exist is to act and so to change. Knowledge as an existent fact consists in the act of showing and leading to an object. According to the Mīmāṁsaka, the *act* of knowing (*jñānakriyā*) refers to an object. For Kant also knowledge involves the synthetic activity of the understanding. Spencer[1] tells us that consciousness arises when the tendencies towards action counteract one another and are therefore thrown back on themselves so as to become conscious of their existence, and knowledge appears as an incident in the adaptation of the organism to the environment. For Bergson also consciousness is a ceaseless creative activity. The voluntarists identify knowing with willing when they hold that cognition is the will when it is thwarted by difficulties and so looks for (*i.e.* thinks) means to overcome them. With the pragmatists knowledge is a belief determined by the will. For neo-idealists like Croce and Gentile[2] knowing is the form of theoretical activity and in thinking we create the thought we think about. Alexander,[3] who is a realist, seems to treat knowledge as a mental act when he says that 'every experience may be analysed into two distinct elements and their relation to one another, namely, the act of mind or awareness and the object of which it is aware, and that the one is an —ing and the other an —ed.' The Behaviourists[4] go to the other extreme and identify knowing with the activity of the body. They hold that consciousness is implicit behaviour, thinking is sub-vocal speaking, and

1. *Principles of Psychology*, Vol. I, Pt. IV.
2. *Cf.* C.E.M. Joad, *Introduction to Modern Philosophy*, Ch. 3.
3. *Space, Time and Deity*, Vol. I, pp. 11-12; Vol. II, p. 86.
4. *Cf.* Watson, *Behaviorism*, Lect. X.; Russell, *Analysis of Mind*, pp. 255 ff.

knowledge is a particular kind of behaviour in animals, or such response to the stimulus as has the characteristics of appropriateness and accuracy.

We may dismiss the behaviouristic contention that knowledge is a particular kind of bodily behaviour. That there is any behaviour, explicit or implicit, can be known only if there is a knowing subject. Behaviour cannot explain knowledge, but presupposes knowledge in order to be understood. Further, from all we know about the conduct of living beings it appears that behaviour arises out of knowledge and is not identical with it. Behaviour may be the objective side of knowledge. It has also a subjective side which is reflected in behaviour or overt action. This is recognised by Russell in his *Outline of Philosophy*, in which he supplements the objective view of knowledge as a way of reacting to the environment, by the subjective view of it as an awareness. The Naiyāyika rejects altogether the act theory of knowledge as a grammatical prejudice, and excludes knowledge from the category of *karma* or action. Even if we suppose that knowledge is an activity, the question will arise: What is the nature of this activity? It cannot be any kind of physical activity, force or motion. Nor can it be a psychical activity. The existence of any activity in the mind or consciousness is a highly questionable fact. According to James,[1] the will is a relation between the mind and its ideas, and in willing there is no innervation or putting forth of energy by the mind into the body. Titchener[2] and some modern psychologists also endorse this view and exclude the will from among the elementary mental processes. The *Bhagavadgītā*[3] anticipates these modern psychologists when it says that 'all actions take place in the material world and it is only egoism that deludes the self into the belief that he is an agent.' In so far as this is true, we cannot speak of knowledge as an activity except by way of metaphor. In knowledge itself as an awareness we find an object that is cognised and a subject or self that cognises it, but not

1. *The Principles of Psychology,* Vol. II. Ch. XXVI.
2. *A Text-Book of Psychology*, Sec. 10.
3. Ad., III, sl. 27.

any activation or energisation. An act is as much an object of knowledge as any physical thing, quality, or action. It is manifested by knowledge, and is not identical with it. On the other hand, knowledge appears as a standing and an accomplished fact which manifests everything that comes before it. It is more like a static illumination than a sweeping flow of conscious stuff. Hence, knowledge is different from action. Among modern writers Moore and Broad refute the act theory of knowledge so strongly advocated by Dawes Hicks.[1]

The second theory with regard to the nature of knowledge is that it is a relation between certain entities. According to Meinong, the Austrian realist, and the Critical realists, knowledge is a relation between three terms, *viz.* a mind, an object, and a content. When I know the table, by mind comes into relation with a physical object through the content of tableness. In *The Problems of Philosophy* Russell seems to accept the view that knowledge is a three-term relation. Some other realists hold that knowledge is a relation between two terms, namely, a mind and any object. Moore reduces cognition to the holding of a relation between a sense datum and a character. Broad also agrees with Moore in this respect and denies the existence of any mental act.[2] Russell in his work *Our Knowledge of the External World* reduces the knowledge-relation to a two-term process, *i.e.* a relation between the mind and the external world. The Neo-Realists go further and reduce knowledge to a relation between one kind of terms. According to them, "knowledge is not a relation between a knowing subject and an object known. It is merely a special sort of relation between object."[3] In the words of the new realists, "Things when consciousness is had of them become themselves contents of consciousness; and the same things thus figure both in the so-called external world and in the manifold which introspection reveals."[4] Russell advocates this theory in *The*

1. *Cf.* L.A. Reid, *Knowledge and Truth*, pp. 186f.
2. *Cf.* L.A. Reid, *op. cit.*
3. *Essays in Critical Realism*, p. 89.
4. *The New Realism* p. 35.

Analysis of Mind. James in his *Essays in Radical Empiricism* reduces knowledge directly to a relation between one type of entities. According to him, knowing can be easily explained as a particular sort of relation into which portions of 'pure experience' may enter. The relation itself is a part of 'pure experience', one of its terms becomes the subject or bearer of the knowledge, the knower, and the other becomes the object known.

The relation theory of knowledge does not stand the test of sound criticism. Although the relation between the subject and the object takes the form of knowledge, knowledge itself is not a relation. All that we seem to be justified in saying is that knowledge appears when the subject becomes related to the object, but it is a new phenomenon other than the subject-object relation. According to the Naiyāyikas, knowledge may be said to arise ultimately out of the relation between the soul and the body. Still, it is not merely a relation between the two, but a new property accruing to the soul therefrom. Whether knowledge can be treated as a quality or not, we shall consider next. The point we are to stress here is that a relation as such is not a cognition but a cognitum, *i.e.* an object of cognition. Of course, when a thing is known, it enters into what we call the knowledge-relation. But this assumes the subject's awareness of the thing as the basis of the relation. So the relation cannot constitute knowledge. As Reid has said, 'knowledge is not itself a relation but the apprehension of relations.'[1] Supposing that knowledge is a relation, we ask: How do we know it? It must be through some other knowledge which, therefore, transcends the relation and is not identical with it. In fact, the subject-object relation does not produce knowledge but only serves to manifest it, just as the contact between the eye and a physical thing serves to manifest its colour but does not produce it.

The third view with regard to knowledge is that it is a quality. According to Descartes and his followers, thought or cognition is the essential attribute of the mind or the soul substance, just as extension is the essential attribute of matter. The Sāṅkhya and the

1. L.A. Reid, *op. cit.*, p. 189.

Yoga system look upon knowledge or cognition as a modification of *buddhi* or the intellect which is its substratum. The Rāmānuja school of the Vedānta takes knowledge as an essential quality of the self. The self is not, as the Advaitins say, itself knowledge but is *qualified* by knowledge. Knowledge is not the essence of the self, but an attribute owned by the self. The Naiyāyikas and the Vaiśeṣikas also advocate the quality theory of knowledge. For them, knowledge is an attribute which inheres in the soul substance which, however, is separable from it.

But the quality theory of knowledge also involves certain difficulties. It cannot account for the reference to objects that is inherent in knowledge. A quality is an intransitive property of a thing. It hangs on the thing and does not point to anything beyond. It is in activity that we find a transition from one to an 'other'. For one thing, to act means aggressively to reach another. But at the same time we must not overlook the distinction between the 'ideal reference' to object that we find in knowledge and any form of physical process or transeunt causality. Knowledge refers to its object and is in this sense a cognition of the object. It does not however move towards it. In it there is no transition from point to point in space. In so far as this is the case, the Nyāya is right in opposing the attempt to identify knowledge with activity. But the view of knowledge as a quality misses the other fact of objective reference that we find in knowledge. Knowledge seems to be what Reid calls ' a self-transitive process.' Its self-transcension is, as Hoernlé points out, directly experienced by us.[1] So, it seems to occupy a position intermediate between quality and activity. To describe its self-transcension or objective reference and, at the same time, demarcate it from physical activity, we may say that knowledge is an 'ideal or theoretical activity.' But after all the characterization of knowledge as an activity, be it physical or ideal or theoretical, is only a symbolic description. While physical activity is real and intelligible, an 'ideal or theoretical activity' can hardly be made intelligible to us. Knowledge is, therefore, neither a quality, nor an activity, nor a relation.

1. L.A. Reid, *op. cit.*, p. 188.

Knowledge is the most fundamental fact of reality. It is the intrinsic character of all reality. Without pausing here to discuss the ontological problem as to the nature and constitution of reality, we may say that reality is a living intelligent system. The ultimate constituents of things are not material but living particles which not only exist and interact with one another, but somehow experience their existence and activity. These many living particles are the differentiations of one universal spiritual life. A pluralistic constitution of things is not inconsistent with the unity of their ultimate ground which is the Absolute Reality. The real is, therefore, an objective system, of which existence and knowledge are two inseparable aspects. It is true that what we know as the consciousness or knowledge of human beings is a specific phenomenon determined by certain conditions as the subject-object relation or the activity of the nervous system and the brain. But while these conditions explain the specific empirical form and character of this or that knowledge, they cannot account for the original sentence or experience which is embedded in reality and conditions those conditions themselves. Hence we conclude that knowledge is present in all reality and is manifested in a specific form in man by the subject-object relation. It does not require to be attached as a quality to any other reality, say, matter or mind or soul. It is just the self-expression of reality. In the words of Bosanquet[1] we may say: "Knowledge is an essential form of the self-revelation of the universe : experience as a whole is the essential form."

2. Classification of Knowledge

Taking knowledge in the most comprehensive sense as the cognition of objects, the Naiyāyikas proceed to distinguish between its different forms, according to the differences in the nature and validity of cognitions. In view of these, knowledge is first divided into *anubhava* or presentation and *smṛti* or memory.[2] In *anubhava* there is a presentational knowledge of objects and so it is felt to be

1. *Logic*, Vol. II, p. 322.
2. Sā dvividhā smṛtiranubhavaśca, TS. and TD., p. 32

given to us. It is original in character and not the reproduction of a previous knowledge of objects. *Smṛti* or memory, on the other hand, is not the presentation of objects, but a reproduction of previous experience. Here our knowledge appears to be due not so much to objects themselves as to our past cognitions of those objects. Each of these has been further divided into valid (*yathārtha*) and non-valid (*ayathārtha*) forms, according as it does or does not accord with the real nature of its object.

Under *anubhava* or presentative knowledge we have the two kinds of valid and non-valid presentations. Of these, the former is called *pramā* and includes all cases of true presentational knowledge of objects. According to the Nyāya, there are four distinct kinds of *pramā* or valid presentation, namely, perception (*pratyakṣa*), inference (*anumāna*), comparison (*upamāna*), and testimony (*śabda*). In each of these there is a presentation of some object as it really is. Hence *pramā,* according to the Nyāya, is not any cognition nor any true cognition as such. It is a valid presentational knowledge of objects.[1] As a matter of usage, however, the word 'knowledge' may be used for *pramā,* according to the context.

There are some cases of knowledge which are presentational in character but not valid. These constitute the class of *apramā* or non-valid presentations (*ayathārthānubhava*), which includes all cognitions that are either false or not-true but not false. Hence, under *apramā* the Nyāya includes doubt (*saṁśaya*) with its varieties of conjecture (*ūha*) and indefinite cognition (*anadhyavasāya*), as well as error (*viparyyaya*) and hypothetical reasoning (*tarka*).[2] It should here be noted that cognitions which do not agree with the real nature of their objects are not always false or erroneous (*bhrama*). There may be cognitions which fail to give us a correct presentation of objects and so are not true (*pramā*). But at the same time they may not make any claim to truth, nor lead to any definite assertion. Such is the case with doubt, conjecture, indefinite

1. Tattvānubhava pramā, *Saptapadārthī*, 140.
2. Ayathārthānubhavastrividhaḥ saṁśayaviparyyayatarkabhedāt, TS. and TD., p. 82 Ūhānadhyavasāyayostu saṁśaya eva, *Saptapadārthī*, 39.

cognition and *tarka*. These are not true indeed, but yet they are not false (*viparyyaya*). It is in view of such facts that the Nyāya divides non-valid presentation (*ayathārthānubhava*) further into doubt (*saṁśaya*), error (*viparyyaya*) and hypothetical argument (*tarka*). Hence, it is not correct to speak of *apramā* or non-valid presentation, always as a case of *bhrama* or error. It becomes so when it definitely contradicts its object *(viparītanirṇaya*).

Memory is not *pramā* or valid knowledge, since it does not refer to presented objects. It may be of two kinds, namely, true and false (*yathārthamayathārtham*). True memory is in accord with the real nature of the objects remembered, whereas false memory does not tally with the real character of the remembered objects. In waking life we have both these kinds of memory. In dreams our cognitions are false memory-cognitions. Dream is a kind of memory that is not in agreement with the real nature of the cognised objects. All knowledge, however, including dream, refers to some real object ; only dream is a false memorial representation of the real.[1]

We may represent the Nyāya classification of knowledge by the following table :

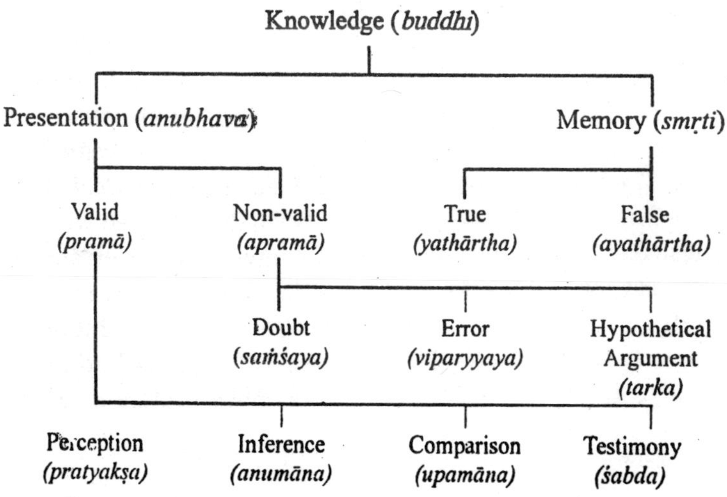

1. TB., p. 30.

3. Memory and Dream

Memory (*smṛti*) is knowledge of one's own past. It is a representative cognition of past experiences due solely to the impressions produced by them.[1] It is thus different from recognition (*pratyabhijñā*) which, according to the Nyāya, is a form of qualified perception and has reference to the direct presentation of some object, although it involves an element of representation.[2] In memory, however, there is only a revival of our past experiences, in the form of ideas and images, in the same form and order in which they were actually experienced by us at a certain point of past time. The ground or condition of this revival is of course the latent impressions left by our past experiences and retained in the soul.[3] When the mind comes in contact with such psychic dispositions (*bhāvanā*) there is a remembrance of the corresponding original experiences. Memory being thus a cognition, by the same self, of what has been once cognised, is an evidence for the soul's permanence. As to the general character of memory we may, therefore, say that it is knowledge arising solely out of the impressions of previous experiences and pertaining to a permanent soul.

While memory has for its general conditions some original past presentation (*pūrvānubhava*) and its impression (*saṁskāra*), it has a number of specific causes that serve either to retain the impressions or revive them in consciousness, and thereby bring about the phenomenon of memory. Among these are: (1) attention (*pranidhāna*) which fixes anything in the mind, (2) association (*nibandha*) which connects different experiences and makes them suggestive of one another, (3) repetition (*abhyāsa*) which secures persistence for the impressions, (4) sign (*liṅga*) that leads the mind to the thing signified, (5) characteristic mark (*lakṣaṇa*) that recalls the class to which an object belongs, (6) similarity (*sādṛśya*) that associates the ideas of like things, (7) ownership (*parigraha*) which

1. *Saṁskāramātrajanyaṁ jñānaṁ smṛtiḥ*, TS., p. 32.
2. TD., p. 33.
3. *Anubhavajanyā smṛtiheturbhāvanā, ātmamātravṛttiḥ*, TS., p 85.

is suggestive of the owner or the thing owned, (8) the relation of dependence (*āśrayāśritasaṁbandha*) of which one term suggests the other, (9) contiguity (*ānantaryya*) which binds together successive phenomena, (10) separation (*viyoga*) that frequently reminds one of what he is separated form, (11) identity of function (*ekakāryya*) that recalls similar agents, (12) enmity (*virodha*) that suggests the rivals in any sphere, (13) superiority (*atiśaya*) that reminds us of what it is due to, (14) acquisition (*prāpti*) that frequently recalls its source, (15) covering (*vyavadhāna*) that suggests what is covered, (16) the feelings of pleasure and pain (*sukhaduḥkha*), (17) desire and aversion (*icchādveṣa*), (18) fear (*bhaya*), (19) need (*arthitva*) that reminds one of their causes and objects, (20) action (*kriyā*) which is suggestive of the agent, (21) the feeling of affection (*rāga*) that often reminds us of its objects, (22) merit (*dharma*) and (23) demerit (*adharma*) that are suggestive of the belief in pre-existence and help or hinder the retention of experiences. These causes of memory cannot be simultaneously operative. Hence recollections are not simultaneous but successive in their appearance in consciousness.[1]

Memory is of two kinds, namely, true (*yathārtha*) and false (*ayathārtha*). It is true when it has its basis in some valid presentation (*pramājanya*) and is in agreement with the real nature of the remembered objects. On the other hand, memory is false when it arises out of such original cognitions as were erroneous (*apramājanya*) and so does not accord with the nature of the objects recalled in it. Thus the truth and falsehood of memory depend on those of the corresponding original presentative cognitions (*pūrvānubhava*) that constitute the ground of all memory.[2] In waking life we have both these kinds of memory. The voluntary or involuntary recollection of past objects, when we are awake, becomes true or false according as it is connected with right or wrong cognitions in the past and so, is or is not in accord with the real nature of the objects remembered.

---

1. NS. and NB., 3.2.44.
2. *Pūrvānubhavasya yathārthatvāyathārthatvābhyām smaraṇamapi ubhayarūpam bhavati*, TM.

Dreams illustrate what is intrinsically false memory. According to the Nyāya, dream-cognitions are all memory cognitions and untrue in character.[1] They are brought about by the remembrance of objects experienced in the past, by organic disorders and also by the imperceptible influences of past desires and actions (*adṛṣṭa*).[2] Hence, dream-cognitions have sometimes a moral value in so far as they produce pleasurable or painful experiences in the self according to the merit or demerit accruing from the actions of waking life. Dream-knowledge, however, is intrinsically false. It is no doubt related to certain objects of the real world. But these objects as cognised in dream are not present to sense. They are either past or remote. Still in dream, objects are actually represented as present. Hence, there is in dream a false cognition of the real when it represents the not-present as the present, the 'that' as the 'this.'[3] It may so happen that dreams sometimes turn out to be true and tally with the subsequent experiences of waking life. But such correspondence between dream-cognitions and waking experience is neither normal nor invariable. Hence dream can never be called *pramāṇa,* or the source of such presentative knowledge as has a real and an invariable correspondence with the object.

The Nyāya account of dream ignores the fact that dream cognitions are as good presentations as our ordinary perceptions. Dreams have not the regularity and orderliness of waking perceptions. But otherwise the two are indistinguishable. The presentative character of dreams has been rightly noted by other systems. The Vaiśeṣika considers dream to be a kind of internal perception due to the inner sense (*manas*) as aided by impressions of past experiences. It is felt as if coming by way of the external senses.[4] The Mīmāṁsā does indeed take dreams as reproductions of past experiences. But it admits that they appear as presentations and are indirectly connected with the real objects of past experiences.

---

1. *Svapne tu sarvameva jñānam smaraṇamayathārthaṁ ca*, TB., p. 30.
2. *Svapnastu anubhūtapadārthasmaraṇaiḥ adṛṣṭena dhātudoṣeṇa ca janyate*, TM.
3. *Doṣavasena taditi sthāna idamityudayāt*, TB., p. 30.
4. PS., pp. 91 f.

The Advaita Vedānta finds in dream a phenomenon of some philosophical significance. In it there is the mental creation of a world under the influence of *avidyā* as aided by the impressions of waking experiences. But the dream-world is quite analogous to the world of sense and the sciences. That the world of our ordinary experience may be a dream is a hypothesis that is admitted even by Russell[1] to be logically possible, though not as simple and preferable as the common-sense belief in an external world. In all this we have a just recognition of the presentative character of dream-knowledge, even though it is eventually condemned as false and erroneous. The Nyāya view of dream is defective in so far as it reduces dream cognitions to false memory. Dream-cognitions are more like perceptions than memory-cognitions. When we recollect a dream we feel 'such and such objects were seen (not merely remembered) in dream last night.' Dream is a kind of false perception. It may sometimes be excited by a physical cause as when a bell ringing causes us to dream of going to school. But although sometimes started by a physical cause dreams do not follow such causes up to their end. Dreams are generally independent of the impressions produced by physical causes on our body. Even when excited by a physical cause, the series of experiences through which a dream progress cannot be traced to a corresponding series of physical causes. Still, our dream experiences are more like perceptions than anything else. These have not indeed the force or *zwang* with which the data of sense come to us. But they seem to possess the vivacity and spontaneity of our ordinary sense perceptions. At least, they are directly given to us like our perceptions. Dreams are experiences which we *have*, and do not arrive at by any process of reasoning. Hence it is that they are called perceptions. But they are false perceptions because they are contradicted by our waking experiences. To the dreamer, however, they appear as true perceptions, because he cannot relate them to his waking experiences and see how they are contradicted by the latter.[2]

1. *Problems of Philosophy*, pp. 34-35 and 191.
2. *Cf.* R.S. Woodworth, *Psychology*, 9th edn., pp. 115-16: "Or you are fully asleep, and then the images that come are dreams and seem entirely real, since contact with the objective situation has been lost."

According to the Nyāya, memory (*smṛti*) is not valid knowledge (*pramā*). We can speak of true and false memory. But even true memory, which gives us a true cognition of some past object, cannot be called *pramā* or valid knowledge. On this point Indian systems of philosophy are divided in their opinion. Some of them consider memory to be as valid as perception and inference, and look upon it as the source of our knowledge of past facts. The Vaiśeṣika accepts memory as valid knowledge distinguished from all forms of wrong cognition.[1] So too the Jaina philosophy counts memory among the forms of valid mediate knowledge (*parokṣa jñāna*).[2] The Advaita Vedānta, we shall see, is not definitely opposed memory being regarded as valid knowledge.

The other systems, especially the Nyāya and the Mīmāṁsā, refuse to recognize memory as valid knowledge (*pramā*). The Mīmāṁsā objection against memory, as we shall see more fully hereafter, is that it gives no new knowledge (*anadhigata*), but is only a reproduction of some past knowledge. The Nyāya, however, does not admit the Mīmāṁsā contention that any knowledge becomes invalid simply because it refers to a previously known object (*gṛhītagrāhītakṛta*). According to it, what makes memory invalid (*apramā*) is the absence of the character of presentation (*anubhūti*) in it. Memory may, in some cases, correspond to real objects. Still it is not valid knowledge, since it does not correspond to given objects and does not arise out of the objects themselves (*arthajanya*). In memory we have not a cognition of given objects but a *re*-cognition of what were given, in the same form and order in which they once existed in the past and have now ceased to exist. That form and order are now past and therefore no longer real, so that between these and their memory-images we cannot speak of a correspondence to the given. Even when an object is first perceived and then immediately remembered, so that perception and immediate memory refer to one and the same object and are spoken of as equally true, we are to observe that the state of memory borrows its validity for the antecedent perception which

1. *Cf.* PS., p. 94; NK., pp. 256-57.
2. *Cf.* TTS., i, 9-13.

produces and fashions it (*yācitamaṇḍanaprāya*).[1] As a matter of fact, however, the object ceases to be given and to be the operative cause of knowledge in memory. The recollection of long past or remote objects is clearly independent of the cooperation of these objects (*anapekṣitārtha*). Memory, being thus based on no given datum (*anarthajanya*), fails to give valid presentational knowledge (*pramā*), and so, is not a source of knowledge (*pramāṇa*).[2] An examination of the view that memory is not valid knowledge is postponed at this stage. We shall come to it after we have got all that the Nyāya has to say about *pramā* and the *pramāṇas*.

4. Doubt (*Saṁśaya*)

Doubt (*saṁśaya*) is the cognition of conflicting notions (*vimarśa*) with regard to the same object.[3] It is the mental reference of two or more contradictory properties to the same object. In it the mind oscillates between different alternate characterizations of some given object.[4] Doubt thus consists in an alternation between different conflicting notions with regard to the same object. The alternatives between which the mind passes in succession in the state of doubt are called *kotis*. These may be two or more in different instances of doubt. Sometimes they are contrary terms (*e.g.* post and man) and sometimes contradictory terms (*e.g.* post and not-post). Doubt arises when with regard to some perceived object there is the suggestion of such conflicting alternatives but no definite cognition of any differentia to decide between them. Hence, doubt has been spoken of as incomplete or indecisive cognition (*anavadhāraṇātmaka*). But doubt is not merely the absence (*abhāva*) of assured cognition (*niścaya*). It is not mere negation of knowledge. It is a positive state of cognition of mutually exclusive characters in the same thing and at the same time.

1. TR. and SS., pp. 43-46.
2. NM., pp. 20-23.
3. NS., 1.1.23.
4. Ekasmin dharmiṇi viruddhanānādharmavaiśiṣṭyajñānam saṁśayaḥ, TS., p. 82.

The state of doubt may be analysed into the following factors. There is first the presentation of some existent object. Next by virtue of association the presented fact calls forth two or more apperceptive systems, each of which tries to appropriate it but is counteracted by the rest. In the absence of any definite cognition of such differentiating characters in the presentation as answer to any of the apperceptive groups, the mind oscillates between them and we have the phenomenon of doubt. Hence doubt supposes the recollection of the differentiating characters of an object but no corresponding presentation of them (*viśeṣasmṛtyapekṣa*). The actual process of mental oscillation in doubt is generally expressed in the form of an interrogation, *e.g.* 'Is the yonder erect figure a man or a post or a tree-trunk?'

Doubt is of five kinds. First, it may arise from the perception of such properties as are common to many things, as when we perceive a tall object at a distance and are not sure if it be a man of a post or a tree-trunk, because tallness is common to them all. Secondly, it arises from the cognition of any peculiar and unique property, as when the cognition of sound makes us doubt if it is eternal or non-eternal, since it is not found in eternal objects like the soul and the atom, nor in non-eternal things like water and earth. Thirdly, it may be due to conflicting testimony, as when the different philosophical theories of the soul leave us in doubt as to the real nature of the soul. Fourthly, it is caused by the irregularity of perception, as when we doubt if the perceived water really exists or not, since there is a perception of water both in a tank and a mirage. Lastly, doubt springs from irregularity of non-perception, as when we are not sure if the thing we cannot see now really exists or not, since the existent also is not perceived under certain conditions.[1] According to the later Naiyāyikas, such as Uddyotakara, Vācaspati and others, there are not five but only three or two kinds of doubt.[2] Irregularity of perception or non-perception is not by itself a cause of doubt. So, also conflict of testimony is

1. NB., 1.1.23.
2. NV. and NVT., 1.1.23.

not an independent cause, but only an auxiliary condition of doubt. In all cases of doubt there is either the perception of common properties or the cognition of something quite new and uncommon. Gaṅgeśa speaks of only two sources of doubt, namely, the suspicion of *upādhi* or condition, and the perception of a property common to many things without any presentation of their differentiating attributes.[1]

According to the Vaiśeṣika, there is fundamentally only one kind of doubt since it is always due to perception of properties common to many familiar objects.[2] Indefinite cognition (*anadhyavasāya*) is a form of knowledge which is quite different and distinct from doubt. Indefinite cognition is incipient knowledge of an object as a mere 'something' without any definition or determination of what that something is. It is illustrated by our ordinary nascent experience, as when we say 'something passed by without our knowing what it was,' or when in the presence of an unfamiliar living being we say 'it must be some kind of animal.'[3] Such indefinite cognition differs from doubt both in origin and essence. Doubt arises from recollection, without any accompanying presentation, of the specific characters of two or more objects, of which we perceive the common properties. The indefinite (*anadhyasāya*), however, is a possible form of cognition with regard to objects whose specific character had never been presented to us. Again, the indefinite does not, like doubt, rest on two or more conflicting notions with regard to the same subject.[4] It should however be noted here that some of the syncretist writers on the Nyāya-Vaiśeṣika include conjecture (*ūha*) and indefinite cognition (*anadhyavasāya*) under doubt. According to Sivāditya and Mādhava, conjecture is that form of doubt, in which one of the conflicting suggested alternatives becomes more probable than the other, as when seeing a tall object in the rice field we say 'it is

1. TC., ii, pp. 210-11.
2. PS., pp. 85 f.
3. NK., p. 183.
4. NL., pp. 45-46; NK., *ibid.*

probably a tall man.' Indefinite cognition is that kind of doubt, in which both the alternatives are implicitly present but neither explicitly thought of.[1] Śaṅkara Miśra in his *Upaskāra* suggests that indefinite cognition arises from cognition of a peculiar property which is not found in other things. Hence it corresponds to the second kind of doubt mentioned by the Nyāya.[2]

Doubt is not valid knowledge (*pramā*). It may sometimes have the character of presentation (*anubhava*) of an object. But it has neither the mark of being an assured definite cognition (*asaṁdigdha*) nor that of a true correspondence with the object (*yathārtha*), and so, does not lead to successful activity. In doubt the oscillation of thought between different ideas has no objective counterpart in the real. Nevertheless doubt is not error (*viparyyaya*). Doubt as a form of cognition, is neither true nor false. It carries with it no definite assertion of any character with regard to its object. It makes no claim to be a true judgment of the object and so the question of its falsity or contradiction does not arise. The value of doubt lies in its being a great impetus to study and investigation. It is the starting-point of a critical knowledge of objects. In this sense it may be said to be the beginning of philosophy. The critical philosophy of Kant is doubtless indebted to the scepticism of Hume.

The Nyāya account of doubt, it will be seen, gives us some important truths. As a mental state, doubt is shown to be different from both belief and disbelief. It neither affirms nor denies anything, but only raises a problem for thought. As such, doubt should also be distinguished from 'the mere absence of belief.' There is absence of belief even when we do not think of anything at all. In doubt, however, we think of two or more alternatives in regard to the same thing. It always has, as the Nyāya-Vaiśeṣika would say, some *kotis* which become contradictory when referred

1. *Ūdhānadhyavasāyayostu saṁśaya eva*, *Saptapadārthī*, 38; *cf.* also sec. 168 and Mādhava's Commentary, *Mitabhāṣinī* on it.
2. *Upaskāra*, 2.2.17.

to the same subject. This point has been rightly noted by Bosanquet[1] when he says "a definite doubt is unquestionably a disjunctive judgment." He observes also that "when a man first doubts and then decides, on such a question as whether the river he sees before him is safe to ford,.....there must be a positive basis of the two or more alternatives as well as one suggested alternative." What this positive basis is or what different bases of doubt there may be have been elaborated by the Nyāya. That the alternatives are exclusive and contradict each other has also been admitted by Bosanquet. But the Nyāya seems to show better insight when it says that doubt is never a definite cognition (*avadhāraṇa*), but an indecisive questioning attitude towards an object.[2] It is not a judgment at all. It does not assert anything. When we are in doubt about anything we do not really know nor do we claim to know what it is. We cannot even say that 'it must be either this or that.' All we can say is: 'Is it this or that?' It is on account of this that doubt is neither true of false. For, as Bradley says, "partial ignorance does not make any knowledge fallacious, unless by a mistake I assert that knowledge as unconditional and absolute."[3]

5. Error (*Viparyyaya*)

Error (*bhrama*) is the reverse of valid knowledge (*pramā*). While valid knowledge is the presentation of an object as what it really is (*tattvānubhava*), erroneous knowledge is the cognition of an object as what it really is not (*atattvajñāna*).[4] In error an object is cognised as having certain characteristics that really fall outside of its being. Hence, it has been described as the wrong apprehension (*mithyopalabdhi*) in which an object is taken for what it is not (*atasminstaditi pratyayaḥ*).[5] The cognitions of a shell as silver, or a rope as a snake, of a post as a man are all cases of error or wrong cognition. In each there is the cognition of an object as other than

1. *Logic*, Vol. I, pp. 35, 279, 356.
2. Kiṁsvidityanyatarannāvadhārayati, NB., 1.1.23.
3. *Principles of Logic*, Vol. I, p. 11.
4. *Saptapadārthī*, sec. 140.
5. NV., 1.1.2.

what it really is. Hence, it may be said that error consists in attributing such characters to an object as are not to be really found in it (*tadabhāvavati talprakāraka*). In it one universal is referred not to its own locus but to that of a different universal. In the cognition of a shell as silver, silverness is referred to a wrong locus, namely, the shell.[1] Hence, it is a false characterisation of the object by the negation of its real characters.

Thus, error is to be distinguished from doubt. Unlike doubt, it is not only non-valid knowledge (*apramā*), but is positively invalid or false knowledge (*bhrama*). An erroneous cognition goes beyond the state of uncertainty in doubt and carries with it a definite assertion (*avadhāraṇa* or *niścaya*) about some presented object. But, then, it is an assertion that contradicts the real nature of its object (*viparītanirṇaya*). It is a false judgment of the real through the attribution of such characters as are excluded by it (*viparītadharmādhyāropeṇa*). We become conscious of error when there is a contradiction between our cognitive and volitional experiences. Erroneous cognitions do not lead to successful activity. The cognition of silver in a piece of shell is found to be erroneous when it fails to lead up to the expected results. It is contradicted and finally sublated by the unexpected experience of failure of the activity concerned in approaching and picking it up. Actions inspired by wrong cognitions fail to realise their ends and thereby expose the invalidity of those cognitions.

6. Theories of Illusion in Indian Philosophy

The explanation of errors of perception has been a perplexing question for all philosophy. The question is this: How are we to explain the false perception of silver in a shell? Is it due to the object itself? Or, is it due to our subjective attitude towards the object? According to the Nyāya, while valid knowledge (*pramā*) is objective in the sense of being grounded in the object itself (*arthajanya*), all error is subjective in so far as it is due to the introduction of a certain foreign character into the object by the

---

1. *Cf.* TD., p. 83; TC., i, pp. 401, 418.

knowing subject (*adhyāropa*). In the case of the mirage, for example, there is nothing wrong in the object. "The object all the while remains while it actually is. In regard to the flickering rays of the sun, when there arises the cognition of water, there is no error in the object: it is not that the rays are not rays, nor that the flickering is not flickering; the error lies in the cognition: as it is the cognition which instead of appearing as the cognition of the flickering rays, appears as the cognition of water, *i.e.* as the cognition of a thing as something which it is not."[1] From this it follows that there is no error in the simple apprehension (*ālocana*) of the object. The object as given in indeterminate (*nirvikalpaka*) perception consists of a number of actually present flickering rays of the sun. But on account of certain defects in the sense organ and the influence of association and memory, the given datum is misinterpreted as water in the determinate (*savikalpaka*) perception of it. Hence the error lies not in the indeterminate perception of the given but in the determinate perception of it as worked up and modified by some representative elements.[2]

The modern school of the Nyāya shows great ingenuity to explain the perceptual character of illusory experience. That in illusion there is the attribution (*āropa*) of a false character to a perceived fact is no doubt true. But the questions that arise are: How do we come to ascribe the false character? How again does this false character appear as something actually perceived in illusion? The Nyāya rightly points out that an illusory experience is a single perception. It is not, as Prabhākara thinks, a complex of perception and recollection with their distinction blurred by obscuration of memory. Thus, when we have the illusion of silver in a shell, we no doubt attribute silverness to the shell which is not its proper locus. But at the same time it is equally doubtless that the silver is somehow perceived and not merely remembered in illusion. This has been very well pointed out by A.C. Ewing when he observes: "The difficulty in the case of perception is not the

1. NV., 1.1.4.
2. NVT., 1.1.4.

mere fact of error, but the demand that we should hold both that what we immediately perceive is numerically identical with a physical object or a part of such an object and yet that it is quite different."[1] To explain illusion, therefore, we have to explain its perceptual character, instead of trying to explain it away.

Taking the illusion of silver in a shell as an illustration, the Nyāya account comes to this. There is first the contact of sense with something present before it. Owing to some defects, the sense apprehends such general features of the thing as its brightness, etc., but fails to discern its peculiar and distinctive features. But the general features being associated with some other thing (here silver) recall the memory-images of the peculiar properties of that other thing. Through such recollection there is a sort of contact (*jñānalakṣaṇa sannikarṣa*) between sense and that other thing (*i.e.* silver). Hence, there is an actual perception of silver in the illusion.[2] The perceived silver is then referred to the locus (*idam*) or the something which is present before and perceived by sense. Hence in the illusion there is perception of both the 'this' and the 'silver', although in different ways.[3] So far there seems to be nothing wrong. The error comes in and the illusion arises when the silver that is perceived elsewhere is referred as a predicate to the 'this' as its subject. It is this determinate knowledge of the 'this' as qualified by 'silverness'' (*viśiṣṭajñāna*) that can account for a man's efforts to gain possession of the illusory object. In recognition (*pratyabhijñā*), in which we say 'this is that man I saw yesterday,' we see how certain presentative and representative elements combine to make up one single perception. Any ordinary valid perception also illustrates how a given sensum combines with associated ideas to make up one percept. But while in these, the combination has its objective counterpart, in illusion the relation between the perceived 'this' and 'silver' is not objectively real. It

1. *Mind*, April, 1930, p. 149.
2. *Cf.* Woodworth, *Psychology*, p. 110: "Memory images, then, are recalled sensations, or have more or less of the quality of sensations."
3. *Cf. Mamatvindriyajanyatvāt jātyasaṁskārācca sākṣātkāritvamevobhayatra*, TC., i, p. 525.

is contradicted and sublated either by a subsequent experience that corrects the illusory experience of silver and shows it to be false, or by the experience of disappointment which ensues when we take possession of it. In the first case the cognition of silver is shorn of its objective (*viṣayāpahāra*), and in the second case we are put in possession, not of the silver, but of the shell (*phalāpahāra*). Hence the error lies not in the presentations concerned in the perception but in the determination of one presentation by another given through association and memory (*jātyasaṁskārāt*). And since this determination results in a judgment of the object as something other than what it is, the Nyāya theory of error is called *anyathākhyāti* or *viparītakhyāti*. According to it, an erroneous cognition is presentational in character and has some basis in facts. But the facts being misplaced and misrelated, error becomes a false apprehension of the real.

The above view of *anyathākhyāti* is common to the Nyāya-Vaiśeṣika. It has been accepted in the main by Kumārila, Rāmānuja[1] and the Jainas. But the Bauddha, the Prābhākara Mīmāṁsā and Advaita Vedānta systems oppose the Nyāya view and propose different theories. Hence, the Naiyāyikas proceed to repudiate the other theories of error. According to the Yogācāras, there is no extra-mental reality, and things are only thoughts or ideas. Reality is a stream of cognitions bifurcated into a subjective and an objective series. Error consists in an illegitimate process of projection of

1. Rāmānuja has proposed an alternative theory of illusion which is distinguished from the above as satkhyāti. According to it, all cognitions are relatively true and none absolutely false. The cognition of silver in a shell is true with reference to the element of silver that it is present in the shell. In every object of the world the elements of all other objects are present in different proportions. So, in the structure of a shell an element of silver is present, although the shell element preponderates in it. Hence, the cognition of silver has an objective basis, and is so far true. But owing to certain defects of the sense organs, there is a distortion of the shell element, and we have the perception of silver in what is really a silver-shell. The perception is wrong, not because it is the cognition of no fact or of the unreal, but because it is a partial view or an imperfect knowledge of the real. (*Cf.* *śrībhāṣya* 1.1.1.)

subjective ideas as objective and extra-mental facts. All cognition of objects thus objectifies the subjective and is therefore erroneous. This view is called *ātmakhyāti* or *jñānākārakhyāti*, since it insists on the sole reality of ideas and looks upon all objects as cognitions wrongly taken for external things.

This theory, however, the Naiyāyikas object, fails to account for the facts of the case. On the theory of subjective idealism of the Yogācāras, there is no difference between knowledge, and the subject and object of knowledge, everything being an idea only. Hence the cognition of silver should appear, not in the form of 'this is silver,' but 'I am silver,' which however is not the case. Then, if everything be an idea we do not know how to account for the difference between an idea and its corresponding percept. Finally, the Nyāya view, that error is the cognition of an object as what it is not, really includes the Yogācāra theory that in error the subjective is taken for the objective and is so cognised as what it is not.[1]

The Mādhyamika school of Bauddha philosophy negates all existence. It holds the *asatkhyāti* view that error consists in the manifestation of the non-existent as existent. The cognition of silver in the shell is erroneous because it manifests the non-existent silver as existent, and we become conscious of this when our first cognition of silver is contradicted by the subsequent cognition of shell. Against this it has been urged by the Naiyāyika that the illusion of silver is not entirely baseless, it cannot arise out of nothing. What is absolutely non-existent cannot produce even the wrong cognition of silver. The illusion of silver is due to something in the nature of the shell. It occurs generally in connection with a shell and the like, but not indifferently with everything. Even if error is a cognition of the non-existent as existent, it is the cognition of it as what it is not. Hence we have in it a case of *anyathākhyāti* which thus includes the *asatkhyāti* of the Mādhyamika. In truth, however, the utterly unreal and non-existent cannot be the object of any knowledge whatsoever.[2]

1. NVT., pp. 85 f.; NM., pp. 176, 545-46.
2. *Ibid.*

The Advaita Vedānta puts forward the view of *anirvacanīyakhyāti*. This does not differ so widely from the Nyāya *anyathākhyāti* as may appear at first sight. While the two views agree so far as the nature and mechanism of illusory perception are concerned, there is difference in one essential point. According to *anirvacanīyakhyāti*, there is in the illusion of silver a contact of the defective sense organ with the glittering shell and then a mental modification answering to the form of 'this object'. Now through the operation of nescience (*avidyā*), as aided by the past impressions of silver, revived by this object's similarity, there is the production of some inexplicable silver which lasts so long as the illusion lasts. It is neither real nor unreal, nor both real and unreal, but indefinable and indeterminable. Hence in the illusion of silver there is an actual cognition of silver. The illusion is presentative in its character so far as it is connected with some silver actually present to consciousness. But while, according to the Nyāya, this presentation of silver is due to association and memory (*jātyasaṁskārāt*), to the Advaitin, it is due to the production of the 'cognised silver' for the time being. To this the Naiyāyikas object that if the silver is actually produced, there would be no illusion but a valid perception. If it be said that the silver is supernatural (*alaukika*) and is erroneously cognised as natural (*laukika*), we have in it just a case of *anyathākhyāti*. If, on the other hand, the supernatural silver is cognised as supernatural, there cannot be anything wrong in the cognition, nor any practical activity in the cogniser to obtain such supernatural silver.[1]

The Prābhākara school of the Mīmāṁsā differs from all others and advocates the view of *akhyāti* or *vivekākhyāti*. According to it, error consists simply in the want of discrimination between perception and image, or between direct apprehension and memory. It is a sort of confused memory (*smṛtipramoṣa*). In the case of the illusion of silver in the shell what happens is that there is first the direct perception of an object with the attribute of brightness, etc. Then through association by similarity the perceived bright object

1. NVT., pp. 85-87; NM., pp. 187 f.

revives the image of silver. Hence the state of cognition has the dual character of percept and image, of something seen and something remembered. On account of certain abnormal conditions, the two things are not kept distinct and are allowed to fuse or coalesce, and we have the resulting cognition of silver referred to the piece of shell. When the illusion is corrected, there is no sublation of the silver but only an explicit recognition of the presentative and representative factors of the wrong cognition. The distinction between the two being cognised, there remains no confusion as to the fact of silver being only remembered and not perceived.[1]

To this theory the Naiyāyika objects that it fails to account for the presentative character of the illusion. So long as we are under the illusion we have a consciousness of the silver as something present and perceived, and not as what was perceived before and is now only remembered. Further, there can be no activity to secure the silver unless there is a positive and determinate cognition of it. A confused knowledge cannot inspire the confidence necessary for practical activity. Non-discrimination, as mere confusion of knowledge, cannot be the ground of such actions as are generally connected with an illusory experience. Hence, illusion must be a single determinate cognition of an object. All this comes out in our subsequent judgment of the illusion as it stands corrected and negated. It is in the form "what I had *seen* is not sliver," and not "what I had remembered is not silver." This clearly shows that the illusion of silver is an error of perception and not of memory. Finally, even on the *akhyāti* theory it must be admitted that in error there is a cognition of the object as what it is not. This will mean that *akhyāti* is but a form of *anyathākhyāti*. Hence the Naiyāyikas conclude that *anyathākhyāti* is the most satisfactory theory of error. It gives us all that the other theories require, but is not vitiated by their faults.[2]

1. *Vide* Jhā, *Prabhākara School of Pūrvamīmāṁsā*, pp. 28-32; *Sadholal Lectures on Nyāya*, Ch. III.
2. NVT., and NM., *ibid*.

Among the theories of perceptual error or illusion as explained above that of the Nyāya seems to be more acceptable than any other. For the Bauddha idealist error consists in the objective appearance of subjective ideas. But this cannot explain the distinction between true and false perception. In both, the object of knowledge is not really other than knowledge or an idea, although it may appear to be so. Hence both must be equally wrong. Further, there being nothing but ideas, one idea may be mistaken for another, but not for that which is no idea all *i.e.* for extra-mental object. Perceptual errors cannot, therefore, be explained on the theory of subjective idealism of the Yogācāra type. "For," as Ewing says, "even in error we are concerned not with our ideas but with external reality,...error is not a mere dwelling on our ideas but an unsuccessful cognising of objects."[1]

The Prābhākara Mīmāṁsakas treat error as the subjective appearance of an object. In it an idea or image of the mind is referred to a given object so as to become one with it. This explanation of perceptual error was once generally accepted in European philosophy. According to most of the Western systems, in illusory perception a real object is modified by subjective factors supplied by the mind through association, memory, emotion, etc. Among modern thinkers, Lossky holds that 'falsity is the subjective appearance of the object since foreign elements can be introduced into the object only by the knowing subject.'[2] Bosanquet only puts the matter in objective terms when he says that 'in falsehood something actual pretends to be something else, or, like a false coin, has not the significance which it claims.'[3] But while this may be accepted as a general definition of error, it does not explain how in perceptual error certain subjective factors, ideas or images, are actually felt as perceived, out there in space. It cannot be said that we do not really perceive the illusory object but only imagine that we do perceive it. Why should we doubt the verdict of

1. *Mind*, April, 1930, pp. 138-39.
2. *The Intuitive Basis of Knowledge*, pp. 227 f., 267 f.
3. *Logic*, Vol. I, pp. 67, 70.

experience here if we do not doubt it elsewhere? And experience clearly tells us that we do perceive the illusory object.

To explain the perceptual character of illusory experience, the Advaita Vedānta supposes the temporary production of certain positive entities of an indeterminate order (*anirvacanīyā prātibhāsikī sattā*). These are neither real nor unreal, but actual facts. The illusory silver is not real, because it is contradicted by a closer experience. It is not unreal, because it is perceived as an actual fact so long as the illusion lasts. Hence, it is an *appearance* which is undeterminable as real or unreal, and is ultimately due to *avidyā* or ignorance. But how ignorance can produce a positive entity and then make us perceive it as an existent fact is left unexplained. Further, as Alexander has pointed out, 'error does not give us a new and more shadowy being than the spatio-temporal reality but is the world of determinate being misread.[1] Moreover, if in illusion certain positive entities are really produced and perceived, we should not be having an illusion, but a true perception.

According to the Nyāya, illusion is a misplaced fact. All the factors of an illusory perception are real and perceived facts, but they are brought into a wrong relation. In the illusory perception of silver, for example, we have an actual perception of a certain locus and some silver, both as real facts. The error arises because the silver perceived at a different time and place, is related to the time and place occupied by the perceived locus, namely, the shell. Some modern realists give a similar explanation of perceptual error. According to Alexander, 'error consists in wrongly combining the elements of reality. Everything which is illusory in the illusion does actually exist in correspondence with the mental activity through which it is revealed; but the personal character of the activity dislocates the real object from its place in things, and refers it to a context to which it does not belong. So when I fancy a horse's body, and complete it with a man's head, the head exists in reality, but not upon a horse's body.'[2] To quote Alexander's own words:

1. Alexander, *Space, Time and Deity*, Vol. I, p. 202.
2. *Essay in Critical Realism*, pp. 135-36.

"Some of our objects are illusory; they are real so far as they are perspectives of space-time, but they contain an element introduced by our personality, and do not belong where they seem to belong."[1] This however does not explain how illusory objects can be perceived at the time and place, to which they do not belong. How can we perceive here and now something which exists elsewhere? W.P. Montague tries to explain this by some distortion of the real object in producing its effect on the brain. He thinks that the so-called sensory illusions result from certain physical or peripherally physiological distortions of the real object underlying.[2] This means that illusory perceptions depend on certain objective and real conditions in the same way in which true perceptions are so conditioned. E.B. Holt goes further than this and establishes the objectivity of error. He thinks that all errors are cases of contradiction or contrariety. The perception not silver is illusory because it is contradicted by the experience of the same object as shell and not silver. But neither the experience of shell nor that of silver is subjective. Both of the contradictory experiences are objective, since the real object itself has contradictory characters. Holt says that "the case of hallucinations is paralleled by such cases as that of mirrored space, wherein sundry mirrored objects occupy the same spatial positions as are occupied by other 'real' objects situated behind the mirror." Hence, we are to say that error consists in entertaining mutually contradictory propositions, of which one may be preferable, but none subjective, because the world is full of such contradictory propositions.[3] On this view, however, the distinction between truth and error becomes insignificant. The same thing may, with equal truth, be called a shell or silver. The Nyāya does not go so far as to say that contradictory characters belong to the same thing or that contradictory propositions are equally objective. It is not the case that the same real has the contrary characters of shellness and silverness. It has really one character,

1. *Space, Time and Deity*, Vol. II, p. 249.
2. *The New Realism* pp. 288-92.
3. *Ibid.*, pp. 369-70.

namely, shellness. But the silver is also a perceived fact. Hence, the crucial question is: How can the silver, which exists elsewhere, be presented here and now? The Nyāya explains this by *jñānalakṣaṇāpratyāsatti* which means a kind of sense-object contact brought about by the revival of the impressions of past experience of an object. Hence, there is a *jñānalakṣaṇa* perception of the silver. As we shall see more fully hereafter, the perception of the silver is a case of what is called "complication" by some Western psychologists. In it the sensation of a particular bright colour calls up, by its previous association, the impression of silver and we have the perception of silver in the shell. The silver does not appear as an idea or image of the mind, but is a content presented by the sensation of bright colour. Still, the perception of the silver is illusory because the character of silverness does not really co-exist with the given sensation of bright colour. It is the presentation of silver in a wrong relation and so an illusion.

7. Hypothetical Argument (*Tarka*)

Tarka is a type of implicative argument by which we may test the validity of the conclusion of any reasoning (or of any judgment). Here we ask whether any contradictions would follow if the given conclusion be accepted as true or rejected as false. If there is any contradiction in accepting it as true we have no doubt that it is invalid. But if in rejecting it as false we are involved in a contradiction, there can be no doubt that the conclusion must have been valid.

The process of reasoning in *tarka* consists in the deduction of an untenable proposition from a certain position (*aniṣṭaprasaṅga*). This has the logical effect of exposing the invalidity of that position and thereby lending support to the counter-position. Thus with regard to the inference of fire from the perception of smoke, there are two alternative positions, namely, that the smoky object is fiery, and that it is not fiery. From the latter position we deduce the proposition that the object is not smoky, which is contradicted by our direct experience. This is expressed in the form of a hypothetical proposition, *viz.* 'if the object be fireless, it must be smokeless.'

Here *tarka* validates the inference of fire through the deduction of an inadmissible proposition from the contrary hypothesis. The proposition is a deduction from the hypothesis in the sense that it follows from it according to a general rule. It is a general rule that whatever has a mark (the *vyāpya*), has that which it is a mark of (the *vyāpaka*). Now the absence of fire is a mark of the absence of smoke. Hence if it be said that there is absence of fire in the object, we cannot resist the conclusion that there is absence of smoke in it, *i.e.* it is smokeless. Such a conclusion, however, is contradicted by direct observation. Hence it is that *tarka* has been defined by the modern Naiyāyikas as the process of deducing from a mark that of which it is a mark, but is false (*vyāpyāṅgīkāreṇa aniṣṭavyāpakaprasañjanrūpaḥ*).[1]

When the proposition established by any method of knowledge (*pramāṅa*) is doubted or disputed, we should have recourse to *tarka* to lay the doubt or end the dispute. In *tarka* we take the contradictory of the proposition in the form of a hypothesis and readily see how that hypothesis leads to a contradiction. Hence *tarka* serves as the limit to doubt (*saṅkāvadhi*). Since, however, the invalidity of a position is not a ground of the validity of its opposite, *tarka* is an aid or auxiliary (*sahakāri*) to *pramāṇa*, but not *pramāṇa* by itself. Thus when on seeing a table we say: 'there is no book on the table', we have a judgment of perception expressed in a proposition. If anyone doubts the truth of this proposition we may effectively dispel it by an argument like this: 'If there were any book on the table, it would have been perceived like the table; but it is not so perceived; therefore it does not exist.' But to argue in this way is not to *know* the non-existence of a book on the table. The knowledge of the book's non-existence is a matter of perception according to the Naiyāyikas. Similarly, to argue that 'if the object be fireless it must be smokeless,' is not to *know* that it is fiery. The knowledge that the smoky object is fiery is acquired by means of inference from smoke as a mark of fire. The hypothetical argument only confirms this inference. Hence *tarka* does not originate true knowledge, *i.e.*

1. TB., p. 32.

is not a *pramāṇa*, although it confirms a *pramāṇa* which brings about the knowledge in question, *i.e.* is auxiliary to the *pramāṇa* (*pramāṇānugrāhaka*).[1]

There are five kinds of *tarka*. These are called *ātmāśraya*, *anyonyāśrya, cakraka, anavasthā* and *tadanyabādhitārtha-prasaṅga*.[2] In all of them the logical form and character of the argument is the same, and they serve the same end of testing the validity of some reasoning or judgment.

Ātmāśraya is an argument that brings out the inconsistency involved in a reasoning which seeks to prove that anything is dependent on itself in respect of its origin or duration or cognition. The argument may be stated in this form: 'If A is the cause of A, it must be different from itself, because the cause is different from the effect.'

Anyonyāśraya is an argument which brings out the contradiction involved in the judgment that two things are reciprocally dependent on each other. The argument may be stated thus: 'If A depends on B, and B depends on A, A cannot depend on B.' To say that 'B depends on A' is virtually to deny that 'A depends on B'. The idea of reciprocal dependence, which is so much favoured by some Western thinkers, is rejected by the ancient Indian thinkers as self-contradictory and absurd.

The third type of *tarka* is called *cakraka*. It consists in exposing the fallacy of a reasoning in which a thing is made to explain the pre-supposition of its own pre-supposition (*tadapekṣyapekṣya-pekṣitva*). If A is pre-supposed in B and B is pre-supposed in C, then to explain A by C is to reason in a circle, because C by its inherent limitations leads us back to A. Starting from A we are referred to C as the ground of its explanation, but to explain C we are brought back to A as its ultimate ground or basis. Here the curve of explanation makes a complete circle in so far as our thought returns to its own starting-point through two or more intermediaries.

1. TB., p. 32.
2. NSV., 1.1.40.

Thus if we admit that perception is pre-supposed in inference and the latter is pre-supposed in testimony, then to prove perception by testimony is to commit the fallacy of circular reasoning. This may well be exposed by a *tarka* like the following: 'If perception depends on testimony, it must be independent of sense-object contact.'

The fourth type of *tarka* is called *anavasthā*. It is an argument which brings out the absurdity of an indiscriminate extension of the fallacy of undue assumption. Here we expose the fallacy involved in the indefinite regress of thought from point to point without any final resting ground (*avyavasthitaparamparāropa*). There is an infinite regress of thought (*anavasthā*) when in an explanation we make use of an indefinite number of principles, each of which pre-supposes its next. Here our thought moves not in a circle, but up a staircase, as it were. Thus if we explain A by B, B by C, C by D, and so on *ad infinitum*, we do not really explain anything. Or, if we try to deduce the ground of inference from inference we are logically committed to the fallacy of infinite regress. The fallacy may be exposed by a *tarka* like this: 'If inference depends on inference for its ground, no inference is possible.'

The last type of *tarka* is called *tadanyabādhitārthaprasaṅga* or *pramāṇabādhitārthaprasaṅga*. It is an argument which indirectly proves the validity of a reasoning by showing that the contradictory of its conclusion is absurd. This may be done by opposing the contradictory of the conclusion to some fact or some universal law. If, therefore, its contradictory be false, the original conclusion must be true and based on a valid reasoning. Take, for example, the inference: 'Whatever is smoky is fiery; this object is smoky; therefore this object is fiery.' If this conclusion be false, then its contradictory, 'this object is not fiery' should be true. But the latter proposition is found to be absurd by the following *tarka*. 'If in the case of this object smoke is not related to fire, then it cannot be an effect of fire. But it must be due either to fire or to not-fire. There is no third alternative here. We do not find it to arise out of not-fire. Hence, if it is not due to fire, it must be either an uncaused effect or a non-existent phenomenon. The first alternative contradicts the law of universal causation and is, therefore, untenable. The second alternative becomes self-contradictory, since it commits us to the proposition that the smoky object is smokeless. For, if A (smoke) be a mark of B (not-fire), and B (not-fire), were a mark of C (not-smoke), then A (smoke) would be a mark of C (not-smoke). In view of such absurdities involved in the contradictory of the original conclusion we must reject it as false and accept the original conclusion as true and as based on a valid inference.

It is to be observed, however, that the Nyāya division of *tarka* into five different kinds is logically unsound. This division has reference to the different kinds of reasoning which may be tested by an argument like *tarka*. But the classification of *tarka* should not be based on the kinds of reasoning that maybe tested by it, because these are unlimited and quite external to the nature of *tarka* as a type of argument. A classification of *tarka* must be based on the logical character of the arguments employed in different cases. Now having regard to its logical character, we find that *tarka* is fundamentally of one kind. In every case in which it is employed it has the form of an inconsistent argument (*aniṣṭaprasaṅga*) developed out of the conclusion of a given reasoning or its contradictory. If this inconsistent argument arises out of the conclusion of the given reasoning, we are convinced that the given reasoning is invalid. If it arises out of the contradictory of the conclusion of a given reasoning, we know for certain that the original conclusion and the given reasoning are valid. As to its logical character, therefore, *tarka* seems to correspond to the antilogism in Western logic. According to some Western logicians,[1] the antilogism is an inconsistent triad of propositions by which the validity of any syllogism maybe determined. A syllogism is proved to be valid if by combining the contradictory of its conclusion with the original premises we get an inconsistent triad. If, however, the resulting triad is consistent, the original syllogism is invalid. It is also admitted by these Western logicians that the inconsistent triad,

1. *Cf.* Chapman and Henle, *The Fundamentals of Logic*, pp. 90 and 102.

like the Naiyāyika's *tarka*, is not itself an argument. It should however be remarked here that the logical form of the argument in *tarka* does not exactly correspond to that of the antilogism. *Tarka* is put into the form of an implicative argument, while the antilogism into that of a categorical syllogism. Again, *tarka* may be employed to test the validity of any reasoning, inferential or otherwise, and it may be developed out of a given conclusion or its contradictory with or without the original premises.

Chapter II

Valid Knowledge and Its Method (*Pramā* and *Pramāṇa*)

1. Definition of *Pramā* or Valid Knowledge

In Chapter II we have considered the different forms of non-valid knowledge (*apramā*). Here, we are to consider the nature of valid knowledge (*pramā*) and the general character of the method of valid knowledge (*pramāṇa*). It may appear to some that the distinction between valid and non-valid or invalid knowledge is not only unnecessary but incorrect. Knowledge, in its strict sense, means a true belief that carries with it an assurance of its truth.[1] Hence, knowledge is always true. It is a tautology to speak of 'valid knowledge' and a contradiction to speak of 'non-valid or invalid knowledge.' The latter is no knowledge at all, since it does not stand for any belief which is true and which gives us an assurance of its truth. When we speak of *pramā* as valid knowledge, we do not forget the strict sense of the word 'knowledge'. But the word 'knowledge' has been used in a narrow as well as a wide sense. Hence in view of the facts that the Nyāya-Vaiśeṣikas use *jñānam* in a very wide sense, that they make a distinction between true and false *jñānam*, and the *pramā* implies something more than knowledge in its strict sense, we propose to use the phrase 'valid knowledge' for *pramā*. As, however, we have already said, the word 'knowledge' may be taken to mean *pramā* according to the context.

Pramā has been defined by the Nyāya as true presentational knowledge (*yathārthānubhava*). It is a definite and an assured (*asaṁdigdha*) cognition of an object, which is also true and presentational in character. Hence, it is that *pramā* excludes all

1. *Cf.* Russell, *Problems of Philosophy*, p. 217.

kinds of non-valid knowledge, such as memory, doubt, error, hypothetical argument (*tarka*), etc. Memory is excluded because it is not presentational (*anubhava*). Doubt and the rest are excluded either because they are not true or because they are not definite and assured cognitions. It appears from this that *pramā* has three main characteristics, namely, assuredness, truth and presentativeness.

As to the first, we may explain it by saying that *pramā* or valid knowledge is a definite categorical assertion as distinguished from all indefinite, problematic and hypothetical knowledge. In *pramā* there is a feeling of assurance or conviction in what is known. That is, valid knowledge is always connected with a firm belief. All assurances or firm beliefs, however, are not *pramā*. In illusion (*bhrama*) we firmly believe in what is false. *Pramā* implies something more than a subjective certainty.

Hence, the second characteristic of *pramā* is that it is true or unerring (*yathārtha*) knowledge. But what makes knowledge true (*yathārtha*)? In answer to this we are told that knowledge is true when it is not contradicted by its object (*arthāvyabhicārī*). This means that knowledge is true when it reveals its object with that nature and attribute which abide in it despite all changes of time, place and other conditions.[1] What is once true of an object is always true of it, no matter what its position in space and time may be. More definitely speaking, to know a thing truly is to know it as characterised by what *is* a characteristic of it (*tadvati tatprakāraka*). We have the truth about a thing when we judge it to be such-and-such, and it *is* such-and-such, *i.e.*, as we determine it by qualities which the thing does in fact possess.[2] Hence, according to the Nyāya the truth of knowledge consists in its correspondence to facts.

So far *pramā* may be said to mean the same thing as knowledge in its narrow sense. Like the latter, it is true belief which is connected

1. NVT., pp. 5, 21.
2. *Cf.* Lossky, *The Intuitive Basis of Knowledge*, p. 227: "We have acquired truth only when the differentiated appearance is composed entirely of elements present in the object itself and nothing has been introduced into it from without."

with an assurance or conviction of its truth. But the Nyāya goes further and adds a third qualification to *pramā*. According to it, *pramā* is not only a true and an assured cognition, but also a presentational cognition (*anubhava*). Otherwise, memory will have to be regarded as *pramā*. Memory knowledge is both true and definitely believed to be true. Still it is not *pramā*, since it is not presentative but representative cognition. What then is *anubhava*? To say, as some Naiyāyikas have said, that *anubhava* is knowledge other than memory is just to beg the question. But the matter has not been left there. We are told by others that *anubhava* is knowledge of *given* facts as distinguished from those that are imagined or supplied by the mind.[1] Or, it may be said that *anubhava* is knowledge which is grounded in and due to the object itself (*arthajanya*). Or again, it may be said that *anubhava* is a cognition that follows uniformly and immediately on the presence of its special cause. This means that a cognition is presentational if it is not separated from the existence of its unique cause by any interval of time. As such, memory cannot be called *anubhava*, because its object is not a given fact, or because it is not due to any influence of the object, or because the impressions (*saṁskāra*), out of which it arises, are not immediately antecedent to it in every case. On the other hand, perception, inference, comparison (*upamāna*) and testimony are all cases of *anubhava* or presentational knowledge. That sense-perception is so, will be generally admitted. But inference and the rest also are, according to the Nyāya, presentational cognitions. Even *prātibha* or intuitive knowledge of future events is regarded as a perception due to the object itself. The Nyāya holds that each of these is a cognition of some objectives facts and is conditioned by those facts. Memory being only a reproduction of past experience cannot be said to be due to its object and is, therefore, other than presentational knowledge (*anubhava*).[2]

Hence, the Nyāya definition of *pramā* or valid knowledge come to this. *Pramā* is a presentational cognition (*anubhava*), in which

1. Tattvamanāropitaṁ rūpam, tasya jñānamanubhavaḥ, *Saptapadārthī*, sec. 64
2. NM., p. 23; TR. and SS., pp. 9-11.

there is a characterisation, in thought, of the object as it is in reality (*yathārtha*), as well as a definite assurance of its being objectively valid (*asaṁdigdha*).

2. Definition of Pramāṇa or the Method of Knowledge

Pramāṇa derivatively means the instrument of valid knowledge (*pramāyāḥ karaṇam*). Hence, generally speaking, we may say that *pramāṇa* is the means or source of right knowledge. It is that which gives us valid knowledge, and only valid knowledge of objects. So, it has been said: "There cannot be by right understanding of things except by means of *pramāṇa*. A subject arrives at the valid knowledge of objects by means of *pramāṇa*, for the existence and nature of objects are to be ascertained only by such cognitions as are based on *pramāṇa*." Again, we are told: "*Pramāṇa* is the cause of valid cognition of objects, inasmuch as it gives us a knowledge of objects as they really are and exist in themselves."[1] "*Pramāṇa* has a real correspondence with objects, in the sense that the nature and attributes of objects, as revealed by *pramāṇa*, are uncontradictorily true of them, despite all variations in time, place and other conditions."[2]

So far we are given to understand, not what a *pramāṇa* exactly is, but what the general character of *pramāṇa* must be. We do not go beyond such general description of *pramāṇa* when we are told by others that "*pramāṇa* is that which is invariably related to *pramā*," or, "to be *pramāṇa* is never to be disconnected from a knower possessing right knowledge."[3] All this means only that *pramāṇa* is the *karaṇa* or means of *pramā* or valid knowledge. What then is a *karaṇa* and how is it constituted? In order to answer the first part of this question we should follow the distinction between *karaṇa* and *kāraṇa*, means and cause.

A cause has been defined as the invariable and unconditional antecedent of an effect (*ananyathāsiddhaniyatapūrvabhāvī*).

1. NB., 1.1.1., 4.2.29.
2. NVT., *ibid.*
3. *Sarvadarśanasaṁgraha*, Chapter on *Nyāya Philosophy*; *Kusumāñjali*, 4-5.

Conversely, an effect is the invariable and unconditional consequent.[1] Or, an effect is what begins to be and thereby negates its antecedent non-existence. There are three kinds of causes, namely, the constituent (*samavāyi*), the non-constituent (*asamavāyi*) and the efficient (*nimitta*). The constituent cause is the substratum in which the effect inheres, *e.g.* the threads of the cloth. The non-constituent cause is the mediate cause of an effect. It determines the effect only in so far as it stands as an inherent attribute of the constituent cause. Its causal efficiency therefore is mediated through its intimate relation to the material or constituent cause. In relation to the effect 'cloth,' the contact of the threads is the non-constituent cause. So, also the colour of the threads is the mediate cause of the colour of cloth. The efficient cause is different from both the constituent and non-constituent causes. It is not merely the passive substratum in which the effect inheres, not any inherent attribute of the substratum that indirectly determines the effect. Rather, it is the agency that acts on both the constituent and non-constituent causes and make them produce the effect. In relation to the cloth, the loom and such other agents constitute the efficient cause. It is the efficient cause that is to be regarded as *karaṇa* or means, because it is principally concerned in bringing about the effect. While the first two are general causes or rather conditions of the effect, the last is the actually operative cause of it. It is the special cause, or simply, the cause of the effect.[2]

Now reverting to the definition of *pramāṇa,* we may say that it is the specific cause of valid knowledge as distinguished from its general causes or universal conditions. *Pramāṇa* is the unique operative cause (*karaṇa*) of right knowledge (*pramā*). It does not, however, follow from this that *pramāṇa* is a simple concept denoting a single thing. On the other hand, we are told that it denotes a complex of many conditions which are partly physical and partly

1. This implies that the relation between cause and effect is a one-one relation, there being only one cause for one effect and one effect for one cause. It thus excludes the idea of a plurality of causes as endorsed by commonsense and ordinary text-books of logic.
2. *Cf.* TB., pp. 2 f. and TS., pp. 35 f.

psychical or mental in nature. In fact, any instance of knowledge involves a long and complicated process which is either physical and physiological or mental or both. The visual perception of a jar, for example, is conditioned by physical contact between the eyes and the object as well as by internal operations of the visual organ, its contact with *manas* or the mind, and that of the latter with the soul. In inferential and verbal knowledge there are such specific psychic conditions as the knowledge of a universal relation and understanding of the meaning of a proposition and so on. Hence, *pramāṇa* is taken to mean the entire complex or collocation of all the specific physical and psychical conditions (*bodhābodhasvabhāvā sāmagrī*) that are actually operative in bringing about a valid and assured cognition of objects (*pramā*). This, however, does not include such universal conditions of all knowledge as subject and object, time and space, etc., within the compass of *pramāṇa* or the method of knowledge. Hence the final definition of *pramāṇa* is that it is the complex of specific conditions, other than the subject and the object, which does not normally fail to produce valid knowledge.[1]

The Vaiśeṣika system defines *pramāṇa* as the unique operative cause (*karaṇa*) of both true presentational knowledge and memory.[2] It would take memory as a distinct *pramāṇa* or method of knowledge like perception and inference. The Nyāya restriction of *pramāṇa* to the ground of presentational knowledge has been set aside and memory has been rightly shown to be an independent method of knowledge by the Vaiśeṣikas.[3]

The Jainas also take *pramāṇa* in a general sense so as to make it applicable to both immediate presentational knowledge (*pratyakṣa*) and mediate knowledge (*parokṣa*) so far as they are true. Under mediate knowledge they include sense-perception, inference, memory and recognition. In this general sense, *pramāṇa* is knowledge that reveals both itself and its object in a way that is not liable to contradiction.

---

1. *Cf.* NM., p. 15.
2. *Smṛtyanubhavasādhāraṇaṁ pramākaraṇaṁ pramāṇam*, TK., p. 6.
3. *Vide infra*., Bk. V, Ch. XX, Sec. 4.

The Advaita Vedānta defines *pramāṇa* as the operative cause (*karaṇa*) of *pramā* or true knowledge. It defines *pramā* in two ways. First, *pramā* means knowledge that has both the characteristics of novelty and uncontradictedness (*anadhigatābādhita*). This means that true knowledge is uncontradicted and original, *i.e.* gives us new information. Secondly, *pramā* is taken to mean simply uncontradicted knowledge of objects. The result is that *pramā* is made to exclude or include memory according as we accept the one or the other way of defining *pramā* or true knowledge.[1]

3. Nyāya Criticism of the Bauddha Views of *Pramāṇa*

It has been generally admitted by all the schools of Indian philosophy that *pramāṇa* is what gives *pramā* and that *pramā* is true knowledge. But there is much difference of opinion among them as to the nature of the truth, which each of them claims for its *pramāṇa*.

The Buddhists generally take the truth of knowledge to consist in its capacity to produce successful activity. *Pramā* or true knowledge (*samyargjñāna*) is harmonious in the sense that there is no conflict between the cognition of an object and the practical activity to obtain it. In fact, all knowledge is meant for some action. We seek knowledge because we want to act effectively in relation to other things. Hence *pramāṇa* or the method of knowledge fulfils its function when it shows an object in such a way as to enable us to act successfully in relation to it. In short, *pramā* is practically useful knowledge, and *pramāṇa* is the source of such knowledge.[2]

To this the Nyāya objects that practical utility (*arthasiddhi*) does not constitute the truth of any knowledge. If it did, the distinction between true and false knowledge would be hard to maintain. The Buddhists suppose that a knowledge is true when it is such presentation (*pradarśaka*) of an object as leads to the actual attainment (*prāpaka*) of it. One this view, all inferences become invalid in so far as the object of inference is not actually presented

---

1. VP., Ch. 1.
2. NBT., Ch. 1.

to senses. Perception may be said to present an object, but it cannot lead to the attainment of the presented object. If the object be a sensum, it must be fleeting on the Bauddha theory of momentariness (*kṣaṇikavāda*). It cannot be made to wait and persist in existence, so that our subsequent activity may put us in possession of it. If however the object be an ideatum or a cogitable entity (*adhyavaseya*), then for the Buddhist, it is no reality but a fiction (*kalpanā*), and we cannot speak of any attainment of it. Further, if with the Buddhist we accept the pragmatist conception of truth and say that whatever is practically useful is true, we must admit that all knowledge about the past and the future is untrue, since it is not connected with any present practical activity. So also with regard to the knowledge that is connected with no activity but the absence of all activity, *i.e.* the attitude of indifference towards the object of knowledge. Some knowledge may involve a tendency towards what is pleasurable, and some a tendency away from what is painful. But there is also a knowledge of what is neutral (*upekṣaṇīya*), with regard to which we remain indifferent. Such knowledge may be as valid as any other, of which the Buddhists can speak, although it is not connected with any useful practical activity. Finally, with the pragmatist definition of true knowledge (*pramā*), the Buddhists cannot but admit the validity of memory and *savikalpaka* perception, since both of them have great practical utility and both lead up to the attainment of their respective objects.[1]

The realistic schools of Bauddha Philosophy, namely, the Sautrāntika and the Vaibhāṣika, define *pramā* as consisting in the identity of content between a cognition and the cognitum.[2] A cognition becomes valid when it has the same content as the object cognised by it. The proper function of *pramāṇa* is to give a true knowledge of objects. But that gives a true cognition of the object which determines the cognition in question to have the same form and structure, in which the object exists, so as to give it the character of objectness (*viṣayatā*). The sense organs, however, which are

1. NM., pp. 23 f. ; TR., pp. 14 f.
2. *Viṣayasārūpyam sākārasya vijñānasya*, NVT., p. 20.

generally supposed to be the organs of knowledge (*jñānakaraṇa*) do not determine our cognitions to have the same content with the objects cognised by them. The cognition of blue colour is not certainly due to the action of the eyes, for the same eyes are operative even in the cognition of colours other than blue. It is the blue content of the object that determine our cognition to be a cognition of blue colour. The content of the object being immpressed on our cognition gives the same content to it, and thereby reveals the object itself as having that content. Therefore, the objective datum (*arthākāra*) is the *pramāṇa* or the source of our knowledge of the object as well as our knowledge of it one way or the other. The content of the object is thus both the ground and the product of knowledge, the means and the end of the process of knowledge. It should not be supposed that there is a contradiction in the same thing being the content of both the object and its knowledge. For here the object is only the object of knowledge and the knowledge is a determination of the object itself. "When a tree is known as *śimśapā,* the nature of the *śiṁśapā* is the content of both the tree and our knowledge of it. It is the object of our knowledge as well as the ground of a discriminative cognition of the object in question. Hence the content of an object (*athākāra*) is *pramāṇa* in so far as it establishes an identity between the object and our knowledge of it."[1]

The Nyāya rejects also the above view of the Bauddha realist. To it, the view that the content of the object is the ground of its knowledge because it ensures correspondence between the two, is not intelligible. It cannot mean that the content of the object reproduces itself as the content of cognition, for the same thing cannot act as a cause in relation to itself. Nor can it mean that the object's content is revealed by its cognition. The content being identical with the cognition need not be revealed or manifested by another act of cognition. Nor again can it be taken to mean that the object's content is what discriminates a cognition and thereby produces a discriminative knowledge of itself. The content and the

1. *Vide* NVTP., pp. 152-54 (Bib. Ind. Edn.).

cognition being identical the one cannot discriminate the other. The law of discrimination requires that the discriminator must be somehow different from the discriminated. When I discriminate a blue colour, I am obviously different from and stand over against the colour which is an object of my thought. All discrimination must take place in this way. The same thing cannot therefore be both the object of knowledge and the content of knowledge.[1]

The Nyāya criticism of the Bauddha view of correspondence between knowledge and its object contains an element of important truth. It has the effect of showing that the correspondence between knowledge and its object has no meaning when, as on the Bauddha view, the two become fused together as one stuff. It is meaningless to speak of correspondence between knowledge and its object, if we take them as identicals or absolute similars. Correspondence between cognition and its object is intelligible when each of them has certain conditions and characters that are wanting in the other, *i.e.* when there are distinctive differences between them. Hence, we cannot accept the view of the new realists[2] that 'the content of knowledge, that which lies in or before the mind when knowledge takes place, is numerically identical with the thing known, and is not in a class by itself. This means that things, when consciousness is had of them, become themselves contents of consciousness and the same things figure both in the so-called external world and in the manifold which introspection reveals. Thus objects literally and actually enter into the mind, and not subjective facts like cognitions or ideas.' On this view, the distinction between knowledge and its object or between truth and error becomes meaningless.

The Bauddha idealists, namely, the Yogācārs give another definition of *pramāṇa*. According to them, consciousness (*vijñāna*) as the principle of self-manifestation is the source of all knowledge (*pramāṇa*).[3] Having no determinations in itself, consciousness

1. *Vide* NVTP., pp. 177 f.
2. *Cf. The New Realism*, pp. 34-35.
3. *Vijñānasyaivānākārasyātmanātmaprakāśanasāmarthyaṃ*, NVT., p. 20.

comes to have certain determinate content in order to manifest itself and thereby gives us knowledge of a world of objects. A *pramāṇa* is that which manifests objects, but manifestation as a conscious process can belong only to that which is intelligent and conscious. The sense organs being unintelligent and unconscious cannot have the power of conscious manifestation. Hence, the intellect itself is to be recognised as *pramāṇa* by virtue of its intelligent nature and capacity of manifestation.[1] It has neither any permanent subject as its locus nor any objects that are external to and independent of it. It is the intellect that accounts for both the subjective and objective aspects of experience. With its beginningless tendencies consciousness is manifested in two series, namely, the objective, consisting of percepts object-ideas, and the subjective, consisting of perceptions of subject-ideas. We need not posit the real existence of objects outside of consciousness. Consciousness may be regarded as manifesting both itself and the so-called objects from within itself. The series of external objects, though not ultimately real, is yet set up by consciousness for the sake of practical activity through the influence of beginningless desires and impressions (*vāsanā*) that are inherent in every finite mind. The diversified contents of experience arise out of the continuous operation of desire, and their bifurcation into the subject-object series is the result of the will to live and act. "As there are ultimately no objects or perceptibles other than the intellect, the intellect itself is to be recognised as manifesting itself and is its own perceptible, luminous with its own light, like light."[2] The intellect or consciousness, therefore, is both *pramā* and *pramāṇa*, the ground of knowledge and the attained knowledge, since it is the cause of manifestation and the object manifested in knowledge.

As against the Bauddha idealists, the Naiyāyikas point out that the definition of *pramāṇa* as the power of self-mainfestation in the nature of consciousness is untenable. A capacity or power is always a tendency to do something not yet accomplished. But self-

1. NVTP., p. 155.
2. *Sarvadarśanasaṁgraha*, Chapter on Bauddha philosophy.

manifestation, being a *fait accompli* inherent in the very nature of consciousness, cannot be said to be the effect of product of any power or capacity. Again, consciousness, as *pramāṇa,* being the ground of the cognition of objects, cannot at the same time become the objects of cognition. One conscious state may become object for another state of consciousness, but the same consciousness cannot be both the cognition of object and the object of cognition. The Yogācāras however take the same consciousness as cause and effect, means and result of the process of knowledge. But it is absurd to speak of the same thing as the subject and the object, the knower and the known.[1]

The force of the Naiyāyika's objection against the Yogācāra view of *pramāṇa* lies in its insistence on a fundamental difference between knowledge or consciousness and its object. Knowledge as manifestation presupposes some object that is manifested by it. As against all idealism the modern realists of the West point out that experience or precipe presupposes existence or esse. For the Naiyāyikas experience or knowledge presupposes some object which may be mental or physical, existent or non-existent. Hence, it is meaningless to speak of knowledge as self-manifestation, *i.e.* a manifestation of itself as object and by itself as subject.

4. Nyāya Criticism of the Mīmāṁsā and Sāṅkhya Views

In the Bhāṭṭa Mīmāṁsā, *pramā* or true knowledge is defined as primary and original knowledge (*anadhigata*). Hence, *pramāṇa* is that which gives us new knowledge, *i.e.* a true cognition of objects of which gives us new knowledge, *i.e.* a true cognition of objects of which we have had no knowledge in the past. Every case of knowledge, if it is to be of any value, should be original in character. It implies a new step, by which we advance from the known to what is not yet known. Real knowledge is a synthetic process adding new contents to the old stock of knowledge. *Pramāṇa* is the means of acquiring knowledge, and so must lead to the acquisition of such knowledge as is not yet attained but is still to be acquired. If

1. NVT., p. 21; NM., p. 16.

the objects are already known, there can be no necessity of acquiring a knowledge of them. The method of knowledge, therefore, must be concerned in knowing what has not been previously known. It follows from this that memory (*smṛti*) cannot be *pramā* or true knowledge, in so far as it is not a new experience but the resuscitation of some old experience. It has no new contents but refers only to the already acquired contents of knowledge.[1]

Here, the Naiyāyikas point out that the definition of *pramā*, as knowledge which has the characteristics of truth and novelty (*yāthārthya* and *anadhigatatva*), is too narrow. It excludes many cases of knowledge which are undoubtedly valid but do not refer to absolutely new objects. Eternal objects, such as space, time, soul, God, etc., cannot be said to be wholly unknown to us. We consider them to be eternal because their non-existence at any time cannot be proved. These have a necessary existence both for our thought and the things of the world. Our present knowledge of such objects comes to us as necessary knowledge. Once we have such knowledge we cannot say either that the objects had no existence before or that we had no knowledge of them prior to this. Rather we think that we had an implicit knowledge of the objects, whatever may be the degree of its clearness or distinctness. They are *a priori* like Kant's categories of the understanding. As Pringle Pattison says: "Mathematical truths, as soon as we realise them, are seen to be necessary, and we seem to have known the always."[2] Plato supposes that our knowledge of them is a recollection. Without going so far it may be said that we have an *a priori* knowledge of eternal entities in the same way in which Russell[3] shows we have an a *priori* knowledge of general principles. Nevertheless, they may be better known or cognised by perception, inference and testimony. But, on the Bhāṭṭa view, no knowledge about these eternal principles can be valid, since it cannot be knowledge of what was not at all known before. Further, our knowledge of

1. *Yathārthamagṛhītagrāhijñānaṁ pramāṇamiti*, SD., p. 45.
2. *The Idea of Immortality*, pp. 46-47.
3. *Problems of Philosophy*, Ch. VII.

ordinary objects is, more often than not, a knowledge of what was previously known. But that does not make them less valid than the most valid knowledge we can have.

Again, the validity of *pratyabhijñā* or recognition as a form of knowledge, becomes inexplicable. To recognise a thing is to know it as what was once known before. In it the object that is now perceived is directly felt as the same thing that was perceived before. We have, for example, the judgment 'this is that man whom I say yesterday'. The 'this' of the present perception is identified with the 'that' of past perception. Recognition cannot, therefore, be a knowledge of what was not known. Still all men including the Bhāṭṭas, admit that recognition is a form of *pramā* or true knowledge. But consistency requires that we must either give up the idea of novelty (*anadhigatatva*) as a characteristic of *pramā* or say that recognition (*pratyabhijñā*) is not true knowledge, *i.e.* is *apramā*. In fact, however, no knowledge is made true or false by reason simply of its originality or unoriginality. The truth of knowledge does not depend on the newness of its object.[1]

In the case of what is called *dhāravāhikajñāna* or persistent knowledge, the Bhāṭṭa definition of *pramā* obviously fails. When the same thing is known by a man for some time there is a continuous series of cognitions with regard to it. Here all the cognitions, which succeed the first and constitute the continuous series together with it, refer to the same thing that has been previously known by the first cognition. We cannot say that each member of the series refers to a new object. Hence, persistent knowledge is, as the Bhāṭṭas themselves admit, valid knowledge, although it is not a knowledge of the new, but of the already known (*adhigata*).[2]

Of course, the Bhāṭṭas contend that the continuous cognition refers to new objects in all its parts. The series of cognitions occurs at different instants of time. The thing as thus connected with different times, though apparently the same, becomes really

1. NM., pp. 21-22.
2. NVT., p. 21.

different objects for our persistent knowledge of it. The successive cognitions are valid in so far as each apprehends the object as qualified by a different time and therefore as something new.[1] The Advaita Vedānta suggests another way out of the difficulty. According to it, persistent knowledge is valid either because its different parts perceive different instants of time or because it is one single cognition as long as it persists and no new mental modification is produced. A continuous cognition is thus one present knowledge manifesting one thing which was previously unmanifested. So the question does not arise as to whether the series of cognitions apprehends new objects or not.[2]

To this the Naiyāyikas object that the instants of time (*kṣaṇa*) cannot be perceived by us. The different instants, entering into the persistent cognition, being unperceived, cannot be said to constitute different objects for the series of cognitions.[3] Were these temoral differences apprehended and wedged into the body of the continuous cognition, its continuity would be broken up and our sense of continuity be lost. As that is not the case, we are to say that in persistent knowledge the series of cognitions refer to one and the same object. Nor can it be urged that persistent knowledge is a single state of cognition enduring for some time. Although from a subjective standpoint continuous cognition may be considered to be one present state of conscious illumination, yet objectively it is a series of cognitions. The present is not a point or one instant of time, which is imperceptible, but a mass or block comprising several instants, while a cognition cannot endure for more than one moment or instant of time. Hence, a present continuous cognition is really a series of cognitions, of which those that succeed the first are admitted by all to be as valid as the first.[4] It cannot be seriously maintained that they open up new aspects of

1. SD., p. 45.
2. VP., Chap. 1.
3. NVT., *ibid.*
4. TC., 1, pp. 379 f. Compare the Nyāya account of 'the present' with James's 'specious present' (*Principles of Psychology*) and Titchener's 'time-field' (*Text-Book of Psychology*).

the object. 'The palm of the hand seen a thousandth time adds no new content to our previous knowledge of it.'[1] In fact the validity of knowledge does not lie in any character of novelty. No knowledge is made true or false by reason simply of its originality or unoriginality. The truth of knowledge does not depend on the newness of its object. The validity of any knowledge comprises three facts, namely, first a correct presentation of the object; second, the practical activity of the knowing subject in response to the presentation, and finally, fulfilment of the activity in relation to the object. These three facts are inseparably bound up with one another, so that with the true presentation of the object, there follows the reaction of the subject and the fulfilment of the reaction by way of its producing the expected results. Now, all the repeated experiences of a thing are equally connected with these three facts. Hence there is no reason to think, as the Bhāṭṭa view will lead us to think, that the first cognition of a thing is valid knowledge while all other subsequent cognitions of it are invalid.[2]

The Prābhākara Mīmāṁsā defines *pramā* or valid knowledge as immediate experience (*anubhūti*). It is different from memory which is due solely to the impressions of past experiences. All immediate experiences have intrinsic validity. There cannot be any question as to the validity of immediate experience, because that is self-evident. Memory, however, is mediate knowledge, being conditioned by past experience. Hence the truth of knowledge (*prāmāṇya*) is guaranteed by its having the character of immediacy.[3]

The Nayāyikas bring forward the charge of inconsistency against the Prābhākara definition of *pramā*. If all cognitions are valid by themselves, there is no justification for treating memory-cognition as invalid on the ground that it is not immediate experience. It is also curious that the Prābhākaras take memory as valid so far as the manifestation of knowledge and the knower is concerned, but invalid with regard to the manifestation of the object.

1. NM. pp. 21f.
2. NVT., p. 21; NM., *ibid.*
3. *Pramāṇamanubhūtiḥ sā smṛternyā*, etc., *Prakaraṇapañcikā*, p. 42.

According to them, every cognition is a triune manifestation (*tripuṭīsaṁvit*). It manifests the subject, the object and itself at one and the same time. Memory as a cognition is valid so far as it manifests the knower and itself (*ātmasvātma*), but invalid so far as it manifests the object (*vedya*). But there is no sense in this invidious distinction. Either memory is wholly valid or it is not valid at all. Further, it is difficult to see what *anubhūti* or immediate experience really means. It cannot mean such knowledge as is not conditioned in its origin by some other knowledge. If it did, *savikalpaka* or determinate perception and inference would become invalid, since these depend on previous experience. Other possible meanings of *anubhūti* also do not stand scrutiny. So, the Prābhākara definition of *pramā* and *pramāṇa* is rejected as unsound by the Nyāya.[1]

In the Sāṅkhya system, it is the function of the intellect (*buddhivṛtti*) that is regarded as *pramāṇa* or the specific cause of true knowledge. The self knows an object through a mental modification that corresponds to the impression produced in the sense organ by the object in question. The object having impressed its form on the sense organ, the mind presents it to the self through a corresponding modification of itself. Hence, the mental function is *pramāṇa* or the source of our knowledge of the object.

The Naiyāyika rejects this view also as untenable. According to him, it is unintelligible how a material and unconscious principle like buddhi can be the locus of the substratum of knowledge. It is the self that has the cognition of objects and not any blind modification of unconscious matter.[2]

The Nyāya criticism of the Bhāṭṭa view of *pramā* as knowledge of what was not previously known raises an important problem of knowledge. The problem is this: Is knowledge a cognition of the known or of the unknown? If it be a cognition of the known, there is no possibility of attaining it. We do not want to know a thing which is already known, and cannot seek to know anything which is absolutely unknown. The Bhāṭṭas would say that since the known

1. TR. and SS., pp. 19 f.
2. NM., p. 26.

need not be known again, all knowledge must be a cognition of what was not known. On the other hand, the Naiyāyikas point out the knowledge need not necessarily be a cognition of what was not previously known. If it were so, we could not speak of the development of knowledge or of a knowledge of the old and the familiar as we have it in recognition. It seems to us that the Naiyāyikas are substantially right in their contention that the knowledge of what is already known is possible. All knowledge, except acquaintance, admits of degrees of determinateness.[1] Our knowledge of objects may pass from an indeterminate cognition of their bare existence to a definite recognition of their nature, character and past history. The more we know of the characteristics of an object, the more determinate is our knowledge of that object. What is known to have certain characteristics may be further known to have other important characteristics. It is in this way that our knowledge of an object develops and becomes more precise and comprehensive. It is true that the other characteristics were not previously known and so impart to the later knowledge a character of novelty. This however does not show that the object itself becomes new whenever we discern new characteristics in it. Rather we are to say that we know the same object which, in a way, we already know. In fact, our response to an absolutely new object is more like a shock of surprise than knowledge in the proper sense.

The Prābhākara view of *pramā* as immediate experience (*anubhūti*) is not really refuted by the Nyāya. Its criticism of this view generally sounds like the *ignoratio elenchi*. What it does is not to attack *anubhūti* as a character of true knowledge, but to show its inconsistency with the Prābhākara account of memory. In fact, the Prābhākara's *anubhūti* and the Naiyāyika's *anubhava* are cognate concepts. Their use of these concepts to exclude memory from *pramā* of valid knowledge appears, as we shall see, to be equally unsound. *Anubhūti* or *anubhava,* as a character of *pramā* does not necessarily imply that memory is not *pramā* or valid knowledge.

1. *Cf.* L.S. Stebbing, *A Modern Introduction to Logic*, p. 24.

The Nyāya should not have found fault with the Sāṅkhya views of the intellect or the mind as an organ of knowledge (*pramāṇa*). On its own showing, *pramāṇa* as the unique cause of *pramā* is a complex of physical and psychical conditions (*bodhābodhasvabhāvā sāmagrī*). Hence, there seems to be nothing wrong merely in taking a material principle like *buddhi* as the means or organ of knowledge (*pramāṇa*).

Chapter III

Factors of Valid Knowledge (*Pramā*)

1. The Subject, Object and Method of Valid Knowledge

Pramā or valid knowledge has been defined by the Nyāya as true presentational cognition (*yathārthānubhava*). It we analyse this conception of *pramā* we shall get three essential factors involved in all valid knowledge. Knowledge as a function implies a subject-object relation. In all knowledge, be it true or false or neither, we see that a subject or knower stands related to an object, in so far as the former has a cognition of the latter. When however we have not *any* knowledge or cognition in view but only true or valid knowledge (*pramā*), there must be another factor, namely, a method of knowledge (*pramāṇa*). Of course, any knowledge, true or false, may be said to be produced by certain conditions or causes. But the cause or ground of wrong knowledge is not *pramāṇa* or a method of knowledge. The cause or the ground of non-valid knowledge (*apramā*) is not, therefore, a factor of valid knowledge (*pramā*) . Hence, we see that the conception of *pramā* or valid knowledge implies three necessary factors, namely, the subject, the object and the method of knowledge (*pramātā, prameya* and *pramāṇa*).[1]

As to the first, namely, the *pramātā*, it has been said that every knowledge involves a subject or knowner, in which knowledge inheres as an attribute. The subject is the substantive ground of all cognitions. It is that which likes and dislikes things and acts accordingly. Hence the *pramātā* is the self conceived as an intelligent agent. It is also independent in the sense that it exists

---

1. *Sādhanāśrayāvyatiriktatve sati pramāvyāptaṁ pramāṇam*, *Sarvadarśana-saṁgraha*, Chapter on Nyāya philosophy.

for itself and is an end to itself. Its independence comes out in the fact that it enjoys and suffers, it is the centre of all activities, and that it directs the course of other things without being determined in its course by them, *i.e.* it is self-determined. The *pramātā* thus described by the Nyāya resembles the self as that is conceived in modern self-psychology.[1] Like it, the *pramātā* is that which knows and strives, enjoys and suffers, remembers and expects; it is an agent, a striver, a desire, a refuser.

Secondly, *pramā* or valid knowledge implies some *prameya* or object, to which the process of knowledge refers or to which it is directed. The object of knowledge may be either existent or non-existent. Both positive and negative facts may become the objects of true knowledge, but the knowledge takes different forms in the two cases. In the case of existent objects our knowledge is positive and does not depend on any objects other than its own. The knowledge of non-existent objects is negative and conditional on the direct apprehension of similar existent objects. "The light of a lamp, which reveals the existence of certain perceived objects in a dark room, manifests also the non-existence of those that are not perceived, for if the latter had existed there, they would have been perceived like the similar perceived objects."[2] Hence just as there can be no knowledge without a conscious subject that knows, so there is no knowledge without an object–a thing or an attribute, a state or a process, a positive or a negative fact that is known. Subject and object (*pramātā* and *prameya*) are strictly correlative factors involved in all knowledge. They are distinguishable no doubt as the knower and the known, but not separable in any act of knowledge.

Thirdly, all true knowledge must be connected with some method of knowledge. In Western philosophy it is customary to analyse the knowledge-relation into the three factors of subject, object and process of knowledge. These correspond respectively to the *pramātā, prameya* and *pramā* in Indian philosophy. In

1. *Cf.* McDougall, *An Outline of Psychology*, pp. 21, 426.
2. NB., I.I.I.

addition to these three, the Nyāya recognises the special cause of knowledge (*pramāṇa*) as an important factor. This is what in Western logic is usually called a method of knowledge and not a factor of it. While it does not overlook their distinction, the Nyāya rightly considers the subject, object, method and resulting state of knowledge (*pramātā, prameya, pramāṇa* and *pramā*) as mutually implicated aspects of the whole truth. Each of these is as essential to knowledge as the rest, and each of them involves the rest by way of logical implication (*prasakti*). So, it has been said that in these four principles, when taken together in one whole but never as disjoined, there is the realisation of truth (*tattvaparisamāpti*). Truth is realised when the subject having known the real by *pramāṇa,* as good or bad or neutral, proceeds to obtain it or avoid it or remains indifferent to it, as the case may be, and ends in actual attainment or avoidance or mere apathy.

The real has thus a value for the knowing subject. Any account of reality as absolutely foreign to our subjective interests and personal values would be a fundamental misconception of it. The different systems of Indian philosophy agree in holding that the world of experience is a system of moral dispensation, in which man has to work out his destiny in obedience to the universal law of moral causation (*karma*). Right knowledge of reality is of supreme importance for man to reach the destination of life. True knowledge is not a passive and lifeless reflection of reality. On the other hand, it is that philosophic view of reality, which has its basis in the vital needs of our spiritual nature and is essentially conducive to the attainment of our supreme life-purpose (*niḥśreyasa*). Herein lies one of the striking points of contrast between Eastern and Western philosophy. In the West, philosophy is generally a matter of intellectual understanding. It is indeed a reflective knowledge of the nature and relations of things and beings. But such knowledge has not always a direct bearing on life and conduct. It is seldom pursued with the excess intention and determined will to solve the problems and work out the final good of life. To the ancient Indian thinkers, however, philosophy was not a mere rational knowledge of things and theories, but a means to the realisation of our life-end, the path to the final goal of life.

2. Distinction of the Method from the Subject and Object of Valid Knowledge

It will appear from the preceding section that the subject (*pramāṇa*), the object (*prameya*) and the method (*pramāṇa*) are all necessary conditions of valid knowledge (*pramā*). No valid knowledge is possible without any one of them. For valid knowledge, the subject and object are as much necessary as the method of it. Hence the question naturally arises: How are we to distinguish the method from the subject and the object and say that the first is the special cause (*asādhāraṇa kāraṇa*) of valid knowledge? Why is it that among the equally necessary factors of knowledge some one should be marked off from the rest and called the unique operative cause (*karaṇa*) of it? How do we know that *pramāṇa* is the most efficient ground (*sādhakatama*) of knowledge, while the other factors are only the general conditions or the logical implications of knowledge?

In the Nyāya system the answer to this question is to be found in two very important considerations. That *pramāṇa* is the special cause and the most important ground of valid knowledge will, in the first place, appear from the following facts.

First of all we see that there is a uniform relation of agreement in presence and in absence between *pramāṇa* and *pramā* as between cause and effect. A *pramāṇa* is always accompanied by valid knowledge which, in its turn, can never arise without the former. Of course, thee can be no valid knowledge without a subject and an object. But every case of the existence of subject ad object is not necessarily a case of the appearance of *pramā* or valid knowledge. On the contrary, in every case in which a *pramāṇa* is operative, *pramā* or valid knowledge must appear as a natural sequel. Thus, a man has no perception of objects in relation to which no sense organ is operative, although he, as subject, and those objects exist side by side. If, however, the objects are in contact with his sense and his mind responds to the sense impressions, he cannot but have perception of those objects.

Secondly, we observe that the *pramātā* or subject arrives at a true knowledge of objects only when it is aided by a *pramāṇa* or an operative cause of knowledge. Contraiwise, we find that the subject and object cannot produce any knowledge in the absence of the *pramāṇa* or the source of knowledge. That is, the subject knows objects only when it makes use of a certain method, but not singly by itself.

Thirdly, we see that *pramāṇa* is the last link in the chain of antecedent conditions that lead to the knowledge of objects. It is the immediate antecedent to the origin of knowledge. The aggregate of psycho-physical conditions, on which knowledge depends, is completed by *pramāṇa,* and knowledge appears immediately as an effect. *Pramāṇa* is the cause of knowledge inasmuch as it is the immediate antecedent, on which knowledge follows first and immediate.[1]

Lastly, it has been pointed out but the Naiyāyikas that a distinction between the different kinds of knowledge is made by reference to the methods of acquiring knowledge. Perception, inference, testimony, etc., are regarded as different kinds of knowledge because they are due to different *pramāṇas* or methods of knowledge. This cannot be due to the subject or the object of knowledge, because these may be the same in what are generally admitted to be different kinds of knowledge. The same subject may know the same object first by inference and then by perception, as when a man confirms the inference of fire in a distant place by approaching it. Hence, the subject and object cannot explain why one kind of knowledge is called perception and another inference. Similarly, we find that the mind's contact with the soul is the common mediate cause of all forms of knowledge. But the mode of this contact is different in different kinds of knowledge. We cannot account for such different modes by the subject and object of knowledge, for they may be the same in two kinds of knowledge. It is the *pramāṇa* that determines the mind's contact with the soul in different ways in the different kinds of knowlede.[2]

1. NV., pp. 5-7; NVT., pp. 22-25.
2. NV., pp. 5-7; NVT., pp. 22-25.

There are two ways of classifying knowledge, *i.e.* by reference to the nature of the objects known, and by reference to the grounds of knowledge. According to the first, we have as many kinds of knowledge as there are kinds of knowables or possible objects of knowledge. This way of distinguishing between the different kinds of knowledge has been followed by the Jainas in their theory of knowledge which divides knowledge broadly into the two kinds of *pratyakṣa* or immediate and *parokṣa* or mediate. Hobhouse also follows the same principle in classifying the methods of knowledge in his *Theory of knowledge.* The second way, however, is generally accepted in Western philosophy. According to this, there are as many kinds of knowledge as there are ways of knowing or specific grounds of knowledge. The Nyāya follows this way along with the Vedānta and some other Indian systems. It shows also that a distinction of knowledge into different kinds cannot be based on the subject or the object of knowledge. The conclusion drawn from this and other facts is that *pramāṇa* or the method is the operative cause of knowledge (*pramā-karaṇam*).

The second consideration, on which the superiority of *pramāṇa* to the other factors of valid knowledge is based, is this. The primary function of knowledge is to give us truth in the sense of real correspondence between idea and object (*arthavattvam*). Now for the fulfilment of this function knowledge is primarily and directly dependent on *pramāṇa* or the operative cause of knowledge. The other factors of knowledge cannot lead to truth except through the aid of *pramāṇa*.[1] The objective validity of knowledge is directly dependent on the efficacy of the method or *pramāṇa* employed to acquire it. The subject or *pramātā* cannot directly produce the validity of knowledge, because as an agent it requires means to bring about this result and cannot itself directly produce the result. Nor can the object or *prameya* be said to produce the state of valid knowledge, for in inference the object is absent and cannot, therefore, be operative in producing a knowledge of itself in the

1. *Arthavati ca pramāṇe pramātā prameyaṁ pramitirityarthavanti bhavanti*, NB., I.I.I.

knowing subject. It may, of course, be said that once we have the truth, we find it as belonging to the subject, the object and the knowledge-relation between the two. Still the subject, the object and the sate of knowledge do not produce the truth, but owe it to the functioning of *pramāṇa* or the ground of knowledge. Hence *pramāṇa* or the method of knowledge is the means or the operative cause (*karaṇa*) of knowledge, as distinguished from the *pramātā* or subject and *prameya* or object which are indeed logically implied in all knowledge but are not directly concerned in producing objectively valid knowledge (*pramā*).[1]

Thus according to the Naiyāyikas, the objective validity of knowledge is due to *pramāṇa* or the method on which it is based. The conscious subject and the cognised object cannot account for the correspondence of knowledge with real facts. The subject and the object participate in truth in so far as they are made to do so by some efficient organ of knowledge, the sense or the reason with which we are endowed. The universal condition of all knowledge is indeed consciousness. But from mere consciousness we cannot deduce the specific modes of knowledge, such as perception of the table, inference of coming rain, verbal cognitions and so forth. Hence while consciousness seems to be the first and the general cause of all knowledge, we require certain specific second causes to explain the particular modes of knowledge and their correspondence to particular objects or facts of the world. Such specific causes of knowledge are called *pramāṇas* in Indian philosophy.

---

1. NVT., pp. 22. 29 f.

Chapter IV

Test of Truth and Error

1. The Problems and Alternative Solutions

In the preceding chapters we have considered the different conceptions of *bhrama* or error and *pramā* or true knowledge. We have also seen that the specific modes of knowledge arise from certain operative causes or specific conditions (*jñānakaraṇa*). These are called *pramāṇa* when the knowledge is true and *apramāṇa* when it is false. Here, we have to consider the following problems as to the truth and falsity of knowledge. Admitting that knowledge depends on certain specific conditions for its origin, how are we to explain its truth or falsehood? How again are we to know its truth or falsehood as the case may be? In other words, the questions are: How is the validity or invalidity of knowledge constituted? And, how is its validity or invalidity known by us? The first question refers to the conditions of origin (*utpatti*), while the second, to the conditions of *ascertainment* (*jñapti*) of truth and falsity.

Generally speaking, two possible answers may be given to the above two questions. First, it may be said that knowledge is both made and ascertained to be valid or invalid by the same conditions which bring about that knowledge (*jñānasāmagrī*). Secondly, it may be said that the truth or falsity of knowledge is both constituted and known by external conditions. On the first alternative, both truth and error would be self-evident (*svataḥ*). On the second alternative, neither truth nor falsehood could be self-evident, but both must be evidenced by something else (*parataḥ*). Or, a distinction may be made between the two cases of truth and falsehood. It may thus be said that while the truth of knowledge is constituted and ascertained by intrinsic conditions (*svataḥ*), its falsity is made so by extrinsic conditions (*parataḥ*). Or, we may just reverse the order and say that while falsity is self-evident (*svataḥ*), truth requires evidence or proof by external conditions (*parataḥ*).

Thus, we came upon four alternative solutions of the problems set forth above. Each of these has been adopted and supported by one or other of the systems of Indian philosophy. The Sāṅkhya accepts the first alternative, namely that both the validity and invalidly of knowledge are self-evident. The Nyāya is generally in favour of the second. *viz.* that neither validity nor invalidity is self-evident, but that both are constituted and known by external conditions. The Bauddhas support the view that falsity is self-evident in knowledge and that external conditions are necessary for truth, if there be any. The Mīmāṁsā and the Vedānta advocate the theory that all knowledge has self-evident validity, while falsehood is due to certain extrinsic conditions.[1]

2. The Nyāya Theory of Extrinsic Validity and Invalidity

According to the Nyāya, knowledge is just the manifestation (*prakāśa*) of objects. As such, it is neutral to truth and falsehood. No knowledge is true or false on its own account, *i.e.* simply because it is produced by certain specific causes (*jñānasāmagrī*). The truth and falsity of knowledge depend respectively on its conformity and non-conformity to objects or facts. A knowledge is true when it corresponds to the real nature and relations of its object; if not, it becomes false, provided it claims to be true. Thus, truth and falsity are characters that appear to be added to knowledge which is indifferent to both, but may have either, according to special circumstances.[2] Hence, the conditions of the validity or invalidity of knowledge must be different from and other than the conditions of the knowledge itself. If knowledge and its validity were conditioned by the same conditions, then error too would become valid knowledge. Even error is a form of knowledge and is conditioned by the conditions of that knowledge. Hence, it should

1. *Sarvadarśanasaṁgraha*, Chapter on Jaimini system.
2. Yathārthetarasādhāraṇo dharmo bodharūpatvam, NM., p. 169.

be as good as valid knowledge. That is, the validity of knowledge being conditioned by the conditions of knowledge itself, there cannot be any false knowledge. On the other hand, if knowledge and its invalidity were due to the same conditions, there can be no valid knowledge. Hence, we must admit that the truth and falsity of knowledge are due to different special conditions other than the conditions or specific causes of knowledge itself.

What then are the special conditions of the validity and invalidity of knowledge? According to the Nyāya, the validity of knowledge is due to the efficiency of the conditions of knowledge (*kārṇaguṇa*), while its invalidity is due to some deficiency in those conditions (*kāraṇadoṣa*). The efficiency or deficiency of the conditions is constituted by certain positive factors. We cannot say that the efficiency of the conditions of knowledge is simply the absence of defects in them (*doṣābhāva*), or that deficiency means only the absence of efficient conditions (*guṇābhāva*). Both efficiency and deficiency stand for certain special positive conditions which modify the general conditions of knowledge and make it true and false respectively. In fact, the specific character of an effect (*kāryaviśeṣa*) is to be explained by some specific character of the cause (*kāraṇaviśeṣa*). Truth as a specific character of some knowledge and falsity as another specific character of some other knowledge must therefore be due to different specific characters of the general conditions of knowledge.[1] Thus, the contact of an object with a sense organ is the general condition of perception. But its validity depends on such special conditions as the health of the sense organ, nearess of the object, sufficient light and sense-object contact. On the contrary, perception is invalid when it general conditions are modified or vitiated by such other special conditions as disease, distance, darkness and slender sense-object contact. Similar is the case with inference and other kinds of knowledge. Hence, both the validity and invalidity of knowledge

1. *Doṣo pramāyā janakaḥ pramāyāstu guṇo bhavet*, etc., *Siddhānta-muktāvalī*, 131; *pramā jñānahetvatiriktahetvadhīnā kāryyatve sati tadviśeṣtvāt apramāvat*, *Kusumāñjali*, pp. 207-09.

are conditioned by extrinsic conditions other than the conditions of knowledge itself (*parataḥ, utpattiḥ*).

Next we come to the question of the ascertainment of validity and invalidity (*prāmāṇyā-prāmāṇyaniścaya*). How is the validity or invalidity of knowledge known? Are they known by the same conditions that constitute knowledge or by any other external conditions? Generally speaking, the Naiyāyikas maintain that the truth and falsity of knowledge are known by certain external conditions other than the conditions of knowledge itself (*parataḥ prāmāṇyāprāmāṇyajñapti*). If the validity of knowledge be known intrinsically by the conditions of knowledge itself, there can be no doubt with regard to the validity of any knowledge. On the other hand, if the knowledge of invalidity be due to the conditions of knowledge itself, there can be no wrong action. That is, if truth be self-evident, there need be no doubt and dispute about knowledge, and if falsehood be self-evident, there should be no illusion and disappointment. In fact, neither truth nor falsehood is known to belong to knowledge just at the time we have that knowledge. As a general rule, the validity or invalidity of knowledge is known some time after the knowledge itself has appeared.[1]

What, then, are the external conditions of the knowledge of validity or invalidity of knowledge? The Naiyāyikas answer that both are known by inference. While knowledge may be internally perceived, its validity or invalidity is to be *inferred* from such extrinsic conditions as its capacity or incapacity to produce successful activity (*pravṛttisāmathya*).[2] Knowledge is known to be valid when it leads to successful activity in relation to its object. We know objects by means of perception, inference, etc. This knowledge sets up certain psycho-physical reactions (*pravṛtti*) in the knowing subject. The success of these reactions, *i.e.* their duly connected with the expected object, is the evidence for the truth of the knowledge. Men sometimes act on wrong knowledge under the belief that it is true and arises out of valid conditions. The

1. TC., I. pp. 184, 233; NM., pp. 160, 169 f.

2. *Prāmāṇyaṁ hi samarthapravṛttijanakatvādanumeyam*, NVTP., 1.1.1.

reason for this confusion between true and false knowledge is some point of similarity between the two. Even wrong knowledge is as good a cognition of objects with their general characters (*sāmānyaparicchedaka*) as right knowledge is such. So, one is apt to be mistaken for the other. But in such cases what distinguishes valid knowledge from the invalid is the test of successful activity. A valid knowledge not only gives us a cognition of some object, but also leads to successful actions on the part of the knowing subject. An invalid knowledge, on the other hand, gives us a cognition of objects indeed, but it fails to lead to successful activity. If our knowledge does not correspond to its object, it cannot be practically efficient in relation to it. In the cases of illusion, hallucination, dream, etc., our knowledge cannot be the basis of effective actions. The Naiyāyikas, therefore, conclude that the truth of knowledge is not self-evident in it, but is evidenced or known by inference from successful activity. By successful activity, they mean the volitional experiences (*arthakriyājñāna*) of the expected object (*phalajñāna*). The perception of water in a certain place is known to be true when by acting on that perception we meet with the expected water. Contraiwise, a knowledge is known to be invalid, when it is contradicted by subsequent volitional experiences (*pravṛttivisaṁvāda*). That is, the invalidity of knowledge is inferred from the failure of the practical activities based on it. The perception of silver in a shell is known to be illusory because the act of picking it up does not give the expected silver. Hence *pravṛttisāmarthya* means that the object as cognised is found present when acted upon by us, *i.e.* it is given to volitional experience just as it was given to the corresponding cognitive experience.[1]

In the case of the knowledge of familiar objects (*abhyāsadaśājñāna*), we do not require the test of successful activity or conative satisfaction (*pravṛttisāmarthya*). In this case it may seem at first sight that the validity or invalidity of knowledge is self-evident (*svataḥ*). A habitual experience is known to be valid or invalid even before we proceed to act upon it and see if it leads to the expected object or not. It would therefore seem that the

1. NM., pp. 171-72.

validity or invalidity of habitual experience need not be known by any inference and, as such, is self-evident. But here the Naiyāyikas point out that it is a contradiction to say that the truth of the familiar is self-evident. The knowledge of the validity of familiar knowledge is conditioned by the conditions of its familiarity. The familiarity of knowledge means its similarity to previous knowledge. Hence, if we have ascertained the validity of the previous knowledge, we may very well know the validity of the present familiar knowledge by an inference based on its similarity to the former (*tajjātīyatva*). What happens here is that the previous verification of knowledge by conative satisfaction becomes a determinant of similar subsequent knowledge. This shows that the validity or invalidity of such knowledge as is not new is known by inference based on essential similarity or generic identity. This inference is, in most cases, implicit and unconscious. But it is never absent. We may put it explicitly in the form of a syllogism like this: 'All knowledge of a known character is valid; this knowledge is of that character; therefore this is valid.' So too, *mutatis mutandis,* for the inference by which we know the invalidity of the knowledge of familiar objects.[1] Hence, the Naiyāyikas conclude that knowledge is both made true or false, and known to be true or false by certain external conditions other than those conditioning the knowledge itself.

3. Objections to the Theory Answered by the Nyāya

According to the Nyāya, knowledge is not ascertained as true or false at its very inception. To have knowledge is not, at the same time, to know it as true or false. The validity or invalidity of knowledge is first known by us when we act upon that knowledge and see if the action is successful or not. But with regard to the test of conative satisfaction (*pravṛttisāmarthya*) as a condition of the knowledge of the validity of knowledge, it may be asked: how do we know that the feeling of satisfaction is true and not false? The perception of water, for example, is to be known as valid when it leads to the volitional experience of the expected results

1. NM., p. 174.

(*arthakriyākhyaphalajñāna*). But how do we know that the volitional experience is valid? Does it not require to be validated by other conditions? If it does, there will be no end of the process of validation and the first perception of water cannot be completely verified.[1]

To this question the Naiyāyikas give two answers. First, it has been said that the experience of expected objects (*phalajñāna*) does not ordinarily require any test of its validity, because there is no doubt about it or because there is the fulfilment of our purpose in it. As for instance, the first perception of water in a mirage requires to be tested because we have doubts about its validity, but that of man going into water need not be further tested, since it is not infected by any doubt and it fulfils the man's expectations.

Secondly, the volitional experience of expected objects may, if necessary, be verified by certain special characteristics of it. Thus, the visual perception of water may be validated by the expected tactual sensations of it, and the latter may be further confirmed by the experiences of bathing, washing, drinking, etc., which are usually associated with water. It may be urged here that a man has the whole series of experiences even in a dream. Hence, it is at least theoretically possible that the first volitional experiences of water as well as those of its usual associated are as invalid as dream experiences. According to the Naiyāyikas, this hypothesis in untenable. There is an obvious distinction between dream consciousness and waking experience. While the latter is clear and distinct, the former is confused and indistinct. Dreams have not the order and uniformity of our waking experiences. Dream experience is contradicted by waking perceptions. There cannot be any retrospection of dream cognitions (*anvyavasāya*). What is cognised in dream cannot be the object of a later dream cognised. In dream all things may be seen but none remembered as what has been previously seen. Hence, the waking volitional experience cannot be reduced to dream.[2]

---

1. NM., p. 172.
2. NM., *ibid.*

The second objection against the Nyāya theory of extrinsic validity is that it involves the fallacy of reasoning in a circle (*parasparāśraya*). The knowledge of the validity of knowledge is said to be conditioned by successful activity, which, in its turn, depends on the knowledge of validity. Successful activity depends on two conditions. First, it depends on a true knowledge of objects. Any knowledge of objects cannot make our actions successful. If it were so, even a wrong cognition of silver should lead to the actual attainment of it. Hence, successful activity must always be due to a true knowledge of objects. Secondly, successful activity requires a right understanding of those objects as means to some end or good. We strive for certain objects only when we know them as the necessary conditions of realising some good. Such knowledge may, of course, be derived from inference. If the present objects are similar to other things which proved to be effective means in the past, we infer that these too will serve as means to the present end. This then implies that successful activity requires a valid knowledge of objects as means to some good. But we cannot know that we have a valid knowledge of objects unless we already know the validity of knowledge means. Hence, it seems that successful activity depends on the knowledge of validity, while the knowledge of validity depends on successful activity. The two being thus necessarily interdependent, neither can be made the ground of the other, and so the validity of knowledge can never be know.[1]

The Naiyāyikas meet the above objection with a just recognition of the difficulties raised in it. According to them, the validity of knowledge is not self-evident, but must be ascertained from certain external conditions. In the case of new objects of experience, such conditions are to be found in the success of the practical activities based on any knowledge. The validity of knowledge is to be known from its capacity to produce successful activity. Hence, prior to any conative verification, the validity of knowledge remains doubtful. It is also true that a valid knowledge of objects is the

1. NM., pp. 163 f.

basis of successful actions in relation to them. An action cannot lead to the expected results unless it is grounded on a true knowledge of some objects as means to some end.

So far the Naiyāyikas admit the contention of the critics. But they point out that this does not lead to the conclusion drawn by them. It does not follow that there can be most successful activity without prior knowledge of the validity of knowledge. A true knowledge of objects is by no means the necessary condition of our action (*pravṛtti*) in relation to them. Any knowledge of objects, right or wrong, is the sufficient ground for producing certain modes of action on the part of the knowing subject. What happens generally is that we act even in the midst of uncertainty and that while acting we may have doubts as to the success of our actions. Even if it be true that to act for ends we must adopt means, it is not always necessary that we must have a true knowledge of the means of actions. A mere *belief* in the means as means will suffice for many voluntary actions.[1] Again, successful activity may be dependent on a valid knowledge of objects. But this does not mean that we must have a knowledge of the validity of the knowledge, by which it is conditioned. To act successfully we must have true knowledge as the basis of our activity. But we may have true knowledge even when we do not know that is true. To have true knowledge is not necessarily to know the truth of that knowledge.[2]

Hence, it follows that we can act when we have some knowledge of an object. The knowledge, by which our action is conditioned, may be true or false without our knowing it as true or false. If then we find that the action is successful, we come to know that the knowledge, on which it was grounded, must have been false. All that is necessary for our actions is that we must *believe* in what we know, and not that we must *verify* it as true before we proceed to act.

1. *Cf.* Stebbing, *Logic in Practice*, p. 99: "Many of our most important actions have to be performed in accordance with beliefs of such a kind (*i.e.*, beliefs more likely to be true)."

2. NM., p. 173.

When we have ascertained the validity of knowledge in some cases, some perceptions and inferences, we may in other similar cases act with an assurance that we have a true knowledge of some objects and that the means of our actions are efficient. Here a present knowledge, a new perception or inference, is known to be valid by reason of its essential similarity with some past valid knowledge. So, it may be said that prior to successful activity we know the validity of our knowledge. But even here it should be noted that the knowledge of validity is not the determinant or the cause (*prayojaka*) of practical activity. Such knowledge may precede activity but it is not a necessary condition of practical activity. If in the face of this, the critic insists that no successful activity is possible without previous knowledge of validity, the reply is that the critical activity itself must stop. The critic cannot be sure of the validity of his contention without the attainment of success. Hence if the attainment of success presupposes knowledge of validity, there cannot be any contention at all. The contending will can have no logical justification at all. The contending will can have no logical justification. There is, therefore, no necessity of the knowledge of validity either for activity as such or for successful activity. The latter does not presuppose the former. Hence, there is no fallacy of circular reasoning involved in the view that successful activity is the test of the truth of knowledge.

The third objection against the Nyāya view of extrinsic validity is that it involves the fallacy of *argumentum ad infinitum (anavasthā)*. If the validity of a knowledge is to be known from an external source, *i.e.* by means of some other knowledge, then we shall have to prove the validating knowledge on the external grounds, and so on *ad infinitum*. Thus, we are to say that the validity of perception is known by inference, that of inference by comparison (*upamāna*), that of the last by testimony, and that of testimony by still other methods of knowledge. Hence, the methods of knowledge must be innumerable. It may be said that to prove the validity of knowledge we need not go beyond the four methods, but prove one individual perception or inference by another perception or inference. Even then we cannot avoid the difficulty of infinite regress. What will happen is that within the circle of the four methods of the Nyāya, the process of validation of one knowledge by another will go on for ever. Thus the perception of water may be known to be valid by inference from successful activity or essential similarity. But how are we to know their validity of the validating inference? It must be by some other perception or inference, and so on *ad infinitum*. To avoid this difficulty the Naiyāyika cannot say that while the validity of the primary knowledge is established by the secondary, that of the latter is self-evident, and so requires no verification. If the truth of the secondary knowledge be self-evident, there is nothing to prevent the primary knowledge from having self-evident validity. Further, it will involve a surrender of the Naiyāyika position that the validity of all knowledge is constituted and ascertained by external conditions. Hence, it seems that on the Nyāya theory of validity, the process of the verification of knowledge will go on as an infinite chain of arguments, in which every link will hang on the next, but the last link is never to be found (*anādiparamparā*).[1]

To this the Naiyāyikas reply that the validity of a knowledge must be known by extrinsic conditions wherever it is necessary to know it at all. But it is not always necessary to ascertain the validity of a knowledge. It becomes necessary when any doubt as to its validity actually arises. Thus when we have the visual perception of water and have any doubt about its validity, we do, of course, ascertain it by inference from some successful activity, *i.e.* by touching or drinking the water. But the validity of the verifying experience requires no further examination or proof. There being no doubt about its validity we do not feel any necessity to prove or ascertain it. Hence the tactual perception of water validates the visual perception of it even when there is no ascertainment of its own validity. When, however, we have any doubt about the validity of the tactual perception, we must establish it by other external conditions, such as the corroborating testimony of different persons. Thus it follows that to know the validity of a knowledge by external grounds, it is not necessary to know the validity of those grounds

1. TC., I, pp. 276-77; NM., pp. 162 f.

so long as they stand undoubted and uncontradicted (*saṁśayābhāva*). If any one still doubts that the validating ground may itself be valid or not, then we have an unmeaning motiveless doubt which has no place in logic.[1]

Lastly, the Nyāya discusses the sceptical contention that there cannot be any valid knowledge. By valid knowledge is meant such knowledge of objects as is due to some method of knowledge (*pramāṇa*). But how is knowledge related to its object in the order of time? Does it precede or succeed or synchronize with the existence of its object (*prameya*)? Knowledge cannot be said to precede its object, since no knowledge appears except as the knowledge of some object. Nor can we say that knowledge succeeds or follows its object. A thing becomes an object to us in so far as it is known. There can be no object which is not the object of some knowledge. Without knowledge there is no object. If a thing can be an object independently of knowledge, there is no need of a method of knowledge for it. Nor again can we say that knowledge and the objects of knowledge co-exist in time. It that were so, all object of the world will be known at the same time, and there can be no desire to increase our knowledge of things. Further, this will contradict the Nyāya view of the serial order of cognitions, from which the existence of *manas* or the internal sense is inferred. Hence it follows that there can be neither knowledge nor a method of knowledge (*pramāṇa*).[2]

This is the sceptical objection against the possibility of knowledge as such. It denies the possibility of knowledge on the ground that the reference of knowledge to its object is inexplicable in the order of time. To this we may, of course, say with Green that, even if knowledge be taken as an event in time, its reference to the object is timeless, so that the question of the temporal relation between knowledge and its objects does not arise. The Naiyāyikas, however, admit that knowledge refers to its object in the order of time. But they point out that the temporal order between knowledge

1. NM., p. 173; TC., I, pp. 277-79, 282 f.
2. NB., 2.1. 8-11.

and its object is indeterminate. It is not the case that knowledge must have a fixed temporal order of priority or posteriority or simultaneity with its object. Knowledge arises out of certain causes and refers to some objects. In some cases knowledge precedes the existence of its object, as when we know something that is to happen in the future. In other cases the object as a physical thing or event may be said to precede our knowledge of it, as when we know that something *was* or had happened in the past. In still other cases knowledge and its object may be said to co-exist or to appear simultaneously in time. This is illustrated by the perception of present facts and, still better, by introspective knowledge of mental contents. Hence, the Naiyāyikas maintain that the time-relation between knowledge and its object cannot be objectively determined as something unalterably fixed like that between cause and effect. It is a variable relation which is to be determined as of this or that kind by actual observation of the instance of knowledge in question. In fact, the same thing can, in different cases, be called the knowledge of object (*pramā*), the object of knowledge (*prameya*) and the operative causes of knowledge (*pramāṇa*), just as the same word may be subject and predicate in different relations and positions. Hence the question of the time-relation between knowledge and the object of knowledge does not necessarily lead to the denial of all knowledge. Further, scepticism, if it is to be consistent, cannot really deny the possibility of knowledge. To deny knowledge is to disbelieve it. But to disbelieve is to *know* that something is not true. Hence the denial of knowledge must have a positive basis in same kind of knowledge. But it is a contradiction to deny knowledge by means of knowledge. This is the Naiyāyika's *reductio ad absurdum* of scepticism.[1]

4. Criticism of the Sāṅkhya View of Intrinsic Validity and Invalidity

According to the Sāṅkhya, truth and falsity are inherent in knowledge. A knowledge is both made true or false and known to

1. NB., 2.1 12-16.

be true or false by the conditions of the knowledge itself. Validity and invalidity cannot be produced in any knowledge *ab extra,* but must belong to it *ab initio*. The one is as much intrinsic or internally conditioned as the other. Hence knowledge must have validity or invalidity on its own account and, as such, these must be self-evident. This view follows from the Sāṅkhya theory of the pre-existence of effects (*satkāryavāda*). According to this, causation is only manifestation of the effect that potentially pre-exists in the cause. A cause can produce only that effect which is inherent in the causal complex. Otherwise, any cause will produce any effect, even the unreal and the fictitious. Hence the validity or invalidity of cognitions as causally determined effects must be regarded as somehow inherent in the cognitions. This means that validity and invalidity are inherent in knowledge. Thus, the validity and invalidity of knowledge are self-evident.[1]

The Sāṅkhya view has been criticized by the Nyāya and the Mīmāṁsā. The latter points out that the theory of causality, on which the Sāṅkhya view of the validity and invalidity of knowledge rests, is itself untenable. Causation or effectutaion has no maning if what caused is pre-existent and so need not really be caused or produced. Causation must be a process of real effectuation, *i.e.* it must be the production of the new or the previously non-existent effect. Further, it is a contradiction to say that both validity and invalidity belong to the same thing, namely, knowledge. How can such contradictory characters belong to the same thing? It cannot be said that while validity is intrinsic to valid knowledge, invalidity is intrinsic to invalid knowledge. Apart from any external conditions, a knowledge cannot determine itself either as valid or invalid. If validity and invalidity are equally intrinsic to knowledge, it must have both at the same time.[2] The Naiyāyikas reject the Sāṅkhya view on the ground that it fails to account for the failure of practical acclivities (*pravṛttivisaṁvāda*). If the validity of knowledge be self-evident, there cannot be unsuccessful activity.

1. SD. and SC., p. 20; NM., p. 160.
2. SD. and SC., pp. 20-21; *Mānameyodaya*, p. 75.

If its invalidity be self-evident, there cannot be any activity at all. The cognition of silver in a shell must be either valid or invalid. If it is valid and known to be valid by itself, then the act of picking it up should not lead to disappointment. On the other hand, if it is invalid and known to be invalid by itself, no one should strive to pick it up. But illusions and disappointments are ordinary and frequent experiences of life. Hence neither the validity nor the invalidity of knowledge is intrinsic and self-evident.[1]

5. Criticism of the Bauddha Theory of Intrinsic Invalidity and Extrinsic Validity

According to the Buddhists, all knowledge is invalid by its very nature. The validity of knowledge *consists* in its capacity to produce successful action. Hence, prior to any successful activity every knowledge is to be treated as invalid. We cannot say that validity belongs to knowledge simply because it has come to be, or has appeared. In that case, error will have to be regarded as valid knowledge, because error too appears as a form of knowledge. That knowledge has been produced does not necessarily mean that there is in it a true cognition of the object, since the knowledge is liable to contradiction. Hence, we are to say that invalidity belongs to knowledge at its inception, and its validity is due to the negation of invalidity by external conditions. In fact, the question of truth and falsity does not arise so long as we are concerned with mere belief. We may know things and believe in them without knowing whether the belief is true or false. The question of the validity of knowledge arises first when a certain belief is contradicted and we apprehend its invalidity. Hence in logic we must start with the invalidity of knowledge.

From a sceptical or rather critical standpoint, the Buddhists take all knowledge as intrinsically invalid and treat validity as an extrinsic character which knowledge comes to have by way of conative verification (*pravṛttisāmarthya*). According to them, the truth of knowledge is constituted by successful activity. Hence, it

1. NM., p. 160; TC., I, p. 184.

follows that prior to successful activity, Knowledge is not-true. When any knowledge leads to successful activity we know that it is not not-true, *i.e.* it is true. So, the Buddhists give a negative definition of truth as what is not false (*avisaṁvādakam*) and conclude that falsity is intrinsic and truth extrinsic to knowledge.[1]

The Naiyāyikas reject the Bauddha view of intrinsic invalidity on the ground that it cannot account for unsuccessful practical activity (*pravṛttivisaṁvāda*). If tne invalidity of knowledge be self-evident, why should a man run after the false, knowing that it is false. Hence there can not be any practical reaction in connection with illusion. Again, if the invalidity of knowledge be due to defects in the conditions of knowledge and be known through contra diction, it cannot be held that it is intrinsically conditioned and self-evident. That invalidity is due to certain extra conditions (*kāraṇadoṣa*) must needs be admitted. Invalidity is not merely the absence of validity, but a positive character of such forms of knowledge as doubt and error. Hence it must be due to some positive conditions other than the causes of knowledge. As such invalidity is not intrinsic to knowledge.[2]

6. Criticism of the Mīmāṁsā Theory of Intrinsic Validity and Extrinsic Invalidity

According to the Mīmāṁsā and the Vedānta, the validity of knowledge is due to conditions that are intrinsic to knowledge, and the knowledge of validity is due to the condition of knowledge itself. This means that knowledge is both made valid and known to be valid by its own intrinsic conditions.

It is the very nature of knowledge to reveal its object. There is no knowledge which does not manifest the nature of some object. Hence, it follows that knowledge requires no other conditions than itself in order to reveal its object. It cannot fail to give us truth if it is to be knowledge at all. For how can it reveal its object without being true? So, we see that knowledge must be valid by its very

1. NBT., pp. 3 f.
2. NM., pp. 160, 169; SD., p. 21.

nature, *i.e.* the very conditions which condition knowledge must also condition its validity. It cannot be said that knowledge is a neutral cognition and that validity and invalidity are its adventitious characters. There is no such thing as a neutral or characterless cognition. Every cognition must be either valid or invalid. There is no third alternative here. A cognition which is neither valid nor invalid is not a fact but a fiction. As for doubt (*saṁśaya*), we are to say that it is not a neutral cognition, but a form of invalid knowledge. Further, if knowledge is not valid on its own account, it can never be made valid on account of any external condition. For the validating condition must itself be validated by other conditions, and these again by still other conditions and so on *ad infinitum*. This means that the validity of knowledge cannot be finally established. Hence, we must either say that knowledge is valid by its very nature or deny that there is any valid knowledge at all. The validity of knowledge must thus be conditioned by the conditions of knowledge itself, *i.e.* it must be intrinsic to knowledge. The only external condition for validity is the negative one of the absence of vitiating factors (*doṣābhāva*). But this does not mean that validity is externally conditioned, since the absence of a thing is not a positive factor that contributes anything towards the validity of knowledge. The absence of vitiating conditions accounts for the absence of invalidity and not for the positive fact of validity. There is no evidence for any positive external condition like special efficacy of the conditions of knowledge (*kārakātirikta-tadgataguṇa*). So we are to say that the validity of knowledge is due to the conditions of knowledge itself (*svarūpasthitahetuja*), *i.e.* it is intrinsic to knowledge.[1]

Similarly, the validity of knowledge must be known from the conditions of knowledge itself. A true knowledge is by itself known to be true. It does not require anything else to show its truth. In fact, the truth of knowledge cannot be known from any external condition. We cannot know it from any special efficacy in the conditions of knowledge (*kāraṇaguṇa*). There is no such thing as

1. VP., Ch. VI; SD., pp. 20, 21, 48.

a special potency of the causes of knowledge. Even if there were such a thing, it cannot be known, since it must pertain to the sense-organs and, as such, must be supersensible. Nor can we know validity from the experience of non-contradiction (*bādhakābhāvajñāna*). Non-contradiction cannot be a test of the truth of knowledge. When we speak of non-contradiction we must mean either of two things, namely, that there is no contradiction for the present or that there cannot be a contradiction at any time. But to know that there is non-contradiction for the present is not to know that the knowledge must be valid. For what is not *now* contradicted may be and often is contradicted in the future. That there cannot be a contradiction at any time is what we can never know unless become omniscient. Absolute non-contradiction is, therefore, an impracticable test of truth. Nor again can the validity of knowledge be known from its coherence with some other knowledge (*saṁvāda*). For this will lead to infinite regress. How can we know that there is real coherence between two cases of knowledge? How again do we know that the second knowledge, with which the first coheres and by which it is tested, is itself valid? To prove the validity of the second we must show its coherence with a third and so on *ad infinitum*. Or, if we stop anywhere and say that the last knowledge or the system of knowledge as a whole has self-evident validity, there is no reason why the first knowledge cannot be said to have the same self-evident truth. It cannot also be said that the coherence of knowledge consists in the volitional experience of expected results. The mere experience of desired objects is no evidence of the validity of knowledge. In dream we have vivid experiences of many desired things. This however does not make dream a valid knowledge at all. Thus, we see that there cannot be any extraneous test of the validity of knowledge, like correspondence, coherence, non-contradiction or pragmatic utility. Hence, knowledge must test or certify its own truth, *i.e.* the validity of knowledge is self-evident.[1]

As to invalidity or falsity, the Mīmāṁsakas and the Vedāntists hold that it is extrinsic to knowledge. While truth is organic to

1. VP. and SD., *ibid.*, NM., pp. 162-65.

knowledge, falsity is accidental and externally conditioned. Thus, the invalidity of knowledge is due to some defects in the conditions of knowledge (*kāraṇadoṣa*). It is only when certain defects vitiate its natural conditions that knowledge fails in its purpose, namely, the attainment of truth. So, invalidity is conditioned by conditions other than those of the knowledge itself. Similarly, the knowledge of invalidity depends on such external conditions as the experience of contradiction and the knowledge of vitiating conditions. This means that knowledge *per se* is valid. If in any case it is rejected as false, that is only because it fails to lead up to certain expected results (*viparītavyavahāraja*), and not because it fails to reveal its object. Every knowledge is intrinsically valid. When any knowledge is, as a matter of practical usage (*vyavahāra*), called false, that is either because it is perceived to arise from certain defects in its natural conditions. The invalidity of knowledge is thus both constituted and known by external conditions other than the conditions of knowledge itself.[1]

In some cases it may so happen that when one knowledge is contradicted by another, we may have some doubt with regard to the second invalidating knowledge and require a third knowledge to resolve the doubt. But even here we are not involved in an infinite regress and bound to give up the idea of the intrinsic validity of knowledge. If the third knowledge is consistent with the first, then the intrinsic validity of the latter remains established as before. What the third knowledge does is not to validate the first by reason of its coherence with it, but to dispel the false doubt raised by the second contradicting knowledge. If, on the other hand, the third is consistent with the second, it confirms the sense of contradiction and the first is known to be invalid. Here the invalidity of the first is known through something other than itself. That the third is consistent with the second does not mean that it validates the second. It means only that the doubt attaching to the second is dispelled by its coherence with the third. Hence, it follows that every knowledge validates itself through itself and is invalidated by some other

1. VP. and SD., *Ibid.*, NM., pp. 162-65.

knowledge. That is, validity is intrinsic to all knowledge, while invalidity is extrinsic and accidental.[1]

The Naiyāyikas reject the first part of the Mīmāṁsā theory, namely, that knowledge is both made valid and known to be valid by its own intrinsic conditions. The validity of knowledge cannot be due to the conditions of knowledge as such. If that were so, there could not be any invalid knowledge, since even invalid knowledge arises from the conditions of knowledge. In fact a valid cognition is more than a cognition as such. Hence, it must be due to some special character of the general conditions of knowledge just as an invalid cognition is due to some positive factors that vitiate the general conditions of knowledge. The mere absence of vitiating factors cannot account for the positive character of validity. Thus the validity of perception is due not merely to the absence of vitiating factors like the diseased condition of the sense organ, but to such positive factors as the healthy condition of the sense organ, etc. Similarly, in all other cases the validity of knowledge is due to some special auxiliary conditions in the specific causes of knowledge (*kāraṇaguṇa*). Such special conditions may not be always perceived, but they may be known from other sources, like inference and testimony. The special efficacy of the sense organs may be known from the medical sciences. Further, if the validity of knowledge be due simply to the absence of vitiating conditions, its invalidity may also be said to be due to the absence of efficacious conditions. As such, we need not say that invalidity is due to external conditions. Again, on the Mīmāṁsā view, all knowledge being intrinsically valid, the distinction between truth and falsehood becomes insignificant. We should not speak of any knowledge as invalid. It cannot be said that when any knowledge turns to be false, it altogether ceases to be knowledge or cognition. A wrong knowledge is as good a cognition as a true one. So, if cognition *per se* be true, there cannot be any wrong cognition. But that there are wrong cognitions, illusions, and hallucinations is an undeniable fact. So it must be admitted that both validity and invalidity are externally conditioned.[2]

1. NM., pp. 166-67.
2. NM., pp. 170-71; SM., 131-36.

Similarly, no knowledge is by itself known to be valid, *i.e.* the validity of knowledge is not self-evident. Thus the cognition of blue does not cognise its truth or validity at the same time that it cognises the blue colour. It does not even cognise itself immediately as a cognition of blue, far less as a valid cognition of blue. On the Bhāṭṭa view, a cognition is not immediately cognised, but is known mediately by inference. If so, the validity of knowledge cannot be immediately known by itself. Nor can we say that with every cognition there follows immediately another cognition which cognises the validity of the first. With the perception of blue, for example, we do not find another cognition immediately following it and cognising its validity or invalidity. There is no introspective evidence for a secondary cognition of validity appearing immediately after the primary cognition of an object. Even if there were such, the validity of knowledge will not be self-evident but evidenced by another knowledge. Further, if the invalidity of knowledge be known from its contradiction, we are to say that its validity is known from the absence of contradiction. On the other hand, if we accept the Prābhākara view that knowledge is self-manifest and guarantees its own truth without reference to anything else, we do not see how there can be doubt and suspicion, or how there can be any failure of practical activity. Since validity is inherent and self-evident in knowledge, every knowledge must carry in it an assurance of its truth and we should have no doubt. Similarly, every knowledge being true and known to be true by itself, there cannot be any disappointment in practical life. But doubts and disappointments are very common experiences of life. If it be said that doubt arises out of contradiction between two cognitions and is resolved by a third cognition, we are forced to give up the idea of self-evident validity. The third cognition may not constitute the validity of the first by reason of its coherence with it, but it at least conditions our knowledge of its validity. So, the validity of one knowledge is known by another knowledge. In fact knowledge only reveals its object. To know that it is valid, *i.e.* it truly reveals the object, we must have some extraneous test like coherence with volitional experience or some accredited past knowledge. Hence, the validity of knowledge must be known from external conditions.[1]

It will appear from the above discussion that the Naiyāyikas are not prepared to accept the theory of intrinsic validity. That truth is intrinsic to and self-evident in *all* knowledge is not admitted by them. But that the truth of *some* cases of knowledge is self-evident is admitted by some Naiyāyikas. There is on this point a difference of opinion between the ancient and the modern exponents of the Nyāya. The older Naiyāyikas insist that a proof of the validity of any knowledge requires the exclusion of other suggested possibilities contrary to it. Hence, we find that they try to establish the validity of every knowledge by external grounds, even at the risk of an infinite regress. To prove the validity of knowledge we need not go beyond perception, inference, comparison and testimony. But one perception or inference must be proved by another individual perception or inference. Hence the same knowledge may sometimes be proved by another and sometimes taken to prove another (*pradīpaprakāśavat*). This seems to be a more empirical and common-sense view of the validity of human knowledge.[2]

Later Naiyāyikas, however, do not insist that every knowledge must be tested and proved before we can accept its validity. According to them, the validity of knowledge need not be proved if there is not the slightest doubt about it (*saṁśayābhāva*). Its validity is practically self-evident so long as it is not contradicted. A motiveless doubt of a possible contradiction is of no account. To say that a knowledge is evidently valid it is not necessary to prove its infallibility or to exclude all other possibilities contrary to it. So, if there be such knowledge as cannot reasonably be doubted we are to say that it has self-evident truth. Of course, when any doubt or dispute arises as to its truth, we must prove it by some extraneous test. Among such cases of knowledge the Naiyāyikas include logical inference and comparison, and cognition of the

1. NM., pp. 170-71; SM., 131-36.
2. NB., 2.1. 17-19.

resemblance between two cognitions (*jñānagatasādṛśyajñāna*), cognition of cognition or self-consciousness (*anuvyavasāya*), and cognition of anything as something or as mere subject (*dharmijñāna*). Inference and comparison (*upamāna*) as logical methods are based on some necessary relation between two terms, namely, a mark and the marked (*hetu* and *sādhya*), a name and its denotation (*saṁjñā* and *saṁjñī*) respectively. Hence, knowledge by inference and comparison is known as necessary knowledge. These become the contents of self-conscious knowledge and, as such, their validity is self-evident. Similarly, the cognition of a cognition or awareness of awareness, the cognition of the similarity between cognitions and the cognition of anything as a mere subject are all cases of self-conscious knowledge. In these we not only know something but also know that we know it. That is, we know that something is known. Hence these cases of knowledge also are necessary knowledge having self-evident validity.[1]

In the case of sense-perception and testimony , however, there cannot be any self-evident validity. These are not based on any necessary relation between two terms. There is no necessary relation between sense-perception and its object or between words and their meanings. Hence we cannot say that to know anything by external perception or testimony is also to know that we know it. These cannot be the contents of self-conscious knowledge and their validity is not self-evident.[2]

It should, however, be noted here that with the Naiyāyikas the self-evident validity of some cases of knowledge does not exclude their liability to error. For the Mīmāṁsaka and the Vedāntist, the self-evident character of a truth means its infallibility which excludes the possibility of any falsification, so that error pertains not to truth but to its applications (*vyavahāra*). For the Naiyāyikas,

1. *Anumānasya... nirastasamastavyabhicāraśaṅkasya svata eva prāmāṇyamanumeyāvyabhicāriligasamutthatvāt*, etc., NVT., pp. 12-13; *Anumānopamānānuvyavasāyadharmijñānānāmapi*...svata *eva prāmāṇyagraha*, etc., NVTP., pp. 119-20; *vide* also TC., I, pp. 277-79, 282-84.
2. *Pratyakṣaśabdavijñānayorna svato 'vyabhicāragraha iti*, etc., NVT., *ibid.*

however, even necessary truths are empirical and so require confirmation by fresh applications (*i.e. pravṛttismarthya*), whenever necessary. But they are different in status from ordinary observation and generalization. They possess the highest degree of certainty which is humanly attainable. Still they may change if, as Hobhouse has said, the constitution of the world changeth. Hence, the Nyāya conception of the self-evident validity of some knowledge is different from the Mīmāṁsā and Vedānata view of the self-evident validity of all knowledge.

7. Indian and Western Theories of Truth

Here we propose to examine the Indian theories of truth, as explained above, in the light of parallel Western theories. With regard to truth there are two main questions, namely, how truth is constituted, and how truth is known. The first question relates to the nature of truth and the answers to it gives us the definitions of truth. The second question refers to the ascertainment of truth and the answers to it give us the tests or criteria of truth.

With regard to these two questions there seem to be two possible answers. Thus it may be said that truth is a self-evident character of all knowledge. Every knowledge is true and known to be true by its very nature. Knowledge does not depend on any external conditions either to be made true or to be known as true. This is the theory of the intrinsic validity (*svataḥ prāmāṇya*) of knowledge as advocated by the Sāṅkhya, Mīmāṁsā and Advaita Vedānta systems of Indian Philosophy. According to the last two schools, the truth of knowledge consists just in its being uncontradicted (*abādhita*). The absence of contradiction, however, is not a positive but a negative condition of truth. Knowledge is both made true and known to be true by its own internal conditions. It is only falsehood that is externally conditioned. So truth is self-evident, while falsity requires to be evidenced by external grounds. The Sāṅkhya goes further than this. It maintains that both truth and falsehood are internally conditioned and immediately known, *i.e.* are self-evident.

There is no exact parallel to the above theory of truth in Western philosophy. It is true that in modern European philosophy knowledge, in the strict sense, is always taken to mean true belief. But truth or validity is not regarded as intrinsic to all knowledge, independently of all external conditions. It is in the writings of Professor L. A. Reid, a modern realist who owns no allegiance to the current schools of realism, that we find some approach to the view that truth is organic to knowledge. But even Reid makes it conditional on knowledge efficiently fulfilling its function, namely, the apprehension of reality as it is. He thinks that truth is nothing else but knowledge doing its job. Thus, he says: "Truth is, indeed, simply,... the quality of knowledge perfectly fulfilling its functions." Again he observes: "If knowledge were not transitive, if we were not in direct contact, joined with reality, then all our tests, coherence, correspondence, and the rest, would be worthless."[1] Here truth is admitted to be a natural function of knowledge, but not as inherent and self-evident in all knowledge. In the theory of intuitionism, we find a close approach to the view of self-evident validity. To the question 'How do we know that a belief is true or valid?' Intuitionism has a simple answer to give, namely, that we know it immediately to be such. As Hobhouse puts the matter: "Intuitionism has a royal way of cutting this, and indeed most other knots: for it has but to appeal to a perceived necessity, to a clear idea, to the inconceivability of the opposite, all of which may be known by simply attending to our own judgment, and its task is done."[2] Among intuitionists, Lossky has made an elaborate attempt to show that truth and falsity are known through an immediate consciousness of their objectivity and subjectivity respectively. For him, truth is the objective and falsity the subjective appearance of the object. But how do we know that the one is objective and the other is subjective? The answer given by Lossky as also by Lipps is that we have "an immediate consciousness of subjectivity" and "an immediate consciousness of objectivity." To quote Lossky's own words: "It is in this consciousness of objectivity and subjectivity, and not...in the laws of identity, contradiction, and

1. L. A. Reid, *Knowledge and Truth*, pp. 185, 199, 204.
2. Hobhouse, *Theory of Knowledge*, p. 488.

excluded middle, that our thought has a real and immediate guide in its search for truth."[1]

It should be remarked here that the above theories of self-evident truth or intrinsic validity give us a rather jejune and untenable solution of the logical problem of truth. They leave no room for the facts of doubt and falsehood in the sphere of knowledge. But any theory of truth which fails to explain its correlate, namely, falsehood, becomes so far inadequate. Further, it makes a confusion between psychological belief and logical certainty. Psychologically a wrong belief may be as firm as a right one. But this does not mean that there is no distinction between the two. Subjective certitude, as such, cannot be accepted as a test of truth. It is true that the theory of intrinsic validity does not appeal to any test of truth other than the truth itself. It assumes that the truth of knowledge is self-evident, and that we cannot think of the opposite. In fact, however, there is no such self-evident truth. It is only in the case of the self that we can speak of self-evidence in this sense. The self is a self-manifesting reality. It is manifest even in any doubt or denial of its reality. Hence self-evidence belongs really to the self only. It is on the analogy of the self that we speak of the self-evidence of any other truth. A truth is self-evident in so far as it has the evidence of the self or is evident like the self. But as we have just said, there is no such self-evident truth other than the self itself. In the case of any other truth, we can always think of the opposite in a sensible way. That 'two and two make five' is not as nonsensical as '*abracadabra*.' Even if the opposite of a certain belief be inconceivable, it does not follow that the belief is infallible. What was once inconceivable is now not only conceivable but perfectly true. Hence, we cannot say that self-evident validity is intrinsic to all knowledge.

The second answer to the question 'How is truth constituted and known?' leads us to the theory of extrinsic validity (*parathaḥ prāmāṇya*). According to this, the truth of any knowledge is both constituted and known by certain external conditions. As a general

1. Lossky, *The Intuitive Basis of Knowledge*, pp. 227-29.

rule, the validity of knowledge is due to something that is not inherent in it. So also the knowledge of validity depends on certain extraneous tests. Validity is thus assigned to one knowledge on the ground of some other knowledge. This is the theory of extrinsic validity as advocated by the Nyāya and the Bauddha systems. In Western philosophy, the correspondence, the coherence and the pragmatist theories of truth all come under the doctrine of extrinsic validity. In each of them the truth of knowledge is made to depend on certain external conditions other than the knowledge itself. According to almost all realists, old and new, it is correspondence to facts that constitutes both the nature and the test of truth.[1] Of course, some realists differ from this general position and hold a different view of the matter. Thus Alexander[2] makes coherence the ground of truth. But in speaking of coherence as determined by reality, he accepts indirectly the theory of correspondence. Reid,[3] on the other hand, treats correspondence to the given only as a test of truth. Russell[4] defines truth in terms of correspondence and accepts coherence as a test of some truths, while others are said to be self-evident. In the philosophy of objective idealism,[5] coherence in the sense of the systematic unity of all experiences is made both the ground and the test of truth. The truth consists in the coherence of all experiences as one self-maintaining and all-inclusive system. It is in this sense that Bosanquet[6] says that 'the truth is the whole and it is its own criterion. Truth can only be tested by more of itself.' Hence, any particular knowledge is true in so far as it is consistent with the whole system of experience. On this view, the truth of human knowledge becomes relative, since coherence as the ideal of the completed system of experience is humanly

1. Vide *The New Realism* and *Essays in Critical Realism.*
2. *Space, Time and Diety*, Vo. II, pp. 251 f.
3. *Knowledge and Truth*, Chap. VIII.
4. *The Problems of Philosophy*, Chaps. XII, XIII; *Our Knowledge of the External World*, p. 58; *The Analysis of Mind*, p. 165.
5. *Vide* Joachim, *The Nature of Truth*, Chap. III.
6. Logic, Vol. II, pp. 265-67.

unattainable. For pragmatism,[1] truth is both constituted and known by practical utility. The truth of knowledge consists in its capacity to produce practically useful consequences. So also the method of ascertaining truth is just to follow the practical consequences of a belief and see if they have any practical value. With this brief statement of the realistic, the idealistic and the pragmatist theories of truth, we proceed to examine the Buddhist and the Nyāya theories of extrinsic validity.

From what we have said before it is clear that the Buddhists adopt the pragmatist theory of truth and reality. For them, practical efficiency is the test of both truth and reality. The real is what possesses practical efficiency (*arthakriyā*) and the true is the useful and so practically efficient (*arthakriyāsāmarthya*). But the pragmatic conception of truth is embarrassed by serious difficulties. The Nyāya criticism of the Bauddha conception of *pramāṇa* has brought out some of these difficulties. Here we may note that to reduce the true to the useful is to make it almost meaningless. It is by no means the case that truth is only a matter of practical utility. The atomic and the electron theories of matter make very little difference in our practical life. Similarly, the different theories of truth involve no great difference in their practical consequences. But in the absence of any other test than that of practical utility we cannot say which one is true and which is false. Further, there are certain beliefs which are admittedly wrong but which are otherwise useful for certain purposes of life. But no one would claim any truth for a wrong belief on account of its practical utility. Hence the Buddhist and the pragmatist theories of truth cannot be accepted as sound and satisfactory.

The Nyāya theory of truth, it will be seen, combines the correspondence, the coherence and the pragmatist theories with certain modifications. According to it, the truth of knowledge consists in its correspondence with objective facts, while coherence and practical utility are the tests of truth in such cases in which we

---

1. James, *Pragmatism*, Lect. VI; Perry, *Present Philosophical Tendencies*, Pts. IV and V.

require a test. It defines the truth of all knowledge as a correspondence of relations (*tadvati tatprakāraka*). To know a thing is to judge it as having such-and-such a character. This knowledge of the thing will be true if the thing has really such-and-such a character; if not, it will be false. The Nyāya view of correspondence is thus different from the new realistic idea of structural correspondence or identity of contents.[1] That knowledge corresponds to some object does not, for the Naiyāyika, mean that the contents of the object bodily enter into consciousness and become its contents. When, for example, I know a table, the table as a physical existent does not figure in my consciousness. This means only that I *judge* something as having the attribute of 'tableness' which really belongs to it. There is a subjective cognition of a physical object. The one corresponds to the other, because it *determines* the object as it is, and does not itself become what it is. If it so became the object itself, there would be nothing left on the subjective side that might correspond to the physical object. Nor again does the Nyāya follow the critical realist's idea of correspondence between character-complexes, referred to the object by the knowing mind, and the characters actually belonging to the object. When we know anything we do not first apprehend a certain logical essence or a character-complex and then refer it to the thing known. Our knowledge is in direct contact with the object. In knowing the object we judge it as having a relation to certain characters or attributes. Our knowledge will be true if there is correspondence between the relation asserted in knowledge, and that existing among facts. Thus my knowledge of a conchshell as white is true because there is a real relation between the two corresponding to the relation affirmed by me. On the other hand, the perception of silver in a shell is false because it asserts a relation between the two, which does not correspond to a real relation between them.[2]

1. *Cf.* Chapter III, Sec. 3, above.
2. *Cf.* "Smith's judgment that it is the light of a ship is true just because 'it,' the light, is in fact so related to a real ship. Jones' judgment (that it is the light of a star), on the other hand, is false, because this thought is

While truth consists in correspondence, the criterion of truth is, for the Nyāya, coherence in a broad sense (*saṁvāda*). But coherence does not here mean anything of the kind that objective idealism means by it. The Nyāya coherence is a practical test and means the harmony between cognitive and conative experiences (*pravṛttisāmarthya*) or between different kinds of knowledge (*tajjātīyatva*). That there is truth in the sense of correspondence cannot, as a general rule, be known directly by intuition. We know it indirectly from the fact that the knowledge in question coheres with other experiences of the same object as also with the general system of our knowledge. Thus the perception of water is known to be valid when different ways of reaction or experiment give us experience of the same water. It is this kind of coherence that Alexander accepts as a test of truth when he says: "If truth is tested by reference to other propositions, the test is not one of correspondence to reality but of whether the proposition tested is consistent or not with other propositions."[1] Hobhouse[2] also means the same thing by 'consilience' as a measure of validity. According to him, validity belongs to judgments as forming a consilient system. Of course, he admits that such validity is relative and not absolute, since the ideal of a complete system of consilient judgments is unattainable. The Nyāya idea of *saṁvāda* or coherence may be better explained as a combination of Reid's methods of correspondence and coherence. If we take the judgment 'that is the light of a ship,' we can test its truth by what Reid calls the correspondence method "of approaching the light and seeing a ship." This is exactly what the Nyāya means by *pravṛttisāmarthya* or successful activity. Or, we can employ, so says Reid, the cheaper coherence, method "of comparing this knowledge with other kinds of knowledge and see if it is consistent with them."[3] In this we have the Nyāya method of testing one knowledge by reference to some other valid knowledge (*tajjātīyatva*). But the Nyāya goes

---

not an apprehension of the existing present complex fact, light-belonging-to-ship."– Reid, *Knowledge and Truth*, pp. 209-10.

1. *Space, Time and Deity*, Vol. II, p. 252.
2. *The Theory of Knowledge*, pp. 499-500.
3. *Knowledge and Truth*, pp. 203-4, 211-12.

further than this and accepts practical utility also as a test of truth. Thus, the validity of the perception of water may be known from correspondence and coherence in the above sense. But it may be further known from the satisfaction of our practical needs or the fulfilment of our practical purposes in relation to water, such as drinking, bathing, washing, etc. But the Nyāya never admits the pragmatist contention that the truth of any knowledge is constituted by its utility or serviceableness. Knowledge is made true by its correspondence to some reality or objective fact. It is true not because it is useful, but it is useful because it is already true. Hence, truth consists in correspondence and is tested by coherence and practical efficiency.

But from the standpoint of the modern Nyāya, all truths do not require to be tested. Some truths are known as such without any test or confirmation. These are manifestly necessary and so self-evident truths. Here the Nyāya view has some affinity with Russell's theory of truth.[1] In both, truth is defined by correspondence to fact, but in different ways. Although truth is thus externally conditioned, some truths are admitted by both to be self-evident. For the Nyāya, however, such truths are only necessary truths or what Russell calls *a priori* principles. Of the different kinds of knowledge by acquaintance–sensation, memory, introspection, etc.–which are admitted by Russell to have self-evident truth, it is only introspection or self-consciousness (*anuvyavasāya*) that is admitted by the Nyāya as having self-evident validity. The validity of self-consciousness is self-evident because there is a necessary relation between consciousness and its contents. When I become conscious of a desire for food, I find that my consciousness is necessarily related to the desire, it is the desire itself as it becomes explicit.[2] Here I not only know something, but know that I am knowing it, *i.e.* the truth of my knowledge is self-evident.

---

1. *The Problems of Philosophy*, Chaps. XI, XII, XIII.
2. *Cf.* C. Hartshorne's article in *The Monist* (Vol. XLIV, No. 2, p. 171): "Must this (feeling) not be admitted to present an obvious dual aspect of being at once subjective and yet a content or object of consciousness, at once a mode and a datum of awareness?"

The different theories of truth discussed above may be shown to supplement one another and be reconciled as complementary aspects of a comprehensive theory. The first requisite of such a theory is the independent existence of a world of objects. If there were no such world, there would be no ground for the distinction between truth and falsehood. Some of our beliefs are true or false according as they are or are not borne out by independent objects or facts. It is because there are certain independent objects, to which our beliefs may or may not conform, that we distinguish between truth and error. Hence we say that truth consists in the correspondence of our knowledge with independent objects or facts. The difficulty on this view, it is generally remarked, is that if the objects are independent of knowledge, we cannot know whether our knowledge corresponds with them or not. How can we know what is outside and beyond knowledge, and see that true knowledge agrees with it? The reply to this is that in the case of external objects, physical things and other minds, we cannot straightway know the correspondence between our knowledge and its objects. Still, we cannot deny the reality of these external objects. But for the independent existence of other things and minds we cannot explain the order and uniformity of our experiences and the similarity of the experiences that different individuals may have under similar circumstances. That some of our experiences represent the real qualities of things may then be known from the fact that they are given in the same way to different persons, or to the same persons through different senses. As Professor Price has shown, "sense-data cohere together in families, and families are coincident with physical occupants."[1] On the other hand, some of our experiences are not taken to represent the qualities of things, because they do not cohere with other experiences of the same individual or of different individuals. The first kind of experiences is considered to be true and objective, while the second is judged to be false and subjective. Similarly, our knowledge of other minds is true when it correctly represents the contents of those minds. It will be false, if what we impute to them forms no part of their actual contents.

1. *Cf. Perception*, p. 302.

This shows that it is correspondence to facts that constitutes the nature of truth, although we cannot directly *know* such correspondence in the case of physical things and other minds. To know this we have to consider if one knowledge coheres with others or the whole body of human knowledge, and also consider if we can successfully act on our knowledge. What is true works, although whatever works is not true. Thus, we know the correspondence of knowledge with facts from its coherence and pragmatic value. But to know that a certain knowledge corresponds with facts is to *know* its truth. It does not constitute its truth. The knowledge becomes true if, and only if, it corresponds with facts. We know or test its truth when we find that it is coherent with other parts of our knowledge and our practical activities. So truth is constituted by correspondence with facts and is tested by coherence and practical activity.

The Vedānta view of truth as uncontradicted experience logically implies the coherence theory of truth. That some experience is uncontradicted means that it is different from the contradicted. But to be different from the contradicted means to belong to the body of coherent knowledge. We do not and cannot rightly judge an experience to be uncontradicted unless we relate it to other experiences and find that it is congruous with them. A dream experience is wrongly judged by the dreamer to be uncontradicted and true, because he cannot relate it to his waking experiences. It cannot be said that a dream experience is true for the time being and becomes false afterwards. What is once true is always true. A dream experience may sometimes be *judged* to be true, but it is really false for all time. And its falsity appears from its incoherence with waking experience. Hence, we are to say that an experience is really uncontradicted when it is related to other experiences and is found to be coherent with them.

It may be urged against the above view that truth consists in correspondence and is tested by coherence, that is either assumes the truth of the testing knowledge, or must go on testing knowledge *ad infinitum*. If knowledge is true when it corresponds with facts, and if the correspondence cannot be directly known, then the truth of every knowledge must be tested by its coherence with others. This, however, means that there can be no end of the process of proving knowledge and, therefore, no final proof of any knowledge. To solve this difficulty we must admit that there is at least one case in which knowledge is, by itself, known to be true. We have such a case in self-consciousness. While the truth of all other knowledge is to be tested by coherence, the truth of self-consciousness is self-evident and requires no extraneous test. The self is a self-manifesting reality. Hence, the contents of our mind or the self are manifested by themselves. They are at once existent facts and contents of consciousness. To become conscious of the contents of one's mind is just to make them explicit. What we are here conscious of are not outside or beyond consciousness. Mental contents not only *are,* but are conscious of themselves. The state of knowledge and the object of knowledge being identical, we cannot strictly speak of a correspondence of the one with the other. Or, if we speak of a correspondence between them, we are to say that it is directly known and so need not be known or tested in any other way. When we feel pain, or know something, or resolve to do anything, we may be conscious of feeling it, or knowing it, or resolving to do it. What we are here conscious of as objects are the objects themselves as they become explicit or conscious of themselves. Similarly, necessary truths and *a priori* principles like the laws of thought, logical and mathematical truths seem to have self-evident validity. The reason for this is that these truths are or express the forms and contents of our own consciousness. They are inherent in or arise out of the nature of our own thought and consciousness, and in knowing them consciousness knows itself, *i.e.* its own forms. They are at once modes and objects of consciousness. In any judgment or knowledge of them, the content and object of consciousness are the same and directly known to be the same. Such knowledge is, therefore, not only true, but also known to be true by itself. Hence we admit that the truth of self-consciousness is self-evident, while all other truths are evidenced by external tests like coherence and pragmatic utility or verification.

II. PERCEPTION AS A METHOD OF KNOWLEDGE (*PRATYAKṢA-PRAMĀṆA*)

Chapter V

Definition of Perception

1. Primacy of Perception over other Methods of Knowledge

Perception (*pratyakṣa*), like inference and the rest, is taken to mean both a form of valid knowledge (*pramiti*) and the means or method of acquiring such knowledge (*pramāṇa*). We are here concerned with them as methods of knowledge. According to the Nyāya, there are four distinct and independent methods or sources of knowledge, namely perception, inference, comparison and testimony. Of these, perception comes first and is the most fundamental. Of course, the primacy of perception over the other methods of knowledge is not due to anything in the nature of the objects of knowledge. So far as the objects of knowledge are concerned, the methods or ways of knowing stand on the same footing in respect of their value and importance. While there are certain objects which may be known by any of the four methods, there are other objects which must be known by a particular method and cannot be known by any other. The existence of fire at a distant place may be known from the testimony of a reliable person. It may also be known by inference from the observed smoke as a mark of fire. Or, if we take the trouble to go up to the place from which smoke issues forth, we have a perception of the fire on the spot. Hence with regard to such objects as the fire, one method of knowledge is as good and valid as any other. Contrariwise, there are certain cases in which a truth is to be known by some special method. Scriptural testimony is the only source of our knowledge about supramundane realities. That there is a future life, a heaven or a hell, is to be believed on the authority of the scriptures and cannot be proved by perception or inference. Similarly, our knowledge of the unperceived cause of a perceived effect is derived neither from testimony nor perception, but from inference. Likewise, perception gives us the knowledge of what is directly present to sense and we do not require any inference or testimony for a knowledge of it. In relation to the objects of knowledge, therefore, the methods are sometimes interchangeable and sometimes exclusive. With regard to any method of knowledge it may be said that some contents of knowledge or some truths can only be given by it, while others may come from this as well as from the other sources of knowledge. Hence, so far as the contents of knowledge are concerned, there is nothing to distinguish one *pramāṇa* or method of knowledge as more fundamental than any other.[1]

Nevertheless there are certain important considerations in favour of the Naiyāyika view that perception is the most primary and fundamental of all the sources of knowledge recognised in any system of philosophy. In the first place, perception is the ultimate ground of all knowledge. It is true that all knowledge does not arise from perception. The empiricists including the Cārvākas are wrong when they suppose that sense-perception is adequate to explain the entire body of human knowledge. According to the Nyāya, perception is not the only source of our knowledge, but it is the basis of the other sources or methods of knowledge. Hence, it has been said that all the other methods of knowledge presuppose perception and must be based on knowledge derived from perception.[2] J.S. Mill recognised this truth when he said that "the truths known by intuition are the original premises from which all others are inferred."[3] For the Nyāya, however, perception is the basis on which we have a knowledge of other truths by inference as well as by comparison and testimony. Inference as a method of knowledge depends on perception. The first step in inference is the *observation* of a mark or the middle term (*liṅgadarśana*), and the *observation* of the relation between the middle and the major

1. NB., 1.1.3.
2. *Sarvapramāṇānāṁ pratyakṣapūrvakatvāt*, NVT., 1.1.3.
3. *A System of Logic*, p. 3.

term. Hence, inference is defined as that knowledge which must be preceded by perception (*tatpūrvakam*).[1] Similarly, *upamāna* or comparison as a method of naming depends on perception of the points of similarity between two objects. So also *śabda* or testimony is dependent on perception inasmuch as the first step in it is the visual or auditory perception of written or spoken words, and such words must come from a person who has a direct or intuitive knowledge of the truths communicated by him. So we see that perceptual knowledge is the ultimate ground of all other knowledge by inference, comparison and testimony.[2]

Secondly, the Naiyāyikas observe that perception is the final test of all knowledge. We may question the truth of the knowledge derived from inference, testimony, etc., but the truth of perception is in a way beyond question. We may know the same thing by means of testimony, inerence and perception. But while the knowledge from testimony and inference requires confirmation by perception, the perceptual knowledge of the thing is in need of no further confirmation. A man may acquire the knowledge of a thing fro some authoritative statement, *i.e.* the testimony of a person. But this generally serves as the starting-point for further reflection on the matter and produces a desire to ascertain the truth in a more convincing way, say, by a process of inferential reasoning. But the inference which confirms the testimony may, in its turn, require further verification by way of direct perception of the object. Perceptual verification is thus the final test of all other knowledge and, as such, perception is the most important of all the methods or sources of human knowledge.[3]

In European philosophy the validity of perception as a source of knowledge is rather overstressed by the empiricists and some modern realists. According to them, the truth of perception is unquestionable and self-evident. Thus J.S. Mill remarks: "Whatever is known to us by consciousness (intuition), is known beyond

1. NS. & NB., 1.1.5.
2. NB. & NV., 1.1.6-7.
3. *Sā ceyaṁ pramitiḥ pratyakṣaparā*, NB., 1.1.3.

possibility of question. What one sees or feels, whether bodily or mentally, one cannot but be sure that one sees or feels,"[1] So also W.T. Marvin thinks that "perception is the ultimate crucial test, and as such, it does not presuppose its own possibility. It simply is; and the man who questions it assumes it in order to do the questioning."[2] Similarly, Russell tells us repeatedly that the truths of perception are self-evident truths, for which we require no test at all.[3] The Naiyāyikas however, do not admit that the validity of perception as such is self-evident and unquestionable. That perception is the final test of all other knowledge does not mean that the truth of perception is self-evident or that it cannot but be true. From the standpoint of common-sense realism they grant that, under normal conditions, what is directly perceived is not doubted and so need not be further proved or tested. When however any doubt arises with regard to the validity of perception, we must examine and verify it as much as any other knowledge.

2. The Buddhist Definition of Perception

The Buddhists define perception as the unerring cognition of a given sensum in complete isolation from all ideata.[4] In it the object of cognition is a unique individual (*svalakṣaṇa*) and the process of cognition is a mere sensing without any element of ideation (*kalpanā*) in it. Vasubandhu, a Bauddha logician of the Yogācāra school (circa 480 A. D.), characterises perception as a cognition that is directly produced by the object, of which it is the cognition.[5] The cognition of fire, for example, is a perception, if and in so far as it is produced and wholly conditioned by fire as an existent fact. On the other hand, the 'cognition of silver' in the presence of an oyster-shell, cannot be called perception, since it is not caused by

1. *A System of Logic*, p. 4.
2. *The New Realism*, pp. 66-67.
3. *The Problems of Philosopy*, Chapter xi; *Our Knowledge of the External World*, p. 72.
4. *Pratyakṣaṁ kalpanāpoḍhamabhrāntam*, *Nyāyabindu*, Chapter 1.
5. *Tato'rthādvijñānaṁ pratyakṣam*, NV. & NVTK., 1.1.4.

the object, of which it claims to be the cognition. The silver is non-existent at the time and place at which it seems to be perceived and so cannot causally determine the cognition in question. So also the inferential cognition of fire is distinguished from perception by the fact that it is not produced directly and exclusively by fire as an objective fact. The inferential knowledge depends on such other conscious and unconscious conditions as the cognition of smoke, the association between smoke and fire, memory of the relation between the two and so on. For the same reason, the Buddhists deny the perceptual character of the so called perceptions of individual objects like the jar, tree, etc. (*saṁvṛtijñāna*).[1] What we directly perceive is not the jar or the tree as a unity of the universal and the particular, but some quality or part of it. What is thus directly sensed is next combined with certain images and ideas of other associated qualities or parts and thereby produces the complex cognition of a jar or a tree. In fact, such complex cognitions (*saṁvṛtijñāna*) are not perceptions, since these are not directly produced but the object alone. Rather, they are wrong cognitions based on the hypothesis of universal essences (*jāti*) underlying the aggregates of parts and qualities constituting individual objects.

Dignāga, the greatest Buddha logician (circa 500 A. D.), brings out the implications of Vasubandhu's definition of perception. If perceptual cognition is solely determined by its object, it must be wholly given and not anywise constructed by the mind. Hence Dignāga defines perception and is not modified by ideas or concepts (*kalpanā*).[2] The concepts of name, class, quality, action and relation do not enter into the perception of an object. What is perceived by us is a unique individual that does not admit of any description by concepts and words. It is just what it is immediately sensed to be. Words and concepts express such aspects of things as are general or common to many things. But a thing is an individual is so far as it excludes all other things from within itself. Hence, what is individual is to be directly felt or intuited, but not expressed by

1. *Ibid.*
2. *Vide Pramāṇasamuccaya*, Chapter 1.

words or concepts. From this it follows that perception is just the cognition of an immediately given datum and is completely free from all subjective or conceptual determinations. It is a pure sensation which cannot be properly described or embodied in verbal judgments.[1]

The Buddhist definition of perception has been criticised and rejected by the Naiyāyikas. It has been pointed out by them that Vasubandhu's definition of perception is too wide. If by perception we are to mean a cognition which is objectively determined (*tato 'rthādvijñānam*), all true knowledge will have to be regarded as perception. As Bosanquet has rightly pointed out, "reality is operative in truth."[2] Thus, a true inference has an objective basis in so far as the conclusion expresses a real relation between two things. So we may say that what is validly inferred is an objective fact which is causally efficient towards the inferential cognition. Similar is the case with the other kinds of valid knowledge. Even the wrong cognition of silver in a shell is not without some objective basis. The wrong judgment, 'that is silver,' is based on the 'that' as an objective fact. Further, on the Bauddha view of universal momentariness (*kṣaṇikavāda*), we do not see how perception can have an objective basis. The object being the cause of perception must be antecedent to it. So when the perception is or appears its momentary cause, namely, the object, must cease to exist. The object cannot therefore be the cause of perception. But if perception be not directly produced by the object, we cannot call it perception at all.[3]

Later Bauddha logicians like Dignāga, Dharmakīrti and others reduce perception to a mere sensation free from all conceptual determination. This, the Naiyāyikas think, is logically indefensible and arbitrary. None of our ordinary perceptions is a pure sensing of the given datum. On the other hand, perception is the interpretation of sensations by associated images and ideas. It is

1. NBT., pp. 7-12.
2. *Logic*, Vol. II, p. 289.
3. NV. and NVT., 1.1.4.

now a commonplace of philosophy that "perception contains not merely sensuous and revived images, but a large element of meaning as well."[1] Perception is not, as the Buddhists think, an unmeaning sensation of an indeterminate real called *svalakṣaṇa*. It has a definite meaning and refers to a determinate object as that is revealed through sensations. It is only because the Buddhists arbitrarily deny the meaning element in perception that they are forced to exclude the complex cognitions of a jar, tree, etc. (*saṁvṛtijñāna*), from the range of perception. As a matter of fact, these are as good perceptions as any other. If, however, we allow with the Buddhists that perception is a matter of pure sensation, we do not understand how it can at all be conceived or logically defined. A pure sensation is an unreal abstraction and not a psychological fact. We cannot point to any of our actual experiences as a case of pure sensation without any element of ideation in it. Such an experience, even if it were real, can hardly be described, far less defined. The Buddhist definition of perception is self-contradictory (*vyāhata*) in so far as it tries to define and determine what is undefinable and indeterminate. Just as what is perfectly unknowable cannot even be known as unknowable, so we cannot consistently determine a perfectly indeterminate experience as perception.[2]

3. The Jaina, Prābhākara and Vedānta Definitions of Perception

It is customary to define perception in terms of sense functioning. The ordinary idea is that perception as a form of

---

1. *Essays in Critical Realism*, p. 91.
2. NV. and NVT., 1.1.4 ; NM., pp. 92-93, 97-100; SD., pp. 38-39.

   The notion of an ineffable sensum, like the Buddhist's *svalakṣaṇa*, has also been repudiated of late by some eminent Western thinkers like Whitehead, Heidegger, Rickert, Bosanquet, Dewey. 'Whitehead speaks of it as the sensationalist fallacy and Heidegger as the illusory notion of mere givenness, untinged with the "concern" which he holds to be constitutive of experience throughout. See Charles Hartshorne's article on "The Intelligibility of Sensations" in *The Monist,* July, 1934, pp. 161-85.

knowledge is essentially dependent for its origin and distinctive character on the stimulation of the sense-organs. There is a departure from this common usage in the definition of *pratyakṣa* or perception given but the Advaita Vedānta, the Prābhākara, Mīmāṁsā and the Jaina system. According to the Prābhākaras, perception is the direct cognition of an object. It is the intuitive or immediate knowledge that we may have of the subject and object of knowledge or of knowledge itself.[1] For the Jainas too, *pratyakṣa* is the direct and immediate knowledge of objects. It is of two kind: *mukhya* or the primary and *saṁvyavahārika* or the practical. The first is quite independent of the mind and the senses. While the origin of the second is conditioned by the mind and the senses, its essence lies in the direct cognition of some object. Hence perception is in its essential nature a direct knowledge of objects.[2]

In the Advaita Vedānta, perception as a *pramāṇa* is the unique cause (*karaṇa*) of perception as a form of valid knowledge (*pramā*). In this sense, the sense organs constitute the *karaṇa* or the unique cause of perceptual cognition. The latter (*i.e. pratyakṣa pramā*), however, is defined as immediate and timeless knowledge (*caitanya*). Such immediate knowledge is the self itself, because it is only in the self that there is pure immediacy of knowledge. The senses are the *karaṇa* or the unique cause of perception as immediate knowledge in so far as the mental modification (*antaḥkaraṇavṛtti*), which manifests it (*i.e. caitanya*), is due to the function of the sense organs. What takes place in perception is this. The *antaḥkaraṇa* or mind goes out through the sense organ which is in contact with a present perceptible object and becomes so modified as to assume the form of the object itself. The mind being a material principle, it is quite possible for it to move and attain the dimension of the object of perception. Perception is the immediate knowledge in which the mental modification is non-

---

1. *Sākṣātpratīthiḥ pratyakṣaṃ meyamātṛpramāsu sā*, *Prakaraṇa-pañcikā*, pp. 52-52
2. *Viśadajñānasvabhāvaṃ pratyakṣam, avyavadhānena pramāṇāntara-nirapekṣatayā pratibhāsamaṁ vastuno'nubhavo vaiśadyam vijñāmasyeti*, etc., *Prameyakamala-mārtaṇḍa*, pp. 57-67

different (*abhinna*) from the object and is lit up by the self's light. The immediacy of perception, however, is not due to its being produced by sense stimulation. If that were so, then inference would have been as immediate as perception, since, according to the Naiyāyikas, the mind as an internal sense is operative in inference. On the other hand, there cannot be any immediate knowledge by intuition, because it is not due to the senses. The connection of perception with sense-stimulation is more accidental than essential.[1]

That there may be immediate knowledge without any stimulation of sense is admitted by many leading philosophers of the West. Any knowledge by acquaintance, Russell[2] thinks, gives us a direct knowledge of things. "Direct cognition," says Ewing,[3] "would be quite possible without direct perception." With regard to perception, however, it is generally held in European philosophy that it is the cognition of an object through sensations. Here the process of perception begins with the action of an external object. The object produces certain modifications in the sense organ and the nervous system and, through these, gives rise to a mental image corresponding to itself. In the Advaita Vedānta the order of the process is reversed. The mind goes out through sense and reaches the object, and there becomes literally changed into the form of the object. On this view, the perplexing question of the correspondence of a mental image to the object, of which it is the image, does not at all arise. The direct apprehension of objects in perception is thus better explained by the Vedānta. It goes further than this and maintains that the essence of perception lies, not in its being produced by sense-object contact, but in the immediacy (*sākṣāttvam*) of the knowledge given by it.

4. The Nyāya Definitions of Perception

The old school of the Nyāya defines perception in terms of sense-object contact (*indriyārthasannikarṣa*). According to it,

1. VP., Chapter 1.
2. *The Problems of Philosophy*, Chapter V.
3. *Mind*, April, 1930, p. 140.

perception is the valid knowledge produced by the contact of an object with a sense organ.[1] This means that perception as a form of valid knowledge is conditioned in its origin by the stimulation of the senses. This definition of perception follows from the etymological meaning of the word *pratyakṣa* or perception. *Pratyakṣa* derivatively means the functioning or operation of the sense organs, each in relation to its particular object (*akṣasyākṣasya prativiṣayam vṛttiḥ pratyakṣam*).[2] In relation to a particular object, the sense may function in two ways. It may function to bring about a contact of itself with the object. In this case, the result is a cognition of the object. Secondly, a sense organ may be operative to produce a cognition of some object. In this case the sense-function consists in sense-cognition, and the result is a judgment of the cognised object as something desirable or undesirable or neither.[3] But even sense-cognition as a form of sense-function is conditioned by sense-object contact. It follows that the fact of sense-object contact is involved in the very meaning of the word *pratyakṣa,* and is common to all perceptions. This common and essential character is made the basis of a definition of perception. For all the older Naiyāyikas, perception is the valid cognition of an object, as distinguished from feeling and volition, and as conditioned by the contact of that object with a particular sense organ.

The above definition perception as knowledge due to sense-object contact is accepted by common sense and many philosophic systems. In the Vaiśeṣika philosophy[4] perception is described as knowledge which is conditioned by the senses. The Sāṅkhya-Yoga system also defines perception in terms of sense-stimulation. According to the Sāṅkhya,[5] perception is the direct cognition of an object by a sense when the two come in contact with each other. The Yoga system holds the same view while emphasising that

1. NS., 1. 1. 4.
2. NB., 1. 1. 3.
3. NB., 1. 1. 3.
4. *Akṣamakṣam pratītyotapadyate prayakṣaṁ*, PS., p 94.
5. *Vide Sāṅkhya-sūtra* and *Pravacanabhāṣya*, 1. 89; *Sāṅkhyakārikā*, 5.

perception is especially a cognition of the particularity of an object. For it, perception is 'a mental modification produced by sense impressions and mainly related to the specific characters entering into the nature of the individual object of perception.'[1] In the *Mīmāṁsā-sūtra* and the Bhāṭṭa school of Mīmāṁsā, perception is defined as 'the cognition which is produced by the efficient contact of the senses with their objects.'[2] Vārṣagaṇya, a follower of the Mīmāṁsā school, reduces perception just to the functioning of the sense organs.[3]

Although the old Naiyāyikas are disposed to find fault with the definition of perception given in the other systems of philosophy, they do not dispute the fact of sense-object contact as constituting the essential nature of perception. Thus the Bhāṭṭa definition is attacked on the ground that it is not limited to valid perceptions but may apply also to doubt and error as forms of perception, in which there is sense-contact with some object.[4] This means that a definition of perception as valid knowledge (*pramā*) should explicitly mention that validity is an essential character of it. But the context makes it unnecessary for the Mīmāṁsaka. Similarly, the Sāṅkhya view is considered by the Naiyāyika to be inadequate, because it does not expressly state the fact of sense-object contact.[5] Such criticism, however, is vitiated by a sophistical spirit. It is true that Īśvarakṛṣṇa does not use just the phrase 'sense-object contact' in his definition (*viz. prativiṣayādhyavasāyo dṛṣṭam*). But this follows clearly when we collate the sūtra and the commentaries on this point. It is therefore unnecessary to dwell at length on the Nyāya criticism of the above definitions of perception. It will suffice for our present purpose to say that the definition of perception as knowledge produced by sense-stimulation or sense-object contact

---

1. *Vyāsa-Bhāṣya* on *Yoga-sūtra*, 1. 7.
2. *Satsṁprayoge puruṣasyendriyāṇām buddhijanma tatpratyakṣam*, *Mīmāṁsā-sūtra*, 1. 1. 4. *Vide also Śāstradīpikā*, p. 35; *Ślokavārttika*, 4. 84.
3. '*Śrotrādivṛttiriti*', *Vārṣagaṇya* quoted in NV. and NVT., 1.1.4.
4. NV. and NVT., 1.1.4.
5. NM., p. 109.

is common to the Nyāya-Vaiśeṣika, the Sāṅkhya-Yoga and the Bhāṭṭa Mīmāṁsā system of Indian philosophy. As we have already said, the same definition of perception is generally accepted in Western psychology and philosophy.[1]

The modern school of the Nyāya takes exception to the old definition of perception in terms of sense-object contact. Gaṅgeśa, the father of modern Nyāya, opposes it on several grounds. First, it is objected by him that the definition is too wide, since it applies to inference and memory as forms of knowledge in which there is sense-object contact. That mind as an internal sense is operative and related to the object known through memory or inference. Secondly, the definition is too narrow in another sense. It precludes the possibility of God's omniscience which is a direct perception of all truth and reality. If there can be no perception without sense-object contact, we can hardly speak of the divine perception, since it is not a sensuous cognition in any sense. Further, we do not find that sense-contact, in one or other form, is common to all perceptions. Again, to define perception in terms of sense-stimulation is to beg the question. What a sense-organ or its stimulation means is to be known from perception. As a matter of fact, we understand what perception is, long before we know what a sense *is*, and which of the senses is concerned in producing it. Hence to explain perception by sense-stimulation is to explain the *obscurum per obscurius.*[2] In view of such defects in the old definition, the modern Naiyāyikas propose to define perception as immediate knowledge. It is the character of immediacy (*sākṣātkāritvam*) that is common to all perceptions. The visual, auditory and other kinds of perception are alike connected with the feeling that something is immediately known by the subject or the knower.[3] Another definition of perception, given by the modern

1. *Cf.* Sir J. H. Parsons, *An Introduction to the Theory of Perception*, p. 3.: "Sensory presentations, as we experience them, invariably evolve percpetion, however naïve it may be, at the start: but there is no percpetion without sensory presentation."

2. TC., I, pp. 539-43.

3. *Pratyakṣasya sākṣātkāritvaṁ lakṣaṇam*, TC., *ibid.*

Nyāya, is that it is knowledge which is not brought about by the instrumentality of any antecedent knowledge.[1] This definition applies to all cases of perception, human or divine. At the same time it excludes all other kinds of knowledge, such as inference, comparison and testimony. Inference is due to the previous knowledge of a fixed relation between two things (*vyāptiñāna*). In *upamāna* or comparison the operative cause of knowledge (*jñānakaraṇa*) is the knowledge of similarity between two things (*sādṛśyajñāna*). Knowledge by testimony is brought about by the understanding of the meanings of words (*padajñāna*). So also memory depends for its origin on some direct experience in the past (*pūrvānubhava*). It is only in the case of perception that our knowledge is not *caused* by previous experience. It cannot be said that perception is entirely undetermined by previous experience. A determinate (*savikalpaka*) perception of an object, as having certain attributes and belonging to a class, is conditioned by the previous knowledge of those attributes as standing for a certain class of things. But even here our perception of the object is only conditioned but not caused by the previous knowledge (*jñānajanya* and not *jñānakaraṇaka*).[2] The present perception of the book before me does not arise out of my previous knowledge about books, although the character of that perception is determined by such antecedent knowledge. At least the perception is not the result of a conscious application of antecedent knowledge to a present case. The Buddhist definition of perception as knowledge which is directly produced by the object alone, excludes all the conscious and unconscious conditions of knowledge from perception except the object. The modern Nyāya, however, excludes all the conscious conditions of knowledge from the definition of perception above given. For it, perception is not entirely undetermined by previous experience. But even if it be determined by previous experience, it is not consciously brought about but that experience. Hence, perception has been defined as the knowledge which is not brought about by the instrumentality of any antecedent knowledge.

1. *Jñānākaraṇakam jñānamiti tu vayam*, TC., I, p. 552.
2. *Op. cit.*, pp. 552-53.

In the syncretist school of the Nyāya, attempts have been made to reconcile the older definition of perception with the modern. Among the ancient Naiyāyikas, Udayana, Vardhamāna and others have suggested that the definition of perception, as given in the *Nyāya-sūtra* in terms of sense-object contact, applies only to ordinary human perception (*laukikamātraviṣayatvāt*).[1] The science of logic is concerned with the conditions or grounds of valid knowledge. It is not interested in the eternal and unconditioned knowledge of the divine being. Hence, the *sūtra* gives a definition of such perception as is due to certain specific causes (*pramāṇa*). In view of this it has been suggested by some syncretist logicians that for normal human perception the definition is that it is knowledge produced by sense-object contact. But when we take perception in a wider sense so as to cover ordinary and extraordinary human perceptions as well as the eternal perception of the divine being, we should define it as immediate (*aparokṣa*) knowledge, or as knowledge which is not brought about by antecedent knowledge (*jñānākaraṇaka*).[2] Keśavamiśra in his *Tarkabhāṣa* goes further and takes the old and modern definitions of perception to mean the same thing. According to him, perception is the source of valid immediate knowledge and immediate knowledge is that which is brought about by sense-object contact.[3] Hence for knowledge there is no distinction between what is immediate and what is sensed. Rather immediate knowledge is just the product of sense-stimulation.

Of the two definitions of perception given above, that proposed by the modern Nyāya seems to be more acceptable. That perception is generally conditioned by sense-stimulation or sense-object contact is true as a matter of fact. Still this fact does not constitute the essential or the universal character of all perceptions. There

---

1. *Vide* Udayana's *Kusumāñjali* and Vardhamāna's *Prakāśa*, 4-5.

2. *Aparokṣapramāvyāptaṁ pratyakṣam anyathā laukikapratyakṣa-mātravivakṣāyāmindriyajanyapramāsādhakatamaṁ pratyakṣam*, TR. and .SS., pp. 57-59.

3. *Sākṣātkāripramākaraṇaṁ pratyakṣam, sākāṣtkāriṇī ca pramā saivocyate yendriyajā*, TB., p.5.

are cases of knowledge which are undoubtedly perceptual in character and yet not brought about by sense-object contact. Instances to the point are to be found not only in the intuition of seers and God's omniscience, but in such abnormal perceptions as illusion, hallucination, dream, delirium and the like. In these cases we have perceptions of objects that are not in actual contact with our senses. No doubt they are all cases of wrong knowledge, but that they are actual perceptions we cannot dispute. When we have such experiences or when afterwards we recollect them, we feel that we did *perceive* certain things which we should not have so perceived. These then are significant experiences which show that perceptual knowledge is not essentially a matter of sense-object contact. Similarly, any ordinary valid perception is found on analysis to contain elements which are not sensations in any sense. When we perceive an orange from a distance, we have a sensation of its colour but not of its smell, taste and touch. Still we perceive all these qualities as constituents of the total percept.[1] Hence, it may legitimately be said that sense-stimulation is not the essence of perception. Wherein that essence lies we may also find in the light of the above instances. They serve to show that we feel sure to perceive anything that is directly presented to us. It does not matter much whether the direct presentation, which we call perception, is right or wrong, is by way of sense or not. Hence we may say that to perceive a thing is to know it immediately. The modern Nyāya hits upon a truth when it defines perception as immediate knowlede, although it recognises the fact that perception is generally conditioned by sense-object contact. The Prābhākara Mīmāṁsā and the Advaita Vedānta are at one with the modern Nyāya in recognising this truth about the essential nature of perception. This is also admitted by Hobhouse when he says that the common and essential character of simple ideas of sensation

1. *Cf.* L. S. Stebbing, *Logic in Practice,* p. 13: "It is true that such judgments ('That is a cow,' 'Here is a pen') go beyond what is directly given to sense, but it does not follow that they are reached by inference. Certainly such judgments may be erroneous. None of these is completely trustworthy, but they are all we *have.*"

and reflection lies, not in their dependence on any sense organ, or any special kind of physiological stimulus, but in their immediate presence of consciousness. Hence while admitting that apprehension, in the sense of sensation or perception, is conditioned by both the sense organ and its stimulation, he defines it as the knowledge of what is immediately present to consciousness.[1]

1. Hobhouse, *The Theory of Knowledge*, Pt. I, Ch. I. Dr. Stebbing seems to endorse the definition of percpetion as immediate knowledge when the observes that in perceptual judgments we merely reord what we take be *directly given. Vide op. cit.*, p. 13.

Chapter VI

Psychology of Perception

1. The Senses (*Indriya*)

From the Nyāya standpoint perception is an immediate valid cognition of reality, due to some kind of sense-object contact. As such, perception involves four operative conditions of causes, namely, objects, senses, mind and self. What objects can be perceived and how they are perceived by us, we shall see in the next chapter. Here we propose to consider, from the Naiyāyika standpoint, the psychological questions as to the nature and function of sense, mind and self in perception.

It is generally admitted that perception is primarily conditioned by the activity of the senses in relation to some objects. Hence, perception is usually defined in terms of sense-stimulation. Even those who refuse to do so have to admit sense-activity as a factor conditioning all perception. But there is some difference of opinion as to the exact nature of the senses and their functions in perception. According to the Buddhists, the senses are the external organs (*golaka*) occupying different parts of the surface of the body.[1] The visual sense, for example, is the pupil of the eye, since objects can be seen only when the pupil is in order but not otherwise. Thus, the endorgans are entrusted by the Buddhists with the function of perception and, therefore, spoken of as the senses. For the Jainas a sense is the physical organ with a specific energy (*śakti*).[2] According to the Sāṅkhyas, the senses are not physical bodies like the pupil called *ahaṅkāra*. They think that a physical (*bhautika*) organ cannot account for the perception of distant objects. In perception the

1. *Golakasyendriyatvamiti Bauddhāḥ*, NSV., 3. 1. 30.
2. *Vide Prameyakamalamārtaṇḍa*, p. 61.

senses must function in direct contact with the objects of perception. But a physical organ like the eye-pupil cannot have direct contact with an object lying at a distance or behind a glass. This is possible only if the sense organ be all-pervading in character and not a limited physical substance. So, the Sāṅkhyas think that the senses are modifications of a subtle all-pervading matter (*ahaṅkārika*) and are themselves all-pervading in character.[1]

The Nyāya rejects both the Bauddha and the Sāṅkhya view about the nature of the senses. It agrees with the Mīmāṁsā and the Vedānta in holding that the senses as neither the end-organs nor modifications of any all-pervading subtle matter. According to these systems the external senses are material substances constituted by the physical elements (*bhautika*) and localised in the different end-organs.[2] In the Nyāya system, a sense is defined as a supersensible organ of knowledge having its locus in the animal organism.[3] A sense cannot itself be sensed or perceived. The existence of the senses is not a matter of direct perception for us. It is by means of inference or reasoning that we know their existence. The eye cannot perceive itself. But that there is a visual sense, follows from the general law that every function is conditioned by some organ. So, it has been said that a sense is what cannot be sensed but must be inferred as an organ necessary for the function of perception. Another definition of sense, given by some Naiyāyikas (*e.g.* Gaṅgeśa and Viśvanātha), is that it is the medium of a contact between the mind and an object to produce such knowledge as is different from memory.[4] This definition, however, is not applicable to mind as a sense, since it cannot be said to be the medium of contact between itself and objects like pleasure and pain. The

1. *Ahaṅkāropādānakamindriyam*, *Tattvakaumudī*, 26. *Cf.* NSV., *ibid.*
2. NS., 1. 1. 12; VP., Ch. VII; SD., p. 36.
3. *Śarīrasaṁjuktam jñānakaraṇamatīndriyamindriyam*, TB., p. 19. *Cf.* H. H. Price, *Perception*, p. 25: "By 'senses' I do not mean 'sense-organs' but 'senses-faculties', *i.e.* the power of being acquainted with this or that kind of sense-datum."
4. SM., 58; TC., I pp. 550-51.

Śāstradīpikā[1] defines sense as what produces a clear and distinct knowledge of the object it is brought in contact with. This definition holds good with regard to all the senses including the mind.

According to the Nyāya and the Mīmāṁsā, there are six sense organs. Of these some are called external and some internal (*bāhymābhyantaram*). There is only one internal sense called *manas* or mind. This will be separately dealt with in another action. There are five external senses, namely, the olfactory, the gustatory, the visual, the cutaneous and the auditory. These senses are physical in character, because they are constituted by the physical elements.[2] But for their physical character we cannot explain the limitation of perception to a particular time and space. If the senses were, as the Sāṅkhyas say, non-physical and all-pervading principles, we should have simultaneous perceptions of all objects in the world. Each sense is capable of revealing the existence of one particular class of objects. A sense organ is constituted by the physical element whose qualities are sensed by it. It possesses the specific attribute of its constituent physical element and is therefore capable of perceiving the qualities belonging to it.[3]

The olfactory sense (*ghrāṇa*) is the organ of apprehending smell. It must have the quality of smell in it in order to apprehend smell in other things. As such, it is constituted by the earth, to which smell originally belongs as an attribute. The sense of smell is said to have its seat in the forepart of the nasal cavity (*nāsāgravarti*).[4] This, however, is contradicted by modern psychology which holds that 'the organ of smell is a muconus membrane lining the roof and part of the walls of the extreme upper portion of the moral cavities'.[5]

The gustatory sense (*rasana*) is the condition of taste sensations. It is constituted by the physical element called water, because it is

1. *Vide* p. 36.
2. NS. and SD., *ibid.*
3. NSV., 3. 1. 32.
4. TB., *Ibid.*
5. *Vide* Titchener, *a Text-Book of Psychology.*

possessed of the specific attribute of that element, *viz.* taste. It is located in the forepart of the tongue (*jihvāgravarti*). But the localisation of the sense of taste in the tip of the tongue does not agree with the finding of scientific psychology. From it we learn that the end-organs of taste, *i.e.* the taste bulbs occur largely in the posterior part of the tongue. The tip on the tongue is especially sensitive to sweet taste. As such, it may be said to be the organ of certain tastes.[1]

The visual sense (*cakṣu*) is the ground of colour-sensations and is itself coloured. It has its locus in the pupil of the eye. It is constituted by a luminous substance called *tejas* or light. In the case of the visual sense the constituent element of light has no manifest form and touch (*anudbhūtarūpasparśa*). The sun as a luminous orb has both form and touch manifest in it. Hence it is that the one cannot be, while the other is, perceived by us. The account of the visual sense given here is in substantial agreement with the modern theory of vision, although it lacks most of its finer details. It will have the support of modern optics which recognises the dependence of visual sensation on the energy of light and the presence of a colouring matter behind the lens, and treats the retina as the organ of vision.[2]

The cutaneous sense (*tvak*) is the source of touch-sensations and temperature-sensations. It is constituted by the physical element *air*, because, like the air, it manifests the quality of touch. The locus or the end-organ of the sense of touch is the whole skin of the body, from head to foot, outside and inside its surface.[3] From a common-sense standpoint no distinction is here made between the different sensations of touch or pressure and those of warmth and cold. In truth, the cutaneous sense is highly complex. Many psychologists distinguish between four cutaneous senses, namely, those of pressure, warmth, cold, and pain.[4] The Naiyāyikas do not

---

1. *Op. cit.*
2. *Op. cit.*
3. TB., pp. 20, 24.
4. Titchener, *op. cit.*

go so far in their account of the cutaneous sense, but describe both pressure and temperature as touch sensations. Nor do they subscribe to the view that the sense of touch is the primitive sense, from which the other external senses develop by increasing differentiation. "Touch," Aristotle observed, "is the mother of the senses." Modern psychologists also think that "starting from this mode of sensibility as a basis the other senses develop by processes of increasing complexity and refinenent."[1] The Naiyāyikas oppose this hypothesis on the ground that the sense of touch cannot, in any degree, perform the function of the other senses in those who are deprived of them.[2]

The auditory sense (*śrotra*) is the source of sensations of sound. It has its seat in the drum of the ear. It is possessed of the quality of sound. As such, it is identical with a portion of the physical element *ākāśa,* as that is present in and limited by the ear-hole. It is not a separate substance, but is a limited portion of *ākāśa* itself, since the quality of sound belongs originally to *ākāśa.*[3] According to the Vedānta, however, sound is not exclusively a property of *ākāśa*, since it is perceived in the air and other elements as well. But it admits that the sense of hearing is constituted by the physical element of *ākāśa.*[4] The Mīmāṁsā differs here from both the Nyāya and the Vedānta in holding that the auditory sense is a portion of space (*digbhāga*) enclosed within the aural cavity.[5] Thus, senses are physical entities constituted by the physical elements.

To the above list of the six senses, recognised by the Nyāya and the Mīmāṁsā, the Sāṅkhya system adds five other senses. These are the five senses of action (*karmendriya*). They are called speech, hands, feet, rectum and the sex-organ, and perform respectively the functions of speaking, prehension, locomotion, evacuation and reproduction.[6] Thus the Sāṅkhya gives us a list of eleven sense-

1. Hollingworth, *Psychology*, p. 456.
2. NB., 3. 1. 51-63.
3. TB., p. 20.
4. VP., Ch. VII.
5. SD., p. 36.
6. *Sāṅkhyakārikā*, 26 & 28.

organs. The Vedānta accepts this with one exception. It excludes the mind or *antaḥkaraṇa* from the list of the senses.[1] The Nyāya objects to this long list on the ground that the assumption of a sense for every function will lead to countless senses. If by sense we mean, as we should, a bodily organ of some special kind of perception (*sākṣātpratīsādhana*), then the organs of action cannot be called sense organs. They do not give us any perceptions of a new thing or quality other than those connected with the six senses of smell, taste, sight, touch, hearing and the mind.[2]

The Naiyāyāyikas' enumeration of the senses, it will be seen, is different from that usually given in Western psychology. Of the six senses enumerated by them, mind as an internal sense finds no place in modern psychology, while a number of internal senses is added to the five external senses recognised by them. These are the kinaesthetic senses. Then we are told that there are certain organic sensations which are derived from the internal organs of the body. These too will have to be regarded as senses if we seriously accept the view of organic sensations. Further, the cutaneous sense is subdivided into the pressure sense, the temperature senses and the pain sense. Of these, the first two, namely, the pressure and temperature senses are included by the Naiyāyikas in the sense of touch, since, according to them, warmth and cold are only different kinds of touch sensations. Hence in addition to the five senses of the Naiyāyikas, we have to admit a pain sense, several kinaesthetic senses and the vital or organic senses. These are supposed to be necessary to explain the sensation of pain, the perceptions of movement and position, resistance and weight, and other organic sensations connected with the abdominal organs, the digestive and urinary systems, the circulatory and respiratory systems and the genital systems.

It seems to me, however, that this long list of the senses, to which Western psychology commits us, has its basis in an unsound epistemology. A careful epistemological analysis of what are called

1. VP., Ch. VII.
2. NVT., p. 531; NM., pp. 482 f.

sensations will show that they are cognitive mental stages which *acquaint* us with the qualities of things. A sensation has, therefore, a cognitive value and has reference to some *given* datum. The cognitive value of a sensation lies in its being the basis of our perception of the thing which produces the sensation. Another characteristic of sensations is that we can have images corresponding to them at the time when they are past. Judged by such criteria, it is very doubtful if we can legitimately speak of a sensation of pain or of kinaesthetic and organic sensations. While touch, warmth and cold are qualities of things, pain cannot be referred to anything as its quality. We feel pain indeed, but do not perceive anything as painful, just as we perceive a rose as red when it produces the sensation of red in us. We can hardly form an image of a pain previously felt in the same way in which we can image a previously experienced colour or sound. Hence pain is better characterised as a feeling, rather than as a sensation. Similarly the so-called organic sensations may be shown to be feelings aroused by certain states of the vital organs, or by the ordinary sensations of pressure, warmth, etc. Thus according to Titchener,[1] 'the sense of satiety, of a full stomach would come from an upward *pressure* against the diaphragm. Thirst appears as a diffuse pressure or as a blend of *pressure* and *warmth*. There are times when the separate heart-beats are clearly sensed as dull throbbing *pressure*.' Titchener says further that 'the special sensations of the genital system appeal first as an *excitement*, then as *gratification* and thirdly as *relief*.' But all these are plainly feeling, and not sensations in the proper sense. Lastly, what are called kinaestehetic sensations are analysable into certain feelings and ordinary sensations produced by different kind of bodily activity. 'A muscular sensation is ordinarily a dull and diffuse *pressure* upon the skin. With increasing intensity it takes on a dragging character and sometimes passes into dull pain.' 'The articular sensation is said to be a massive complex of sensations in the wrist-joint whose quality is not distinguishable from that of cutaneous *pressure*.' The perceptions of the movement and position of our limbs, with closed eyes, and those of the weight

1. *Vide A Text-Book of Psychology*, pp. 160-92.

and resistance of other bodies are said to be based upon the articular sensations. But we have no specific sensations of movement and position, resistance and weight. In fact, none of them can be treated as a sense-datum like colour and sound. Hence we require no separate senses for their perceptions. If, then, the so-called muscular and articular sensations can be analysed into sensations of pressure and feelings of strain and pain, we see no reason why we must admit separate senses for them. We admit different external senses for the different kinds of sensations, like colour, sound, etc., because we cannot analyse any of them into any other. The sensations of one sense are quite distinct from those of any other sense. But even those who speak of the kinaesthetic senses would admit that 'the kinaesthetic sensations are, in general, very like the cutaneous, and in one case, indistinguishable from cutaneous pressure.' Supposing that there are kinaesthetic senses, we ask: What sensa or sense-qualities do they acquaint us with? Certainly, movement and position, resistance and weight are not sensa like colours and sounds. There being no other distinct sensa for them, we are to say that the kinaesthetic sensations, like the alleged sensation of innervation, are really feelings produced by bodily movements. Accordingly, the so-called kinaesthetic senses will have to be regarded as organs of action and not of sensation.

2. Function of the Senses

The function of the senses is to produce perception of objects. For a sense organ, to function is to give us immediate knowledge about certain objects. How, then, do the senses function to give us perception of objects? Is the activity of the senses conditioned by their contact with the objects of perception? Or, do they give us perception of objects without any contact with them?

According to the Buddhists, the senses function without direct contact with the objects of perception. They are all "distance receptors" (*aprāpyakāri*), and do not require immediate contact with their objects. This is especially seen in the case of the senses of sight and hearing. We see far-off objects that cannot have any direct or approximate contact with the eyes. We hear sound produced at a long distance from our ears. Similarly, the eye perceives objects much larger than itself and so incapable of being covered by it. Again, the eye and the ear can perceive the distance and direction of sights and sounds respectively. This they could not, if, like the senses of smell, taste, and touch, they were in immediate contact with their objects. Lastly, many of us can, at the same time, see the same object or hear the same sound from different places. Conversely, one man can, almost at the same time, see two things or hear two sounds, fairly apart from each other. This shows that the senses of sight and hearing may function without actual contact with their respective objects.[1]

According to the Nyāya, Sāṅkhaya, Mīmāṁsā and Vedānta systems, the senses can perceive only such objects as are in direct or indirect contact with them (*prāpyakāri*). This is obvious in the case of the so-called lower senses, namely, touch, taste and smell. Sensations of touch and taste arise only when the sense organs are in immediate contact with their respective objects. To taste a thing is to place it in direct contact with the tongue. To touch a thing is to bring it in contact with the skin. Sense-object contact as a condition of olfactory sensation is no less real, although it may sometimes be less obvious. If the smelling object be in our immediate surrounding, there is obvious contact of it with the olfactory organ. If it be at a distance from us, then the odorous particles given off by the object are brought in actual contact with the sense organ by currents of air.[2] In the case of the lower senses, all systems of philosophy admit a direct sense-object contact. It is also admitted that the senses of smell, taste and touch remain passive in their end-organs where they are met by their respective stimuli. The remaining two senses of sight and hearing also act in contact with their objects, although not quite as directly as the rest. According to the Vedānta, the sense of hearing travels to the sounding objects and gives us sensations of sound.[3] The Nyāya, however, agrees

1. NV. and NVT., 1. 1. 4.
2. NM., p. 479.
3. VP., Ch. I.

with modern science in holding that sound-waves sent by the object are received into the ear-passage and there perceived as sound.[1] According to both the Nyāya and the Vedānta, the visual sense reaches out to its object and gives us colour-sensations. This is why the eye and the ear can perceive the distance and direction of their respective objects. While in modern science visual sensation is believed to be due to the transmission of light-waves from the object to the eye, in Indian philosophy it is explained by the emanation of light-rays from the eye to the object. Ordinarily the colour-rays are not visible, but are inferred as the medium of sense-object contact in visual perception. Still we may perceive them under certain special circumstances, as when they emanate from the eyes of cats and other animals in a dark night. The uninformed and the uncultured may not admit sense-object contact in the perception of distant objects, because the medium of such contact is imperceptible. But that there cannot be any perception without sense-object contact is implied in all cases of obstructed sense-activity (*āvaraṇopapatti*). We cannot see things hidden behind and opaque body. Again, what seems to be a simultaneous perception of objects occupying different places, is really a case of different perceptions occurring in quick succession. We perceive a near object earlier than a remote one, because our senses take a longer time to reach the latter. Hence, sense-object contact is a condition of all perceptions.[2]

According to all the Naiyāyikas, sense-object contact (*indriyārṭhasannikarṣa*), which is the cause of perception, is of six kinds. First, we have a case of direct contact which consists in the conjunction (*saṁyoga*) between sense and its object. In the visual perception of a substance like the jar, there is an immediate contact of the eyes with the object. The visual sense finds its way to the jar and becomes conjoined with it. Secondly, there may be an indirect contact of sense with its object through the mediation of a third term that is related to both. When we see the colour of the jar, our

1. BP., 165-66.
2. NV. and NVT., 1. 1. 4; NM., pp. 479 f.

eyes come in contact with the colour through the medium of the jar. The jar is conjoined with the eyes on the one hand, and contains the colour as an inherent quality of it, on the other, Here the contact between sense and object is due to the object's (here colour) inseparable relation to what is conjoined with sense. Hence, this sense-object contact is called *saṁyukta-samavāya* or a relation of inherence in what is conjoined to sense. Thirdly, sense-object contact may be more indirect than what we find in the preceding case. It may be due to the mediation of two terms which, by their relation, connect sense with its object. When by means of the eyes we perceive a universal like 'colourness' (*rūpatvādisāmānya*) inhering in the jar's colour, there is contact of the eyes with the object 'colourness' through the medium of the two terms 'jar' and 'colour.' This sense-object contact is called *saṁyukta-samaveta-samavāya,* since it is due to the object's inherence (*samavāya*) in something (here colour) which is inseparably related to (*samaveta*) what (here jar) is conjoined (*saṁyukta*) to sense. The fourth case of indirect sense-object contact is called *samavāya* or inherence. Here the sense is in contact with its object in so far as the object inheres as a quality in the sense itself. This is illustrated in the auditory perception of sound. The ear's contact with sound is due simply to the latter's inherence as a quality in its own substance, *ākāśa*, which constitutes the auditory sense. In the fifth case sense-object contact is called *samaveta-samavāya* or the relation of inherence in that which inheres in sense. Here the sense is in contact with its object through the medium of a third term that is inseparably related to both. Thus, in the auditory perception of the universal 'soundness' (*śabdatva*), the ear is in contact with the object 'soundness,' because it inheres in sound which, in its turn, inheres as a quality in the ear. The last type of sense-object contact is called *viśeṣaṇatā* or *viśeṣyaviśeṣaṇabhāva.* In it the sense is in contact with its object in so far as the object is a qualification (*viśeṣaṇa*) of another term connected with sense. It is by means of such sense-object contact that the Naiyāyikas explain the perceptions of non-existence (*abhāva*) and the relation of inherence (*samavāya*).[1] It

1. BP. and SM., 59-62.

takes different forms according to the different ways in which the mediating term is related to sense. Thus it is called *saṁyukta-viśeṣaṇatā* when the object is abjectival (*viśeṣaṇa*) to that which is conjoined (*saṁyukta*) to the sense organ. This is illustrated by the visual perception of the non-existence of a jar in a certain place. Here the eye is in contact with non-existence as a qualification (*viśeṣaṇa*) of the place which is in conjunction (*saṁyukta*) with the eye. Similarly, it is called *saṁyukta-samavetaviśeṣaṇatā* when the sense is related to an object that is abjectival (*viśeṣaṇa*) to what inheres (*samaveta*) in that which is conjoined (*saṁyukta*) to sense. Thus, in the perception of the non-existence of sound in the odour of the earth, our sense is in contact with the non-existence as a qualification of odour which inheres in the earth as conjoined to the sense. Or, it may be called *samavetaviśeṣaṇatā* when the object of perception is a qualification (*viśeṣaṇa*) of that which inheres (*samaveta*) in sense. Thus when we perceive that there is no odour in sound, our sense is in contact with the non-existence of odour as a qualification of sound which inheres in the auditory organ. So too with regard to the other forms of this kind of sense-object contact. These have been collectively called *viśeṣaṇatā* or the contact of sense with that which is adjectival to another term connected with sense.[1] The Vedāntins also recognise these six kinds of sense-object contact. But they do not admit the perception of non-existence *abhāva* and inherence (*samavāya*).[2] We shall discuss this point afterwards.

With regard to perception, it has been asked: What is the *karaṇa* or the unique cause of perception? Is it sense or sense-object contact or something else? According to the older Naiyāyikas,[3] sense-object contact (*sannikarṣa*) is the *karaṇa* of perception, since it is the immediate antecedent to the appearance of the phenomenon of perception. The contact of sense with its appropriate object does not normally fail to produce a perception of it. Hence it is that sense-function or sense-contact should be recognised as the *karaṇa*

1. SM., 61.
2. VP., Chaps. I and VI.
3. NB., NV. and NVT., 1. 1. 3-4.

or specific cause of perception. Modern Naiyāyikas, however, hold that the sense organ is the *karaṇa* of perception.[1] A *karaṇa* is unique operative cause of an effect (*vyāpāravadasādhāraṇakāraṇa*). It is something that produces the effect by its operation and not the operation itself. The senses are such causes as produce perception by their activity or contact with the objects. As such, it is the sense (*indriya*) that should be called the *karaṇa* of perception. Keśava Miśra reconciles these views by reference to the different kinds of perception. He thinks that sense and sense-object contact are the *karaṇas* of *nirvikalpaka* and *savikalpaka* perceptions respectively. Even *nirvikalpaka* cognition may be taken as *karaṇa* in relation to cognitions of the values of object for us (*hānopādānopekṣā-buddhayaḥ*). Other however, think that sense is the *karaṇa* of all kinds of perception.[2]

3. The Nature and Function of the Mind (*Manas*)

It is with some hesitation that we use the word *mind* for *manas* in connection especially with the Nyāya philosophy. In Western philosophy mind is generally taken to mean both the subject of consciousness or the self and the totality of conscious states and processes in which the self is manifested. In this sense mind corresponds roughly, not to the *manas,* but to the *ātman* or soul in the Nyāya system. Of course, among European thinkers there are some, the materialists and some behaviourists, who reduce mind or self to a function of the body. Thus understood, mind stands for just what the Cārvākas mean by *ātman* or the self. In deference to the common usage of language we propose to use the word *mind* for *manas* pointing out the differences in their meaning.

According to the Nyāya-Vaiśeṣikas, *manas* or mind is a sense like the senses of taste, smell, etc. It is an internal sense having its locus in the heart (*hṛdayāntarvarti*).[3] In the Sāṅkhya and Mīmāṁsā systems also mind is treated as an internal (*āntara*) sense.[4] The

1. BP, and SM., 58.
2. TB., p. 5.
3. TB., p. 20.
4. SD., p. 36.

Sāṅkhya considers it to be an unconscious product of subtle matter (*ahaṅkāra*).[1] For the Nyāya-Vaiśeṣikas, mind is an eternal substance which is different from the physical substances. Unlike the external senses, mind is non-physical (*abhautika*), *i.e.* it is not constituted by any of the physical elements of earth, water, etc. It is not, like the external senses, possessed of any specific attribute of the physical elements, nor is it limited to the perception of any particular class of objects. As an internal sense it is concerned in all knowledge in different ways. It is atomic and exists in contact with the soul (*aṇvātmasaṁyogi*). The mind as a sense cannot be perceived, but is known by inference (*na pratyakṣamapi tvanumānagamyam.*)[2]

Just as external perception depends on the external senses, so internal perception depends on an internal sense, called *manas*. Every perception requires the contact of an object with its special sense organ. We have perceptions of such subjective facts as pleasure, pain, desire, aversion and the like. These perceptions cannot be due to the senses of sight, hearing, etc., since they arise even without these senses. Hence there must be an internal sense to produce internal perceptions.[3] The mind is also a condition of external perception. The external senses can perceive objects only when they are in contact with the mind. To perceive an object the mind must attend to it through the senses. We do not perceive things in a state of absentmindedness, even though our senses be in physical contact with them.[4] So also the mind is a condition of such subjective states and processes as doubt and dream, memory and inference, etc.[5] Some Naiyāyikas hold that although the mind is a condition of all knowledge, yet it does not act as a sense in the case of memory, inference, etc., because that will render them indistinguishable from perception.[6] But it may be said that in

1. *Sāṅkhyakārikā*, 27.
2. NB., 1. 1. 4; TB., pp. 23, 30.
3. BP., 57, 85.
4. TB., *ibid.*
5. NB., 1. 1. 16.
6. TC., I, p. 550; SM., 51.

memory and inference the mind gives us a knowledge of objects, not by its contact with them, but through some other knowledge, as a past experience and the understanding of a universal relation (*vyāpti*). Hence, memory and inference are not cases of perception, although they are dependent on the function of the mind as a sense.[1]

That *manas* or the mind *is* and is atomic follows also from the order of succession among our cognitions. At any moment of our waking life various objects are acting upon our body. All the external senses may thus be in contact with their objects at the same time. But we cannot have more than one cognition at one moment. Hence, it follows that the senses of smell, taste, etc., must come in contact with some internal organ in order to produce cognitions. This internal organ is *manas* or the mind. It has no extension or magnitude (*avyāpi*), because it cannot cone in contact with more than one thing at one time. If the mind were an extended organ, it would have had simultaneous contact with more senses than one and we could have many perceptions at one and the same time. This being not the case, we are to say that the mind is atomic (*aṇuparimāṇa*).[2]

The Vedānta view of the mind is different from those of the other systems. According to it, *manas*, is that function (*vṛtti*) of the *antaḥkaraṇa* which is concerned in the state of doubt. The same *antaḥkaraṇa* is called *buddhi, ahaṅkāra* and *citta,* according as it functions respectively in the states of decision (*niścaya*), conceit (*garva*) and recollection (*smaraṇa*). It is the *antaḥkaraṇa* which performs these and other mental functions, such as cognition, feeling, desire, etc. Hence by the *mind* we are to understand, not *manas,* but *antaḥkaraṇa* as conceived by the Vedāntist. According to him, the mind is not an atomic substance, but an inert principle of limited dimension (*paricchinna*). Although inter (*jaḍa*) in itself, it manifests pure intelligence (*caitanya*) and is therefore regarded as intelligent in a secondary sense (*jñānatvopacāra*). The mind is not a sense (*indriya*) whose existence is proved by inference from

1. SD., p. 36.
2. NB., 1. 1. 16, 3. 2. 60-63; BP., 85.

the perception of pleasure, pain, etc. Direct knowledge of perception is not due to sense-object contact. We have a direct perception of the mind when we perceive the qualities of pleasure, pain, etc., in it. And a perception of these mental states does not require any internal sense, called manas in the other systems.[1]

It is to be observed here that the view of mind as sense is not acceptable. Those who take the mind as internal sense deny that it is a physical (*bhautika*) thing of any kind. So the mind as sense cannot be a physiological apparatus like the brain or any part of it that is directly correlated to conscious processes. The mind as a non-physical sense is analogous to the 'inner sense' conceived as a special faculty of inner experience in traditional Western psychology.[2] But the one is quite as unnecessary as the other to explain the facts of consciousness. It is the internal perception of pleasure, pain, etc., that is held to require an internal sense. But if by sense we mean, as the Naiyāyikas do mean, a medium of contact between mind and an object, then the mind itself cannot be a medium of contact between itself and objects like pleasure, pain, etc. The medium must be something else which should be called sense and not the mind. In truth, however, no internal or 'inner sense' is necessary for the perception of pleasure, pain and other psychical processes. These are held by the Naiyāyikas to be attributes of the self. As such, they are parts of the conscious life of the self and are, by their very nature, conscious or perceived facts. The Vedānta is right in holding that the mind (*antaḥkaraṇa*) perceives itself and its functions without the help of any internal sense. It agrees with modern psychology in holding that mind is just the totality of conscious states and processes. It is involved in some difficulty by making conscious phenomena qualities of a material substratum. How can the *antaḥkaraṇa,* which is inert and material in itself, become a conscious and an intellignet mind? 'By the self's relation to or reflection in it,' says the Advaita Vedāntist. The self (*ātman*), which is neither mind nor matter, is the ground of both mental and material phenomena. The Advaita

1. VP., Ch. I.
2. *Vide* Klemm, *A History of Psychology.*

Vedāntist would thus agree with the new realists who hole that mind and matter are not two oppose substances but different arrangements of the same neutral stuff. Or, as Russell has said: "Matter is not so material and mind not so mental as is generally supposed."[1] If so, mind and matter need not be two contradictory terms or irreconcilable opposities, but may become related to each other. Hence mental functions may belong to an apparently material substratum like the *antaḥkaraṇa*.

4. The Self and its Function in Perception

By the self (*ātmā*) we are to understand the individual soul (*jivātmā*) in connection with perception. The self, in this sense, has been conceived in different ways by different schools of philosophy. We find four main views of the self in Indian philosophy. We find four main views of the self is either the body with the attribute of intelligence or the aggregate of the senses of sight, hearing, etc. This is the materialistic conception of the self. The Buddhists reduce the self to the mind as a stream of thought or a series of cognitions. Like the empiricists and the sensationalists, they admit only the empirical self or the 'me.' Among the Vedāntists, some, the Advaitavādins, take the self as an unchanging, self-shining intelligence (*svaprakāśa caitanya*) which is neither subject nor object, neither the 'I' nor the 'me.' Other Vedāntists, the Viśiṣṭāvaitavādins, however, hole that the self is not pure intelligence as such, but an intelligent subject called the ego or the 'I' (*jñātāhamartha evātmā*).[2]

The Nyāya-Vaiśeṣikas adopt the realistic view of the self. According to them, the self is a unique substance, to which all cognitions, feelings and conations belong as its qualities or attributes.[3] Desire, aversion and volition, pleasure, pain and cognition are all qualities of the self. These qualities cannot belong to the physical substances, since they are mental. Hence, we must

1. *The Analysis of Mind*, p. 36.
2. *Vide Śrībhāsya*, 1. 1. 1.
3. NS., 1. 1. 10; PS., pp. 30 f.

admit that they are the peculiar properties of some substance other than the physical substances. The self is different in different bodies, because their experiences do not overlap but are kept distinct. The self is indestructible and eternal (*nitya*). It is ubiquitous or infinite (*vibhu*), since it is not limited in its activities by time and space.[1] The body or the external senses cannot be called self because intelligence or consciousness cannot be their attribute. The body, by itself, is unconscious and unintelligent. The senses cannot explain all mental functions. Imagination, memory, ideation, and like are independent of the sense of sight, hearing, etc. The mind too cannot take the place of the self. If the mind be, as the Nyāya-Vaiśeṣikas hold, an atomic substance, then the qualities of pleasure, pain, etc., in it must be as imperceptible as the mind itself. If, of the other hand, the mind be a series of cognitions, each manifesting itself, then memory becomes inexplicable. No member of a mere series of cognitions can know what has preceded it or what will succeed it (*vāsanāyāḥsaṁkramāsaṁbhavāt*). 'A succession of ideas is not an idea of succession.' The Advaita Vedāntin's idea of the self as eternal, self-shining intelligence is no more acceptable to the Naiyāyikas than that of the Buddhists. There is no such thing as pure intelligence unrelated to some subject and object. Intelligence cannot subsist without a certain locus. Hence the self is not intelligence as such, but a substantial principle owning intelligence as its attribute. The self is not mere knowledge, but a knower, an ego or the 'I' (*ahaṁkārāśraya*).[2] Still knowledge or intelligence is not an essential and inseparable attribute of the soul. The soul is, in itself, neither material nor mental, but a neutral substance which comes to have the attribute of intelligence or consciousness in its relation to the body.[3]

According to the Nyāya, the self is the fundamental ground of all mental functions. It is involved in all cognitions, affections and volitions. All the experiences of an individual, whether cognitive

1. BP., 51.
2. BP. and SM., 48-50.
3. NV., 1. 1. 22; NM., p. 432.

or otherwise, must inhere in the self and cannot be separated from it. What are know as innate faculties of the mind, the reflexes, instincts and inborn feelings of fears, hatred, etc., are all conditioned by the past experiences of a self in this or a previous life.[1] Even the body and the senses cannot function unless they are connected with the self. Hence the self is called the guiding principle of the body and the senses (*indriyādyadhiṣṭhātā*).[2] In the case of external perception the self comes in contact with the object through the medium of the mind and the external senses. When we have the perception of an external object, the self is in contact with the mind, the mind with the external sense concerned, and the external sense with the object of perception.[3] In the case of internal perception the mediation of external sense is unnecessary. Here the object is in contact only with the internal sense, called *manas*. We shall consider internal perception later on.

Like the older school of Western realism, the Nyāya-Vaiśeṣika system accepts the substantialist theory of the self. But their view of the self differs from that of the realists in two important respects. For the realists consciousness or intelligence is an essential and inseparable attribute of the soul. The soul cannot exist without the attribute of consciousness. For the Nyāya-Vaiśeṣikas, however, the soul is in itself an unconscious substance. Consciousness is an accidental property of the soul, due only to its temporary connection with the body. Then, while the realists conceive the individual soul at least to be a limited substance, the Nyāya-Vaiśeṣikas take all souls as unlimited and all-pervading substances (*vibhu*). But the Nyāya view of the self is untenable. If the soul be a substance we do not understand how it can exist without its distinctive attribute of consciousness and still be called the self. Without consciousness the soul is indistinguishable from matter. Again, to say that the soul is in itself pure substance is to say that it is a substance without attributes, which, however, is a contradiction. Further, if the soul

1. NS., 3. 1. 19 ff.
2. BP., 47.
3. TB., p. 5.

be an independent entity of the realistic type we cannot explain its relation to consciousness or mind or body. The soul-substance is not in its own essence related to anything else. Hence it can only be externally related to other things through the medium of a third thing. In perception it is said to be related to the object through the medium of the senses. But how are we to explain its relation to the mind or other senses? That must be by some other medium. Again, that medium must require another and so on indefinitely. So, we are to give up the idea of the self as a neutral substance externally related to consciousness. In truth, the self is a self-conscious reality. We may call it a substance in the sense of an existing 'continuant,' but that continuant is psychical and not physical. It is not a metaphysical surface on which consciousness is accidentally reflected. Rather consciousness or intelligence is the intrinsic character of its existence, the core of its being. It is not indeed the passing thought, which James proposes to call the self. The Naiyāyika is right in insisting that fleeting ideas or cognitions cannot take the place of the permanent self. So, also an unconscious substance cannot be the conscious self. We should say tnat the self is the intelligent reality or being which is the ground of all thought and experience. It is the eternal self-manifesting real which witnesses, but is not involved in, the flow of events.

Chapter VII

Ordinary Perception and Its Objects

1. Different Kinds of Perception and the Categories of Reality (*Padārtha*)

Taking perception as a general name for all true cognitions produced by sense-object contact the Naiyāyikas distinguish between different kinds of it. First we have the distinction between *laukika* or ordinary and *alaukika* or extraordinary perceptions. This distinction depends on the way in which the senses come in contact with their objects. We have *laukika* or ordinary perception when there is the usual sense-contact with objects present to sense. In *alaukika* perception, however, the object is such as is not ordinarily present to sense but is conveyed to sense through an unusual medium. Ordinary perception, again, is of two kinds, namely, external (*bāhya*) and internal (*mānasa*). That former is due to the external senses of sight, hearing, touch, taste and smell. The latter is brought about by the mind's contact with certain objects. Thus we have six kinds of ordinary perception, namely, the visual, auditory, tactual, gustatory, olfactory and the internal.[1] In this chapter we propose to consider the objects of external and internal perceptions. The special cases of perception, called *alaukika,* will be discussed in a later chapter.

According to the Nyāya-Vaiśeṣikas, there are two main types of reality, namely, being and non-being (*bhāvo 'bhāvaśca*). Being as a category (*padārtha*) stands for all that *is,* or for all positive realities. Similarly, non-being stands for whatever is *not, i.e.* for all negative realities. That a thing is *not*, or does not exist is as much a real fact as that it *is,* or does exist. Hence *abhāva* or non-

1. SM., 52, 63.

existence is as good a category of reality as *bhāva* or being. There are six kinds of being or positive reality. These are substance (*dravya*), quality (*guṇa*), action (*karma*), the universal (*sāmānya*), particularity (*viśeṣa*), and the relation of inherence (*samavāya*). Of these, the first three are existents. These participate in existence (*sattā*). On the other hand, the universal, particularity and the relation of inherence are positive realities but not existent fact. These do not participate in existence (*sattā*). They possess being but not existence. Hence there are two types of being or positive reality, *viz.* the existent and the subsistent. Of the six kinds of positive reality recognised by the Nyāya-Vaiśeṣikas, the first three are existents and the last three subsistents. Thus we have altogether seven categories of reality, namely, substance, quality, action, the universal, particularity, the relation of inherence and non-existence.[1] All objects of the world or all realities have been brought under these seven categories by the Nyāya-Vaiśeṣikas. Their scheme of the classification of realities may be compared to that of the modern realise. Among modern realsts Russell [2] Alexander[3] and others recognise the reality of negation or nonexistence. According to them, negative or non-existent facts are as real and objective as positive facts. It is also held by them that among positive facts some have existence in a particular time and space, while others have subsistence only in so far as these are free from limitation to one particular space and time. According to them, universals and relations are such subsistent realities. But for the Naiyāyikas, particularity also is a subsistent fact and the relation of conjunction (*saṁyoga*) has existence as an attribute of the substances related by it.

All realities, we have said, are brought under the seven categories. But all of them cannot ordinarily be object of perception. Hence, with regard to the different objects included under each of the categories we have to distinguish between those that are perceived and those that are imperceptible.

---

1. Bp. and SM., 2, 14.
2. *The Analysis of Mind*, pp. 275-76.
3. *Space, Time and Deity*, pp. 200-22.

2. Perception of Substances or Things (*Dravya*)

A substance is defined as the constitutive cause of things or as the substratum of qualities.[1] There are nine kinds of substances. These are: earth, water, light, air, *ākāśa,* time space, soul and mind.[2] Of these, the first four stand for both the atoms of earth, water, light and air, and the compounds formed by these atoms. The atoms of earth, etc., cannot be perceived. A compound of two atoms, called *dvyaṇuka* or the dyad, is also imperceptible, because, like an atom, it has no dimension and manifest quality (*mahattva* and *udbhūtava*). Mind (*manas*) as another atomic substance is not an object of ordinary sense-perception. So also *ākāśa,* time and space are, according to the Nyāya-Vaiśeṣikas, imperceptible substances.[3] *Ākāśa* is an all-pervading medium which is inferred from the phenomena of sound. Space and time are conceived as two receptacles of unlimited dimension holding all things and events within them. These two are the most fundamental conditions for the existence of finite objects and are therefore called the origin of all that is originated (*janyānāṁ janakaḥ*). Each of these is said to be one, eternal and infinite.[4] As infinite wholes these cannot be perceived, since the conditions of perception, *viz,* limited dimension and manifest quality, are absent in them.

It follows from the above that the perceptible substances are earth, water, light, air and the soul. Of these, the soul is the object of internal perception which we shall consider afterwards. With regard to air as a substance, there is some difference of opinion among the Naiyāyikas. According to the older Naiyāyikas, there are two conditions of the external perception of a substance, namely, that it must have a limited dimension and manifest colour (*mahattve sati udbhūtarūpavattvam*).[5] On this view, air becomes imperceptible, since it has no manifest colour in it. Its existence is

1. *Samavāyikāraṇaṁ dravyam, guṇāśrayo vā*, TB., p. 20.
2. Bp., 3.
3. TB. and TM., Ch. I.
4. BP. and SM., 44-46.
5. TM., Ch. I.

therefore to be known by inference from the quality of touch which subsists in the air. According to the modern Naiyāyikas, however, colour is not a condition of all external perception of substances. It is only in the visual perception of substance that manifest colour is an essential condition. The sense of touch also perceives substances in which the quality of touch is manifest (*udbhūtasparśa*). Hence, we may have a perception of air as a substance possessing the quality of manifest touch.[1]

Aditting that we have a perception of the substances of earth, water, light and air, it should be noted that what we perceive is neither an atom (*paramāṇu*) of earth, etc., nor a compound of any two atoms only (*dvyaṇuka*). To be perceived, a substance must have a limited diṃension. It must be neither infinite like space, etc., nor infinitesimal like an atom of the compound of two atoms. Hence, the perceptible substances are finite things from the triad (*trasareṇu*) upwards. A triad (*tryaṇuka*) is a compound of three dyads or three compounds of two atoms each. It is the minimum perceptible substance in Indian philosophy. As a matter of fact, therefore, the substances that are perceived by the external senses are complex finite things like the jar, table, tree, etc.

In the external perception of substances or finite things the senses come in direct contact with the things. This sense-object contact is called *saṁyoga* or conjunction. Of the five external senses, it is the sense of sight and touch that can give us a perception of things. The eye perceives things that have manifest colour, *i.e.* are visible. The sense of touch perceives things that possess manifest touch or are tangible. In both cases the perceived thing is conjoined to the sense. They are not always or inseparably related but are two substances that come in actual contact with each other at the moment of perception (*ayutasiddhyabhāvāt*). The other senses of taste, smell and hearing cannot give us perceptions of things. These can perceive the qualities of taste, etc., but not the substances or things, in which the qualities inhere. Hence, we have only visual and tactual perceptions of physical things. To perceive a thing is to

1. SM., 56.

perceive it as having a limited dimension in space. The organs of sight and touch, being extended, can perceive things as having a limited extension. The other senses cannot perceive extension and are therefore incapable of perceiving things as extended in space.[1]

The things that are perceived by the external senses possess a limited dimension (*mahattva*). This means that they are made up of parts (*avayava*). The magnitude of a thing depends on the aggregation of a number of parts composing it. Hence, it seems that to perceive a thing we must perceive all its component parts at one and the same time. But a simultaneous perception of all the parts of a thing is not possible. In the visual perception of a tree, for example, the eye comes in contact with only a part of its front side. There is no contact of the eye with the other sides of the tree or other parts that fall outside the visual field. How then can we have a perception of the tree when only a part of it is actually perceived?

This question has troubled psychologists for a long time. The answer given by the associationists is generally accepted by other schools of psychology, such as structuralism, functionalism and self-psychology. According to the associationist psychology of Hume, Mill and others, a thing is an aggregate of its parts. We perceive the different parts one after the other and it may be, on different occasions. It is because the different parts are always found to go together that their corresponding ideas become associated in our minds. Hence, the perception of one part recalls the ideas of the other parts, and all of them associated together give us the perception of the tree. According to other psychologists, the perception of the tree is no doubt due to the combination of the presented part with ideas or representations of the other parts. But this combination is effected, not by the association of ideas, but by

1. *Gandhāśrayagrahaṇe to ghrāṇasyāsāmarthyam*, etc., SM., 53; *ghrāṇarasanśrotrāṇī dravyāgrāhakāṇi, cakṣustvaṅmanāṁsi dravyagrāhakāṇi*, TK., p. 9. H. H. Price also thinks that our beliefs concerning material things are based upon visual and tactual experiences, and that other modes of sense-experience, *e.g.* hearing and smelling cannot by themselves give us any knowledge of the material world. See his *Perception*, p. 2.

the synthetic activity of the mind or the self. Among Indian thinkers the Buddhists adopt the associationist explanation of the perception of things as wholes made up of parts.

Here the Naiyāyikas point out that the associationist explanation fails to account for the perception of a thing. According to it, the perception of a thing consists in having ideas or images of other parts when one part of it is actually perceived. But these other parts are as far from being the thing as the perceived part itself. Further, to think of the other parts as connected with the perceived part is not to perceive them, but to infer the unperceived from the perceived. Hence, what we call the perception of a thing is really an inference or remembrance of it. It cannot be said that to perceive a thing the mind is to synthesise the presentation of a part with the representation of other parts. In that case we have a mental construction and no perception of the thing. So, the Naiyāyikas maintain the we have a direct perception of the thing as a whole also with the perception of any part of it. According to them, a thing is not a mere aggregate of parts (*avayasamūha*), but a whole which is distinct from any or all of the parts constituting it (*dravyāntara*). It subsists in the parts not by fractions, but wholly and indivisibly. To perceive any part of a thing *as part* is also to perceive the whole to which it belongs. When we perceive a book we apprehend it directly as a whole of parts. We have not to construct it from successive perceptions of different pats or from perception of some and ideal representation of others. If we have not a direct perception of the thing as a whole, we cannot perceive it at all. It we are to construct the thing from sense-impressions of its parts, perception would become inferential knowledge.[1]

Some modern psychologists confirm the Nyāya view of the direct perception of a thing as a whole. H. H. Price[2] rejects the associationist and the rationalist explanation on this point and holds that in perception 'what we accept is not simply a surface (though this is the most that can be present to our senses) but a complete

1. NB., 2. 1. 28-34.
2. *Perception*, pp. 153-54.

material thing as a whole. When we sense the sense-datum the house just presents itself to us as a whole, without any reasoning or passage of the mind.' Similarly, the Gestalt psychologists[1] show that the perception of a thing, say an orange, is not a colour experience somehow combined with the experiences of a certain shape, taste, touch and smell. On the other hand, it is a whole of experience which gives us knowledge of the thing as a whole, *i.e.* as a round fruit, soft to touch and with sweet acid taste. We try to account for this whole of experience by saying that it is a compound of certain simpler ideas like those of colour, taste, smell, etc. But here we fail to notice that the experience-whole is what we have to start with and the simpler ideas are discovered by subsequent analysis. Hence, we are to say that there is first the perception of a thing as a whole and that its parts are next perceived by focussing attention on this or that aspect of it.

But while the Naiyāyikas are right in holding that we have the direct perception of a thing as a whole, they seem to limit arbitrarily the range of such perception to the tactual and the visual field. They deny the capacity of perceiving things to the senses of taste, smell and hearing. But it is dogmatic to say that tasting or smelling or hearing a thing is not perceiving it. It is true that taste, smell and sound are the qualities of substances or things. But so also are colour and touch. Hence, if the senses of sight and touch can perceive things when they sense their colour and touch, there is no reason why the other senses should fail to perceive things when they perceive their other qualities. This is all the more necessary for the Naiyāyikas who hold that perceive a quality the sense must first come in contact with the substance, of which it is the quality. For the perception of a quality, the sense must be related, through the substance, with the quality (*saṁyukta-samavāya*). But if there is contact of sense with the substance there must be a perception of it. Even if it be said that perception is not determined by sense-object contact but by the character of immediacy, we have to admit that the senses of taste, smell and hearing give us a perception of

1. *Psychologies of* 1925; Köhler, *Gestalt Psychology.*

things. An appeal to direct experience shows that the gustatory, olfactory and auditory cognitions of things are as immediate as their visual and tactual perceptions.

3. Perception of Attributes (*Guṇa*) and Actions (*Karma*)

An attribute (*guṇa*) is defined as that which exists in a substance and has no quality or activity in it.[1] A substance exists by itself and is the constituent (*samavāyi*) cause of things. An attribute depends for its existence on some substance and is never constitutive of things. It is a non-constituent (*asamavāyi*) cause of things in so far as it determines their nature and character, but not their existence. All attributes must be owned by substance. So, there cannot be an attribute of attributes. An attribute is itself attributeless (*nirguṇa*). An attribute is a static property of things. It hangs on the thing as something passive and inactive (*niṣkriya*). So, it is different from both substance and action. There are altogether twenty-four kinds of attributes. These are: colour (*rūpa*), taste (*rasa*), smell (*gandha*), touch (*sparśa*), sound (*śabda*), number (*saṅkhyā*), magnitude (*parimāṇa*), differentia (*pṛthaktva*), conjunction (*saṁyoga*), disjunction (*vidhāga*) remoteness (*paratva*), nearness (*aparatva*), fluidity (*dravatva*), viscidity (*sneha*), knowledge (*buddhi*), pleasure (*sukha*), pain (*icchā*), aversion (*dveṣa*), effort (*prayatana*), heaviness (*gurutva*), merit (*dharma*), demerit (*adharma*), and faculty (*saṁskāra*).[2]

All attributes do not admit of sense perception. Hence we are to exclude the imperceptible attributes from the objects of perception. Faculty (*saṁskāra*), is of three different kinds: velocity (*vega*), which keeps a thing in motion; mental disposition (*bhāvanā*), which enables us to remember and recognize things; and elasticity (*sthitisthāpaka*), by which a thing tends towards equilibrium when disturbed. Of these, mental disposition and elasticity are regarded as imperceptible attributes. So, also merit (*dharma*) and demerit (*adharma*) are considered to be supersensible

1. *Dravyāśritā jñeyā nirguṇā niṣkriyā guṇāḥ*, BP., 86.
2. BP., 3-5.

attributes of the soul.[1] With regard to effort (*prayatna*) some Naiyāikas make a distinction between three different kinds of it, namely, vital effort (*jīvamayoni*) which maintains the flow of life (*prāṇasaṁcārahetu*), and positive and negative volitions (*pravṛtti* and *nivṛtti*). According to them, vital effort (*jīvanayoni prayatna*) is an attribute which is not perceived, but inferred as the causes of vital functions. Modern Naiyāyikas, however, do not recognise the attribute of vital effort.[2] Almost all the Indian systems agree in holding that heaviness or weight (*gurutva*) is a quality which cannot be perceived, but must be inferred.[3] The reason why these qualities are treated as imperceptible is that they cannot be perceived by any of the senses recognised in Indian philosophy. They are supersensible entities and hence there cannot be any kind of contact between these and our senses. In the Jaina system, however, light and heavy are treated as touch-sensations.[4]

The remaining attributes are regarded as capable of being perceived by the sense. But those belonging to the soul, such as knowledge, pleasure, pain, desire, aversion and volition, are the objects of internal perception which we shall afterwards consider. These apart, the attributes that are left are the objects of external perception. Some of them are perceived only by one sense, and some by two senses. Thus colour (*rūpa*) is perceived only by the eye. Taste (*rasa*) is a quality of substances that is perceived only by the gustatory sense (*rasana*). Smell (*gandha*) can be perceived only by the olfactory sense (*ghrāṇa*), and touch only by the cutaneous sense (*tvak*). The perception of these four attributes has two conditions, namely, that they must be manifest (*udbhūta*) and that they must belong to substances possessing a limited dimension (*mahadvṛttitva*).[5] In the perception of these attributes the second form of sense-object contact (*viz. saṁyukta-samavāya*) obtains.

1. BP., 93-94.
2. SM. and *Dinakarī*, 149-52.
3. BP., 153.
4. *Cf. Pañcāstikāyasāra*, Ch. II.
5. Bp., 53-56, 92-93.

The attributes come in contact with their respective senses through their inherence (*samavāya*) in the things that are conjoined (*saṁyukta*) to the senses. Conjunction or direct contact is possible only between two substances. Hence, there cannot be any direct contact of the attributes with their special senses. But the attributes of colour, etc., inhere in certain things or substances, such as a jar, an orange, a table, etc. When these things come in actual contact (*i.e.* are conjoined) with the eye, etc., there is a perception of the qualities of colour, taste, smell and touch as inhering (*samaveta*) in them.

Sound is an attribute of *ākāśa,* and is perceived only by the auditory sense (*śrotra*). In the perception of sound the forth kind of sense-object contact (*viz. samavāya*) holds good. Sound is perceived when it comes in contact with the auditory sense. This contact cannot be a relation of conjunction (*saṁyoga*), since one of the terms is an attribute. The sense of hearing is a portion of *ākāśa,* in which sound inheres as an attribute. Hence the contact of sound with the auditory organ means its inherence (*samavāya*) in the latter.[1] Sound is first produced by the conjunction or disjunction of things. But this sound cannot be perceived unless it reaches the passage of the ear. So, the first sound produces other sounds which either undulate towards the ear or move in straight lines in all directions (*vīcitaraṅganyāyena kadambamukulanyāyena vā*). In this way the series of sounds meets the ear. The last number of the series which strikes upon the ear-drum is perceived, while the first and the intermediate ones are not perceived. So it is not correct to say that we perceive sound at a distance.[2] The Vedāntist, however, thinks that in the perception of sound it is the ear the meets sound and not *vice versa.* We are not wrong when we say that we hear the sound of the distant drum. For there is nothing to contradict the obvious experience of distant sounds.[3]

---

1. BP., 53, 60.
2. BP., and SM., 165-66.
3. VP., Chap. I.

The attributes that admit of perception by both the senses of sight and touch are number, magnitude, differentia, conjunction, disjunction, remoteness, nearness, fluidity, viscidity and velocity.[1] These are perceived by the eye when connected with light and manifest colour, and by the tactual sense when connected with manifest touch.[2] Of visible and tangible things there may be respectively a visual and tactual perception of their number, etc. In the perception of these qualities we have the second kind of sense-object contact, *viz. saṁyuktasamavāya.* The objects (*i.e.* number and the rest) come in contact with the senses through their inherence (*samavāya*) in certain things that are conjoined (*saṁyukta*) to the senses.

In the perception of magnitude (*parimāṇa*) we are to admit a further fourfold contact between sense and the things concerned. By magnitude is here meant a limited dimension that he longs to ordinary things like tables and jars, and neither the unlimited dimension to he all-pervading substances, nor the minute dimension of atoms and dyads, for these are imperceptible. The magnitude of ordinary sensible things is due to the number and magnitude of their component parts. Hence to perceive the magnitude of a thing we are to perceive the coexistence and relative position of the constituent parts. This is rendered possible by four kinds of contact (*cattuṣṭayasannikarṣa*); that between the different parts of an extended sense organ and the different parts of the thing, that between the different parts of the sense organ and the whole of the thing, that between parts of the thing and the whole of the sense organ and that between the whole of the sense organ and the whole of the thing.[3] It is by virtue of such contacts between sense and things that we can perceive their magnitude from a distance. The Naiyāyika has to take the help of so many kind of sense-object contact because he believes in the direct visual perception of the magnitude of distant things. The muscular sensation of movement

1. BP. and SM., 93.
2. *Ibid.,* 54-56.
3. TB., p. 6.

is not admitted by him as a factor in the perception of magnitude or limited extension.

Differentia (*pṛthaktva*) is a positive character of things. That one thing is different from another, *e.g.* a cow and a horse, does not simply mean that the one is not the other. Difference does not consist in the mutual negation (*anyonyābhāva*) of two things. One thing is different from other things, not simply because it excludes or negates them, but because it has a distinctive character of its own whereby it is differentiated from them. This distinctive character constitutes its differentia from other things. Differentia is thus an objective character or attribute of things and is perceived in things that are perceptible.[1] The Vedānta, however, takes difference to be a case of mutual non-existence and holds that it is known not by perception, but by non-perception (*anupalabdhi*).[2] Modern Naiyāyikas also do not treat difference as a separate quality, but reduce it to mutual non-existence.[3]

Conjunction (*saṁyoga*) is a relation (*sambandha*) that is perceived as an attribute of the things related by it. Disjunction or separation (*vibhāga*) is not a relation (*sambandha*). Rather, it is the negation of the relation of the relation of conjunction between two things. It is also perceived as an attribute of the things which are disjoined. Space and time as infinite wholes are imperceptible substances. But the remoteness or nearness of things in time and space is a perceptible quality of the things. Things are far or near in space according as they are separated from our body by a larger or smaller number of contacts with space-points. Similarly, things are near or remote in time according as they have a smaller or lager number of contacts with time-instants. Such position in time and space becomes an attribute of things and is perceived by the senses of sight and touch.[4] Fluidity, viscidity and velocity are the qualities of certain things and are perceived by the senses of sight

1. SM., 114.
2. VP., Ch. VI.
3. *Dinakarī*, 114.
4. BP., 54-56, 121-24.

and touch like other perceptible qualities. Here, again, the modern Naiyāyikas do not recognise remoteness and nearness as separate qualities, since these are due to varied contacts of an object with points of time and space.[1]

Action (*karma*) is physical movement. Like an attribute, it inheres only in substance.[2] It is different from both substance and attribute. Substance is the support of both action and attribute. An attribute is a static character of things, but actions are dynamic. While an attribute is a passive property that does not take us beyond the thing it belongs to, an action is a transitive process by which one thing reaches another. So it is regarded as the independent cause of the conjunction and disjunction of things. An action has no attribute because the latter belongs only to substance. All actions or movements must subsist in limited corporeal substances (*mūrtadravyavṛtti*). Hence there can be no action or motion in the all-pervading substances. There are five kinds of action such as throwing upward, throwing downward, contraction, expansion and locomotion (*utkṣepaṇāpakṣepaṇākuñcanaprasāraṇagamana*). These actions belong to such substances as earth, water, air, light or fire and the mind. Those inhering in the mind are imperceptible, since the mind is so. The action or motion of the perceptible substances can be perceived by the senses of sight and touch. In the perception of movement the second kind of sense-object contact, *viz. saṁyukta-samavāya* is operative. The senses come in contact with movement through their conjunction with the things in which it inheres.[3]

4. The Universal (*Sāmānya*), Particularity (*Viśeṣa*) and the Relation of Inherence (*Samavāya*)

There are three views of the universal or the class-essence in Indian philosophy. In the Bauddha philosophy we have the

1. *Dinakarī*, 124.
2. *Calanātmakaṁ karma, guṇa iva dravyamātravṛtti*, TB., p. 28.
3. BP., 54-56.

nominalistic view. According to it, the individual alone is real and there is no class-essence or universal other than the particular objects of experience. The idea of sameness that we may have with regard to a number of individuals of a certain class is due to their being called by the same name. It is only the name that is general, and the name does not stand for any positive essence that is present in all the individuals. It means only that the individuals called by one name are different from those to which a different name is given. Thus certain animals are called cow, not because they possess any common essence. But because they are different from all animals that are not cows. So, there is no universal but the name with a negative connotation.[1]

The Jainas and the Advaita Vedāntins[2] adopt the conceptualistic view of the universal. According to them, the universal does not stand for any independent entity over and above the individuals. On the other hand, it is constituted by the essential common attributes of the individuals. Hence the universal is not separate from the individuals, but is identical with them in point of existence. The two are related by way of identity. The universal has existence, not in our minds only, but in the particular object of experience. It does not, however, come to them from outside, but is just their common nature. On this view, "individuals have," as Mill says, "no essences."[3]

The Nyāya-Vaiśeṣikas accept the realistic view of the universal. According to them, universals are eternal entities which are distinct from, but inhere in many individuals (*nityatve satyanekasama-vetatvam*).[4] The universal is the basis of the notion of sameness that we have with regard to all the individuals of a certain class. It is because there is one single essence present in different individuals that they are brought under a class and thought of as essentially the

1. *Vide* TB., p. 28; *Six Buddhist Nyāya Tracts,* Pt 5, on *Sāmānyadūṣaṇa-dikprasāritā.*
2. VP., Ch. I; *Outlines of Jainism,* p. 115; *Prameyakamala.,* Ch. IV.
3. J. S. Mill. *A System of Logic,* p. 73.
4. SM., 8.

same.[1] Like Plato's "ideas," or "essences" of the mediaeval realists, *sāmānya* or the universal is a real entity which corresponds to a general term or class-concept in our mind. Some of the modern realists also hold that 'universal is an eternal timeless entity which may be shared by many particulars.' The Naiyāyikas agree further with the modern realists in holding that universals do not come under existence (*sattā*). These do not exist in time and space, but have being and subsist in substance, attribute and action. There is no universal subsisting in another universal (*sāmānyāna-dhikaraṇatvam*), nor is there any universal for particularity (*viśeṣa*), inherence (*samavāya*) and non-existence (*abhāva*).[2] Modern realists, however, do not sensible objects are capable of being perceived by the senses, admit with the Naiyāyikas that all universals pertaining to. According to the former, we can perceive only such universals as may be called "sensible qualities," as for example, colour, whiteness, hardness, etc.[3]

According to the Naiyāyikas, the universals that subsist in supersensible objects are imperceptible (*atīndriyavṛttīnia-tīndriyāṇi*). The universals that inhere in perceptible objects (*pratyakṣavṛttīni*) are perceived by the senses which perceive their locus. The universals of substances or things (*dravya*) are perceived by the senses of sight and touch provided they are visible and tangible things respectively.[4] Thus, jarness (*ghaṭatva*), treeness (*vṛkṣatva*) and manhood are universals that inhere respectively in all individual jars, trees and men. When perceiving any of these individuals, we directly cognise also the universal inhering in it. Here the second form of sense-contact, *viz. saṁyukta-samavāya,* functions. The universal "jarness" comes in contact with the visual or the tactual sense through its inherence (*samavāya*) in the jar that is seen or touched and is thus conjoined (*saṁyukta*) to the sense concerned.

---

1. TB., p. 28; PS., p. 164.
2. BP. and SM., 14, 15.
3. *Vide*, Russell, *The Problems of Philosophy,* Chs. IX, X.
4. TK., p. 9.

The perception of universals pertaining to attributes (*guṇa*) and actions (*karma*) generally takes place through the third kind of sense-contact, *viz. saṁyukta-samaveta-samavāya.*[1] When perceiving such qualities as a red colour, a fragrant smell, a sweet taste and a hard touch, we also know directly, *i.e.* perceive the universals of colour, smell, taste and touch as such. Similarly, when we perceive a particular kind of movement we know directly what motion in general is. To perceive anything as thrown upward or downward, is also to perceive anything as thrown upward or downward, is also to perceive the universal of upward or downward impulsion (*utkṣepaṇativādi*). Smellness (*gandhatva*) as a universal pertaining to different kinds of smell is perceived by the olfactory sense. Taste (*rasatva*) as the genus of different kinds of taste is perceived by the gustatory sense. Similarly, the universals of colour (*rūpatva*) and touch (*sparśatva*) are perceived by the senses of sight and touch respectively. The universals pertaining to other sensible attributes and actions or movements are perceived by both the senses of sight and touch.[2] These universals are perceived when they come in contact with the senses through their inherence in attributes or actions which inhere in certain things that are conjoined with the senses. When, for example, I see a white paper, I perceive the universal 'whiteness' as intimately related to the particular kind of white colour in the paper which is in conjunction with my eyes. Soundness (*śabdatva*) as the genus of different kinds of sound is perceived by the auditory sense through the fifth kind of sense-contact, *viz. samaveta-samavāya.* The universal 'soundness' is in contact with the ear through its inherence (*samavāya*) in sound which inheres as a quality (*samaveta*) in the auditoy sense.[3] The universals of actions or motions belonging to perceptible things are perceived by the senses of sight and touch through the third kind of sense-contact, *viz. saṁyukta-samaveta-samavāya.* The universal 'motion' is in contact with the visual or cutaneous sense

---

1. TB., p.6; BP., 54-56, 59-60.
2. BP., 53-56.
3. BP. 53, 61.

in so far as it subsists in a particular kind of movement inhering (*samaveta*) in something that is seen or touched (*i.e.* is cojoined with the visual or tactual sense).[1]

According to the Vedānta, the universal, as constituted by the common attributes of the individuals, is perceived along with the perception of the individuals. The perception of the different kinds of universals is mediated by different kinds of sense-contact. The universal of substances is perceived by *saṁyuktatādātmya,* that of attributes or actions by *saṁyuktābhinnatādātmya,* and that of sound by *tādātmyavadabhinna* forms of sense-object contact. These three forms correspond respectively to the second, third and fifth forms of sense-contact admitted by the Naiyāyikas. But where the latter speak of the relation of inherence (*samavāya*), the Vedāntist puts in the relation of identity, since inherence is not admitted by him as a distinct category and the relation between substance and attribute, or universal and particular is said to be one of identity (*tādātmya*), so that they require no *tertium quid* like inherence to relate the one to the other.[2]

Particularity (*viśeṣa*) is the extreme opposite of the universal (*sāmānya*). It is the ultimate ground of the differences of things from one another. Things are ordinarily distinguished from one another by means of their component parts or aspects. But the differences of parts or aspects rest on those of other smaller parts or finer aspects. In this way we are led to the ultimate differences of the simple substances, beyond which we cannot go. The ultimate differences are due to certain unique characters which distinguish one thing from all other things of the world. Particularity is such unique character of the simple and eternal substances.[3] It is completely different from universals or the things coming under any universal. Hence by particularity we are to understand the unique individuality of space, time, *ākāśa*, minds, souls, and the atoms of earth, weter, light, and air. Particularity is thus eternal

---

1. BP., 54-56.
2. VP., Ch. I.
3. BP. & SM., 10.

and subsists in the eternal substances (*nitya-nityadravyavṛttiḥ*).[1] There are innumerable particularities, since the individuals in which they subsist are innumerable. Other things are distinguished by their particularities, but the latter are distinguished by themselves (*svata eva vyāvṛttāḥ*). Hence particularities are so many ultimates (*antyāḥ*) in the analysis and explanation of things. There cannot be any perception of them, since they are supersensible entities (*atīndriyāḥ*).[2] Some modern Naiyāyikas, however, do not admit that particularity is a distinct category. If the particularities can be distinguished by themselves, without having any distinguishing character in them, the eternal substances also may be distinguished by themselves without requiring any character like particularity (*viśeṣa*).[3]

There are two main relations recognised in the Nyāya-Vaiśeṣika philosophy. These are the relations of conjunction (*saṁyoga*), and inherence (*samavāya*).[4] A relation is here conceived as a positive connection between two facts. Hence, it is that the commonly recognised negative relations of disjunction, spatial and temporal separation, etc., are treated as qualities and not relations. Conjunction (*saṁyoga*) is a transient relation between two things which may and normally do exist in separation from each other. Two balls moving from opposite directions meet at a certain point of space. The relation which holds between them when they meet is one of conjunction. It is a temporary contact between two things which may again be separated (*yutasiddha*). So long as it is, it exists as a quality of the terms related, but it does not affect the existence of those terms. It makes no difference to the existence of the balls whether they are conjoined to each other or not. Thus conjunction is an external relation which exists as an accidental quality of the terms related by it.

---

1. TB., p. 28; PS., p. 168.
2. TS., pp. 11, 88.
3. *Dinakarī*, 10.
4. TB., p. 2.

Samavāya is an eternal and natural (*ayutasiddha*) relation between two facts, of which one inheres in the other.[1] It is a necessary relation in so far as the related terms or at least one of them cannot exist without being related to the other. Like conjunction, it is distinct from the terms related by it.[2] But while conjunction exists as an adventitious quality of the related terms, *samavāya* does not *exist* as a quality but always *subsists* between the things related. The relation of *samavāya* holds between such entities as whole and part, attribute or action and substance, the universal and the individual, particularity and the simple eternal substances. Of these pairs, the first cannot exist without being related to the other. The whole is always related to its parts, attribute or action is inseparably related to some substance, the universal must always subsist in the individual, and so particularity (*viśeṣa*) in the simple substances.[3] But the part can exist without being actually related to the whole. A substance may have being without relation to its attributes or actions.[4] So, we see that *samavāya* is a necessary relation for one of the relata and not for both. It cannot be called an internal relation, since the related entities are not affected by it. It stands as a natural link between two facts, each of which has a distinct of its own. A substance and its attribute are not made to be such by their relation to each other. Hence, like conjunction, *samavāya* is an external relation. But, unlike conjunction, it is not produced, nor does it exist as a quality in time and space. It always subsists between two facts, which are naturally related to each other. Some modern realists treat relations as universals that do not exist but subsist.[5] For the Naiyāyika, however, the relation of conjunction is an attribute and has existence in time and space. The relation of inherence is a subsistent fact but

1. *Ayutasiddhayoḥ sambandhaḥ samavāyaḥ* etc., TB., p.2; *samavāyatvaṁnityasaṁbandhatvbam* etc., SM., 11.
2. *Svasaṁbandhibhinno nityaḥ saṁbandhaḥ samavāyaḥ,* TM., Ch. I.
3. BP. and SM., ii.
4. *Dravyaṁ nirguṇameva prathamamutpadyate paścāt tatsamavetā guṇā utpadyante*, etc., TB., p. 3.
5. Russell, *The Problems of Philosophy,* Ch. IX.

not a universal. It is a category distinct from the universal and the rest. Both conjunction and inherence are objects or perception. The relation of inherence is perceived by the senses of sight and touch. In perceiving this relation there is contact between sense and object by way of *viśeṣaṇatā.* We directly perceive that the cloth inheres in the threads. But the contact of the relation of inherence with our sense is indirect. It comes in contact with the sense of sight or touch through being adjectival to the threads which are conjoined with either of them.[1] The Vaiśeṣikas, however, hold that *samavāya* cannot be perceived, but must be known by inference. They agree with the Naiyāyikas in maintaining that *samavāya* is one and eternal. We cannot distinguish between different kinds of *samavāya,* because it is the same in all cases.[2] Some modern Naiyāyikas, however, contend that *samavāva* is not of one, but many different kinds, since one thing is found to inhere in other things in different ways.[3]

Svarūpasaṁbandha[4] is a third relation admitted by the Naiyāyikas. It has been introduced to explain such cases of connection between things as are neither conjunction (*saṁyoga*) nor inherence. Unlike the relations of conjunction and inherence, *svarūpasambandha* is not distinct from the terms related by it. Rather, the relation is itself constituted by one of the relata. What is the relation between an object and our knowledge of it? In cannot be inherence, since knowledge, as a quality, inheres not in the object, but in the soul. Nor can it be conjunction, because that is possible only between two substances, while knowledge is an attribute and not a substance. Nor can we say that we do not require any relation. The two being distinct entities require somehow to be related. Hence it is said that a new relation, called *svarūpasambandha,* is to relate the two. The object is related to knowledge in so far as it is known. The relation of knowledge to the object is thus the object itself as

1. BP., 54-56, 62.
2. PS., pp. 172-176.
3. *Dinakarī,* 11.
4. SM., 11; *Nyāyakośa,* p. 1057.

know (*arthasvarūpa*). The object as known is what we mean but its relation to knowledge, so that the relation is constituted by the object, or is due to the nature of the object itself.

The Nyāya doctrine of *samavāya* has been severely criticized and rejected by the Advaita Vedāntin. Śaṅkara in his commentary on the *Brahma-Sūtra* shows that the necessity of the category of *samavāya* arises from the Naiyāyika's conception of a thing as a collection of distinct and different entities like substance, attribute, action, the universal and particularity. If these are so many distinct entities, we have to explain how they are united in the thing so as to make it one whole. This cannot be explained by the relation of conjunction, since it is a case of the dependence of attribute, action, etc., on substance, while conjunction is a relation between independent substances which can exist in isolation. So we have to introduce a new relation to explain the intimate connection between a substance and its attributes, actions, etc., and this is *samavāya* or the relation of inherence. But if attributes, actions, etc., are distinct and different from substance, there is no more reason to suppose that they depend on substance than there is to think that such independent objects as man, horse, and cow, depend on one another. If, on the other hand, attribute and the rest depend on substance and cannot exist without it, we should say that they are not different entities but only different aspects of the substance itself. The same thing is called by the different names of attribute, action, etc., according to its different organizations (*saṁsthāna*), in the same way in which the same man is a father, a son, a brother, etc., under different conditions. A substance and its attribute or action, the universal and the individual, the whole and the part are such that we cannot have any experience of the one without the other. They are inseparable both in our experience and in point of existence. It follows from this that they are not different entities, but aspects of the same thing. To say that they are distinct and different entities which require to be related by *samavāya,* which also is a distinct entity, is to court the fallacy of infinite regress (*anavasthā*). How is *samavāya* itself related to each of the terms related by it? To explain this we have to bring in new relations which being distinct entities will also require other relations and so on *ad infinitum*. Hence, we are to say that attributes, actions, universals, etc., are not independent entities, but aspects of the same substance, and that we do not require a new relation like *samavāya* to relate them to substance.

The Vedāntin's criticism of the Nyāya view of *samavāya* seems to miss the essential point. From the standpoint of a common-sense realism the Naiyāyika maintains the distinction between a substance and its attributes or actions, the universal and the individual, the whole and the part. It may be conceded to the Vedāntin that we have no experience of attributes and actions without a substance, of the universal without the individual, of the whole without its parts. It may also be admitted by us that attributes, actions, universals, etc., do not exist except in a substance. But from this we cannot conclude that a substance is identical with its attributes and actions, or that it is an aggregate of the aspects of attribute, action, universal, etc. Two entities may be inseparable and yet not identical, only if they are different and distinct in our experience. We cannot, indeed, have any experience of attributes without a substance. But the same experience tells us that a substance is distinct from its attributes, and the attributes are distinct from the substance. A substance is not an attribute, nor a group of attributes. There can be no attributes without some substance. Hence, the existence of attributes presupposes the distinct reality of a substance. That we ascribe different sense qualities to the same substance also shows that the substance is not identical with any of them, but is distinct from them all. What we mean by a subsatance is, therefore, different from what we mean by an attribute. The substance stands for the 'continuant' or the reality underlying the changing characters of a thing, and the attributes stand for its properties or powers of manifesting certain characters under certain conditions. Although an attribute is not a substance, yet it is inseparably related to or rooted in it. This inseparable relation or the fact of subsistence of the attribute in a substance is *samavāya*. The same reasoning applies *mutatis mutandis* to the relation between substance and action, the universal and the individual, the whole and the part, particularity and the particulars. In each case we have an inseparable relation between two distinct and different entities. It is a relation like *saṁyoga* or conjunction. But, unlike *saṁyoga* which is a quality, *samavāya* is a special relation that cannot be reduced to any other category. It is not a substance because it has no qualities. It is not a quality because it is not limited to substances, nor does it qualify substances. For the same reason it cannot be regarded as an action. It is not a universal nor particularity, because it is neither the common essence of many things nor the peculiarity of anything. It is the objective fact of an inseparable connection between two other facts which are distinct and different. Hence we have to admit a separate category called *samavāya* or the relation of inherence.

5. Perception of Non-existence (*Abhāva*)

The above categories of substance and the rest stand for positive realities, whether existent or subsistent. The category of *abhāva* stands for all negative or non-existent facts. These facts are as real and objective as positive facts, only they have no being. While positive facts are, *i.e.* possess being, negative facts are not, *i.e.* possess being, negative facts are not, *i.e.* possess non-being.[1] *Abhāva* or non-existence is defined as that which is not inherence and cannot be in the relation of inherence to anything else (*asamavāyatve satyasamavāyaḥ*).[2] It is not inherence because it does not subsist as a positive fact. It cannot have the relation of inherence to anything, because non-existence cannot be the constitutive element of anything and also because inherence is possible only between two positive entities.

As to the nature of non-existence their are different conceptions. According to the Sāṅkhya and the Prābhākara Mīmāṁsā, the non-existence of one thing in another means the mere existence of the latter. For example, the non-existence of a jar on the table means

1. *Abhāvatvaṁ dravyādiṣaṭkānyonyābhāvavattvaṁ*, SM., 12.
2. *Sarvadarśanasaṁgraha*, Chapter on Vaiśeṣika system.

the existence of the table *per se*. Hence, non-existence is the mere existence of a locus (*adhikaraṇkaivalyam*).[1] The Nyāya objects to this view and treats non-existence as an entity distinct from its locus (*atiriktapadārtha*). It non-existence were the simple existence of the locus, it would become indistinguishable from existence. The table exists as much when the jar is non-existent as when it is existent on the table. So we may speak of a jar's non-existence on the table even when it actually exists there. Non-existence is not the locus as such, but an objective character (*viśeṣaṇa*) of it.[2] It is not, like the colour of a table, a *guṇa* or attribute of the locus. It is only abjectival to or a determination of the locus which exists as a positive entity. Non-existence or negation is thus a real and distinct entity which is adjectival to some positive fact. According to the Vedānta and the Bhāṭṭa Mīmāṁsā also, non-existence is an entity distinct from the locus. All objects have two characters, a positive and a negative. A thing exists positively in itself and is characterised negatively by the absence of other things in it. This absence or non-existence of other things in not the mere existence of the thing in itself. If the non-existence of a jar on the ground were the mere existence of the ground, we cannot speak of its non-existence when there is a cloth on the ground and so no cognition of the mere ground. On the other hand, we may speak of the jar's non-existence even when it exists on the ground, for the ground as such exist while their is a jar on it. Hence non-existence is something distinct from its locus.[3]

Abhāva or non-existence is of four kinds, namely, *prāgabhāva, pradhvaṁsābhāva, atyantābhāva,* and *anyonyābhāva*.[4] Some Naiyāyikas, however, bring the first three under the head of *saṁsargābhāva* and recognise only two kinds of non-existence.[5] *Saṁsargābhāva* or the negation of a connection is that which is

1. TKD., p. 50; SD., pp. 83-84.
2. TC., I, pp. 693 f.; SM., 2 and 12.
3. SD., pp. 83-84.
4. TS., p. 89. *Cf.* VP., Ch. IV.
5. NVT., 2. 2. 12; BP. and SM., 12.

different from *anyonyābhāva* or the negation of identity. In the one the connection between two things is denied, in the other we deny the identity or sameness of two different things or concepts.

Prāgabhāva or antecedent non-existence is the non-existence of a thing prior to its production, *e.g.* the non-existence of an effect in the cause. So long as the effect is not produced, it is non-existent in the cause. This kind of non-existence is said to be without a beginning but not without an end (*anādiḥ sāntaḥ*). It is subject to cessation (*vināśya*).[1] The effect never existed before its production, so that its non-existence has no beginning. Its production at any time means the end or cessation of its previous non-existence. *Prāgabhāva* thus refers to the past non-existence of a thing and implies the possibility of its future existence. Like the past it has no beginning but has an end, since it ends just when the thing begins to exist. The present existence of a thing ends its past non-existence, just as the past has its end in the present.

Pradhvaṁsābhāva or consequent non-existence is the non-existence of a thing posterior to its destruction, *e.g.* the non-existence of an effect when it is destroyed. This kind of non-existence has a beginning but no end (*sādiranantaḥ*). It is subject to origin in time (*janya*), but not to cessation.[2] When a jar is broken its existence ends, and its non-existence begins but can never be ended, because the same jar cannot be brought back to existence. *Pradhvaṁsābhāva* may thus be said to refer to the future non-existence of a thing in relation to its present existence. Like the future it has a beginning but no end. It begins just when a thing's present existence ceases, and continues for all time to come just as the future begins with the cessation of the present and extends indefinitely forwards. Thus while *prāgabhāva* is beginningless, *pradhvaṁsābhāva* is endless. The one is an infinite series backwards, the other is an infinite series forwards. The one has an end, while the other has a beginning. That is, an infinite series may have an end or a beginning. Kant in his first 'antiomy' failed to see

---

1. SM., 12; TB., p. 29; TS., p. 89.
2. *Ibid.*

this when he argued that what is infinite can neither begin nor end. This antinomy may be solved in the light of the Naiyāyikas' finding that some infinite series have ends.

Atyantābhāva or absolute non-existence is the negation of a connection between two things for all time (*nityasaṁsargābhāva*). It is subject neither to origin nor to cessation (*ajanyāvināśī*).[1] Thus it is both beginningless and endless. This is illustrated by such cases of non-existence as a hare's horn, the colour of air, etc. The non-existence of a connection between horns and the hare, or colour and the air is true at all times, past, present and future. Thus *atyantābhāva* or absolute non-existence is not a cipher which is the property of a general term that applies to no object.

Anyonyābhāva or reciprocal non-existence is the negation of identity, or the difference between two things, *e.g.* a jar is not a cloth.[2] A jar and a cloth mutually exclude each other, and so each is non-existent as the other. *Anyonyābhāva* stands for this mutual negation of the relation of identity between two things. Like absolute non-existence (*atyantābhāva*), reciprocal or mutual non-existence (*anyonyābhāva*), is eternal, *i.e.* both beginningless and endless (*ajanyāvināśī*). But the distinction between the two is this. Absolute non-existence as a material aspect. In it there is the affirmation of something actual (*e.g.* the hare or the air), and the negation of a relation with regard to it (*e.g.* the relation between hare and horn, or colour and air). On the other hand, reciprocal non-existence is only a logical or formal negation with reference to the relation of identity between two things which need not be actual. That 'X is not Y,' 'a red star is not a blue star' is true even if no such things actually exist. In absolute non-existence we deny the connection between two things, while in reciprocal non-exeistence the identity or sameness or two things or concepts is denied. The opposite of absolute non-existence is a connection between two things, while that of reciprocal non-existence is the

1. *Nityasaṁsargābhāvatvamatyantābhāvatvam*, SM., *ibid.; traikāliko 'bhāvo' tyantābhāvaḥ*, TB., *ibid.*
2. *Anyonyābhāvastu tādātmyapratiyogiko 'bhāvaḥ, ibid.*

identity between them.[1] The proposition 'there is no colour in the air' implies the absolute non-existence of colour in the air. The opposite of this will be a proposition which connects colour with the air, *e.g.* 'there is colour in the air.' The proposition 'a jar is not a cloth' implies the difference of the one from the other. The opposite of this will be a proposition which identifies the two, *e.g.* 'a jar is a cloth.'

As to how non-existence or negation is known by us, there is a sharp difference of opinion among the different systems of Indian philosophy. According to the Bhāṭṭa Mīmāṁsā and the Vedānta, non-existence is known by non-perception of what should have been perceived (*yogyānupalabdhi*). It cannot be known by perception. Perception requires sense-object contact. But there cannot be any contact of sense with non-existence or negation. It is not, in some cases at least, known by inference. When we know the non-existence of a jar on the ground before us, we have a direct knowledge which is not mediated by any inferential reasoning. In such cases our knowledge of non-existence comes from non-perception as a distinct source of knowledge.[2] As we have already said, non-exsistence is, according to the Bhāṭṭa Mīmāṁsā and the Vedānta, both an objective character of things, and a character of the presentation of things. But it is not perceived like the whiteness of snow or the redness of a rose. On the other hand, we have an immediate feeling of it as a character of the presentation just when we have that presentation. This subjective feeling of the presented character *as distinct* or the discriminative feeling of it is what we mean by our knowledge of it. *Anupalabdhi* is this subjective feeling and is an independent source of the knowledge of non-existence.

The Vaiśeṣika and the Prābhākara school hole that non-existence is known by inference. According to the former the non-existence of the cause is inferred from the non-existence of the effect, just as its existence is inferred from that of the effect.[3] In the

1. TS and TD., pp. 89 f.
2. VP., Ch. VI; SD., pp. 86-87.
3. PS., p. 111; *Upaskāra*, p. 228.

Prābhākara Mīmāṁsā also non-perception is not regarded as a distinct source of the knowledge of non-existence. Rather, the non-perception of a thing is the condition from which we infer its non-existence.[1] The Sāṅkhya[2] and the Nyāya system agree in holding that non-existence is known by perception. According to both, non-existence is an objective determination (*pariṇāma* or *viśeṣaṇa*) of some positive entity (*bhāvapadārtha*) and can be perceived by the senses. The Nyāya explains the perception of non-existence as due to an indirect sense-object contact called *viśeṣaṇatā*. The non-existence of a jar on the ground is an abjective or determination (*viśaṣaṇa*) of the ground which is its substantive (*viśeṣya*). This non-existence comes in contact with our sense through being abjectival (*viśeṣaṇa*) of the ground which is in conjunction (*saṁyukta*) with the sense. Thus non-existence is perceived as an abjective or objective character of some positive thing which is in contact with our sense.[3] That for the knowledge of non-existence there must be a contact of sense with its locus is also admitted by the Vedānta. And, that the knowledge of non-existence is aided by non-perception is admitted by the Nyāya. We know that a jar does not exist on the ground when we feel that it must have been perceived if it were on the ground.[4] Thus, the Nyāya and Vedānta agree in holding that to know non-existence there must be a perception of the locus and non-perception of what does not exist in it. But while the Nyāya takes non-perception (*anupalabdhi*) as an auxiliary condition (*kāraṇa*) of the perception of non-existence, the Vedānta takes it as the unique cause (*karaṇa*) of the knowledge of non-existence. For the Nyāya, the senses which perceive the locus do also perceive non-existence as determinant (*viśeṣaṇa*) of it. For the Vedānta, the senses are solely concerned in the perception of the locus and do not go further than that. And while the senses perceive a certain locus, the ground, they do *not perceive* a jar on

1. SD., pp. 83 f.
2. TKD., pp. 50-51.
3. TB., p. 6; TC., I, pp. 574-76.
4. *Yadi syādupalabhyetetyevaṁ yatra prasajyate*, Bp., 62; *yogyānupalabdhyā abhāvaḥ pratyakṣaḥ*, TM.

it. This non-perception, therefore, of what might have been perceived if it existed, is the source of our knowledge of the jar's non-existence.[1]

Among Western thinkers it is now generally recognised that negative facts are as real as positive facts. But there is much difference of opinion as to how negation or non-existence is known. According to Alexander,[2] 'negation is not merely a subjective attitude of the mind. That is only an instance of negation, in the region of mental acts. Negation or negativity is a real character of things, which means exclusion or rejection. Not-white is the character which excludes or is different from white. This then would support the Nyāya view that non-existence is perceived as a determination of some positive entity. This seems to be implied also in the view of negation held by Bradley and Bosanquet. Bradley[3] says: "The affirmative judgment qualifies a subject by the attribution of a quality, and the negative judgment *qualifies* a subject by the explicit rejection of that same quality." According to him, 'the truth of the negative lies in the affirmation of a positive quality. In "A is not B" the real fact is a character *x* belonging to A, which is incompatible with B. The basis of negation is really the assertion of *a quality that excludes* (*x*). It is not the mere assertion of the quality of exclusion (not-B).' So too Bosanquet[4] holds that affirmation is prior to negation as supplying the reality within which alone negation has a meaning. In this sense the non-existence of a jar on the ground will be equivalent to the existence of the ground as such. It is to be observed, however, that while the ground is perceived, its exclusion of a jar is not so perceived. The fact of there being no jar on the ground may be a given fact, but it is not given by way of sense perception. As Russell[5] has said, negative facts are real but not sensible facts. That 'A is not B,' or that 'a jar

1. *Vide* TC., I, Ch, on Anupalabdhi; VP., Ch. VI.
2. *Space, Time and Deity,* p. 200.
3. *The Principles of Logic* Vol. I, pp. 116-17.
4. *Logic,* Vol. I, p. 281.
5. *The Analysis of Mind,* p. 276.

does not exist on the ground' is more primarily a subjective feeling of privation with regard to A, or the ground, than a perception of any sensible fact. Hence, the Vedānta seems to be nearer the truth when it takes non-perception (*anupalabdhi*) as an independent source of the knowledge of non-existence or negation.

6. Internal Perception and its Objects

Internal perception is due to the internal sense or *manas*. Hence, it is called *mānasa* or *āntara pratyakṣa*. It is the knowledge of mental fact brought about by their contact (*sannikarṣa*) with the inner sense or *manas*. Thus *mānasa* or internal perception is, like introspection the source of our direct knowledge about mental or subjective facts. But while modern introspectionists take introspection to consist in the mind's knowledge of its own contents, the Naiyāyikas treat internal perception as knowledge of certain subjective facts other than, but due to, the mind as a sense. Generally speaking, the self and its contents are the objects of internal perception. These are perceived when they come in contact with *manas* or the mind. In introspection the mind or self turns back on itself and perceives what is going on there without requiring any sense. The Naiyāyikas, however, like the older introspectionists, believe that the self requires an "inner sense" to perceive psychical facts, just as it requires the external senses to perceive external objects.

Among the objects of *mānasa* or internal perception the *Bhāṣāpariccheda* mentions the feelings of pleasure and pain, desire and aversion, cognition or knowlede and all kinds of mental effort or volition.[1] To these we may add the universal of each of these attributes, their non-existence and inherence in the self, and the self itself.[2] All of these are perceived when there is contact (*sannikarṣa*), in some form or other, between them and the internal sense of *manas*. Let us now consider the process involved in the perception of these objects.

---

1. *Manogrāhyaṁ sukhaṁ duḥkhamicchā dveṣo matiḥ kṛtiḥ*, BP., 57.
2. TK., p.9.

According to the Nyāya, pleasure and pain, desire and aversion, cognition and volition are attributes of the self. Their relation to the self is one of inherence (*samavāya*). They are perceived when the mind as a sense comes in contact with them. This sense-object contact is not one of direct conjunction (*saṁyoga*). It is an indirect contact called *saṁyukta-samavāya.* Pleasure, pain and the rest as particular facts, come in contact with the mind through their inherence (*samavāya*) in the self which is conjoined (*saṁyukta*) with the mind. Similarly, the universal of pleasure, pain, etc., are perceived through that kind of indirect sense-contact which is called *saṁyukta-samaveta-samavāya.* The universals of pleasure and pain (*sukhatvaduḥkhatva*) subsist in particular pleasures and pains by way of inherence (*samavāya*). The particular pleasures and pains exist in the soul as its inherent attributes (*samavetaguṇāḥ*). Hence the mind comes in contact with the universals of pleasure and pain through their inherence in what inhere in the soul which is conjoined to the mind. In perceiving any particular pleasure or pain we do perceive its pleasureableness or painfulness quite as directly, although the pleasure ableness or painfulness quite as directly, although the process of perception is more mediated and complicated.[1] So also, we perceive that pleasure, pain, etc., inhere in the self so long as they exist or are present. And just as we perceive the existence so also we perceive their non-existence or absence. That 'I am unhappy,' or 'I have ceased to be angry' is as much a matter of direct perception as that 'I am happy' or 'I am angry.' The process of perception is, however, somewhat different. The perception of the inherence (*samavāya*) of pleasure and pain, as also of their non-existence (*abhāva*) in the self is mediated by the indirect sense-object contact called *viśeṣaṇatā*. Both the inherence of a present pleasure and the non-existence of a past one are determinations (*viśeṣaṇa*) of the self. They are perceived when the mind as sense comes in contact with them through its conjunction with the self which has those determinations.[2] It is only in the perception of the self that there is a direct sense-object

1. *Vide* SM., 57; TB., p. 6.
2. TB., p. 6.

contact. The self as a substance come in actual contact (*saṁyoga*) with *manas* or the mind as another substance, and thereby becomes an object of internal perception.[1] It cannot be perceived by the external senses, since it possesses neither a limited dimension (*mahattva*) nor any manifest (*udbhūta*) colour or touch.[2] According to some Naiyāyikas, the pure self cannot be an object of perception. The self is perceived only as related to some perceptible attribute like cognition, pleasure, etc. We do not perceive the self as such but as feeling or knowing or doing something. Hence the self is perceived through the perception of this or that state of consciousness. While one's own self can be perceived, other selves can only be inferred from their bodily actions or behaviours.[3] According to the Vedānta, pleasure, pain, desire, aversion and volition are perceived, but their perception requires no sense organ like *manas* or the mind. They are the different parts or aspects of the *antaḥkaraṇa*. As such, there is a natural identification between these and the *antaḥkaraṇa* or the mind. This identification means a perception of all that is identified with the *antaḥkaraṇa*. In short, mental states are perceived facts because they are mental, and so do not require any sense to perceive them.[4]

As to the question how cognition or knowledge is known, there is a sharp difference of opinion among philosophers. Some thinkers who deny the possibility of introspection would say that knowledge can never be known. This is the position taken up by Comte, Dunlap and others. Comte thought that knowing cannot be known, since it involves a division of the mind into two parts, which is impossible. So too, Dunlap, in his article "The case against Introspection,"[5] urges that there is a dualism of subject and object, that the subject can never become object, and therefore there can be no awareness

---

1. *Manasāntareṇendriyeṇa yadātmaviṣayakaṁ jñānaṁ janyate 'hamiti tadā mana indriyamātmārthaḥ, ibid.*
2. BP. and SM., 49-50.
3. *Ibid.*
4. VP., Ch. I.
5. *Psychological Review,* Spt., 1912.

of an awareness. He says: "Knowing there certainly is; known, the knowing certainly is not." Again he says: "I am never aware of an awareness." But if this is so, how do we know that there is any knowledge or awareness at all? Dunlap says that it is 'by being aware of somethings?' This means that when I am aware of something I am aware of being aware of it. To know something is thus to know that something is known. Hence, it cannot be denied that knowledge is somehow known, be it by introspection or not. As Russell[1] has pointed out, 'the statement "I am aware of a colour" is assumed by Dunlap to be known to be true, but he does not explain how it comes to be known.'

Hence, the next question is: How is it that knowledge is known? According to the Śāṅkhya, the Prābhākara Mīmāṁsā and the Advaita Vedānta, knowledge is known by itself. Cognition or knowledge is a conscious fact and it is the very nature of consciousness to be aware of itself. The point has been elaborated by the Prābhākaras in their theory of *tripuṭīsaṁvit* or triune manifestation.[2] According to it, every knowledge manifests itself at the same time that it manifests an object and the knowing subject. It is at once a manifestation of three things, namely, knowledge, the object and the knower. The Jainas also take a similar view with regard to the nature of knowledge. The Advaita Vedānta takes knowledge or consciousness to be the essence of the self, the very stuff of it. As such knowledge is self-manifest and self-shining (*svaprakāśa*).[3] It does not require any thing else to manifest or know it. On this view, every cognition is self-cognised, and consciousness is full and complete awareness of something by a self. But that 'every knowledge is self-conscious knowledge,' or 'to be aware of something is also to be aware of that awareness' is a proposition which is not borne out by psychological facts. Subconscious or unconscious experiences of the mind cannot be said to be full and explicit awareness of themselves. Further, as Russell[4]

1. *The Analysis of Mind*, p.115.
2. *Vide Prakaraṇapañcikā*, p. 59.
3. *Vide* VP., Ch. I.
4. *The Analysis of Mind*, pp. 115-16.

has remarked, it is highly probable that children and the higher animals are away of objects, but not of their own awareness.

According to the Bhāṭṭa Mīmāṁsā[1] knowledge cannot be directly known. We can never know any knowledge immediately by itself or by any introspection called internal perception. That we have an awareness or a knowledge of some object is no doubt a matter of knowledge for us. But this latter knowledge is not at all immediate and perceptual knowledge; it is only mediate and inferential knowledge. When we are aware of something, it comes to have the character of 'being an object of our knowledge' (*jñātatā*). But how can a thing have this character of 'being known,' unless there was previously some knowledge of it? Hence from the character of 'being known' or 'being cognised' in the known object we infer the antecedent existence of knowledge or cognition. Thus, knowledge is neither self-manifested nor directly perceived, but inferred from the character of 'knownness' or 'cognisedness' (*jñātatā*) in the object that has been known or cognised. The Naiyāyikas reject this view on the ground that 'knowness' cannot be a character of objects, for objects acquire no character from their relation to knowledge.

The Naiyāyikas, as we have already seen, hold that knowledge is known by introspection or internal perception (*mānasa pratyakṣa*). According to them, cognition or knowledge manifests its objects, but not itself. It points beyond itself and can never be directed to itself. Hence cognition or knowledge cannot be self-manifested. It does not, however, follow that knowledge cannot be at all known or manifested. Just as an object is manifested by a cognition of it, so one cognition is manifested by another that follows it and makes it an object to itself. First there is the cognition of an object (*vyavasāya),* and then another cognition coming after it cognises the first *i.e.* there is an after-cognition (*anuvyavasāya*) of the first cognition.[2] It follows that every cognition is not

1. *Vide* SD., pp. 56-57.
2. TR., p. 53; TD., p. 32.

necessarily cognised, that awareness of an object is not always an awareness of itself. It is only when the self or mind attends to, and casts an introspective glance at it, that one cognition or knowledge is known or perceived. This view of the Naiyāyikas has the support of many modern introspectionists like Stout, Laird and others. Thus Stout observes: "Psychical states as such become objects only when we attend to them in an introspective way. Otherwise they are not themselves objects, but only constituents of the process by which objects are cognised."[1] So too, Laird says: "Certainly, our cognitive processes are, in their usual exercise, processes with which (not at which) we look; and none of them, perhaps, can look at itself. It does not follow, however, that *another* (introspective) look cannot be directed towards this process of looking..."[2] This means that one cognition is known by another by way of introspection. But for the Naiyāyikas, introspection involves a peculiar difficulty. It supposes the simultaneous presence of two cognitions, which is not admitted by the Naiyāyikas. Hence we are to say that the cognition, which is cognised by another cognition, is past in relation to the second cognition which is present. This implies that introspection is really memory or retrospection of what is past. But there cannot be any memory without a previous perception corresponding to it. Hence we are committed to the view that every cognition somehow cognises itself. It may not have an explicit awareness of itself but only an implicit or vague feeling of its presence. As Stout has elsewhere said: "The stream of consciousness *feels* its own current."[3] Hence, the way in which cognition or knowledge (or for the matter of that, the mind) knows itself is quite different from that in which it knows an object external to itself. This has been very well recognised by Alexander in his distinction between an enjoying and a contemplating consciousness. He says that 'in any experience the mind enjoys itself and contemplates its object, that the mind is not a contemplated object

1. *A Manual of Psychology*, p. 134.
2. *Contemporary British Philosophy*, First Series, p. 227.
3. *Analytic Psychology*, Vol. I, p. 160.

to itself, and that introspection is not contemplation.[1] Hence, we conclude that knowledge is known directly by itself. This knowledge of knowledge however is neither an explicit manifestation nor a definite perception of it, but a feeling or an enjoying consciousness of itself.

1. *Space, Time and Deity,* Vol. I, pp. 12-17.

Chapter VIII

Three Modes of Ordinary Perception

1. *Nirvikalpaka* and *Savikalpaka* Perception

As we have noticed in a previous chapter, perception has been divided by the Naiyāyikas into two broad classes, namely, *laukika* or the ordinary and *alaukika* or the extraordinary. This division depends on the nature of the sense-object contact that is involved in all perceptions. Ordinary perception again, has been divided into the six kinds of olfactory, gustatory, visual, tactual, auditory and mental perceptions. Such classification of ordinary perceptions has reference to the senses concerned in perception. According to another classification, ordinary perception is of two kinds, namely, *nirvikalpalka* or the indeterminate and *savikalpaka* or the determinate. Here the principle of classification is the character of the perceptual knowledge which arises from sense-object contact. To these two kinds of perception we may add *pratyabhijñā* or recognition as a special form of determinate perception. Thus keeping in view the nature of perception, the Naiyāyikas distinguish between three modes of ordinary perception, namely, the *nirvikalpaka*, the *savikalpaka* and *pratyabhijñā*. Extraordinary perception being explicit and definite knowledge, has but one mode, namely, *savikalpaka* or determinate.[1]

While the distinction between *nirvikalpaka* and *savikalpaka* perceptions is generally recognised in Indian philosophy, there is much difference of opinion, among the different systems, as to their exact nature and validity. The grammarian philosophers (*śābdikas*) along with other take the extreme view that all perceptions are *savikalpaka* or determinate, since every perception

1. *Alaukikaṁ tu . . . savikalpakameva*, *Nyāyakośa*, p. 499.

must be expressed in a verbal proposition and is consequently predicative in its character. This is met by another extreme view, held by the Buddhists and some Vedāntists, that *nirvikalpaka* or indeterminate perception alone is valid, while *savikalpaka* or determinate perception is false knowledge. Between these two extremes we may place the other systems of philosophy which accept both *nirvikalpaka* and *savikalpaks* perceptions as true knowledge. Thus, among the different theories of perception in Indian philosophy there seems to be a sort of gradation from the most abstract to the most concrete view of perception.

In the Advaita Vedānta system we seem to have the most abstract view of *nirvikalpaka* perception. According to it, *nirvikalpaka* is the knowledge of pure being (*sanmātram*). It is a cognition of the 'this' or the existent as such, but not as determined by anything. To determine a thing is to characterise it by this or that quality and is thus to distinguish it from other things having different qualities. All this, however, is the work of discriminative thought (*vikalpa*). Prior to discrimination there cannot be any cognition of an object as such-and-such, *i.e.* as a determinate reality. Hence, *nirvikalpaka* perception must be the cognition of pure indeterminate being. It is in *savikalpaka* perception that an object is determined by certain qualities and is distinguished from different objects. But all objects being ultimately one undifferentiated unity of consciousness (*caitanya*), their distinction or difference is only an appearance. The view of the world as a plurality of independent reals is not only opposed to scriptual testimony, but also logically untenable and self-contradictory. Hence we are to say that *savikalpaka* gives us a knowledge of appearances, while *nirvikalpaka* gives us the ultimate truth.[1]

The epistemology of the Neo-Advaita Vedānta is in agreement with the general metaphysical position of the earlier school. From the *vyāvahārika* or practical standpoint it makes a distinction between *savikalpaka* and *nirvikalpaka* perceptions. According to it, *savikalpaka* is the knowledge of a thing as qualified by an

1. *Vide* Rāmānuja's commentary on the *Vedānta-sūtra*, 1. 1. 1; SD., p. 40.

attribute (*vaiśiṣṭyāvagāhi*). In it the thing is related as subject to the attribute as its predicate. Hence the essence of *savikalaka* perception is the determination of its object by way of predication. The perception of an object *as* a jar is *savikalpaka*, since the quality of 'jarness' is prediated of the object. On the other hand, *nirvikalpaka* is the knowledge of a thing as not related to anything, not even to itself (*saṁsargānavagāhi*). It is the knowledge of the identity of a thing as excluding all relations. Hence in *nirvikalpaka* perception there cannot be any predication of the object in terms of the subject-predicate or substantive-abjective relation (*viśeṣya-viśeṣaṇa-saṁbandha*). As instances of such *nirvikalpaka* or non-relational knowledge, the Vedāntist mentions the propositions 'this is that man,' 'that art thou.' When in the presence of a man we have it said 'this is that Devadatta,' we have the perception of Devadatta as the same identical man. This knowledge of the man is *nirvikalpaka*, since its object is not qualified by or related to anything. What we apprehend here is the simple identity of the man in the past and the present, but not his relation to any time, space, or anything else. It is true that the man may have certain attributes and is related to this or that time and space. But in the perception in question we are not at all concerned with his relation to any attribute, but only with his identity as such. It may be urged here that since the knowledge is grounded on a proposition (*vākyajanya*), it cannot but be relational in character. A proposition is the assertion of a relation between two things, of which one is the subject and the other perdicate. Hence the knowledge 'this is that man' must be *savikalpaka* or predicative. To this the Advaita Vedāntist replies that a proposition which asserts the identity of an object does not come under the law of predication. When we say 'this is that man' we do not predicate 'that man' of 'this.' It is not the case that we relate 'this man' with 'that man,' but simply assert the identity between the two. An identity proposition (*akhaṇḍārtha vākya*) thus gives us non-predicative or non-relational knowledge (*nirvikalpaka jñāna*).[1] Thus, we see that, according to the Advaita Vedānta, *nirvikalpaka* perception is a judgment of identity

1. VP., Ch. I.

expressed in a proposition, The identity that is perceived in *nirvikalpaka* does not pertain to any of the specific attributes of parts of the perceived object. It refers only to the identity of the object as an unrelated essence, *i.e.* as pure being. But while the 'identical' perceived in *nirvikalpaka* is an abstract unity of being, our knowledge of it is a propositional judgment of the non-predicative order (*akhaṇḍārtha vākya*). The Vedāntist further holds that *nirvikalpaka* perception is self-manifest or self-conscious knowledge. It is perceived by itself (*pratyakṣa*), and does not require any other knowledge to manifest or perceive it. It follows also that we have first the *savikalpaka* perception of an object as related to certain qualities and then a *nirvikalpaka* perception of it as a unity that remains identical with itself under different conditions.

According to the Buddhists, *nirvikalpaka* is the only type of valid perception. It is such cognition of an object as contains no element of thought or ideation in it (*kalpanāpoḍham*).[1] Ordinarily, knowledge involves two elements, namely, the given or the sensed and the menat or the ideated. The Buddhists hold that what is given is a unique individual (*svalakṣaṇa*) that belongs to no class and is not related to anything.[2] We may call it by a name, bring it under a class and think of it as having certain qualities, actins and relations. But its name, class, quality, action and relation are not any part of what is directly given; these are the contribution of our mind (*kalpanā*) to the given experience. Hence, *nirivikalpaka* perception is a cognition of the given datum as such, *i.e.* as not modified by any idea or concept like those of its name, class, etc. (*nāmajātyādyasaṁyutam*). It is a pure sensation of the simples of experience and does not lend itself to any verbal expression (*abhilāpasaṁsargāyogyapratibhāsam*). As contrasted to this, *savikalpaka* perception is a verbalised experience, in which the object is determined by the concepts of name, class, relation, etc. Here we think of the object as a complex of parts and attributes,

1. Dignāga, *Pramāṇasamuccaya,* Ch. I; NBT., pp. 9 f.
2. *Cf.* "*Apare tu svalaksaṇamātragocaraṁ nirvikalpakamicchanti,*" SD., p. 41.

bearing a certain name and having certain relations. Such knowledge, however, is false, since it is not due to the given object, but to our conceptual construction of it.[1] Thus, the Buddhists reduce *nirvikalpaka* to pure sensation which is valid but blind, and *savikalpaka* to conceptual knowledge definite but false. Be it noted, however, that the Buddhists's *nirvikalpaka* as a cognition of the simples or unique individuals of experience is less abstract than the Advaitin's *nirvikalpaka* as a cognition of pure being.

In the Mīmāṁsā, the Sāṅkhya and the Nyāya-Vaiśeṣika system we have what may be called a concrete view of perception. According to these realistic schools, what is given in perception is not, as the Advaitins think, a pure unity of being or the abstract identity of the 'this' and 'that' of experience. Nor is it, as the Buddhists suppose, the unique individual, the bare particular or the mere 'this' of experience. On the other hand, it is held in these systems that any perception, *nirvikalpaka* or *savikalpaka,* is a direct cognition, of the real individual which is a unity of the universal and the particular. The distinction between *nirvikalpaka* and *savikalpaka* is not due to any difference in the contents of perception, but to the way in which the same contents of experience may be ordered and arranged. As we shall see, however, there is some difference of opinion as to the nature and structure of *nirvikalpaka* perception between the Bhāṭṭa Mīmāṁsā and Sāṅkhya systems, on the one hand, and the Prābhākara and Nyāya-Vaiśeṣika systems, on the other.

According to the Sāṇkhya and the Bhāṭṭa Mīmāṁsā, both *nirvikalpaka* and *savikalpaka* are equally valid and necessary modes of perceptual knowledge. By *nirvikalpaka* they mean that cognition which spontaneously arises at the first moment of contact between sense and object.[2] It is a knowledge of the object as one individual whole of generic and specific attributes. There is no differentiation

1. NVT., 1. 1. 4; Mādhavācāryya, *Sarvadarśanasaṁgraha.* Chapter on *Bauddha philosophy. Vide* also NM., pp. 92 f.
2. *Akṣasannipātānantaramaviviktasāmanyaviśeṣavidhāgaṁ saṁmugdha-vastumātragocaramālocanjñānam*, SD., p. 40

between the universal and the particular that are combined in the body of the individual. Hence there is only an apprehension of the individual as an indefinite object (*sammugdhavastumātra*), but no definite understanding of it as this or that kind of object (*vastuviśeṣa*).[1] *Nirvikalpaka* perception thus resembles the perception of children and dumb persons. Like the latter perception, it is a simple apprehension of an object as something, but not as this or that kind of thing. So, likewise, it cannot be expressed in words, *i.e.* embodied in propositions. Thus *nirvikalpaka* perception is a simple apprehension, in which the 'this' of experience is brought under the general idea of 'something' (*vastusāmānya*). It is a judgment without words, *i.e.* a non-propositional judgment.[2] That *nirvikalpaka* is a real mode of perception appears from the fact that it is the basis of what we call reflex actions and *savikalpaka* perceptions. When a man suddenly withdraws his finger from a pricking pin, we cannot say that there is in him a clear understanding of the pricking object as a pin. Yet without some knowledge of the object his action remains unintelligible. What prompts the man's action in this case is properly described as *nirvikalpaka* perception of 'something pricking him'. Again, *savikalpaka* perception is understood by all as the predicative knowledge of an object (*vaiśiṣṭyāvagāhi jñāna*). In it the homogeneous indefinite object of *nirvikalpaka* perception is analysed into the universal and the particular (*sāmānya-viśeṣa*), and the two are then related by way of predication. Thus, when I perceive an animal as a cow, my perception is *savikalpaka*, since I definitely predicate 'cowness' of the animal before me. Now such predication is possible only through comparison of the animal in question with other objects of our past experience and recollection of their respective class-names. But the impetus to the acts of comparison and verbal memory must be given by a previous cognition of the animal as some kind of thing. This first *nirvikalpaka* cognition of the animal as something (*vastusāmānya*) is necessary for the subsequent *savikalpaka*

1. *Sammmugdham vastumātrantu prāggṛhṇantyavikalpitam, tatsāmānya-viśeṣbhyām kalpayanti manīṣiṇaḥ*, TKD., 27
2. *Ibid.*

understanding of it as this particular kind of thing (*vastuviśeṣa*), *i.e.* as a cow. The indefinite individual of the first experience is analysed into 'this thing' as a particular, and 'cowness' as a universal in relation to it and qualifying it as a predicate. This is the *savikalpaka* knowledge of the thing in terms of the substantive-abjective relation, and it is expressed as a verbal judgment of the form: 'this is a cow.'[1] Thus, we see that, according to the Sāṅkhya and Bhāṭṭa Mīmāṁsā schools, *nirvikalpaka* and *savikalpaka* are but two stages in the perception of the same fact. The former is a stage of unverbalised judgment of an object as an individual whole, while the latter is a verbal judgment of it by way of predication.

In the Nyāya-Vaiśeṣika and Prābhākara Mīmāṁsā systems we find a theory of perception which is in substantial agreement with that just explained above. According to the Nyāya-Vaiśeṣikas, ordinary perception is of two kinds, namely, *nirvikalpaka* and *savikalpaka,* both of which are equally valid and grounded in reality.[2] They hold that *nirvikalpaka* is not merely a cognition of the bare particular (*svalakṣaṇa*), since it manifests the universal (*sāmānya*) as weel. If the universal is not cognised at the *nirvikalpaka* stage, our knowledge of it at a subsequent *savikalpaka* stage becomes inexplicable. But for a direct knowledge of the universal as a unity of the individuals we could not recognise them as similar and group them together into one class. The universal cannot be constructed by our mind at any stage of our knowledge, unless we start with it as a directly given fact.[3] Nor again, is

1. SD. and SC., p. 40; TKD, 27.
2. Some commentators on the Nyāya system think that the distinction between *nirvikalpaka* and *savikalpaka* is not recognised in the *Sūtra, Bhāṣya* and *Vārttika,* and that it was introduced into the Nyāya philosophy by later logicians. Vācaspati Misra, however, in his *Tātparyaṭīkā* (p. 125) traces trhe distinction to *Nyāya-Sūtra,* 1. 1. 4. Following his teacher, Trilocana, he takes the words *avyapadeśyam* and *vyavasāyātmakam* contaned in this sūtra to mean respectively *nirvikalpaka* and *savikalpaka* percpetions. Later Naiyāyikas follow Vācaspati in this interpretation of the *sūtra* and hold that it distinguishes between *nirvikalpaka* and *savikalpaka* as two kinds of ordinary perceptions.
3. NM., p. 98.

nirvikalpaka a knowledge of the abstract universal (*sāmānyamātra*), or of pure being (*sattā*). Our first cognition of a thing is not merely an apprehension of its unity, but also of its differences. When we perceive anything, its manifoldness is as much manifest to consciousness as its unitary character. It is cognised as a unity of many parts, qualities and aspects. Likewise, if nothing but mere being (*sattā*) be the content of immediate apprehension, we do not know how to account for our knowledge of the particulars (*viśeṣa*) of experience. Further, pure being which is nothing in particular cannot be the object of our knowledge.[1] Hence, we are to admit that in *nirvikalpaka* perception there is a cognition of both the universal and the particular, the generic and specific properties of an object as such.[2] It is a knowledge of the perceived object with all the wealth of its concrete characters in themselves. It cognises the universal or the class-essence present in the object of perception as well as its colour, form, structure and other specific characteristics. Thus the *nirvikalpaka* or indeterminate perception of an orange is the cognition which is produced immediately after the contact of the senses with the object, and which manifests its generic and specific properties in their isolation. It gives us a knowledge of the orange, not *as orange,* but as the grouping of a certain colour, taste, smell, etc., with a certain universal called orangeness.[3] But while both the universal and the particulars constituting an object are cognised in *nirvikalpaka* perception, they are not brought under the substantive-adjective relation (*viśeṣyaviśeṣaṇasaṁbandhānavagāhi*).[4] In *nirvikalpaka* perception these are cognised as unrelated units of reality. Here then the object of perception is not known *as* an individual *related* to a certain universal. It is not judged as an individual belonging to a certain class and bearing that class-name. Hence, *nirvikalpaka* is the

---

1. *Ibid.*
2. *Sāmānyaviśeṣeṣu svarūpālocanamātraṁ pratyakṣam*, PS., 187; *nirvikalpakam . . . sāmānyaṁ viśeṣaṁ cobhayampi gṛhṇāti*, NK., p. 189.
3. SM., 58.
4. *Avyapadeśyaṁ jātyādisvarūpāvahi na tu jātyādīnā, mitho viśeṣaṇa viśeṣyabhāvāvagāhīti*, NVT., p. 125.

knowledge of an object as not characterised in any way (*niṣprakāraka*).[1] It is an apprehension of the object as 'something', but not as related to a class and called by a name (*nāmajātyādiyojanāhīnaṁ...kiñcididamiti*).[2] Hence, it is not a judgment of the object in terms of the subject-predicate relation (*vaiśiṣṭyānavagāhi*). On the other hand, it is a simple apprehension of the existence and attributes of an object without any corresponding judgment of it in words, or by why of predication.

According to some linguistic thinkers there cannot be any *nirvikalpaka* perception in the sense of an unverbalised experience as explained above. They hold that we cannot think things except through words. All objects are inseparably connected with the words by which they are denoted. To cognise a thing is to know it as such-and-such and so to relate it to a denotative word (*vācakaśabda*). Likewise, we can act in relation to a thing only when we know it precisely as of this or that kind, *i.e.* determine it by means of a class-name. In fact, all our cognitions are embodied in verbal propositions, such as 'I know a colour,' 'I have a taste,' 'it is a smell,' and so on. All cognitions being thus inseparable from verbal and expressions, there can be no *nirvikalpaka* or unverbalised cognition.[3] The Nyāya-Vaiśeṣikas repudiate the linguistic contention on the following grounds. In the case of children and dumb persons there is undoubtedly a knowledge of many objects, but no verbal expression of that knowledge. Even in the case of grown up persons, who are in the habit of expressing their thoughts in words, there is such a thing as sensation which is a bare apprehension of something, but no verbal judgment of it. The first stage of perception is a sensory cognition arising just with the contact between sense and object. Like the perception of the child or the dumb person, it does not require and has not the

1. *Namajātyādiyojanārahitaṁ vaiśiṣṭyānavagāhi niṣprakārakaṁ nirvikalpakam* TC., I, p. 809.
2. *Nirvikalpakaṁ viśeṣyaprakārādirahitaṁ vastusvarūpamātrajñānam* TM., Ch. II.
3. NB., 1. 1. 4.; NK., p. 189

time to develop into verbal judgment. The verbal expression of sensory cognitions is a later stage of perception, which serves the purpose of social intercourse and communication. The linguistic contention that objects are inseparable from their corresponding words leads to absurd consequences. If it were true that all objects are inseparably connected with all the words denoting them, even children and idiots should know all those words when they perceive the objects. It follows also that a man who perceives the words 'colour,' 'sound,' etc., should have a knowledge of the objects denoted by them, even though he may be deprived of their special sense organs. Hence the Naiyāyikas conclude that all cognitions need not necessarily be verbally expressed knowledge. As a matter of fact, what enables us to recall the words with which an object is associated is a previous *nirvikalpaka* cognition of it as an existent fact. Our first experience of an object is a simple apprehension of its existence apart from any verbal association. Such simple unverbalised experience is the ground of our subsequent judgment of it in words or predicative propositions. Hence *nirvikalpaka* is a real stage of perception.[1]

According to the Naiyāyikas, *nirvikalpaka* is a real but not a perceived fact (*atīndriya*).[2] It is a conscious, but not a self-conscious state. The Naiyāyikas hold that to be self-conscious means, for a conscious state, to be perceived by another state of consciousness. In self-consciousness (*anuvyavasāya*) one cognition is cognised by another which follows the first and apprehends it as an object to itself. But there cannot be a cognition of *nirvikalpaka* cognition. To cognise a cognition is to know it explicitly as a cognition of this or that object. To become conscious of a mental state is to refer it explicitly to the self, on the one hand, and some definite object, on the other. Thus my awareness of a perception (*anuvyavasāya*) appears in the form 'I know this jar,' or 'I know this table.' *Nirvikalpaka* perception is a knowledge of the uncharacterised object. It is an undifferentiated feeling of the indefinite. As such, it

1. NB. and NK., *ibid.*
2. *Jannirvikalpākhyaṁ tadatīndriyamiṣyate*, BP. and SM., 58.

cannot be known as a perception or this of that object. Hence the Naiyāyikas differ from the Advaitins in holding that *nirvikalpaka* perception cannot be perceived or directly known.[1] Although we cannot perceive it, we can logically proved it. The existence of *nirvikalpaka* perception is proved by inference. In *savikalpaka* perception an object is known as related to certain qualities. But we cannot know the relation between a thing and its qualities unless we previously know these in themselves. *Nirvikalpaka* is this prior knowledge of the thing and its qualities as unrelated entities. It is the ground of our *savikalpaka* or relational knowledge about the thing. Hence we must admit *nirvikalpaka* as the first stage of all grades of perception, since a simple cognition of existents as such is the precondition of all comples cognitions of their different relations. Thus the reality of *nirvikalpaka* is inferred from *savikalpaka* perception.[2]

With regard to *savikalpaka* perception, the Nyāya-Vaiśeṣikas agree with others in holding that it is the cognition of an object as qualified by certain attributes (*viśiṣṭajñāna*). In it the object of perception is known as characterised by some qualities. So, it is a judgment in which certain attributes are related to the object by way of predication, *e.g.* 'this is a cow.'[3] Here the attribute of cowness is predicated of the presented object. Hence *savikalpaka* perception is always expressed in a proposition, of which the subject is the thing perceived and the predicate is the attribute present in the thing. From this it follows that the contents of *savikalpaka* perception are the same as those of the *nirvikalpaka*. It is the same object that is cognised in both. But while in the former the object and its attributes stand in the subject-predicate relation, in the latter they are not so related. Hence the two differ, not in their object or content, but only in point of predication. *Savikalpaka* is a judgment

1. *Nirvikalpakaṁ na pratyakṣam . . . vaiśiṣṭyānavagāhijñānasya pratyakṣaṁ na bhavati, ghaṭamaṁ jānāmīti pratyayāt*, etc., SM., 58.
2. *Viśiṣṭavaiśtyajñānaṁ prati hi viśeṣaṇatāvacchedakaprakārakaṁ jñānaṁ karaṇam*, etc., TC., I, p. 812.
3. *Savikalpakaṁca viśiṣṭajñānaāṁ yathā gaurayamiti, ibid.*, p. 839. *Savikalpakaṁ nāmajātyādiyojanātmakam*, TB., p. 5

of the object in words or propositions, but *nirvikalpaka* is a judgment of it not in words or propositions. The one is a predicative, which the other is non-predicative judgment of the same object or fact.[1]

While *nirvikalpaka* is the first, *savikalpaka* is the second stage of an ordinary perception. The first stage develops into the second in the case of all normal individuals who know the use of any language. The process of development from the one to the other is explained by association and memory. In the case of the perceptional judgment: 'this is a cow,' the first step is the contact of sense with the object, which immediately leads to a *nirvikalpaka* perception or simple apprehension of the cow as something definite. The indefinite object of *nirvikalpaka* perception being associated with a certain class-name in our past experience revives the word-image answering to that name. With this we remember the class-name of the perceived object and call it by that name. It is here that we have a *savikalpaka* perception of the object expressed in the proposition 'this is a cow.'[2] The Buddhists deny the validity of the *savikalpaka* mode of perception. They contend that what is given in perception is a bare particular which belongs to no class and bears no name, *i.e.* has no relations. Its class, name, etc., are only thought relations which do not exist in the object, but are introduced into it by the thinking subject to meet the needs of our practical life.[3] From the standpoint of the Nyāya realism, however, there is no error in the *savikalpaka* perception of an object as qualified by certain attributes and called by a name. According to it, what is given in *nirvikalpaka* perception is neither a characterless nor an uncharacterisable object, although it be not so far characterised in any way. In reality the object is a concrete individual in which certain particulars or specific attributes are united which certain

1. *Tasmāt ya eva vastvātmā savikalpakasya gocaraḥ sa eva nirvikalpakasya śabdollekhavivarjitaḥ. . . Iha śabdānusandhānamātramabhyadhikaṁ param, viṣaye na tu bhedo'sti savikalpayoḥ*, NM., p. 99.
2. *Vide* NVT., p. 128; NK., p. 192.
3. *Vide* NVT., pp. 133 f., and TR., pp. 60-61.

particulars or specific attributes are united with a certain class-essence or universal. While in *nirvikalpaka* the object is apprehended as an undifferentiated whole of the universal and the particulars, in *savikalpaka* these are analysed, unfolded and recombined into the substantive-adjective relation. Hence it cannot be said that *savikalpaka* is concerned only with thought-relations which have no objective basis. Rather, it unfolds all that is implicitly involved in the *nirvikalpaka* stage and expresses it in the form of a proposition. It does not add anything that is not contained in the object itself. It represents no change or development in the object of perception. On the other hand, it marks a change in the perceptive consciousness of the object, a development of it from a dumb feeling of 'something there' to an articulate expression of the feeling as a cognition of this or that definite thing. Hence *savikalpaka* is as valid as, but more expressive than, *nirvikalpaka* perception.[1]

Yet another theory of perception, which we have to consider now, presents what may be called the most concrete view of perception. It takes up the extreme position that all perceptions are *savikalpaka* or determinate and that there is no such thing as a perfectly indeterminate (*nirvikalpaka*) perception. This view of perception is shared by the Cārvākas, the Jainas, the ancient Śābdikas and the Viśiṣṭādvaita Vedānta of Rāmānuja. According to Rāmānuja, to know a thing is to know it as possessed of certain attributes. A thing's existence cannot be separated from its nature and attributes. To know the 'that' or existence of a thing is also to know the 'what' or the nature of its existence. All knowledge is, therefore, a definite cognition of some object as related to a certain class and qualified by certain attributes. It is always a determinate (*savikalpaka*) cognition of the object as this or that kind of thing. There cannot be any knowledge of the perfectly indeterminate. That which is no thing in particular cannot be the object of our knowledge. Hence, there is no such thing as indeterminate (*nirvikalpaka*) knowledge in the sense of a cognition of what is not determined or characterised in any way (*nirviśeṣa*). There being

1. *Vide* NVT., pp. 137-44; NM., pp. 64-69

thus no absolutely indeterminate knowledge, the distinction of *nirvikalpaka* and *savikalpaka* perception is a relative distinction. It is a distinction between two perceptions, both of which cognise an object as somehow qualified and determined (*saviśeṣaviṣaya*). But while in *nirvikalpaka* the object of perception is partially determined, in *savikalpaka* it is determined more fully and clearly. Thus the *first* perception of a cow is *nirvikalapka* in the sense of being a cognition of it as an animal of a certain make-up, or of some kind, but not of this or that particular kind. On the other hand, the perception of the same object, in the case of an adult who knows cows as a class, will be *savikalpaka* in so far as the object is here further determined and definitely known as belonging to the class of cows. *Savikalpaka* and *nirvikalpaka* perceptions are thus cognitions, not of the characterised and uncharacterised, but of the more or less definitely characterised object.[1]

The Cārvākas, the Śābdikas and the Jainas go further than Rāmānuja and hold that *nirvikalpaka* perception is not real in any sense. According to the Jainas, all true knowledge must be a definite and an assured cognition of objects (*vyavasāyātmakaṁ jñāam*).[2] What distinguishes true knowledge from doubt, error and the rest is the fact that it is a firm belief which is also true. It is a definite judgment of an object as this and not as that.[3] In it there is a definite affirmation or denial that an object is or is not such-and-such. In the so-called *nirvikalpaka* perception, however, there is no such definite assertion of anything about any object. Hence, it cannot be recognised as a form of valid knowledge. Further, all knowledge being implicit in an manifested by the self, perception is only conditioned and not produced by the function of the senses. Every perception, just when it occurs, will be a complete manifestation of the object. In perception there need not be a transition from an initial stage of vague and unorganised sense-impression to that of

---

1. *Pratyakṣasya nirvikalpakasavikalpakabhedabhinnasya na nirivśeṣavastuni pramāṇabhāvaḥ*, etc., *Śrībhāṣya*, 1. 1. 1.
2. *Vide Prameyakamalamārtaṇḍa*, 1.
3. *Tanniścayātmakaṁ samāropaviruddhatvādanumānavat*, *ibid.*, 3.

distinct and determinate knowledge. All true perceptions are, therefore, determinate (*savikalpaka*) cognitions of objects as they really are in themselves.[1]

The same conclusion has been reached by the Śābdikas or grammarian philosophers on the ground of the intimate relation between thought and language. According to them, all objects are inseparably connected with the words or terms denoting them. All our thoughts and cognitions of things are expressed in words and propositions. We cannot think of things except through their corresponding denotative terms.[2] Bhartṛhari, a grammarian philosopher, lays it down as a general rule that there can be no thought without language and that all knowledge must be verbalised experience.[3] It follows, therefore, that all our perceptions must be cognitions of objects as denoted by certain names or words. They must be expressed in propositions, in which the perceived thing and its qualities are related as subject and predicate. Hence, there can be no *nirvikalpaka* perception in the sense of a cognition which is independent of verbal expression and free from association with words or general terms.[4] All perception is thus *savikalpaka* or determinate knowledge of objects as qualified by the attributes predicated of them. The Cārvākas recognise only *savikalpaka* or determinate perception, in which we cognise object as possessed of a number of perceptible qualities. For them, *nirvikalpaka* perception is a hypothesis which cannot be verified by actual experience. It is something which cannot be perceived and is therefore unreal.

With this we pass from the extreme view of perception as blind sensation to what appears to us to be another extreme view of it as

1. *Ibid.*, p. 8.
2. *Sarve'rthāḥ sarvathā sarvadā sarvatra nāmadheyānvitāḥ*, etc., NVT., p. 125.
3. *Na so'sti pratyayo loke yaḥ śabdānugamādṛte, anuviddhamiva jñānaṁ sarvaṁ śabdena gamyate*. (Bhartṛhari, *Kārikā* quoted in *siddhāntacandrika*, pp. 39-40).
4. NVT., pp. 125-26.

a fully developed judgment expressed in a predicative proposition. This is met by an intermediate position that distinguishes between two modes of perception, namely, the *nirvikalpaka* and the *savikalpaka,* of which the former is simple apprehension or judgment of an object without words, and the latter a predicative judgment of it in a word-proposition. This intermediate position seems to be a more reasonable view of perception. The pure sensation, to which the Buddhists reduce perception, is a psychological myth. Then the linguistic view of perception as always a fully developed propositional judgment is contradicted by such perceptions as ante-date language, *e.g.* the perceptions of children and higher animals. Even it the case of adults who know a language, an indefinite cognition of an object as given in sensation may very well precede a definite perception, in which it is recognised as a particular kind of thing. According to most of the Indian systems, the former is the *nirvikalpaka* and the latter the *savikalapaka* mode of perceptual knowledge. It is also generally held by them that there is no room for error in *nirvikalpaka* perception, since it is a bare apprehension of the given object without any judgment of it as this or that. Hence, it is always true. It is the *savikalpaka* perception of an object as a particular kind of thing that is liable to error, since our judgment here may not conform to the real nature of the object.[1]

2. Recognition (*Pratyahjiñā*) as a Mode of Perception

Recognition may be understood in two senses. In a wide sense, recognition means understanding the nature or character of a thing. In this sense, to recognise a thing is to know it as such-and-such, as when I know that the animal before me is a cow. It is generally admitted that recognition in this sense is an ordinary mode of

1. Jayanta Bhaṭṭa, however, maintains that liability to error is common to both *nirvikalpaka* and *savikalpaka* perceptions. The illusions of sense, like the percpetion of two moons, are instanced by him as cases of *nirvikalpaka* perception which are erroneous. (*Vide Nyāyamañjarī*, p. 97.)

perception, which is called *savikalpaka* and which relates a thing and its qualities by way of prediction. In a narrow sense, however, recognition means knowing a thing as that which was known before. To recognise thus means to cognise once again that which we are aware of having cognised before. *Pratyabhijñā* is recognition in this sence. It consists in knowing not only that a thing is such-and-such but that it is the same thing that we saw before. According to the Naiyāyikas, *pratyabhijñā is* the conscious reference of past and a present cognition to the same object. I see a jar, recognize it as something that was perceived before, and say 'this is the same jar that I saw.'[1]

With regard to the nature of *pratyabhijñā* or recognition the question is: Is it a simple or a complex cognition? Is it a case of pure perception or memory? According to the Buddhists, recognition is a mechanical compound of perception and memory. It cannot be called perception, because it relates to a past object with which there cannot be any sense-contact. It cannot be called pure memory which refers only to the past, while recognition refers to a present object as the 'this.' Nor can we say that recognition is a synthesis or unitary product of perception and memory. Perception and memory arise respectively out of sensation and imagination, and are incapable of fusing into a single effect. Admitting that recognition is a unitary product, what is the nature of its object? If the object be past, then recognition is not different from memory. If it be in the future recognition becomes a form of imagination (*saṅkalpa*). The object cannot be a merely present fact, since in recognition the object is identified with something of our past experience. To say that the object of recognition exists in the past, present and future is a contradiction in terms. Hence the Buddhists conclude that *pratyabhijñā* is a dual cognition including both perception and memory which refer respectively to the two aspects of an object as 'this' and 'that', iṣ as present and past.[2]

---

1. *Pūrvāparayorvijñānayorekaviṣaye pratisandhijñānaṁ pratyabhijñānam*, etc., NB., 3. 1. 7., 3. 2. 2.
2. NM., pp. 448-49.

The Jainas take *pratyabhijñā* to mean recognition in the sense of both understanding the nature of an object and knowing that it was perceived before. To recognise a thing is to know that it has this or that property, or that it is the same as what was seen before. It is not true to say that *pratyabhijñā* is a dual cognition consisting of perception and memory. Although conditioned by perception and memory, it is a new kind of knowledge which cannot be resolved into them. The testimony of introspection clearly tells us that *pratyabhijñā* is a unitary cognition and a distinct type of knowledge. What the Naiyākas call *upamāna* or comparison is, according to the Jainas, a form of *pratyabnijñā* as understood by them.[1]

According to the Naiyāyikas, *pratyabhijñā* consists in knowing that a thing now perceived is the same as what was perceived before.[2] That *pratyabhijñā* or recognition, in the second sense, is a single psychosis appears clearly from the fact that it refers to one and the same object. The cognitions of a jar and a cloth are two different psychoses, because they are evidently related to two different objectives. Recognition refers to only one thing and is therefore a simple and unitary cognition. The unique cause (*karaṇa*) of the phenomenon of recognition is constituted by the senses and the effects of past experience. Recognition is brought about by sense-impressions as modified by the effects of previous experience of an object.[3] It gives us the knowledge of an object as existing in the present and as qualified by its relation to the past.[4] A thing's relation to past time or a past experience is a character which qualifies its present existence. To know this is just to know that we have perceived it before, *i.e.* to recognise it. Hence recognition is a special mode of *savikalpaka* perception. In all but the *nirvikalpaka*

---

1. *Vide Prameyakamalamārtaṇḍa*, pp. 97-100.
2. *So'yaṁ devadatta ityatītavartamānakālaviśiṣṭaviṣayakaṁ jñānam pratyabhijñā*, *Mitabhāṣiṇī*, p. 25.
3. *Saṁskārasahitamindriyamasyāḥ pratīteḥ karaṇam* etc., NM., p. 459.
4. *Atītakālaviśiṣṭo vartamānakālāvacchinnaścārtha etasyāmavabhāsate*, *ibid*.

mode of perception there is the influence of past experience on our present knowledge. All *savikalpaka* or determinate perceptions of objects consist of certain given or presentative elements and certain representative factors like ideas and images of similar objects experienced in the past. In an ordinary *savikalpaka* perception the representative factors do not remain distinct but are assimilated with the presentative elements to make up one percept. In *pratyabhijñā* or recognition, the representative factor has the form of a definite recollection of some past experience of an object and modifies the present perception of it. Still it is perception, since it is brought about by sense-object contact.[1] Hence, the Naiyāyika concludes that recognition is a kind of qualified perception, in which the present object is qualified by a distinct recollection of its past experience. The Mīmāṁsakas and the Advaita Vedāntins also hold that recognition is a kind of perception. The Mīmāṁsakas, however, do not distinguish it from an ordinary *savikalpaka* perception. According to them, recognition is that kind of perception in which the object is determined by the name by which it is called, *e.g.* 'this is Devadatta.'[2] For the Advaitin, *pratyabhijñā* is a perception of the *nirvikalpaka* kind, since there is in it no predication of any thing about the perceived object, but an assertion of its identity amidst changing conditions.[3]

1. *Pūrvābhijñānaviśiṣtagrāhyamāṇamiṣyatāṁ pratyabhijñānam*, NM., p. 461.
2. SD., p. 43.
3. VP., Ch. I.

Chapter IX

Extraordinary Perception (*Alaukika Pratyakṣa*)

1. *Sāmānyalakṣaṇa* or the Perception of Classes

In the ancient school of the Nyāya we do not meet with the distinction between *laukika* or ordinary and *alaukika* or extraordinary perception. This distinction appears in the modern Nyāya beginning with Gaṅgeśa. In *laukaia* or ordinary perception there is a normal sense-contact with objects present to sense. In *alaukika* perception, however, the objects are not actually present to sense, but are conveyed to it through an extraordinary medium. In it there is a special kind of sense-object contact (*alaukika-sannikarṣa*). Extraordinary perception is of three kinds, namely, *sāmānyalakṣaṇa, jñānalakṣaṇa* and *yogaja*.

Sāmānyalakṣaṇa is the perception of a whole class of objects through the generic property (*sāmānya*) perceived in any individual member of that class. Thus when we perceive something *as* a pot we judge it as belonging to the class of pots. But to know that the thing belongs to the class of pots is also to know all other pots belonging to the same class. To say that 'this is a pot' is to know, by implication, what all other pots are. Hence in perceiving one thing as a pot we perceive all other pots. But the other pots are not present to sense in the same way in which one is present. How then can there be any perception of the other pots? If there is to be any perception of the other pots, they must be in some sort of contact (*sannikarṣa*) with our sense. According to the Naiyāyikas, when we perceive one pot we perceive the universal 'potness' as its defining property. It is this perception of the universal 'potness' in the present pot that serves the purpose of contact (*āsatti*) between sense and all other pots. The knowledge of the universal (*sāmānyajñāna*) is here the medium of sense-object contact, by which we have a perception of all pots when one is perceived.[1] It may be objected here that *sāmānyalakṣaṇa* perception would make each of us omniscient. If all the objects of a class are known with the perception of any of them, we should know all knowable objects when we perceive anything of the world as belonging to the class of knowables. The Naiyāyikas reply that in *sāmānyalakṣaṇa* we perceive only one member of a class as an individual with its specific and generic properties, while the other members are known as possessing the generic property or the universal alone. Hence we cannot expect to have that full and detailed knowledge of all things, which is implied by omniscience.

That *sāmānyalakṣaṇa* is a type of real perception is supported by the Naiyāyikas on the following grounds. Without it we cannot explain the knowledge of universal propositions (*vyāpti*), which is presupposed in inference. How do we know that all smoke are related to fire? We cannot know this if our perception be limited to particular smokes, for any number of particulars will not make up the universal. Hence we must admit that while perceiving one smoke as related to fire, we perceive all smokes, through the universal 'smokeness,' as so related. It cannot be said that it is unnecessary to assume that we perceive all smokes as related to fire, because we cannot even doubt if *all* smokes are related to fire or not, unless all smokes are somehow presented to us when we do perceive one as related to fire.[2] Again without *sāmānyalakṣaṇa* we cannot explain negative judgments of perception like 'this cloth is not a pot,' 'this is not a cow,' etc. To say that 'this is not a cow' is to know the class of cows, *i.e.* all cows. This can be known only if when perceiving one cow we perceive all other cows through the universal 'cowness' as perceived in the present and perceived cow. Further, we cannot explain the voluntary effort to attain a pleasure without the help of *sāmānyalakṣaṇa*. To strive consciously for a pleasure is somehow to know it as something to be, but not yet,

---

1. *Āsattirāśrayāṇāṁ tu sāmānyajñānamiṣyate*, etc., BP. and SM., 64-65
2. T.C., II, pp. 290f. SM. 65.

experienced. But how can we know a pleasure which we have not yet had? This is possible if, when experiencing one pleasure, we know all pleasures through the universal 'pleasurableness' as belonging to the perceived pleasure.[1]

The Nyāya view of *sāmānyalakṣaṇa* has been severely criticised and finally rejected by the Vedānta. According to it, *sāmānya* or the universal is a group of essential and common attributes belonging to a number of individuals. While the universal, as such, may be perceived along with the perception of an individual, it does not give us a perception of all the individuals possessing the same universal. Nor is there any valid ground to believe that in perceiving one individual we must perceive all other individuals of the same class. Thus in inference, say of fire from smoke, it is sufficient if we know 'smokeness' as related to 'fireness.' It is not at all necessary for us to know that *all* smokes related to fire. If all were known, then there would be no need for any inference in a particular case. Similarly, the negative judgment 'this is not a cow' is quite possible if we only know what 'cowness' is and not what all cows are. So, too, there may be a conscious pursuit of some future pleasure if the pursuer knows it to be similar to his previously experienced pleasures. For this, there need not be a *sāmānyalakṣaṇa* perception of all pleasures when one is actually perceived.[2]

Now, we are to observe that the reality of *sāmānyalakṣaṇa* as a type of perception depends on the presentative knowledge, if any, of a class of things. If there is any such knowledge with regard to a whole class of things, we have to admit *sāmānyalakṣaṇa* as a type of genuine perception. It is pointed out by the Naiyāyikas that any knowledge of the genus or the class does not justify us in believing in *sāmānyalakṣaṇa*. To know the general character of an atom is to have only a *conceptual* knowledge (*mānasabodha*) of all atoms. Similarly, we may *think* of the class of pots in a dark room. But that does not mean that we have a presentation of all

1. *Ibid*., pp. 238-90.

2. *Vide Advaitasiddhi*, pp. 137-39.

pots through any sense for which we require the help of a *sāmānyalakṣaṇa* perception. It is only when in perceiving some individual object there is the presentation of the class of objects to which it belongs that we have to admit *sāmānyalakṣaṇa* to explain the presentative knowledge of that class. Hence the crucial question is this: Is there any presentative or direct knowledge of a class of things? The Naiyāyikas contend that there is such a knowledge and seek to prove it on such grounds as we have explained above. Before we come to these we may state the following facts as more or less non-controversial.

When I know an individual as belonging to a certain class I know the universal or class-essence underlying it. To know the universal, however, is to know a character or group of characters which belongs to all the members of the class. So, in knowing the universal I know all the individuals of that class—past, present and future—as participating in that universal. To know a horse *as* horse is to know horseness, and to know horseness is to know that it belongs to all horses, or to know all horses as possessing it. Again, a knowledge of the class seems to be implied in any generalisation. When from such particular cases as 'A is mortal,' 'B is mortal,' 'C is mortal,' and so on, we conclude that '*all* men are mortal,' we somehow know that mortality is true of the *class* of men. Now the question is: How do we know anything about the whole of a class of things from the observation of some of its members? In other words, how do we get general propositions from the observation of particular facts?

In Western logic this is explained by inductive inference.[1] The Naiyāyikas, however, hold that the knowledge of the class or the general proposition is given by perception of an extraordinary kind. The Vedāntins, on the other hand, argue that a generalisation is the statement of an invariable relation between universals and that it is known through the observation of their concomitance in one or more instances. Thus, the general proposition 'all men are mortal,' or 'whatever is smoky is fleary' is the expression of an invariable

1. *Vide* Mill, *A System of Logic;* Stebbing, *Logic in Practice*, pp.19-20.

relation between manhood and mortality, or smokeness and fireness. We have a knowledge of such general propositions when in any particular instance we find manhood to be related to mortality, or smokeness to fireness. The Vedānta view of generalisation thus corresponds to what is know as "intuitive inducation" in Western logic[1] and is explained as a "process by means of which we apprehend a particular instance as exemplifying an abstract generalization," as when 'from the apprehension of *this red patch* as being darker than *that pink patch* we may know immediately that every such red patch (*i.e.* redness) is darker than every such pink patch (*i.e.* pinkness).' It seems to me that while the abstract principles of mathematics may be taken as statements of necessary relations between certain universal concepts, all our empirical generalisations, including those here given, are truths about classes of things. In fact, such principles are what may be better called the necessary laws of thought rather than truths about any universal that has a denotative reference to a class of thing. But, if we take the above cases as abstract generalisations exemplified in particular instances, we do not understand how they can be called, as some Western logiciancs have called them, "intuitive induction." If by such induction we are to mean "the *immediate apprehension* of an axiom by means of its exemplification in a particular instance," we must admit that there is no room for any induction or inference or reasoning in it. If we have an immediate knowledge of anything, there is no need for any inference or reasoning with regard to it. A description of such knowledge as "intuitive induction" seems to me to be no less objectionable than a description of it as "perceptual inference." If, however, by "intuitive induction" we mean the intuitice knowledge of a general principle through a particular instance, we should made it plain that such instance is not the basis of an *inference* with the regard to the general principle. Rather, the general principle is apprehended along with the particular instance, although an explicit statement of it may be separated from the latter by an interval of time. To guard against a possible

1. *Vide* Stebbing, *A Modern Introduction to Logic*, p. 243.

misunderstanding, therefore, it is better to characterise our knowledge of the general principles of logic and mathematics as intuition than to call it an "intuitive induction."[1]

Our ordinary generalisations, however, are different from the abstract principles of logic and mathematics. While the latter are truths about certain universal concepts, the former are truths about classes of things. When we lay down the proposition 'all men are mortal,' or 'all smoky objects are fiery,' what we really want to convey is, not that there is a necessary relation between manhood and mortality, or between smokeness and fireness, but that mortality is true of the class of men, or that all smokes are connected with fire. Such propositions are empirical generalisations in the sense that these are assertions about whole classes of things, which are true, and that these are arrived at from observation of particular instances. But what is the nature of the process of knowledge that is involved when we generalise from 'some' to 'all' in a logically valid way? Is it any kind of induction? If so, it must be either 'perfect induction' or "Induction by Simple Enumeration." A 'perfect induction' is one in which 'from the consideration of each of the members of a *limited* class we pass to a generalisation concerning all the members of that class.' This is exemplified when on examining every boy of a class one says "all the boys of this class are intelligent." With regard to this Stebbing[2] says: 'Mr. Johnson has suggested the convenient name *summary induction* for this mode of *inference*, and that it is certainly a more appropriate name than "perfect induction."' It seems to me that both the names are equally inappropriate, and that for the same reason. A summary of a number of observed facts is not an induction at all. To call it an induction, be it perfect or summary, is to misjudge its epistemic character as inferential. If on examining every patient in a sick-

1. This is really admitted by Dr. Stebbing although there seems to be some wavering at certain places. *Cf.* "Thus we may be said to *see* the general principle in apprehending the particular case." "The *intuition* is of the form but it relates to the material exemplified in the form" (italics mine). --*A Modern Introduction to Logic*, pp. 96-97, 244.

2. *A Modern Introduction of Logic*, p. 244.

room a physician says "all the patients in this room have got fever," then his judgment is not to be described as an induction or inference in any sense. It is but a memory synthesis like the one we have when we understand the meaning of a sentence by a synthesis of its constituent words and their meanings as that is effected by memory. Hence, our knowledge of a general proposition like 'all men are mortal' cannot be called a "perfect induction," even if it were possible for us to examine all men. But that is not possible as a matter of fact, since in man we have, not a limited, but an unlimited class that has "an infinite number of members."

Let us next consider whether an empirical generalisation like 'all men are mortal' can be explained by "Induction by Simple Enumeration." "Generalisation from a number of examined instances which are not assumed to constitute *all* the instances of the given class is now usually known by the name 'Induction by Simply Enumeration.' "[1] Such induction may, therefore, be put in this form: 'A, B, C are mortal; therefore, all men are mortal.' But this is not a form of valid inference. It obviously violates the general rule of inference that we must not go beyond the evidence, since in this inference the conclusion makes a statement about *all* men on the ground of what is observed in *some* men. Further, if it were a form of valid inference, it would validate any argument that might be put in this form, just as the form of deduction guarantee the validity of a reasoning that may be put in any of them. While, however, we accept the argument 'all men are mortal, because A, B, C are mortal,' we do not acquiesce in the proposition 'all men are white, because A B, C are white.' But why? If we examine the two arguments we shall see that the distinction between them is this. In the first, mortality which is found in some men is predicated of all men. In the second, whiteness which is observed in some men is predicated of all men. But then, we find A, B, C to be mortal, not because they are A, B, C, but because they are men. On the contrary, we know that A, B, C are white because they are A, B, C, and not simply because they are men as such. This means that

1. *Op. Cit.*, p. 245.

while mortality is related to the essential nature of A, B, C, whiteness is not so related to them. That individual men like A, B, C possess a certain essential common nature which is to be found in all men is borne out by the fact that we put together all men into the class 'man' and exclude all other animals from that class. If, then, we find that mortality is related to the essential nature of some men, we know that all men must be mortal. That is, we know all men to be mortal when we know that mortality belongs to the essential nature of some men like A, B, C. But the first knowledge does not *follow* from the second To know mortality to be related to the essential nature of some men is just to know that it is related to all men or the class of men. 'What is related to the essential nature of some men must be related to all men' is a truth which is known *directly* or *immediately*, and for which we require no inference or reasoning. Hence our knowledge about the whole class is here an intuitive knowledge due to the knowledge of the class-essence or the universal. It cannot be said that the knowledge of the class-essence or the universal is got by inductive inference. The latter presupposes the former and so cannot be the ground of it. It seems to me that the universal, underlying a class of things is either directly known or never known. Observation of and experiment on things help us to *find* or *discover* the universal that is in them, but not to *make* or *construct* it our of them. And when by observation and experiment we find that the universal or class-essence is related to something, we know *at once* that all the members of the class are related to that thing. According to the Naiyāyikas, it is the perception of the whole of a class as related to an attribute, which is simultaneous with the perception of the class-essence as so related. To distinguish it from ordinary sense perception they call it *alaukika* or extraordinary perception. If this be, as it very likely is, so, what is known as inductive inference may be reduced to the Naiyāika's *sāmānyalakṣaṇa* perception in the sense of intuition of a general proposition through the knowledge of the class-essence or the universal.[1]

1. Some Western logicians fully reealise the futility of all induction as a form of valid inference. They do not, however, so clearly realise the

The Naiyāyikas further point out that without the perception of the whole of a class of things the problem of generalisation cannot even arise. If, when perceiving a particular smoke as related to fire, we ask 'are *all* smokes related to fire?' it is because the class of smokes is somehow presented to us. It cannot be said that we merely *think* of *all* smokes as a concept or general idea, and that there is no presentation or direct experience of them. We can think of such particular smokes as were previously experienced by

---

implication of this futility. If there is no *form* of inductive inference, there can be no such thing as inductive inference in logic. If this be admitted, as it should be, then the problem of generalisation takes a different form. A generalisation is no longer a matter of inference, but is to be explained by way of intuition. That our knowledge of general principles is intuitive will be admitted by many. But very few, if any, will admit that an empirical generalisation also is a matter of intuition based on the knowledge of class-essences or universals. Some Western logicians, however, seem to tend towards this view when they try to establish a general proposition on the ground of the knowledge of "important resemblances" or "common properties" or "class-characters" of things. Consider, for example, the following statements from Dr. Stebbing: 'Such classes as *swans* and *men* differ from such classes as *scarlet things* and *sour things* in the fact that every member of the class *swan*, for instance, has several properties in common with all the other members, whereas the members of the class *scarlet things* have few properties in common which are not also possessed by things that are not scarlet. Such classes as *swans* are called by Mill, "natural kinds." 'Simple enumeration is not, then, to be regarded as a process *simply of counting;* it is a countion of instances *recognised as having certain properties in common.* The inference is dependent upon recognition of *resemblances.*' (*A Modern Introduction to Logic,* pp. 248-49.) 'It is the fact that certain properties are found together that makes class-names so useful. If we know that there is a set of properties such that no member of the set is every found without other members of the set, then we have a basis for inference. It is because this appears to be the case with natural kinds that generalisation about natural kinds, such as *crows, acids, men,* seems to be plausible.' (*Op. cit.,* p. 251.) "As Mr. Keynes points out: 'Scientific method, indeed, is mainly devoted to discovering means of so heightening the known analogy that we may dispense as far as possible with the methods of pure induction.' " (*op. cit.,* p. 256.) *Cf.* also Latta and Macbeth, *The Elements of Logic,* p. 268.

us. But the idea of particular smokes always falls short of the class of smokes or *all* smokes. And there cannot be any idea of the class of smokes without a corresponding direct experience of it. It is only when, in perceiving one smoke as related to fire, *all* smokes are presented to us through the perception of the class-essence 'smokeness,' that we can legitimately ask the question: Are *all* smokes or the class of smokes related to fire? Hence, we conclude that *sāmānyalakṣaṇa* is a type of genuine perception. It should, however, be borne in mind that we have not such a perception whenever we perceive any individual possessing a class-essence. It is only when the perception of the class-essence of an individual has a direct reference to the class of things to which it belongs that we have to admit a *sāmānyalakṣaṇa* perception of that class of things through the perception of the class-essence. In what cases other than those mentioned above there is such a reference is a matter of phenomenological observation which we need not discuss here.

2. *Jñānalakṣaṇa* or Acquired Perception

The second type of extraordinary perception is called *jñānalakṣaṇa.* It is the perception of an object which is in contact with sense through a previous knowledge of itself.[1] When on seeing something a man says: 'I *see* a piece of fragrant sandalwood,' he has an immediate knowledge or perception of its fragrance. This cannot be explained without the help of *jñānalakṣaṇa*. How can he perceive the fragrant sandalwood, seen at a distance? Its fragrance is not then smelt by him and so does not come in contact with the sense of smell. Nor can there be any ordinary contact between smell and the sense of sight. Still he perceives it as fragrant sandalwood lying at a distance. Hence we are to say that there is some extraordinary contact between fragrance and the sense of sight. Here our past experience of fragrance in the sandalwood does the work of contact between sense and object. Our past knowledge of fragrance (*saurabhajñāna*) brings about the present

1. *Viṣayī yasya tasyaiva vyāpāro jñānalakṣaṇaḥ*, BP., 65.

perception of it, although it is not actually smelt by us. It cannot be said that the present perception of fragrance as a particular is brought about by *sāmānyalakṣaṇa* cognition of the class of fragrants. The latter cognition supposes an ordinary perception of the genus of fragrance through sense-contact which is not to be found in the present case.[1] Thus, we see that in both *sāmānyalakṣaṇa* and *jñānalakṣaṇa* perceptions sense-object contact is mediated by some kind of knowledge. In the former, the knowledge of a universal and, in the latter, some past experience is the medium of contact between sense and the perceived objects. But the distinction between them is this. While in *sāmānyalakṣaṇa* the knowledge of the universal leads to the perception of the individuals in whihc it inheres (*āśraya*), in *jñānalakṣaṇa,* a past knowledge leads to the present perception of its own object (*yadviṣayakaṁ jñāanṁ tasyaiva pratyāsattiḥ*).[2]

The Naiyāyikas explain illusions by the help of the theory of *jñānalakṣaṇa* perception. The illusory silver is perceived because it is presented through our previous knowledge of silver as seen at some other time and place. But the Vedānta objects to the Nyāya theory of *jñānalakṣaṇa.* It argues that to recognise *jñānalakṣaṇa* as a type of genuine perception is to reduce ordinary inference to perception. If the fragrance of sandalwood be perceived because we have a previous knowledge of it as connected with sandalwood, then in the inference of fire from smoke, the fire may be said to be said to be perceived since we have also a previous knowledge of it as related to smoke. There is nothing to distinguish between the two cases. In the one we have a perception of sandalwood and a previous knowledge of its relation to fragrance. In the other, we have a perception of smoke and a similar knowledge of its relation to fire. Hence if the fragrance be in extraordinary contact with sense and so perceived, there may be such an extraordinary perception of fire and, for the matter of that, of all objects of inference. So, the Vedānta holds that our knowledge of the fragrance

1. SM., 65.
2. *Ibid.*

of sandalwood, seen at a distance, is due to inference and not any extraordinary perception like the Naiyāika's *jñānalakṣaṇa.*[1]

Now let us consider whether the knowledge of the fragrant sandal that is involved in the judgment "I *see* a fragrant sandalwood" is really a case of perception as held by the Naiyāyikas, or a case of inference as urged by the Vedāntins. Students of Western philosophy will readily recognise that such knowledge is of the same kind as what is called "complication" by some psychologists. The judgment " I *see* a fragrant sandalwood" is in fact equivalent to the judgment "The sandalwood" *looks fragrant.* " And this is really another instance of what Stout, Ward and Wundt call "complication," and illustrate by such judgments as "Ice looks cold," "The armour looks hard, smooth and cold."[2] We may go further and say that the Naiyāyika's *jñānalakṣaṇa* is similar to the visual perception of distance, since the eyes have "no independent means of apprehending those relations of surfaces and lines which presuppose the third dimensioı.. ' If there can be a visual perception of distance, coldness, hardness, etc., there can also be a visual perception of fragrance. Hence the fundamental question to be discussed here is this: Can there be, and is there in fact, a *visual* perception (*i*) of distance, (*ii*) of coldness, hardness, etc., and (*iii*) of fragrance.

With regard to the first case (*i*), J. S. Mill[3] was strongly of opinion that 'the perception of distance by the eye is, in reality, an inference grounded on experience; though in familiar cases it takes place so *rapidly* as to appear exactly on a par with those perceptions of sight which are really intuitive, our perceptions of colour.' Modern psychology, however, has outgrown this view and finds no difficulty in admitting that there is a visual perception of distance. With regard to the other cases, however, there is much difference of opinion among philosophers, both Indian and Western. While

1. VP., Ch. I.
2. *Vide* Stout, *A Manual of Psychyology*, p. 102; Wundt, *Human and Animal Psychology*, pp. 285-86.
3. *A System of Logic*, p. 4.

the Advaitins would bring all such cases under inference, the Naiyāyikas are in favour of treating them as genuine perceptions. Among modern thinkers some psychologists like Stout, Ward and Wundt take at least the sencod group of cases (*ii*) as a form of perception, although, to distinguish it from ordinary perception, they give it the name of "complication." Many other psychologists, however, would reduce them to some kind of rapid or implicit inference. As for the third case (*iii*), the Naiyāyikas are perhaps the only realists who would say that we have a visual perception of fragrance.

How are we to deal with the second and the third case? We have to raise two questions, *viz.* (*i*) how are we to distinguish between perception and inference, and (*ii*) where are we to draw the line between perception and inference?

Perception may be defined as an immediate knowledge of objects or a knowledge of objects which is not brought about by any other knowledge. On the other hand, inference is the indirect knowledge of an object through the mediation of some sign which is known to be always related to it. In both perception and inference there is an interpretation of some daum. In both we may distinguish between a given and a suggested content. In perception there is a synthesis of some sensuous elements and some non-sensuous presentations. But in perception these two elements are *not kept distinct.* They fuse into one whole or form parts of one complex object. There is no transition of consciousness from the one to the other. We do not think of the one apart from and independently of the other. The one immediately suggests the other and gives rise to the cognition of an object as one whole, of which they are the parts. Thus in an adult's visual perception of a rose, the sensory element, namely its colour, immediately presents its other qualities, namely, its touch and smell, and the sensed and the presented elements blend into the perception of the rose.

Inference is distinguished from perception by the fact that it gives us a knowledge of some fact through the mediation of some other fact on the basis of a uniform relation between them. Of these two facts the second suggests the first through a knowledge of their uniform connection with each other. But the suggestive fact and the suggested fact remain *distinct* and we are conscious of a transition of thought from the one to the other. These do not fuse into one whole as they do in perception. Rather, they stand out as two wholes or two distance facts, either of which is though of independently of the other. Thus in the inference of fire from smoke my mind passes from one thing to another which is distinct from it and is thought of independently of it. Hence, the distinction between perception and inference is briefly this: Perception is the integral immediate consciousness of an object. Inference is a multiple mediated consciousness of an object which may be expressed as a this-therefore-that consciousness.

In view of the above distinction between perception and inference we can not admit the Advaitin's contention that to recognise *jñānalakṣaṇa* as a form of perception is to obliterate the distinction between perception and inference. When we pass such judgments as 'the rose looks soft,' 'the stone looks hard,' we do not pass from the colour of the rose or the stone to its tactual quality. Likewise, when we say 'ice looks cold,' or 'the sandal looks fragrant,' there is no transition of thought from ice to coldness, or from the sandal to its fragrance. We do not say "because ice, therefore cold," or "because sandal, therefore fragrant." On the other hand, coldness or fragrance is a part of the presentation of the ice or the sandal. What we say is: "I see the cold ice or the fragrant sandal," just as we say "we see the distant hill.' In the inference of fire from smoke, however, there is a transition of our thought from smoke to fire as two distinct object. We never say "I see the fiery smoke." In fact, the fire is here only *thought of* by us and not presented to us. To recognise *jñānalakṣaṇa,* therefore, as a form of perception is not to ignore the fundamental distinction between perception and inference.

It may indeed be contended here that while in the visual perception of a rose or a stone or a block of ice, there is a presentation of some tactual quality, there is no such presentation of fragrance in the visual perception of sandalwood. To this we are to say that if the eye can present a tactual quality like softness or hardness or coldness which it is not fitted, by nature, to perceive, there is no inherent impossibility in the eye being made competent to perceive smell. We are, therefore, to consider under what condition or conditions perception takes place. When we have discovered these conditions, we shall see that, although logically perception and inference are two fundamentally distinct ways of knowing, yet from the psychological standpoint, it is not possible to draw the line between them.

As we have already said, perception is constituted by the union of certain sensuous elements with certain non-sensuous presentations into one whole. The sensuous elements are the given and the non-sensuous elements are presented by the given. As a general rule, perception occurs when there is either a natural or a habitual association between the sensuous and the non-sensuous elements of perception, so that the one immediately calls up the other and the two are fused into one whole of presentation of some object. By 'natural association' I mean an association, in our minds, of one sense quality with such other sense qualities as are, by nature, connected with it. It follows naturally from this that such associations will be most frequently experienced by us and therefore ingrained in our minds. The question as to how many senses and sense qualities there are, is not relevant for our present purpose. We adopt here the universally accepted view that there are five senses and five corresponding sense qualities, namely, smell, taste, colour, touch and sound. Taking these sense qualities in the order in which they have been mentioned here, we may say that there is a natural connection of that which precedes to those which succeed it, but not *vice versa*. Thus a smelling object has generally some taste, colour, touch and sound. But a sounding object like space or air has no colour, taste and smell. So also, to smell a thing is generally to see and touch it. But to see a thing is not to taste or smell it so generally. Hence, it is that a smell or taste sensation naturally calls up the colour and touch of an object.

On the other hand, a 'habitual association' is the association, in our minds, of one sense quality with those which are not, by nature, connected with it. Hence, it is less frequently experienced by us and is, in many cases, looser than a natural association.[1] Still when a habitual association between them is once formed in our minds, one sense quality immediately calls up others and all of them are combined into the perception of an object. Thus sound is not naturally connected with touch as there is sound in space but no touch. So also, touch has no natural relation to colour, as there is touch in the air but colour. Similarly, there is no natural connection of colour with taste and smell. Thus there is colour in light but no taste and smell. Hence, it is that an association of colour with smell is looser than that of smell with colour, with which it is naturally connected. While the mere smell of kerosene immediately suggests its colour, the latter by itself hardly suggests the former. But by repeated experiences of their uniform connection with one another a habitual association between them may be established in our minds, and one sense quality may present another which is not naturally connected with it. It is in this way that the sound of a bell presents its tactual and visual qualities and we have the auditory perception of a bell, just as the sight of the bell presents its tactual and auditory qualities and we have a visual perception of it. Thus, we say "I hear the bell," just as we say "I see the bell."

The two alternative conditions of perception, *viz.* a natural and a habitual association between its two elements, are realised in the life of an individual through repeated experiences of the objects of the world. When we speak of a natural association between them we do not mean that it is congenital, so that the association is formed in the mind of every individual from his or her birth. If it were so, every baby should have as good perceptions as any grown-up person. All that we mean by a natural association is that it has a

---

1. This is also admitted by some Western thinkers, *Cf.* Stout, *A Manual of Psychology,* pp. 102-03: In the qualification of actual touch experience by revived visual experience we find the union of the constituents of the comples *much losser.' Cf.* also Bosanquet, *The Essentials of Logic,* p. 31: 'The judgement of sight perception, "That (which I see) is a cab," though its terms are *more inextricably interwoven,* has just the same elements in it as the judgment of sound perception, "That (which I hear) is a cab." '

basis in the constitution of things and that it is most frequently met with in the experiences of an individual. If, therefore, both natural and habitual associations are produced by repeated experiences, two important consequences would follow: (1) It follows that the knowledge of the same object may, *under the same objective conditions*, be a matter of perception or inference for different individuals, according as there is or is not a natural or a habitual association as the basis of their knowledge. (2) It follows that, *under the same objective conditions,* the knowledge of the same object may at first be a matter of inference and subsequently of perception, and *vice versa,* for one and the same individual. The knowledge of a rose from its sight a perception for the person in whom the repeated experiences of roses have established a natural or a habitual association between its colour and touch and smell. The knowledge of the same rose, under the same external conditions, will be an inference for another person when, for want of repeated experiences, its colour does not immediately call up its touch and smell, but suggests them as distinct ideas or images on the ground of its similarity to the colour of roses. For illustration we may refer to the difference between our knowledge of a new variety of the rose and thatof the gardener who presents it to us. An armour may *look* hard, smooth and cold to an adult who is familiar with it. A child may just *imagine* it to have these or very different tactual qualities. The fragrance of sandalwood may be directly known from its sight by those who are closely acquainted with it, but for others its fragrance. When I go to a foreign country I can barely *infer* the distance and size of an object from its visual appearance, but a native of the country who is familiar with the environment has a perception of these from the same position, which is essentially visual. If, however, I stay there for some months and become familiar with the environment, I may have a visual *perception* of the same facts under the same objective conditions. For the illustration of the converse case, *i.e.* the relapse of perception into inference, we may refer to (*i*) any case of senility in which a person has but a doubtful inferential knowledge of things and persons under the same objectuve conditions under which he or she once used to perceive them, and (*ii*) the common though curious instance of forgetfulness in which we fail to recognise an old acquaintance whom we have not seen for many years and try to *infer* his identity by putting certain questions to him and judging their answers.

The foregoing discussion leads us to the conclusion that there cannot be an absolute line of demarcation between perception and inference. We cannot say that under the same objective conditions the knowledge of an object must always be a perception for every individual and that it can never be otherwise. Nor can we aver that such knowledge must always be an inference for all individuals and that it can never be a perception for any. On the contrary, we are to admit that it may be either, for different individuals, or for the same individual at different stages of his or her life, according to his or her or their mental equipment.

In view of the answers which we have given to the two questions stated above we justified in saying that, under certain conditions, it is quite possible that there may be a presentation of fragrance in relation to the activity of the visual sense. When these conditions are fulfilled, there is nothing to prevent the eye from giving us an *immediate* knowledge of fragrance. And that is why of all people the Vedāntins must admit that there may be a visual perception of fragrance, since, according to them, perception is just immediate knowledge and not any cognition produced by sense stimulation. Hence we admit that there may be a visual perception of fragrance, just as some psychologists believe that there is a visual perception of hardness, coldness and the like. Since, however, such perceptions are brought about by senses which are not ordinarily capable of perceiving their objects, it is better to call them extraordinary and put them in a separate class as *jñānalakṣaṇa* perception or complication.

3. *Yogaja* or Intuitive Perception

The third kind of extraordinary perception is called *yogaja*. It is the intuitive perception of all objects–past, distant and future–

due to some supernormal powers generated in the mind by devout meditation (*yogābhyāsajanito dharaviśeṣaḥ*). In the case of those who have attained spiritual perfection (*yukta*), such intutive knowledge of all objects is contant and spontaneous. In the case of others who are on the way to perfection (*yuñjāna*), it requires the help of concentration as an auxiliary condition.[1]

The reality of *yogaja* perception is generally accepted in Indian philosophy on the authority of the scriptures (*Śruti* and the like)[2] But there is nothing absurd or strange in the concept of an intuitive knowledge of all things. As concepts analogous to *yogaja* we may mention the theological ideas of eternity and omniscience. Or that of intuition in the philosophy of Spinoza and Schelling. Again, it is a psychological fact that by concentration we may expand the span of our consciousness so as to cognise a number of object at one and the same time. It is also a matter of common observation that sometimes we forget do the right at the right moment. In many case, the reason for this is that our mind is distracted by or scattered over many other things. Sooner or later, however, we detect such lapses just when the distraction is over and the mind becomes calm and collected. Similarly, when we recollect something by an efforts of attention we see how concentration of the mind helps to manifest the past and the distant. In truth, consciousness is, in its own nature, of unlimited span. The limitations of our consciousness are due, not to anything in the nature of consciousness itself, but to the physiological conditions under which it has to work in us. Such considerations suggest that it is possible for the human consciousness to have an instantaneous knowledge of all things, provided it can get over its organic limitations and natural distractions. But granting that such knowledge is possible, can we speak of it as perception in any sense? It is not certainly the ordinary perception of an object which is present to and affects our senses. What is past, distant or future cannot be the object of our ordinary sense perception. Still we cannot say that intuitive knowledge is

1. BP. and SM., 65-66.
2. *Ibid.*

due to inference or any other kind of reasoning. Intuitions came to us with the spontaneity and vividness of a lightning flash, as it were. In all respects they are more like the given contents of our knowledge than the products of our imagination, thought or reasoning. Hence if we are to classify intuitive knowledge at all, we are to say that, like the knowledge by clairvoyance, it is perception of an extraordinary kind.

III. THE THEORY OF INFERENCE (*ANUMĀNA-PRAMĀṆA*)

Chapter X

Nature of Inference

1. Definition of *Anumāna* or Inference

Anumāna literally means such knowledge as follows some other knowledge. It is the knowledge of an object due to a previous knowledge of some sign or mark (*liṅga*).[1] The previous knowledge is the knowledge of the *liṅga* or mark as having a universal relation with the *sādhya* or major term and as being present in the *pakṣa* or minor term.[2] Hence, *anumāna* has been defined in the Nyāya system as the knowledge of an object, not by direct observation, but by means of the knowledge of a *liṅga* or sign and that of its universal relation (*vyāpti*) with the inferred object.[3]

The object of inference is some fact which follows from some other fact because of a universal relation between the two. With regard to something of our experience we wand to know by means of *anumāna* that which may not be perceived but is indicated by what is perceived in it. *Anumāna* as a *pramāṇa* is , therefore, the source of our knowing through the medium of a sign or mark that a thing has a certain character. It leads to the knowledge of a thing as possessing a character, say fire, because of its having another character, smoke, which we apprehend and which we know to be always connected with it. Thus in anumāna we arrive at the knowledge of an object through the medium of two acts of knowledge or propositions.

All systems of Indian philosophy agree in holding that *anumāna* is a process of arriving at truth not by direct observation but by

---

1. *Mitena liṅgena liṅgino 'rthasya paścānmānamanumānam*, NB., 1. 1. 3.
2. *Vyāptiviśiṣṭa-pakṣadharmatājñānajanyam*, etc., TC., II, p. 2.
3. NM., p. 109.

means of the knowledge of *vpāpti* or a universal relation between two things. The Nyāya view is stated already. According to the Vaiśeṣikas, *anumāna* is the knowledge derived from the perception of a *liṅga* or sign which is uniformly connected with something else, such as cause, effect, co-effects and correlative terms.[1] The Buddhists take *anumāna* to consist in the perception of that which is known to be inseparably connected with another thing. Such inseparable connection between two things is due either to the law of causality or the principle of essential identity (*tadutpatti* and *tādātmya*).[2] So also the Jainas hole that *anumāna* is the method of knowing an unperceived object through the perception of a sign and the recollection of its invariable concomitance with that object.[3] The Sāṅkhya and the Yoga, the Mīmāṁsā and the Vedānta system too define *anumāna* as the knowledge of one term of a relation, which is not perceived, through the knowledge of the other term which is perceived and is explicitly understood as invariably related to the first term.[4] In *anumāna* what is perceived leads us on the knowledge of what is inferred through the knowledge of a universal relation (*vyāpti*) between the two.

2. Distinction between Perception and Inference

Perception and inference are equally valid methods of human knowledge (*pramāṇa*). But while perception is independent of any previous knowledge, inference depends on previous perception. Inference is sometimes defined as knowledge which is preceded by perception.[5] It depends on perception for the knowledge of the *liṅga* or the middle term as subsisting in the *pakṣa* or the minor term. It depends on perception also for the knowledge of *vyāpti* or the universal relation between the middle and major terms of

1. PS., pp. 99 f.
2. *Nyāyabindu,* Chapter. II.
3. *Prameyakamalamārtaṇḍa,* p. 101.
4. TKD., 5; VB., 1. 7; SD. and SC., p. 60; VP., Ch. II.
5. NS., i. 1. 5.

inference.[1] It is only when we have observed two things to be always related that from the perception of the one we infer the existence of the other. Thus, inference is knowledge derived from some other knowledge, while perception is not derived from any other knowledge. That is, inference is mediate and perception immediate knowledge of an object.

All perception is essentially of one kind, namely, that it is a knowledge of what is given. But there are different kinds of inference based on different kinds of *vyāpti* or universal relation. Perception is generally due to some contact of our sense organs with the objects perceived by us. It gives us knowledge of only those objects which lie within the range of the senses. Hence, it is limited to the here and the now, *i.e.* to present objects. Inference, on the other hand, is due to the knowledge of *vyāpti* or universal relations among objects. It is by means of such universal principles that inference gives us a knowledge of objects beyond the reach of our senses. It extends our knowledge from the present to the past, distant and future. Ordinarily we perceive objects that are in actual contact with our senses, but we infer those that are not open to sense perception.[2] Perception usually excludes inference but not *vice versa.* What is perceived or directly known does not ordinarily require to be known indirectly by means of inference. Inference functions with regard to neither what is absolutely unknown nor what is definitely known. It relates to objects that are doubtful, *i.e.* objects which we have reasons to believe in, but which are not yet established facts. Hence inferences generally require confirmation by means or perception.[3]

3. The Constituents of Inference

Form the definition of inference (*anumāna*) it will appear that there must not be less than three propositions and more than there

---

1. NB., 1. 1. 5.
2. NV., 2. 1. 31.
3. *Agnerdṛṣṭatvena saṁdehasyānudayāt. Saṁdigdhaścārtho 'numīyate,* TB., p. 8.

terms in any inference. In inference we arrive at the knowledge of some unperceived character of a thing through the knowledge of some *liṅga* or sign in it and that of *vyāpti* or a universal relation between the sign and the inferred character. There is first the knowledge of what is called the *liṅga* or mark in relation to the *pakṣa* or the subject of inference. This is generally a perceptual judgment relating to the *liṅga* or middle term with the *pakṣa* or minor term of inference (*liṅgadarśana*), as when I see that the hill is smoky, and infer that it is fiery.[1] It is a proposition in which the *liṅga* is predicated of the *pakṣa* and thus corresponds to the minor premise of a syllogism. Secondly, inference requires the knowledge of *vyāpti* or a universal relation between the *liṅga* and the *sādhya*, or the middle and major terms. This knowledge of the *liṅga* or middle term as always related to the *sādhya* or major term is the result of our previous experience of their relation to each other. Hence it is a memory-judgment in which we think of the *liṅga* as invariably connected with the *sādhya* (*vyāptismaraṇa*), *e.g.* 'all smoky objects are fiery,' Thirdly, we have the inferential knowledge (*anumiti*) as resulting from the previous knowledge of the *liṅga* and that of its universal relation (*vyāpti*) with the *sādhya.* It is a proposition which relates the *pakṣa* or minor term with the *sādhya* or major term, *e.g.* 'the hill is fiery.' The inferential cognition (*anumiti*) is a proposition which follows from the first two propositions and so corresponds to the conclusion of the syllogism.[2]

Corresponding to the minor, major and middle terms of the syllogism, inference in Indian logic contains three terms, namely, *pakṣa, sādhya* and *hetu.* The *pakṣa* is the subject under consideration in the course of the inferential reasoning. Every inference proceeds with regard to some individual or class of individuals about which we wand to prove something. Hence the *pakṣa* is that individual or class about which we want to establish something or predicate an

1. It should be observed here that the first step of inference may be either the percpetion of the middle term or a proposition stating that the meddle term is related to something.
2. SM., 66-67; NM., p. 109.

attribute which is suspected but not definitely known to be present in it.[1] That which possesses the inferable character is called *pakṣa* or minor term of inference, *e.g.* ' the hill' when we want to prove that it is fiery. In relation to the *pakṣa* or minor term in any inference, a *sapakṣa* or positive instance is that which is decisively proved to be related to the inferable character, *e.g.* 'the hearth' in relation to 'the hill.'[2] Contrariwise, a *vipakṣa* or negative instance is that which is definitely known to be characterised by the absence of the inferable character, *e.g.* 'water' as marked by the absence of 'fire'[3]

While the *pakṣa* is the subject, the *sādhya* is the object of inference. It is that which we want to know or prove by means of any inference. The *sādhya* is that character of the *pakṣa* or minor term which is not perceived by us, but indicated by some sign present in it. In short, it is the inferable character of the minor term and thus corresponds roughly to the major term of the syllogism. It is that character which is predicated of the minor term in the resulting inferential knowledge or the conclusion of the syllogism.

With regard to the exact nature of the *sādhya* there is some difference of opinion among the different systems of Indian philosophy. According to the Advaita Vedānta, what is inferred is the unperceived character of the subject or minor term of inference. In the inferential knowledge that 'the hill is fiery,' it is 'the fire' that is inferred and not 'the hill' which is but perceived. The Buddhists contend that 'the fire' cannot be the object of inference from smoke. We know it just when we know the smoke as related to fire. So there remains nothing more to be inferred. Nor do we infer the relation between 'the fire' and 'the hill.' We cannot speak of a relation unless there are two things to be related. But in inference we have only one thing, namely, the hill, since the fire is not perceived. The hill being perceived cannot be said to be the object of inference. What is therefore inferred is 'the hill as

1. *Saṁdigdhasādhyavān pakṣaḥ*, TS., 44. *Cf. Nānupalabdhe na nirṇīte'rthe nyāyaḥ pravartate, kintu saṁśayite*, NB., 1. 1. 1.
2. *Niścitasādhyavān sapakṣaḥ*, TS., 44.
3. *Niścitasādhyābhāvavān vipakṣaḥ*, *ibid.*

possessed of fire.[1] The Mīmāṁsakas also hold that what we infer is the subject or minor term as related to the predicate or the major term.[2] The Naiyāyikas however maintain that the object of inference may be different in different cases. What is inferred may be either the subject or minor term as related to the major term, or the major term as related to the minor, or the middle term taken as a particular individual and related to the major term.[3] When we perceive smoke in a hill, what we know by inference is either 'the hill as related to fire,' or 'fire as related to the hill.' But when the site or the smoke cannot be perceived, what we infer is that the perceived individual smoke is to fire.[4]

The third term of inference is called the *liṅga* or sign because it serves to indicate that which we do not perceive. It is also called the *hetu* or *sādhana* in so far as it is the ground of our knowledge of the *sādhya* or what is inferred. Like the middle term of a syllogism, it must occur at least twice in the course of an inference. It is found once in relation to the *pakṣa* or minor term and then in relation to the *sādhya* or the major term. It is through a universal relation between the *hetu* and the *sādhya,* or the middle and major terms that the *pakṣā* or minor term, which is related to the middle, becomes connected with the *sādhya* or major term.[5] That is, the *pakṣa* is related to the *sādhya* through their common relation to the *hetu* or middle term. There are five characteristics of the middle term.[6] The first is *pakṣadharmatā,* or its being a character of the *pakṣa.* The middle term must be related to the minor term, *e.g.* hill is smoky (S is M). The second *sapakṣasattva* or its presence in all positive instances in which the major exists. The middle must be

1. *Pramāṇasamuccaya,* Chapter II. *Vide* also NVT., pp. 179-80.
2. *Tasmāt dharmaviśiṣṭasya dharmiṇaḥ syāt prameyatā, Ślokavārttika,* Chapter on Inference. *Agniviśiṣṭastu parvato.........anumeyaḥ*, SD., p. 63.
3. NB. and NV., 1. 1. 36.
4. *Vide* NVT., p. 182.
5. *Vyāptibalenārthagamakaṁ liṅgam*, TB., p. 7.
6. *Vide* NM., p. 110; 1. 2. 4.

distributively related to the major, *e.g.* all smoky objects are fiery (M is P). The third is *vipakṣāsattva*, or its absence in all negative instances in which the major is absent, *e.g.* whatever is not fiery is not smoky (No not-P is M). The fourth is *abādhitaviṣayatva*, or the uncontradictedness of its object. The middle term must not aim at establishing such absurd and contradictory objects as the coolness of fire or the squareness of a circle. The fifth character of the middle is *asatpratipakṣatva,* or the absence of counteracting reasons leading to a contradictory conclusion. These five characteristics, or at least four of them, must be found in the middle term of a valid inference. If not, there will be fallacies. We shall have to consider these points more fully later on.

Chapter XI

Grounds of Inference

1. The Logical Ground of *Vyāpti* or Universal Relation

In inference our knowledge of the *sādhya* or major term as related to the *pakṣa* or minor term depends on the knowledge of *vyāpti* between the middle and major terms. It is on the ground of *vyāpti* or a universal relation that the middle term leads to the knowledge of the inferred object (*vyāptibalenārthagamakaṁ liṅgam*). Every inference is thus logically dependent on the knowledge of *vyāpti*. Hence, the questions that we have to consider here are: (*i*) What is *vyāpti*? and (*ii*) how is it know?

With regard to the first question we have to say that *vyāpti* literally means the state of pervasion or permeation. It thus implies a correlation between two facts, of which one is pervaded (*vyāpya*) and the other pervades (*vyāpaka*). A fact is said to pervade another when it always accompanies the other. Contrariwise, a fact is said to be pervaded by another when it is always accompanied by the other. It follows from this that the *vyāpaka* or the pervader is preset in all the places in which the *vyāpya* or the pervaded is present. In this sense smoke is pervaded by fire, since all smoky objects are also fiery. But while all smoky objects are fiery, all fiery objects are not smoky, *e.g.* the red-hot iron ball. Similarly, all men are mortal, but all mortals are not men, *e.g.* birds and beasts. A *vyāpti* between terms of unequal extension, such as smoke and fire, men and mortals, is called *asamavyāpti* or *viṣamavyāpti*. It is a relation of non-equipollent concomitance between two terms, from one of which we may infer the other, but not *vice versa*. Thus, we may infer fire from smoke, but not smoke from fire. As distinguished from this, a *vyāpti* between two terms of equal extension is called *samavyāpti* or equipollent concomitance. Here the *vyāpti* holds between two terms which are coextensive so that we may infer either of them from the other. Thus there is a *samavyāpti* between cause and effect, substance and attribute. We may infer the cause from the effect, the substance from the attribute, or *vice versa.* Thus, whatever is produced is non-eternal, and whatever is non-eternal is produced.

It will appear from the above that *viṣamavyāpti* is a universal proposition, of which only the subject is distributed, *i.e.* taken in its entire extension. A *savyāpti,* on the other hand, is a universal proposition which distributes both the subject and the predicate. They would thus correspond respectively to the universal affirmative and universal negative propositions in Western logic. It is to be noted however that there are some universal affirmative propositions which distribute both their subject and predicate. Thus, 'whatever is produced is non-eternal,' 'men are rational animals' are cases of *samavyāpti* or universal affirmative propositions in which both the subject and the predicate are distributed.

For any inference the minimum condition is some kind of *vyāpti* between the middle and major terms. It does not matter whether the *vyāpti* is *sama* or *viṣama, i.e.* equipollent or non-equipollent. This satisfies the fundamental law of syllogistic inference that one of the premises must be universal. Now the *vyāpti* between the middle and major terms means generally a relation of coexistence (*sāhacarya*) between the two, *e.g.* wherever there is smoke there is fire.[1] Every case of coexistence, however, is not a case of *vyāpti.* Thus, all the children of a certain father may be dark. But this does not mean that there is *vyāpti* or a universal relation between a particular parentage and dark complexion. In many instances fire may coexist with smoke. Still there is no *vyāpti* or vniversal relation between fire and smoke, since there may be fire without smoke. The reason is that in such cases the relation of coexistence is dependent on certain conditions (*upādhi*) other than the terms related. Thus the darkness of complexion is determined by certain

1. *Yatra dhūmastatrāgniriti sāhacaryaniyamo vyāptiḥ*, TS., p. 45.

physiological conditions, and the presence of smoke in fire is conditioned by moisture in the fuel. Hence we are to say that *vyāpti* is that relation of coexistence between the middle and major terms which is independent of all conditions (*upādhi*).[1] It is an invariable and unconditional relation (*niyata anaupādhika sambandha*) of concomitance between the middle and major terms. This means that there is no exception to the relation of concomitance between the two, no exception to the relation of concomitance between the two, no instance in which the middle is present without the major. Hence, *vyāpti* as the logical condition of inference may be defined either positively or negatively. Positively speaking, *vyāpti* is the uniform existence of the middle term in the same locus with the major term such that the major term is not absent in any locus in which the middle term exists. In the terminology of the Navya Nyāya, *vyāpti* is such a relation coexistence between the middle and major terms that the major is not a counter-entity to any negation abiding in the middle, *i.e.* it is none of those things which are absent in the locus of the middle term.[2] *Vyāpti* has been negatively defined as the non-existence of the middle term in all the places in which the major term does not exist.[3] That there is *vyāpti* between the middle and major terms means that the middle (M) never is, if the major (P) is not. These two definitions of *vyāpti* give us two universal propositions, one positive and the other negative, *e.g.* 'all cases of smoke are cases of fire,' and 'no case of not-fire is case of smoke' (All M is P, and No not-P is M). This means that the *vyāpti* or universal proposition which is the ground of inference may be either affirmative (*anvaya*) or negative (*vyatireka*). Hence *vyāpti* is said to be of two kinds, namely, *anvaya* or affirmative and *vyatireka* or negative. While in *anvaya-vyāpti* or the universal affirmative proposition the middle term is *vyāpya* or subject and the major is *vyāpaka* or predicate, in *vyatireka-vyāpti* or the universal negative proposition the contradictory of the

1. *Vide* TB., pp. 7-8.

2. *Athavā hetumanniṣṭhavirahāpratiyoginā sādhyena hetoraikādhikaraṇyaṁ vyāptircuyate*, BP., 69. *Vide* also TC., II, p. 100. *Cf.* VP., Ch. II.

3. *Vyāptiḥ sādhyanadanyasminnasaṁbandhaḥ*, etc., BP., 68.

vyāpaka or predicate becomes *vyāpya* or subject and the contradictory of the *vyāpya* or subject becomes the *vyāpaka* or predicate.[1] Thus 'whatever is smoky is fiery,' or 'All M is P' is an *anvayavyāpti,* of which the corresponding *vyatireka-vyāpti* will be 'whatever is not-fiery is not-smokey,' or 'All not-P is not-M.' The logical ground of inference then is *vyāpti* in the sense of a universal proposition which may be either affirmative of negative.

So much the definitions of *vyāpti*[2] or the universal relation between the middle and major terms of inference. The next question is: How is *vyāpti* known? How do we pass from particular cases of the relation between smoke and fire to the univerral proposition 'all cases of smoke are cases of fire'? This is the problem of induction, which is not separately treated in Indian logic, but is made a part of the general theory of inference. Indian systems of philosophy take inference as a process of reasoning which is not only formally valid but also materially true. Hence, in an inference of any kind the question arises: How do we get the universal proposition *(vyāpti),* on which inference depends?

The Cārvākas, who are radical empiricists, contend that all knowledge is limited to particulars. We cannot pass from the knowledge of particular cases of the relation between two objects to that of all possible cases. There is no successful method of generalisation from particulars. Perception, which is the only source of human knowledge, does not help us to establish a universal proposition. It is limited to present facts and cannot tell us anything about the past, distant and future. Hence, from perception we know what is true of a thing or a limited number of things. That is, perception gives us particular, but no universal propositions. If perception cannot give us a knowledge of *vyāpti* or universal

---

1. *Vide* TB., p. 9.
2. Gaṅgeśa in his *Tattvacintāmaṇi* discusses at length the definitions of *vyāpti,* numbering twenty in all. Of these he rejects all but one as either too wide or too narrow or otherwise objectionable. The last definition of *vyāpti,* accepted by him as valid, has been noted above, along with another to cover both the cases of *anvaya* and *vyatireka vyāpti* or the universal affirmative and the universal negative proposition.

proposition, inference and the other alleged sources of knowledge certainly cannot do so. All sources of knowledge except perception depend on *vyāpti* or a universal relation between two things and cannot, therefore, be made the ground of our knowledge of it. To take them as such is to reason in a vicious circle.[1]

The Buddhists meet the Cārvāka contention in two ways. First, they point out that Cārvākas' refutation of inference is itself a process of reasoning which, on their own admission, depends on some kind of *vyāpti*. As such, it practically amounts to a refutation of their own position, namely, that no process of reasoning including inference is valid. As a matter of fact, the Cārvākas employ the method of inference more than once in their philosophy. For example, it is by means of inference that they can know that other people differ form them with regard to the question of inference, or that other sources of knowledge are as fallacious as inference, or that God, soul, etc., do not exist because they are not perceived.[2]

Next the Buddhists proceed to show how *vyāpti* or a universal proposition may be based on the principles of causality and essential identity (*tādātmya* and *tadutpatti*).[3] When two things are related as cause and effect, they are always and everywhere related to each other. There can be no exception to their relation, since the cause cannot be separated from its effect, nor the effect from its cause. To say that there is no necessary relation between the cause and the effect, or that there may be an effect without its cause is not admissible, because such a hypothesis involves self-contradiction and makes life impossible. Hence we are to take the law of causality as a universal law. To determine whether the relation between two objects is causal or not, we are to apply the test of *pañcakāraṇī*. According to it, there are five steps in the determination of a causal relation. First, the effect is not perceived before it is produced. This means that the effect is an event which appears after another phenomenon that is its cause. The causal phenomenon is thus

1. *Vide Sarvadarśanasaṁgraha*, Chapter I.
2. *Op. cit.*, Ch. II.
3. *Op. cit.*, Ch. II; *Nyāyabindu*, Ch. II.

antecedent to the effect phenomenon. Secondly, the cause is perceived, *i.e.* there is a change in the existing order of things. Thirdly, the effect phenomenon appears in immediate succession. Fourthly, the cause is made to disappear. Fifthly, the effect disappears in immediate succession.[1] The Buddhist method of determining the causal relation corresponds to Mill's method of difference in its double application. If, all other conditions remaining the same, the appearance of one phenomenon is immediately followed by that of another, and its disappearance is immediately followed by that of another, and its disappearance is immediately followed by the disappearance of the other, then the two are related as cause and effect. When once we know them to be related as cause and effect, we may very well take them as universally related. Similarly, the principle of essential identity (*tādātmya*) is another ground on which we may base a universal proposition. A thing is always related to what is identical with it. Identity does not mean a mere repetition of the same thing, *e.g.* 'A is A.' Nor can there be any identity between things that are absolutely different, *e.g.* a horse and a cow. By identity we mean the relation between two different things that coexist in the same locus (*sāmānādhikaraṇyam*). Thus, there is identity between the genus and the species coming under it, or the class and the individuals included in it. A *śiṁspā* is identical with a tree, in so far as the two refer to the same object. From this we know that all *śiṁśapās* are trees, since *śiṁśapās* will cease to be *śiṁśapās*, if they are not trees.[2] Thus, *vyāpti* or a universal proposition is to be based on the necessary principles of causality and identity. Experience, or observation and non-observation cannot be the sure ground of generalisation. Empirical knowledge, however well founded, can never be necessary and universal, There is an element of doubt and uncertainty in all emirical generalisations. Causality and identity being the presuppositions of all experience are

---

1. *Kāryasyotpatteḥ prāganupalaṁbhaḥ* etc., *Sarvadarśanasaṁgraha,* Ch. II.

2. *Sarvadarśanasaṁgraha* and *Nyāyabindu, ibid.* The word *śiṁśapā* occurring in these texts means a kind of tree which is also *śiśu.*

necessary and universal truths, to which all sense experience must conform. Hence any generalisation based on either of these two principles is universally valid and not open to any doubt.

That Naiyāyikas criticise and reject the Bauddha method of ascertaining *vyāpti* on the following grounds. According to the Buddhists, *vyāpti* or a universal relation between the middle and major terms is to be deduced from the relation of causality or identity between the two. This, however, is not true. There are many cases of *vyāpti* or universal relation which is independent of the motions of causality and identity. Thus there is a universal tradition of succession between day and night, or between the different seasons, or between sunset and the appearance of stars. Similarly, we find a universal relation of coexsistence between a certain substance and it attributes, or between a certain colour and a certain taste. Here we have *vyāpti* or a universal relation between terms which are neither cause and effect nor identical with one another, but from one of which we can validly infer the other. Further, the relation of identity between two things can hardly be treated as a ground of inference from the one to the other. If the two things be identical, then both must be equally perceived or inferred. The tree being identical with the *śiṁśapā* must be perceived just when we perceive the latter, and so need not be inferred. For the same season, if we infer the tree from the *śiṁśapā* and say "all *śiṁśapās* are trees," we should be able to infer the *śiṁśapā* from the tere and say "all trees are *śiṁśapās*." The two things being identical, we should be able to infer either of them from the other. Nor again does the abstract principle of causality help us to draw inferences in particular cases. Granting that there is a universal and an unconditional relation between the cause and effect, it is extremely difficult for us to determine whether the relation between two particular things is causal or not. The test of *pañcakāraṇī* recommended by the Buddhist is not an absolute guarantee for there being a causal relation between two things. That test applies when all the conditions of a certain relation remain the same. But it is only with regard to the known or the perceptible conditions that we may be sure whether they remain the same or not. With regard to the imperceptible conditions we cannot be absolutely certain that no change in these corresponds to a change in the relation between two things. Thus in the relation of fire to smoke it is just possible that an invisible agent (*piśāca*) always intervenes between the two and produces the smoke. Moreover, thee is such a thing as a "plurality of causes," which makes it hazardous to infer any particular cause for any single effect. Thus we may admit that fire is the cause of smoke in a particular case, and yet say that it is not a cause in other cases, or that there are other causes producing smoke in other instances. Hence it is not always safe to infer a particular cause from an effect as such.[1]

According to the Vedānta,[2] *vyāpti* or a universal proposition is the result of an induction by simple enumeration. It rests on the uncontradicted experience of agreement in presence between two things. When we find that two things go together and that there is no exception to their relation, we may take them as universally related. The Nyāya agrees with the Vedānta in holding that *vyāpti* is established by means of uncontradicted experience of the relation between two things. It is based, not on any a *priori* principle like causality or identity, but on the uniform experience of concomitance between two objects. The Nyāya, however, goes further than the Vedānta and supplements the uncontradicted observation of agreement in presence by that of agreement in absence and *tarka* or indirect proof.[3] The Nyāya method of induction or generalisation may be analysed into the following steps. First we observe that there is a uniform agreement in presence (*anvaya*) between two things, or that in all the cases in which one is present the other also is present. Secondly, we see that there is uniform agreement in absence (*vyatireka*) between them, *i.e.* in every case in which the one is absent, the other also is absent. So far we see that the two things go together both in their presence and absence, or that there

1. NVT., pp. 158-64; NM., pp. 113-127
2. VP., Ch. II.
3. *Vyabhicarasyāgraho'tha sachacāragrahastathā heturvyāptigrahe tarkaḥ kvacicchaṅkānivartakaḥ*, BP., 137.

is positive and negative conincidence between them (*sahcāra*). Thirdly, we do not observe any contrary instance in which one of them is present without the other (*vyabhicārāgraha*). From this we conclude that there must be a natural relation of invariable concomitance between the two things.[1]

Still, we are not sure if their relation is dependent on any condition (*upādhi*) or not. *Vyāpti* or a universal relation between two things is that relation of concomitance between them which is independent of all *upādhis* or conditions. An *upādhi* or condition is a term which is coextensive with the major but not with the middle term of an inference.[2] Thus, when one infers the existence of smoke from fire, he relies on a conditional relation between fire and smoke, since fire is attended with smoke on condition that it is fire from 'wet fuel.' It will be seen here that the condition of 'wet fuel' is always related to the major term 'smoke,' but not so related to middle term 'fire,' as there are cases of fire without 'wet fuel.' Hence to make sure that a certain of uniform concomitance between two things is a *vyāpti* or a universal relation, we must eliminate all conditions. This can be done by repeated observation (*bhūyodarśana*) of their agreement in presence and absence under varying circumstances. Here if we see that there is no material circumstance which is present or absent just when the major term is present or absent, we are to understand that its conconitance with the middle term is unconditional. In this way we can exclude all the suspected conditions of a relation of concomitance between the middle and major terms and say that it is a relation of *vyāpti* or unconditional concomitance.[3] If even after repeated observation we have any doubt as to there being *vyāpti* or a universal relation between the middle and major terms, we are to have recourse to *tarka* or indirect proof to end such doubt. Thus, the universal proposition, 'all cases of smoke are cases of fire,' may be proved

1. SM., 137.
2. *Avyāptasādhano yaḥ sādhyasamvyāptirucyate sa upādhiriti*, *Sarva-darśanasaṁgraha*, Chapter I. *Vide* also BP., 138.
3. *Vide* TB., pp. 7-8.

indirectly by disproving its contradictory. If this universal proposition be false, then its contradictory, 'some cases of smoke are not cases of fire,' must be true. This means that there may be smoke without fire. But the supposition of smoke without fire is contradicted by the known relation of causality between fire and smoke. To say that there may be smoke without fire is to say that there may be an effect without its cause, which is absurd. If any one has the obstinacy to say that sometimes there may be effects without causes, he must be silenced by the practical contradictions (*vyāghāta*) involved in the supposition. If there can be an effect without a cause, what should he constantly seek for fire to produce smoke or for food to alleviate his hunger? Thus its contradictory being proved to be false, the universal proposition 'all cases of smoke are cases of fire' comes out as true, *i.e.* there is *vyāpti* or a universal relation between smoke and fire.[1]

So far the Naiyāyikas try to establish *vyāpti* or a universal proposition by the method of simple enumeration supported by *tarka* or a hypothetical reasoning which indirectly proves its *tarka* or a hypothetical reasoning which indirectly proves its validity. By examining a number of positive and negative instances of agreement in presence and absence between two things, they conclude that there is a universal relation between them. This conclusion is then indirectly confirmed by showing that a denial of the universal relation between these two things leads to contradictions. But as we have already seen in connection with their theory of *sāmānyalakṣaṇa* perception, a general proposition like 'all smoky object are fiery' cannot be logically proved by "Induction by Simple Enumeration." In simple enumeration we pass from *some* observed cases of the relation between two things to a statement about their relation in *all* cases. Thus, from some observed cases of the relation between smoke and fire we infer that all smokes are related to fire. But this inference is not valid, since it viloates the general rule of inference that we must not go beyond the evidence. The method of simple enumeration cannot, therefore, conclusively establish *vyāpti*

1. *Vide* SM., 137; TC., II, pp. 210-12.

or a universal proposition. Hence the question is: How from the observation of some smokes as related to fire do we know that all smokes are related to fire? The Naiyāyikas explain this by the help of *sāmānyalakṣaṇa* perception. The universal proposition 'all smokes are related to fire' cannot be explained by the perception of particular instances of smokes as related to fire, for any number of particulars cannot make up the universal. For this we require a perception of the whole class of smokes as related to fire. We have such a perception through the perception of the universal 'smokeness' as related to fireness.' In perceiving particular smokes we perceive the universal 'smokeness' inhering in them. But to perceive 'smokeness' is to perceive, in a non-sensuous way, all smokes so far as they possess the universal 'smokeness.' Hence the universal proposition 'all smoky objects are fiery' is given by a non-sensuous perception of all smokes as related to fire through the perception of smokeness as related of fireness.[1]

The Nyāya method of establishing *vyāpti* brings out the importance of class-essences or universals for induction. It shows how the validity of a generalisation from the particulars of experience depends ultimately on the discovery of certain common essences or universal characters of particular things. From the observation of a limited number of instances of the relation between two things we cannot know anything for certain about all possible instances of them unless we find that the things possess a certain essential nature which is the basis of their relation in some cases. The particular objects of experience lend themselves to a generalisation when they are recognised as instances of a class and possessed of some essential common nature. A number of things are arranged in one class in view of such common essence or universal which is present in all the members of that class, but absent in those of a different class. Hence if in some cases we see

1. *Sāmānyalakṣaṇāṁ vinā dhūmatvena sakaladhūmānāṁ vahnitvena sakalavahnīnāṁ ca bhānaṁ kathaṁ bhavet tadarthaṁ sāmānyalakṣaṇā svīkriyate,* etc., SM., 65. *Vyāptigrahaśca sāmānyalakṣaṇāpratyāsattyā sakaladhūmādiviṣayakaḥ,* etc., TC., II, pp. 153-54.

that something is related to the essential nature or the universal underlying a class, we know that it is related to all the members of that class. The observation of particular instances is important because it helps us to find the universals underlying different classes of things and their relations with one another. Hence, the problem of induction is the problem of the discovery of class-essences or universals exemplified in particular things. As we have already remarked, some Western logicians are slowly recognising the truth of the Nyāya view that an inductive generalisation must be based on the knowledge of class-essences or universals embodied in particular things. But they do not go so far as to say with the Naiyāyikas that an empirical generalisation from particular instances is a matter of non-sensuous intuition based on the perception of universals. They would generally treat it as an inference from known resemblance or as a perfect analogy. Mr. Eaton, however, goes further and maintains that the first step in induction is a direct perception of the universal in the particular. He says: "Induction proceeds from the particular to the general, but not from the sheer particular. The particular must be seen to embody some characters or relations, to exemplify some form. Given a particular, let us say a blinding streak of light, and another particular, a loud crash following immediately after, we must be able to characterise these occurrences and frame a generalization 'lightning is followed by thunder,' in order that induction may have a beginning. The most primitive of all inductive steps can be described as the direct perception of the universal in the particular. A generalization *relevant* to particulars must be framed if it is to be tested, and this primary relevance of a generalization to particulars cannot be manufactured from particulars as mere *thises* and *thats*. There is no process by which this relevance can be inferred. It can only be directly apperhended."[1] To this first stage of the inductive procedure, Mr. Eaton adds a second, in which isolated generalisations are made more probable by the elimination of irrelevance and by fresh evidence, and a third, in which generalisations reinforce one another by entering into logically

1. R. M. Eaton, *General Logic*, p. 496.

organised systems.[1] It is to be observed, however, that a generalisation is framed at the very first stage, and that the second and third stages only help us to test and confirm it. Hence so far as the knowledge of the general proposition is concerned, we are to say that it is given to us by way of a direct perception of the universal in the particular.

2. The Question of *Petitio Principii* in Inference

As we have already seen, every inference involves the knowledge of *vyāpti* or a universal relation between the major and the middle term. Without a universal relation between the two, no valid conclusion can be drawn from the premises. It is only when we know that smoke is universally related to fire that we can conclusively prove the existence of fire in a hill in which we see smoke. Otherwise, the inference will be inconclusive and invalid. On the other hand, it would seem that if we know smoke to be universally related to fire, we already know the smoke in the hill to be related to fire. The truth of the universal proposition 'all cases of smoke are cases of fire' involves, may, depends on the truth of the proposition 'this case of smoke is a case of fire.' Thus it would seem that the major premise of an inference, which is a universal proposition, assumes what we want to prove in the conclusion, *i.e.* an inference involves the fallacy of *petitio principii* or begging the question.

The above dilemma of inference has been anticipated and solved in Indian philosophy. The solution is generally based on the distinction between the knowledge of the universal and that of the particulars coming under it. When we know that smoke is always related to fire, we know them in their general character as two universals. This does not imply that we know the relation between all particular smokes and fires. Thus the Mīmāṁsakas[2] argue that the knowledge of *vyāpti* or a universal relation between smoke

1. *Op. cit.*, p. 501.
2. *Vide* SD., pp. 62-63.

and fire does not necessarily involve any knowledge of a particular instance of fire, *e.g.* the fire in a hill. When we know the universal proposition 'all cases of smoke are cases of fire,' we do not know anything about the hill, far less, about its relation to fire. If that were not so, or, if we knew anything about the fire in the hill, there could be no necessity for the perception of smoke in the hill, in order to know the existence of the fire in it. Hence, it follows that the conclusion of the inference, namely, 'that hill is fiery,' is a new knowledge which is not involved in the knowledge of its premises. The Naiyāyika view of *vyāpti* as covering all the individual cases of a relation seems to commit inference to the fallacy of *petitio principii.* Thus, it has been held by the Naiyāyika that when we know the *vyāpti* or the universal relation between smoke and fire, we know all the individual cases of smoke to be related to fire. Otherwise, we cannot account for the inference of fire from the smoke in hill. If we do not know that the hill-smoke is related to fire, we couldn't possibly pass from the one to the other. But then the difficulty is that if we already know the hill-smoke to be related to fire, there is no room for an inference to arrive at a new truth. The conclusion of such an inference will only repeat what is already stated in the premises. This difficulty in the Nyāya view of inference may however be explained. According to the Naiyāyika, to know that smoke is universally related to fire is indeed to know that 'all cases of smoke are cases of fire.' But the knowledge we have of all fires and smokes is mediated by the knowledge of the universals 'fireness' and 'smokeness' (*sāmānyalakṣaṇāpratyāsatti*). This means that we know all fires and smokes in so far as they participate in 'fireness' and 'smokeness,' *i.e.* in their general character without any reference to their specific characters. So, while the *vyāpti* gives us a knowledge of the relation between smoke and fire in general, an inference based on it gives us the knowledge of the relation of fire to a particular object, namely, the smoky hill. The major premise of the inference 'all cases of smoke are cases of fire' does not by itself lead to the conclusion that there is fire in the hill. It is only when the major premise is combined with the minor,' there is smoke in the hill,' that we draw the conclusion 'there is fire in the hill.' This shows that the truth of the conclusion is not epistemically involved in that of the major premise or the universal proposition. Hence, we are to conclude that inference is neither inconclusive nor a *petitio principii,* since it gives us a new knowledge.[1]

3. The Psychological Ground of Inference *(Pakṣatā)*

Just as inference depends on the knowledge of *vyāpti* or a universal relation between the middle and major terms, so it depend on the relation of the middle term with the minor term.[2] In inference the minor term becomes related to the major through its relation to the middle term. Every inference proceeds with regard to some object about which we want to establish something on the ground of *vyāpti* or a universal proposition. Hence, the minor term is as much necessary for inference as the middle term. The minor term being called *pakṣa* in Indian logic, *pakṣatā* is treated as a necessary condition of inference. If there is to be any inference, there must be a *pakṣa* or a minor term. Hence the question is: Under what conditions do we get the minor term of an inference? Or, under what conditions do we draw inference with regard to anything? While the validity of inference depends on *vyāpti,* its possibility depends on *pakṣatā*. Inference takes place when there is a *pakṣa* or subject of inference, it becomes valid when based on *vyāpti* or a universal relation between the middle and the major term. Hence while *vyāpti* is the logical ground of inference, *pakṣatā* is its psychological ground or condition.

From the fact that the minor term is an object about which we *want to infer* something, it will appear that the two obvious conditions of a minor term are the absence of certainty about something (*siddhyabhāva*) and the will to infer it (*siṣādhayiṣā*). The old Naiyāyikas[3] and the Vedāntists[4] accept both of these

1. TB., p. 11; TC., II, pp. 290-91.
2. *Anumānasya dve aṅge vyāptiḥ pakṣadharmatā ca*, etc., TB., p. 11. *Vyāpyasya parvatādivṛttitvaṁ pakṣadharmatā*, TS., p. 46.
3. *Na nirṇīte'rthe nyāyaḥ pravartate kintu saṁśayite*, NB., 1. 1. 1. *Saṁdigdhasādhyadharmā dharmī pakṣaḥ*, TB., p. 11.
4. *Pakṣatvam tu sādhyasaṁdehavattvam sādhyagocarasādhakamānābhāvavattvam vā, Advaitasiddhi,* p. 29.

conditions when they say that *pakṣatā* consists in the presence of doubt about the *sādhya* or the major term (*sādhyasaṁdeha*). We have a *pakṣa* or a minor term when we are in doubt whether a certain subject is related to the *sādhya* or the major term. Now doubt implies not only the absence of certain knowledge about something but also a positive desire or will to know it. Hence doubt as a condition of inference involves both the absence of certainty about something and the desire to have certain knowledge about that thing.

The modern Naiyāyikas take exception to the above view of *pakṣatā*. According to them, neither the absence of certainty nor the will to infer is a necessary condition of inference. There may be inference even in the presence of certainty. A logician may, if he so will, infer the existence of an elephant from its trumpeting voice even when he has perceived it and so acquired certain knowledge about it. Or, a man may infer the existence of the self even when he has acquired certain knowledge about it from the scriptures. Again, there may be inference even when there is no will to infer, as when one involuntarily infers the existence of clouds from the roar of thunder. This case shows also that the presence of doubt is not an essential condition of inference, since there is in it no previous doubt as to the existence of clouds in the sky. Thus, we see that inference takes place under the following conditions: (*a*) when there are absence of certainty and presence of the will to infer; (*b*) when there is absence of both certainty and the will to infer: (*c*) when there is presence of both certainty and the will to infer. But no inference takes place when thee are presence of certainty and absence of the will to infer. Hence to combine the first three cases and exclude only the last, we are to say that inference takes place in all cases exception that in which thee are presence of certainty and absence of the will to infer. This is expressed by the modern Naiyāyikas by saying that *pakṣatā* consists in the absence of that condition in which there are the presence of certainty and absence of the will to infer.[1]

---

1. *Siṣādhayiṣāviraha-viśiṣṭasiddhyabhāvaḥ pakṣatā. Yatra siddhirnāsti tatra siṣādhayiṣāyām satyāmasatyāmapi pakṣatā. Yatra siṣādhayiṣāsti*

The conditions of valid inference have of late been discussed by some Western logicians. All of them, however do not sufficiently realise the importance of the psychological condition of inference, which Indian logicans discuss so thoroughly under the theory of *pakṣatā.* Russell seems to think that all that is necessary for inference is the logical condition of a relation of implication between propositions. According to him, the psychological element, namely, our *knowledge* or the propositions and their relation, is not a necessary condition of inference. Thus he says: 'It is plain that where we validly infer one proposition from another, we do so in virtue of a relation which holds between the two propositions whether we perceive it or not: the mind, in fact, is as purely receptive in inference as common sense supposes it to be in perception or sensible objects.'[1] Some other Western logicians like Mr. Johnson and Dr. Stebbing[2] have recognised the importance of both the logical and psychological conditions of inference. According to them, there are two kinds of conditions for any valid inference. The first kind of conditions refers to the propositions and the relations that hold between them. These conditions are said to be independent of the thinker and are called by Mr. Johnson the "constitutive conditions." In order that the proposition *q* may be formally inferred from *p*, it is necessary that *p* should logically imply *q* and also that *p* should be true. The other kind of conditions refers to the relation of the propositions to what the thinker may happen to *know.* Since in inference a thinker passes from something *known* to something *inferred,* it follows that the propositions and their relations must be known by us. It follows also that what is *inferred* must not be already known as true or false. In order that *q* may e validly inferred from *p,* it is necessary that *p* must be known to be true, and also that *p* must be known to imply *q* without its being known that *q* is true. These conditions are dependent upon the relation of the thinker

---

tatra siddhau satyāmasatyāmapi pakṣatā. Yatra siddhirasti siṣādhayiṣā ca nāsti tatra na pakṣatā, etc., SM., pp. 309-10. *Vide* also TM., Ch. II; TC. II, pp. 407-32.

1. Russell, *Principles of Mathematics*, p. 33.
2. Stebbing, *A Modern Introduction to Logic*, pp. 215-16.

to the involved in inference, and are called "the epistemic conditions" of inference.

It would appear from the above that there is a consensus of opinion among logicians, both Indian and Western, that a valid inference must satisfy at least two conditions, namely, that there must be a true proposition and that it must imply another proposition. There is, however, some difference of opinion among them as to how these conditions conditions inference. While a realist like Russell seems to think that they condition inference even when they are not known, Indian logicians maintain that they can condition inference only when they are known by us. According to them, while perception may be said to be conditioned, by the *existence* of the sense organs, inference is conditionea not by the mere fact, but by the *knowledge* of something as a sign and that of its invariable relation to something else, although the reality of these things and their relation is independent of our mind.[1] These two views seem to be reconciled by Mr. Johnson who holds that for inference there must not only be a true proposition and a relation of implication between propositions, but that these must be known by the thinker who is inferring.

With regard to what we have called the psychological conditions of inference, there is a sharp difference of opinion among logicians. The question here is: Under what conditions does inference take place? The answer given to this question by the old Naiyāyikas and the Vedāntins is that inference takes place when there is a doubt about what is to be inferred. This is perhaps the most plausible view that would be readily accepted by common sense. No man takes the trouble to infer or prove anything unless he is in doubt about it. This view, however, is contradicted by the inference of clouds from the sudden roar of thunder, since it is not preceded by any doubt in the mind of the thinker who infers.

But then it may be said that want of certainty, if not a positive state of doubt, is the essential condition of inference. In the

---

1. *Sā (vyāptiḥ) ca sattayā cakṣurādivannāṅgabhāvaṁ bhajate kintu jñātatayā*, *Sarvadarśanasaṁgraha*, Ch. I. *Cf.* also BP., 66; VP., Ch. II.

Advaitasiddhi this view is accepted as an alternative to the first given above, when it says that *pakṣatā* consists in the absence of proof relating to what is to be inferred.[1] Among Western logicians, Dr. Stebbing also supports this view when she says: "Since inference is a process in which a thinker passes from something known to something *inferred,* it is clear that we would not say we had *inferred* *q* if we had already asserted *q*. It is, therefore, obvious that *q* must not be *known* to be true, and equally obvious that *q* must not be *known* to be false."[2] There is a strong presumption in favour of this view. Inference as a source of knowledge aims at giving us certain knowledge about things. So, it is obvious that if we want to know anything by inference, it is because we lack certain knowledge about it.

Now, let us consider if the second view can explain all the cases of inference mentioned by the modern Naiyāyikas. There seems to be no difficulty so far as the first two cases are concerned. In the first case (*a*), we have inference when there is the absence of certainty together with the will to infer, *e.g.* the inference of future rain from the appearance of dark clouds in the sky. In the second case (*b*), we have inference when there is the absence of both certainty and the will to infer, *e.g.* the inference of clouds from the roar of thunder. While there is the absence of certainty in both these cases, the will to infer is absent in the second. This seems to suggest that the absence of certainty is the essential condition, and the will to infer only an accidental condition of inference. But when we come to the third case, we are confronted by an exception to the rule that every inference is conditioned by the absence of certainty. Thus, in case (*c*), we have inference when there is certainty together with the will to infer. If this be so, we have to reject the view that the absence of certainty is an essential condition of inference and recognise the importance of the will to infer as a condition of inference. But the question is: Is there really any case in which inference takes place in spite of certainty and in virtue of

1. *Sādhyagocarasādhakamānābhāvavattvam vā*, *Advaitasiddhi*, p. 29.
2. *A Modern Introduction to Logic*, p. 215.

the will to infer? The examples cited by the Naiyāyikas are rather doubtful cases. Thus, it may be said that if a logician infers the existence of an elephant perceived by him, it must be because he has some doubt, however slight, about the truth of his perception. Similarly, we may say that when a person infers the existence of the self known by him through the scriptures, it must be because he is not absolutely sure of the truth of his scriptural knowledge. But there are certain cases of inference which may be taken as crucial instances. The path described by a falling body may be deduced by a physicist from certain laws of motion, even when he sees it and has no doubt about the reality of what he sees. We might prove, to a person who doubted the correctness of our memory, that it rained yesterday, by pointing to other facts with which rain is necessarily connected.' A lawyer may produce evidences to prove a case of which he has a personal knowledge. Some theorems of Geometry prove what is otherwise obvious or clearly perceived. At least, the geometrician who proves them has no doubt about their truth. It is true that in some of these cases there is some doubt in the mind of the person or persons for whom these inference are made. But we must frankly admit that there is no doubt in the mind of the person who makes the inference. It cannot be said that the presence of doubt in one mind conditions the process of inference occurring in a different mind. Hence, we are to admit that there may be inference in the face of certainty, only if we have the will to infer. It may, of course, he asked here: What does the will to infer aim at in such a case? To this we reply that it aims at demonstrating a known fact by showing its necessary connection with other facts. It cannot be said that the demonstrative knowledge of the fact being absent before, the inference of certainty. So, far as the knowledge of the fact is concerned, its demonstration adds nothing to the certainty with which it was otherwise known before. Nor can we say that what the demonstrative inference proves is not that there is such-and-such a fact, but that such-and-such a fact *follows from* certain other facts. That a fact follows from other facts is no part of the conclusion of an inference, but a part of its grounds or premises. Hence, we are to say that the conclusion of the demonstrative inference states the same fact that was previously known by perception or memory, only it arrives at the fact by way of inference. And, as prof. Creighton says: "It is not necessary for inference that the conclusion reached should be a fact which was not hitherto known,"[1] So, we conclude that the modern Naiyāyikas are justified when they emphasise the function of will in inference, and define *pakṣatā* as the absence of the condition in which there is certainty, but no will to infer.

4. *Liṅgaparāmarśa* as the Immediate Cause of Inference

As we have already seen, every inference must involve at least three steps. There is first the knowledge of the middle term as related to the minor term (*liṅgajñāna*). Secondly, there is the knowledge of an universal relation between the middle and the major terms (*vyāptijñāna*). Lastly, there is the conclusion, in which the major term is predicated of the minor term. The conclusion is the result of inference as a process of reasoning. Now the question is: What is the special cause (*karaṇa*) that brings about the conclusion? It is the knowledge of the *liṅga* or the middle term? Or, is it the knowledge of *vyāpti* or the universal relation between the middle and major terms?

According to the older logicians, including the Buddhists, the Jainas and same Naiyāyikas, it is the knowledge of the *linga* or the middle term that leads to the conclusion.[2] Hence the middle term, known as such, is to be taken as the *karaṇa* or operative cause of inference. For the Mīmāṁsakas and Vedāntists, the knowledge of *vyāpti* or the universal relation between the middle and major terms is the *karaṇa* or special cause of inference. The knowledge of *vyāpti* is revived in our mind when we see the *liṅga* or the middle term as related to the *pakṣa* or the minor term, and this leads to the conclusion. On this view an inference will include the following steps: (1) the knowledge of *vyāpti* or the universal relation between

1. *An Introductory Logic*, p. 432.
2. *Vide* SM., p. 286.

the middle and major terms, *e.g.* all cases of smoke are cases of fire; (2) the perception of the minor term as qualified by the middle term, *e.g.* the hill is a case of smoke; (3) a revival of the impression of *vyāpti* previously acquired, without any necessary recollection of it; and (4) the conclusion that the minor term is related to the major term, *e.g.* the hill is a case of fire.[1]

According to the modern Naiyāyika, the *liṅga* or the middle term cannot be the *karaṇa* or operative cause of inference. The middle term may be a thing of the present or the past or the future. But it cannot function in an inference when past or future. The middle term cannot lead to the conclusion except through the knowledge of *vyāpti* or the universal relation between it and the major term. Hence the knowledge of *vyāpti* or the universal relation between the middle and major terms should be taken as the special cause (*karaṇa*) of inference. But the knowledge of *vyāpti* does not immediately lead to the conclusion. It has for its function (*vyāpāra*) a synthetic view of the middle term as related to the major, on the one hand, and the minor, on the other (*liṅgaparāmarśa*).[2] This is called *tṛtīyaliṅgaparāmarśa, i.e.* a consideration of the middle term for the third time. The middle term, *e.g.* smoke, is known first when we acquire the knowledge of its invariable relation with the major term 'fire' in the kitchen, etc. It is known for the second time in relation to the minor term, *e.g.* the hill. It is considered for the third time when we know it as that character of the minor term which is universally related to the major, as when we say 'the hill is possessed of such smoke as is always related to fire.'[3] It is through

1. *Vide Siddhāntamuktāvalī* with *Dinakarī*, pp. 288-89. *Cf. Vedānta-Paribhāṣā*, Chapter. II: *"evem ca 'ayaṁ dhūmavān' iti pakṣadharma-tājñāne 'dhūmo vahnivyāpya' ityanubhavāhitasaṁskārodbodhe ca sati 'vahnimān' ityanumitirbhavati, na tu madhye vyāptismaraṇaṁ tajjanyaṁ 'vahnivyā-pyadhūmavānayam' ityādi viśeṣaṇaviśiṣṭajñānam........"*
2. *Vyāpārastu parāmarśaḥ karaṇaṁ vyāptidhīr bhavet*, etc., BP. and SM., 66-67.
3. *Mahānasādau dṛṣṭāne...dhūmajñānaṁ prathamam, tataḥ parvatādau dhūmaṁ dṛṣṭvā vyāpyatvena tatsmaraṇaṁ dvitīyaṁ, tatastatraiva vyāpyatvena dhūmasya parāmarśvahnivyāpyadhūmavāna yamityevaṁrūpo jāyata iti tṛtīyatvam, Tarkakaumudī*, p. 10.

such *liṅgaparāmarśa* or knowledge of the middle term as universally related to the major and as characterising the minor, that the knowledge of *vyāpti leads* to the conclusion. Hence while the knowledge of *vyāpti* is the special cause (*karaṇa*) of inference, *liṅgaparāmarśā* is the immediate cause (*caramakāraṇa*) of the conclusion.[1] Some modern Naiyāyikas go further and say that *liṅgaparāmarśa* itself is the operative cause (*karaṇa*) of inference.[2] On this analysis inference involves the following steps: (1) the knowledge of *vyāpti* or the universal relation between the middle and major terms, *e.g.* all cases of fire; (2) the perception of the minor term as related to the middle, *e.g.* the hill is a case of smoke; (3) a recollection of the *vyāpti* between the middle and major terms; (4) a contemplation of the middle as correlating the major and minor terms, *e.g.* the hill is a case of smoke pervaded by fire; (5) the conclusion relating the minor term with the major, *e.g.* the hill is a case of fire.[3]

As it has been pointed out by Dr. D.M. Datta, the Nyāya view of *liṅgaparāmarśa* as the immediate antecedent of the conclusion agrees with Bradley's analysis of inference.[4] According to Bradley, an inference is always an ideal construction resulting in the perception of a new condition. The premises of inference are the data, and the process of inference consists in joining them into a whole by an ideal construction. "We must fasten them together, so that they cease to be several and are one construction, one individual whole. Thus instead of A-B, B-C we must have A-B-C." Take for example the inference: 'Man is mortal and Caesar is a man and therefore Caesar is mortal. In this inference "there is first a

1. *Vide* TC., II, pp. 521-51.
2. Vide *Tarkasaṁgraha*, p. 50.
3. *Yena puruṣeṇa mahānasādau dhūme vahnivyāptirgṛhītā paścāt sa eva puruṣaḥ kvacitparvatādāvavicchinnamūlāṁ dhūmarekhāṁ paśyati, tadanantaraṁ dhūmo vahnivyāpya ityevaṁrūpaṁ vyāptismaraṇaṁ tasya bhavati paśācca vahnivyāpyadhūmavānayamiti jñānaṁ bhavati sa eva parāmarśa ityucyate tadanantaraṁ parvato vahnimānityanumitirjāyate, Siddhāntamuktāvalī*, pp. 284-86.
4. *Vide The Six Ways of Knowing*, p. 207.

construction as Caesar-man-mortal, and then by inspection we get Caesar-mortal."[1] So also the Naiyāikas hold that without *liṅgaparāmarśa* as a synthetic correlation of the minor, middle and major terms we cannot explain the transition from the premises to the conclusion. If no such synthesis was required, then the premises could, even in their isolation, lead to the conclusion.[2] The Vedāntists, however, contend that the two premises, taken together, lead to the conclusion. When I see smoke in a hill and remember that smoke is always related to fire, I am at once led to the knowledge that there is fire in the hill. It is not necessary for me to stop and say further, 'the smoke in the hill is a smoke pervaded by fire.'[3] As we shall see it more fully larter on, in the case of inference for oneself we do not require anything more than the major and minor premises to arrive at the conclusion. There is a natural transition of thought from these premises to the conclusion. When, however, we are to demonstrate the truth of the conclusion to other persons, we must state the identity of the middle term occurring in the two premises and exhibit it in a third premise which relates the same middle to the minor and major terms. Here we assert that the same M which is always related to P is present in S. Hence, we conclude that *liṇgaparāmarśa* is not an essential condition of all inferences, although it serves to make an inference most cogent and convincing.

1. Bradley, *The Principles of Logic*, Vol. I, p. 259.
2. SM., 63.
3. VP., Ch. II.

Chapter XII

Classification and Logical Forms of Inference

1. *Svārtha* and *Parārtha* Inferences

In Indian logic an inference is a combined deductive inductive reasoning consisting of at least three categorical propositions. All inferences are thus pure syllogisms of the categorical type which are at once formally and materially valid. Hence, we have not a classification of inferences into deductive and inductive, immediate and mediate, syllogistic and non-syllogistic, pure and mixed. The Naiyāyikas give us three different classifications of inference. According to the first, inference is of two kinds, namely, *svārtha* and *parārtha*. This is a psychological classification which has in view the use or purpose which an inference serves. According to another classification, inference is said to be of three kinds, namely, *pūrvavat, śeṣavat* and *sāmānyatodṛṣṭa*. This classification has reference to the nature of the *vyāpti* or the universal relation between the middle and major terms of inference. *Pūrvavat* and *śeṣavat* inferences are based on causal uniformity, while *sāmānyatodṛṣṭa* is based on non-causal uniformity. According to a third classification, inference is distinguished into *kevalānvayi*, *kevala-vyatireki* and *anvaya-vyatireki*. This classification is more logical inasmuch as it depends on the nature of the induction by which we get the knowledge of *vyāpti* or the universal proposition involved in inference. These different kinds of inference we shall have to consider one after another.

All inferences must have one of two ends in view. They are meant either for the acquisition of some new knowledge on our part or for the demonstration of a known truth to others. Accordingly, all inferences are classed under the two heads of *svārtha* or inference for oneself and *parārtha* or inference for others.[1] An inference is called *svārtha* when it aims at the knowledge of an unperceived object on the part of a man who employs that inference. In this kind of inference a man seeks only to reach the conclusion for himself by relating it to the major and minor premises. This is illustrated in the case of a man who infers the existence of fire in a hill because he first perceives a mass of smoke in it and then remembers that there is a universal relation between smoke and fire. On the other hand, an inference is *parārtha* when it aims at demonstrating the truth of the conclusion to other people. In this inference there is a justification of the conclusion through a justification of the middle term that leads to it. It is here specifically pointed out that the same middle term which is universally related to the major is also present in the minor term. The conclusion is thus found to follow necessarily from a synthesis of the major and minor premises. This synthesis is embodied in a third premise which relates the minor, middle and major terms of the inference. A *parātha anumāna* is illustrated when a man having inferred the existence of fire in a hill lays it down as a thesis and proves it as a conclusion following from the major and minor premises and their combination into a third premise.[2]

2. *Pūrvavat, Śeṣavat* and *Sāmānyatodṛṣṭa* Inferences

In the *Nyāya-sūtra*[3] inference is distinguished into three kinds, namely, *pūrvavat, śeṣavat* and *sāmānyatodṛṣṭa*. There are different views with regard to the nature of these inferences. According to one view, a *pūrvavat* inference is that in which we infer the unperceived effect from a perceived cause. Here the *liṅga* or the middle term is related to the *sādhya* or the major term as its cause and is, therefore, antecedent to it. In this inference we pass from the knowledge of the antecedent cause to that of the consequent effect. This is illustrated when from the presence of dark heavy

1. *Taccānumānaṁ dvividham, svārthaṁ parārthaṁ ceti*, TB., p. 9.
2. TS., pp. 46-49.
3. *Vide* NS., 1. 1. 5.

clouds in the sky we infer that there will be rainfall. A *śeṣavat* inference is that in which we infer the unperceived cause from a perceived effect. Here the middle term is related as an effect to the major term and is, therefore, consequent to it. In this inference we pass from the knowledge of the effect-phenomenon to that of the antecedent causal phenomenon. This is illustrated in the inference if previous rain from the rise of the water in the river and its swift muddy current. It will be observed here that in both *pūrvavat* and *śeṣavat* inferences the *vyāpti* or the universal relation between the major and middle terms is a uniform relation causality between them. These inferences thus depend on scientific inductions. In *sāmānyatorṣṭa* inference, however, the *vyāpti* or the universal relation between the major and middle terms does not depend on a causal uniformity. The middle term of the inference is related to the major term neither as a cause nor as an effect. We infer the one from the other, not because they are causally connected, but because they are uniformly related to each other in our experience. This is illustrated when one infers that the sun moves because, like other moving object, its position changes, or; when we argue that a thing must have some attributes because it is like a substance. Here the inference depends not on a causal connection, but on certain observed points of similarity between different objects of experience. So, it is more akin to an analogical argument than to syllogistic inference.

According to a second interpretation, a *pūrvavat* inference is that which is based on previous experience. If two things have always been found to be related in the past, then from the perception of the one we infer the existence of the other, as when we infer fire from smoke. Similarly, a *śeṣavat* inference is taken to mean inference by elimination, in which the inferred character is the residuum of a process of elimination which excludes other characters. This is illustrated when one argues that sound must be a quality because it cannot be a substance or an activity or a relation and so on. So also *sāmānyatodṛṣṭa* inference is explained as that in which we do not perceive that relation between the major and middle terms, but find the middle to be similar to objects which are related to the major term. This is illustrated when one argues that the soul-substance exists because the quality of consciousness must, like other qualities, inhere in a substance.[1] According to a third view[2] these three kinds of inferences may be taken to mean *kevalānvayi, kaevala-vyatireki* and *anvaya-vyatireki* inferences which we are to consider next.

3. *Kevalānvayi, Kevala-vyatireki* and *Anvaya-vyatireki* Inferences

In view of the different methods of establishing *vyāpti* or a universal relation between the major and middle terms, inferences have been classified into the *kevalānvayi*, the *kevalavyatireki* and the *anvaya-vyatireki.* An inference is called *kevalānvayi* when it is based on a middle term which is only positively related to the major term. Here the knowledge of *vyāpti* between the middle and major terms is arrived at only through the method of agreement in presence (*anvaya*), since there is no negative instance of their agreement in absence.[3] This is illustrated in the following inference:

> All knowable objects are nameable;
>
> The pot is a knowable object;
>
> Therefore the pot is nameable.

In this inference the major premise is a universal affirmative proposition in which the predicate 'nameable' is affirmed of all knowable objects. This universal proposition is arrived at by simple enumeration the positive instances of agreement in presence between the knowable and the nameable. Corresponding to this universal affirmative proposition we cannot have a real universal negative proposition like 'No unnameable object is knowable,' for we cannot point to or name anything that is unnameable.[4] The minor

---

1. *Vide* NB., 1. 1. 5.
2. *Vide* NV. and NSV., 1. 1. 5.
3. *Yatra sādhyavyatireko na kutrāpyasti sa kevalānvayi*, TM., Ch. II.
4. TB., p. 10.

premise and the conclusion of this inference are also universal affirmative propositions and cannot be otherwise. Hence with regard to its logical form the *kevalānvayi* inference is a syllogism of the first mood of the first figure, technically called Barbara.

A *kevala-vyatireki* inference is that in which the middle term is negatively related to the major term. It depends on a *vyāpti* or a universal relation between the absence of the major term and that of the middle term. Accordingly, the knowledge of *vyāpti* is here arrived at only through the method of agreement in absence (*vyatireka*), since there is no positive instance of agreement in presence between the middle and major terms excepting the minor term.[1] This may be illustrated by the following inferences:

(1) No non-soul is animate;
All living beings are animate;
Therefore all living beings have souls.[2]

(2) What is not different from the other elements has no smell;
The earth has smell;
Therefore, the earth is different from the other elements.[3]

Symbolically put the inferences stand thus:

No not-P is M;
S is M;
Therefore S is P.

In the second inference above, it will be seen, the middle term 'smell' is the differentia of the minor term 'earth.' An inference which is thus based on the differentia (*lakṣaṇa*) as the middle term is also called *kevala-vyatireki*.[4] In it the minor term is co-extensive

---

1. *Kevalavyatireki tvasatsapakṣo,* etc., TC., II, pp. 582 f. *Vyatirekavyāptau tu sādhyābhāvo vyāpyaḥ hetvābhāvo vyāpakaḥ,* TM., Ch. II.
2. *Vide* TB., p. 10.
3. *Vide* TS., p. 52.
4. *Lakṣaṇamapi kevalavyatireki hetuḥ*, TB., p. 10.

with the middle. Hence we have no positive instance of the coexistence of the middle with any term but the minor.[1] So, there can be *vyāpti* or a universal relation only between the absence of the middle and the absence of the major term. We cannot point to any positive instance of agreement in presence between the major and middle terms, except those covered by the minor term. Hence the major premise is a universal negative proposition arrived at by simple enumeration of negative instances of agreement in absence between the major and middle terms.[2] The minor premise is a universal affirmative proposition. But although one of the premises is negative, the conclusion is affirmative, which is against the general syllogistic rules of Formal Logic. Hence we see that *kevala-vyatireki* inference is not any of the valid moods of syllogism recognised by Formal Logic. The validity of such inferences, however, has been admitted by Bradley as a special case of negative reasoning.[3]

An inference is called *anvaya-vyatireki* when its middle term is both positively and negatively related to the major term.[4] In it there is *vyāpti* or a universal relation between the presence of the middle and the presence of the major term as well as between the absence of the major and the absence of the middle term. The knowledge of the *vyāpti* or the universal proposition, on which the inference depends, is arrived at through the joint method of agreement in presence and in absence (*anvaya* and *vyatireka*). The *vyāpti* or the universal proposition is affirmative (*anvayi*) when it is the result of an enumeration of positive instances of agreement in presence between the middle and major terms. It is negative (*vyatireki*) when it is based on the simple enumeration of negative

1. *Yatra sādhyaprasiddhiḥ pakṣātirikte nāsti, sa kevalavyatireki*, TM., Ch. II.
2. *Vide* TB., p. 10.
3. *Vide* Bradley, *The Principles of Logic*, Vol. I, pp. 274-82.
4. *Yatra sādhyaṁ sādhyābhāvaśca anyatra prasiddhaḥ so 'nvayavyatireki*, etc., TM., Ch. II.

instances of agreement in absence the middle and major terms.[1] The difference between the universal affirmative and universal negative propositions (*anvaya-vyāpti* and *vyatireka-vyāpti*) is that the subject of the affirmative proposition becomes the predicate, and the contradictory of the predicate of the affirmative proposition becomes the subject in the corresponding negative proposition.[2] Hence, an *anvaya-vyatireki* inference may be based on either a universal affirmative or a universal negative proposition as its major premise. It is illustrated in the following pair of inferences:

(1) All cases of smoke are cases of fire;
The hill is a case of smoke;
Therefore, the hill is a case of fire.

(2) No case of not-fire is a case of smoke;
The hill is a case of smoke;
Therefore, the hill is a case of fire.

The Vedāntists do not recognise the above classification of inference into *kevalānvayi, kevala-vyatireki* and *anvayavyatireki*. According to them, inference is logically of one kind, namely, *anvayi*. An inference must be based on *vyāpti* or the universal relation between the middle and major terms. The knowledge of *vyāpti* is arrived at through the observation of agreement in presence between the middle and major terms with the non-observation of any contrary instance. Hence for the Vedāntists, both the premises as also the conclusion of an inference must be universal affirmative propositions. That is, all inferences must be in the technical form of Barbara. But there cannot be any *kevalānvayi* in the sense of an inference in which the major term is a character that is not anywhere non-existent. In *kevalānvayi* the middle term is only positively related to the major term, since there is no case of their absence. This, however, is not true. The whole system of finite categories

1. *Sa cānvayavyatirekī, anvayena vyatirekeṇa ca vyāptimattvāt*, etc., TB., p. 9.
2. *Idid.*

being transcended and negated in Brahman or the Absolute, we cannot have any term which is never non-existent. As for the Nyāya view of *vyatireki,* the Vedāntists contend that as a reasoning based on a universal negative proposition, it is not to be regarded as an inference, but as *arthāpatti* or postulation. An inference is a knowledge of the major term through that of the middle term. This knowledge is based on the *vyāpti* or the universal relation between the presence of the middle and the presence of the major term. When one infers fire from smoke he depends on the knowledge of *vyāpti,* not between the absence of fire and the absence of smoke, but between the presence of smoke and the presence of fire. There being no such thing as *vyatireki* inference which is but a synthesis of the *anvayi* and *vyatireki* forms of inference.[1] According to the Naiyāyikas, however, *arthāpatti* is not a separate method of knowledge, but a form of inference. We shall have to consider this question more fully hereafter.

4. The Logical Form of Inference

All the systems of Indian philosophy agree in holding that the syllogism represents the typical form of an inferential reasoning. In inference we arrive at a truth through the medium of some other truths. Like the conclusion of a syllogism, inferential knowledge is a deduction from certain propositions. There is however some controversy among the different systems as to the number of the constituent parts or propositions entering into an inference (*avayava*).

According to some old Naiyāyikas, there are ten members or constituent parts of an inference. These are: (1) *jijñāsā* or the desire to know the truth, (2) *saṁśaya* or doubt about the real nature of a thing, (3) *śakyaprāpti* or the capacity of the *pramāṇas* to lead to true knowledge, (4) *prayojana* or the purpose of making an inference, (5) *saṁśaya-vyudāsa* or the removal of all doubts about the truth of an inference, (6) *pratijñā* or the first proposition, (7)

1. *Vide* VP., Ch. II.

hetu or the reason, (8) *udāharaṇa* or the example, (9) *upanaya* or the application of the example, and (10) *nigamana* or the final conclusion.[1]

The above view of the syllogism as consisting of ten parts or members (*daśāvayava*) has been criticized and rejected by the later Naiyāyikas, from Vātsyāyana downwards. According to them, the first five factors, mentioned above, are unnecessary for proving anything by means of an inference. They represent not so much the logical steps in drawing a conclusion as the psychological or epistemological conditions involved in inference. Thus the desire to know (*jijñāsā*) may be taken as a condition of all knowledge, by which we want to realise some end. But such desire does not prove anything to any person and cannot, therefore, be regarded as a factor of inferential reasoning. Similarly, doubt is the impetus to a desire to know the truth and is, in this sense, a condition of knowledge. But to doubt is not to prove anything. The validity of all knowledge depends on the validity of the methods of knowledge (*śakyaprāpti*). But the validity of the methods cannot be put forward as a pat of the argument to prove a conclusion. So also the purpose or the end, which an inference serves, is no part of the inference itself. The removal of doubt (*saṁśaya-vyudāsa*) consists in repudiating all views which contradict the conclusion of an inference. This serves to lend indirect support to the conclusion, but does not really prove it. Hence, it has been held by the Naiyāyikas that the syllogism consists of the last five members mentioned above, since they are all necessary for proving of demonstrating a truth.[2] The Sāṅkhya[3] and Vaiśeṣika[4] systems also accept this view of the syllogism as consisting of five members or propositions. The five members of the syllogism have been explained by the Naiyāyikas as follows:

1. NB., 1. 1. 32.
2. NS. and NB., 1. 1. 32.
3. *Vide Sāṅkhya-sūtra,* 5. 27.
4. In Praśastapāda's *padārthadharmasaṁgraha* (p. 114) the five members of the syllogism are called *pratijñā, apadeśa, nidarśana anusaṁdhāna* and *pratyāmnāya.*

(1) The first member of the syllogism is called the *pratijñā* or the propositum. It is just a statement of one's position and consists in the assertion of some unperceived quality or character in relation to some object of experience. The assertion may be affirmative or negative. Hence, in the *pratijñā* a certain predicate is either affirmed or denied of a certain subject, *e.g.* 'the hill is fiery,' or 'sound is not eternal.' The *pratijñā* includes a subject (*pakṣa*) and a predicate (*sādhya*), but no copula or verb to relate the two, e.g. '*parvato vahnimān*' (the hill fires). It thus corresponds to a proposition without any copula. It is to be proved and established by other propositions in the course of the inference. The *pratijñā* simply tells us what the subject of the inference is and what we want to infer or prove with regard to it.[1]

(2) The second member of the syllogism is called the *hetu* or the reason. It consists in the statement of the mark or the sign (*liṅga*) which being present in the subject or the minor term suggests that the latter possesses a certain property predicated of it. It is the assertion of the middle term by which we know that the *pakṣa* or the minor term is or is not related to the *sādhya* or the major term. It may thus be called the middle premise or the middle proposition of the syllogism. But while the *pratijñā* is a proposition of two terms, the *hetu* is a one term proposition. Thus for the proposition 'the hill is fiery,' the *hetu* or the middle proposition is '*dhūmāt*,' *i.e.* 'because of smoke.'[2]

(3) The third member of the syllogism is called *udāharaṇa* or the example. It consists in the assertion of a universal relation (*vyāpti*) between the major and middle terms with reference to some apposite instances. The *hetu*

---

1. NS. and NB., 1. 1. 33.
2. *Ibid.*, 1. 1. 34-35.

or the middle term proves the presence or the absence of the major in the minor only as it is connected with the minor, on the one hand, and universally related to the major, on the other. Hence the universal relation between the major, and middle term must be duly asserted as an essential member of the syllogism. The assertion is a universal proposition which may be either affirmative or negative. It is a universal affirmative proposition when it indicates the agreement in presence between the major and middle terms as supported by a positive instance, *e.g.* 'all cases of smoke are cases of fire, to wit, the kitchen.' It takes the form of a universal negative proposition when it shows the agreement in absence between the two, as supported by a negative instance, *e.g.* 'no case of not-fire is a case of smoke, to wit, the lake.'[1] The third member of the Nyāya inference thus corresponds to the major premise of the syllogisms in the first figure. As a universal proposition supported by certain instances, the third member of the syllogism is found to be an inductive generalisation based on actual facts of observation. It thus shows that an inference is both deductive and inductive, formally valid and materially true. As Dr. Seal rightly observes: 'It harmonises Mill's view of the major premise as a brief memorandum of like instances already observed, with the Aristotelian view of it as the universal proposition which is the formal ground of the inference.'[2]

(4) The fourth member of the syllogism is called *upanaya* or the application. It consists in the application of the universal proposition with its example to the subject or the minor term of the inference. While the third member of the syllogism states the universal relation

1. *Ibid.*, 1. 1. 36-37. *Cf.* Vyāptipradarśanaviṣayo dṛṣṭṭntaḥ, NVT., p. 304.
2. *The Positive Sciences of the Ancient Hindus*, p. 252.

between the major and middle terms, or between their absence, the fourth member shows the presence or the absence of the middle in the minor term. It may thus be called the minor premise of the syllogism, and may be a universal affirmative or negative proposition. It is affirmative when it is the application of an affirmative major premise with a positive instance, *e.g.* 'so, like the kitchen, the hill is smoky.' It is a negative proposition when it is the application of a negative major premise with a negative instance, *e.g.* 'unlike the lake, the hill is not not-smoky, *i.e.* it is smoky.' The fourth member of the syllogism is not merely a repetition of the second or the middle proposition. It brings out the identity between the middle term mentioned in the second member and that which is stated to be universally related to the major in the third member of the syllogism. As such, it is a synthesis of the second and third members of the syllogism. It shows that the same middle which is universally related to the major term is also present in the minor term, and is, therefore, very useful for the purpose of proof.[1]

(5) The fifth and the last member of the syllogism is called *nigamana* or the conclusion. Here the preceding four steps are brought to a point so as to demonstrate the truth of the first proposition, with which the inference starts. It consists in the re-statement of the *pratijñā* or the propositum as proved by the major and minor premises, *e.g.* 'therefore, the hill is fiery.' It should not be supposed that the conclusion is an unmeaning repetition of the first proposition. What is at first put forward as a hypothesis or bare assertion is asserted in the conclusion as a firmly established truth. What appears in the first proposition as a judgement to be proved, does indeed re-appear in the conclusion, but

1. NS. and NB., 1. 1. 38; TR., pp. 181 f.

as something proved and demonstrated by other propositions.[1]

The logical form of an inference or the syllogism, according to the Naiyāyikas, may be illustrated in the following ways:

(1) S is P;
∵ S is M;
M is P;
S is M;
∴ S is P.

Or,

The hill is fiery;
Because it smokes;
Whatever smokes is fiey, *e.g.* the kitchen;
So, the hill smokes;
Therefore, it is fiery.

(2) S is P;
∵ S is M;
No not-P is M;
S is not not-M;
∴ S is P.

Or, The hill is fiery;
Because it smokes;
Whatever is not-fiery does not smoke, *e.g.* the lake;
Not so the hill (*i.e.* the hill does smoke);
Therefore, the hill is fiery.

The Mīmāṁsakas and the Vedāntists join issue with the Naiyāyikas on the question of the parts or members of a syllogism.[2]

1. TR., pp. 181 f.
2. *Vide* SD., p. 64; VP., Chap. II.

They agree with the Naiyāyikas in holding that the syllogism is necessary only for *parārthānumāna* or demonstrative inference and that *svārthānumāna* or inference for oneself requires no verbal statement in the form of the above syllogism. But they decline to accept the Nyāya view that the syllogism consists of five members or propositions. According to them, a syllogism does not require or than three members to carry conviction to anybody. The two essential conditions of a valid inference are *vyāpti* or a universal relation between the major and middle terms and *pakṣadharmatā* or the presence of the middle term in the minor. Hence the full force of a syllogism comes out in the body of three affirmative propositions, two of which stand for the grounds of inference and one for the conclusion. These three propositions are either the *pratijñā, hetu* and *undāharaṇa,* or the *udāharaṇa*, *upanaya* and *nigamana*.[1] Hence, we will have two forms of the syllogism, which may be put thus:

(1) S is P;
∵ S is M;
All M is P.

Or, The hill is fiery;
Because it smokes;
Whatever smokes is fiery, *e.g.* the kitchen.

(2) All M is P;
S is M;
∴ S is P.

Or, Whatever smokes is fiery, *e.g.* the kitchen;

1. The Buddhists go further than the Mīmāṁsakas and the Vedāntists in reducing the syllogism to two propositions only, namely, the *udāharaṇa* and the *upanaya,* but no *nigamana* or conclusion. As Mr. Joseph and Dr. Stebbing also point out, we may sometimes put an argument in the form of a single proposition as when we say 'if wishes were horses, beggars could ride.' (*Cf.* Joseph's *An Introduction of Logic*, p. 352; Stebbing's *A Modern Introduction to Logic*, p. 110).

The hill smokes;

Therefore, it is fiery.

It will be observed here that in the first form of the syllogism given above, the inference stars form the conclusion, and then the premises are stated to justify it. In the second form, the premises are given first and then the conclusion is drawn from them. That inferences may take both forms has been recognised by some modern Western logicians like H.W. B. Joseph,[1] L. S. Stebbing,[2] F. M. Chafman and Paul Henle.[3] But it will be admitted by all that while the second form (in which the premises comes first and the conclusion last) has a rigidly formal character, it is the first (in which the conclusion comes first and the premises last) that is ordinarily used by us when we actually infer anything. "In ordinary speech we more often state the conclusion first and then state the premises. This gives emphasis to the conclusion and also aids in showing the direction of our argument."[4] If this be so, then we must say that the Nyāya form of inference, in which the conclusion-to-be-proved comes first and the premises last, is the natural or actual form of reasoning. But it should be remarked that the first proposition cannot be strictly called the conclusion, since a conclusion is what follows from certain grounds or premises. So, it seems better to speak of it, like the Naiyāyika, as just a *pratijñā* or probandum, *i.e.* something to be proved. This proposition stands out as the conclusion when it is seen to follow logically from certain other premises. That there must be two such premises, *viz.* the major and the minor, all logicians would readily admit. And that there must also be a third premise to synthesis these two seems to be admitted only by a logician like Bradley.[5] It will, however, be admitted by others that there is no logical necessity for any thinker to infer the existence of fire in a hill unless it is shown that the

1. *An Introduction of Logic*, pp. 255-56.
2. *A Modern Introduction to Logic*, pp. 82, 84.
3. Chapman and Henle, *The Fundamentals of Logic*, p. 98.
4. *Op. cit.*
5. *The Principles of Logic*, Vol. I, p. 259.

smoke in it is just that real natural smoke mises. These three premises together with the conclusion and illusion, like the mirage, then we cannot conclude that there *is* fire in the hill, although we may *think* that there is. So if there is to be no gap in the chain or reasoning that is to establish the conclusion, we are to have a third premise to bring out the identity of the middle term in the preceding two premises. These three premises together with the conclusion and the probandum give us the five-membered form of the Nyāya syllogism which, therefore, seems to be both psychologically correct and more conclusive for demonstration.

Chapter XIII

Fallacies of Inference

1. Distinction between a Valid and an Invalid Reason

In Indian logic the fallacies of inference are all material fallacies. So far as the logical forms of inference are concerned, there can be no fallacy, since they are the same for all valid inferences. An inference, therefore, becomes fallacious by reason of its material conditions. The Nyāya account of the fallacies of inference is accordingly limited to those of its members or constituent propositions, and these have been finally reduced to those of the *hetu* or the reason.[1] For the purpose of proof as inference is made to consist of five members, namely, *pratijñā, hetu, udāharaṇa, upanya* and *nigamana*. As such, the validity of an inference depends on the validity of the *pratijñā* and other constituent parts of it. If there is anything wrong with any of its members, the syllogism as a whole becomes fallacious. Hence, there will be as many fallacies of inference as there are fallacies of its component parts, from the first proposition down to the conclusion. So, we may speak of fallacies of the *pratijñā,* etc., as coming under the fallacy of inference (*nyāyābhāsa*).[2] But it must be admitted that the validity of an inference depends ultimately on the validity of the *hetu* or reason employed in it. So, also the

---

1. *Cf.* The Aristotelian classification of fallacies into those in *dictione* and those *extra dictionem.* This agrees with the Nyāya classification in excluding the formal fallacies of undistributed middle, illicit process, and so on, from the list of fallacies.

2. The word *nyāyābhāsa* has been used by Vātsyāyana in a technical sense to mean all such inferences as are opposed to precption and scriptural testimony. (*Vide Nyāya-Bhāṣya,* 1. 1. 1.). Here, however, it is used in its literal sense to mean the fallacies of inference.

members of a syllogism turn out to be right or wrong according as they elaborate a right or wrong reason. The fallacies of inference ultimately arise out of the fallacious reason. So, the Naiyāyikas bring the fallacies of inference under the fallacies of the reason (*hetvābhāsa*) and consider a separate treatment of the inferential fallacies due to the propositum, example, etc. (*pratijñābhāsa, dṛṣṭāntābhāsa*) as unnecessary and superfluous.[1]

Now, the question is: What is a fallacious middle (*hetu*)? How are we to distinguish between a valid and an invalid middle? Literally speaking, *hetvābhāsa* or the fallacious middle is one that appears as, but really is not, a valid reason or middle term of an inference. It appears a valid ground of inference because it satisfies some of the conditions of a valid middle term. But on closer view it is found to be fallacious because it does not fulfil all the conditions of a valid ground of inference.[2] As we have seen before, there are five conditions of the *hetu* or the middle term of an inference. First, the middle term must be a characteristic of the minor term (*pakṣadharmatā*). Secondly, it must be distributively related to the major term, *i.e.* the major must be present in all the instances in which the middle is present (*sapakṣasattva*). Thirdly, and as a corollary of the second condition, the middle term must be absent in all cases in which the major is absent (*vipakṣāsattva*). Fourthly, the middle term must not relate to obviously contradictory and absurd objects like the coolness of fire, etc. (*abādhitaviṣayatva*). Fifthly, it must not itself be validly contradicted by some other ground or middle term (*asatpratipakṣatva*). Of these five conditions, the third does not apply to the middle term of a *kevalānvayi* inference, because it is such that no case of its absence or non-existence can be found. Hence, with regard to it we cannot say that the middle term must be absent in all cases in which the major is absent, Contrariwise, the second condition does not apply to the middle term of a *kevalavyatireki* inference since here the middle term is always negatively related to the major term. Thee is a universal relation between the absence of the middle and that of

1. *Vide* TR., p. 236; NM., p. 572.
2. *Vide* NV., 1. 2. 4.

the major term. Of such a middle term we cannot say that wherever it is present the major must be present. It is only in the case of *anvayavyatireki* inferences that the middle term must satisfy all the five conditions. Hence, it has been said that a valid middle term is one that satisfies the five or at least the four conditions as explained above.[1] As contrasted with this an invalid middle term (*hetvābhāsa*) is that which violates one or other of the conditions of a valid ground of inference (*hetu*). It may be employed as the *hetu* or the middle term of an inference, but it fails to prove the conclusion it is intended to prove. There are different forms of the fallacious middle according to the different circumstances under which it may arise. All fallacious middle terms have been classified under the heads of the *savyabhicāra, viruddha, prakaraṇasama* or *satpratipakṣa, sādhyasana* or *asiddha, kālātīta* and *bādhita*.[2] Keśava Miśra observes that the fallacies of definition such as *ativyāpti* or 'the too wide,' *avyāpti* or 'the too narrow' and *asaṁbhava* or 'the false' also come under the fallacies of the middle term.[3]

2. The Fallacy of *Savyabhicāra* or the Irregular Middle

The first kind of inferential fallacy is called the *savyabicāra*. In it the *hetu* or the middle term is found to lead to nc one singie

---

1. *Vide* NSV., 1. 2. 4; NM., p. 110.
2. In both the old and the modern schools of the Nyāya, the inferential fallacies have been calssified under five heads. The first four kinds of fallacies bear the same names or at least the same significance in both the schools. The last kind of fallacy, however, is not only called by different names, but bears substantially different meanings in the two schools. It is in view of this fact that I have taken the two names to stand for two kinds of fallacies of the middle term. Hence, we get six kinds of fallacies in place of the five enumerated in the Nyāya treatises. *Vide Nyāya-sūtra*, 1. 2. 4.; *Tattvacintāmaṇi*, II. p. 778.) In the Prābhākara Mīmāṁsā the fallacies of the middle term are called the *asādhāraṇa, bādhita, sādhāraṇa* and *asiddha* (*vide* Jhā, *Prabhākara School of Pūrva Mīmāṁsā*, p. 46). In *Pudārthadharmasaṁgraha* the fallacies are called the *asiddha, viruddha, sandigdha* and *anadhyavasita*.
3. *Vide* TB. p. 37.

conclusion, but to different opposite conclusions. This fallacy arises when the middle term violates its second condition, namely, that it must be distributively related to the major term. This condition requires that the middle term must be pervaded by the major term, or that the major must be present in all the cases in which the middle is present. The *savyabhicāra hetu,* however, is not uniformly concomitant with the major term. It is related to both the existence and the non-existence of the major term. It is therefore called *anaikāntika* or an irregular concomitant of the *sādhya* or the major term. Hence from such a middle term we can infer both the existence and the non-existence of the major term.[1] Of such *savyabhicāra* or irregular middle there are three kinds, namely, the *sādhāraṇa, asādhāraṇa* and *anupasaṁhārī.* The *sādharaṇa* or the ordinary fallacy of the irregular middle occurs when the middle term is in some cases related to the major and in the other cases related to the absence of the major.[2] This is illustrated in the following syllogism:

> All knowable objects are fiery;
>
> The hill is knowable;
>
> Therefore, the hill is fiery.

Here the middle term 'knowable' is indifferently related to both fiery objects like the kitchen, and fireless objects like the lake. All knowables being thus not fiery we cannot conclude that a hill is fiery because it is knowable. Rather, it is as much true to say that, for the same reason, the hill is fireless.

The second form of the *savyabhicāra* is called *asādhāraṇa* or the extraordinary. It is a peculiar form of the fallacy of the irregular middle. In it the middle term is related neither to things in which the major exists nor to those in which it does not exist.[3] Hence, from such a middle term we can infer neither the existence nor the non-existence of the major term. Or, such a middle term may be employed to prove both the existence and the non-existence of the

---

1. Anaikāntikaḥ savyabhicāraḥ, NS., 1. 2. 5.
2. *Sādhāraṇaḥ sādhyavat tadanyavṛttiḥ*, etc., NSV., 1. 2. 5.
3. *Asādhāraṇaḥ sapakṣavipakṣavyāvṛttaḥ* etc., *ibid.*

major term. This is illustrated when one argues that sound is eternal because there is *śabdatva* or 'soundness' in it. Here the middle term 'soundness' is related only to the minor term 'sound.' It is found neither in eternal objects like the soul nor in other non-eternal things like the pot. Hence, we do not know if soundness is universally related to the eternal or the non-eternal. The middle term being undistributed one way or the other cannot lead to any valid conclusion.

The third form of the *savyabhicāra* is the *anupasaṁhārī* or the indefinite.[1] Here the middle term is related to a minor term that stands not for any definite individual or class of individuals, but indefinitely for all objects. Hence the distribution of the middle term cannot be proved either positively or negatively. To prove that the middle term is distributively related to the major we are to point out either the positive instances of their agreement in presence or the negative instances of their agreement in absence. Since, however, the minor term stands for all possible objects, we cannot go beyond them and get any case in which the middle coexists with the major, or the absence of the major is concomitant with that of the middle term. This is illustrated in the inference that 'all objects are eternal, because they are knowable.' The validity of this inference depends on the validity of the major premise, namely, 'all knowables are eternal.' But the validity of the major premise cannot be proved, since beyond all objects we have no instances of the concomitance between the knowable and the eternal.

3. The Fallacy of Viruddha or the Contradictory Middle

There are two different explanations of the fallacy of *viruddha*. According to the *Nyāya-sūtra* and *Bhāṣya,* the fallacy of the *viruddha* consists in the opposition of one doctrine to a previously accepted doctrine, both belonging to the same system of thought.[2] It is a contradiction between the different parts or doctrines of a system of philosophy. As an example of this Vātsāyana cites two

1. *Anvayvayatirekadṛṣṭāntarahito 'nupasaṁhārī*, etc., TS., p. 56.
2. *Siddhāntamabhyupetya tadvirodhī viruddhaḥ*, NS., 1. 2. 6.

contradictory statements from the *Yoga-bhāṣya,* namely, (*i*) that the world ceases from manifestation because it is not eternal, and (*ii*) that even then it exists because it cannot be destroyed.[1]

In the above sense the *viruddha* as a fallacy means the contradictions and inconsistencies involved in any school of philosophy. As such, however, it is not an inferential fallacy, but the fallacy of self-contradiction in which any theory or philosophy may be involved. Hence the first explanation of the *viruddha* as given above does not appear to me to be acceptable.

According to the later Naiyāyikas, from Uddyotakara downwards, the *hetu* or the reason is called *viruddha* when it disproves the very proposition which it is meant to prove.[2] This happens when a middle term exists, not in the objects in which the major exists, but in those in which the major does not exist. That is, the *viruddha* or the contradictory middle is that which is pervaded by the absence of the major term.[3] The result is that such a middle term instead of proving the existence of the major in the minor term, which is intended by it, proves its non-existence therein. It contradicts and sublaters the *pratijñā* or the proposition which it is employed to prove and establish. Thus if one argues 'sound is eternal, because it is caused,' we have a fallacy of *viruddha* or the contradictory middle. The middle term 'caused' does not prove the eternality of sound, but its non-eternality, because all that is caused is non-eternal. Hence, the distinction between the fallacies of the *savyabhicāra* and the *viruddha* is that while in the former the middle term is universally related neither to the existence of the major nor to its non-existence, in the latter the middle term is universally related to the non-existence of the major term. As a consequence of this, the *savyabhicāra* or the irregular middle only fails to prove the conclusion, whereas the *viruddha* or the contradictory middle disproves it or proves the contradictory proposition.

---

1. *Vide* NB., 1. 2. 6.
2. *Pratijñāhetvorvā virodhaḥ* etc., NV., 1. 2. 6.
3. *Sādhyābhāvavyāpto heturviruddhaḥ* etc., TS., p. 57.

4. The Fallacy of *Prakaraṇasama* or the Counteracted Middle

The third inferential fallacy is called the *prakaraṇasama*. Literally, it means a reason which is similar to the point at issue (*prakaraṇa*). We have a point at issue when there are two opposite views with regard to the same subject, both of which are equally possible, so that they only give rise to a state of mental vacillation as to the truth of the matter. Now when a middle term does not go further than producing a state of mental oscillation between two opposite views we have a case of the *prakaraṇasama* middle. This happens when one reason seeks to prove the existence of the major in the minor, but there appears some other reason to prove the non-existence of the major, and both of them are found to be equally strong. Here the opposed reasons counteract each other, but neither can sublate the other. They may indeed be employed as the middle terms of an inference, but each being neutralised or counterbalanced by the other (*satpratipakṣita*) fails to establish a sure conclusion and is therefore fallacious. Hence the *prakaraṇasama* is also called *satprtipakṣa* or that which is opposed by an equally strong *hetu* or middle term.[1] This is illustrated in the following arguments: 'sound is eternal, because the properties of the non-eternal are not found in it'; and 'sound is non-eternal, because the properties of the eternal are not found in it.' Here both the inferences are fallacious, because there is nothing to distinguish between the two middle terms leading to opposite conclusions.[2] The two middle terms being counteracted by each other cannot lead to any definite conclusion and we are left with the same question with which we started, namely, whether sound is eternal or non-eternal. The fallacy of the *prakaraṇasama* is distinguished from that of the *savyabhicāra* by the fact that while in the latter one and the same character of the minor is taken as a middle term that may lead to opposite conclusions, in the former two different characters of the minor are taken as the middle terms

---

1. *Yasmāt prakaraṇacintā sa nirṇayārthamapadiṣṭaḥ prakaraṇasamaḥ*, NS., 1. 2. 27. *Yasya pratipakṣabhūtaṁ hetvantaraṁ vidyate sa prakaraṇasamaḥ, sa eva satpratipakṣaḥ* etc., TB., p. 36.
2. *Vide* NB., 1. 2. 7.

leading to oppositer conclusions. It is also distinguished from the *viruddha* or contradictory middle which by itself proves the opposite of what it is intended to prove, while here the opposite conclusion is proved by a different middle term (*hetvantara*).[1]

5. The Fallacy of *Asiddha* or the Unproved Middle

The fourth kind of fallacy is called the *sādhyasama* or the *asiddha*. The word *sādhyasama* means a middle term which is similar to the *sādhya* or the major term. The *sādhya* is a character which we want to prove in relation to the *pakṣa* or the minor term. Hence the *sādhyasama* stands for a middle term which requires to be proved as much as the major term. This means that the *sādhyasama* middle is not a proved or an established fact, but an *asiddha* or unproved assumption.[2] The fallacy of the *asiddha* occurs when the middle term is wrongly assumed in any of the premises and so cannot be taken to prove the conclusion. It follows that the premises which contain the false middle become themselves false. Thus, the fallacy of the *asiddha* virtually stands for the fallacy of false premises, which is a form of the material fallacies in Western logic.

There are three main forms of the fallacy of *asiddha*, namely, (*i*) the *āśrayāsiddha*, (*ii*) *svarūpāsiddha* and (*iii*) *vyāpyatvāsiddha*.[3] Of these, The *aśrayāsiddha* is a middle term which has no *locus standi*. One condition of a valid middle term is that it must be present in the minor term. The minor term is thus the locus of the middle. Hence if the minor term is unreal and fictitious, the middle cannot be related to it. The result is that the minor premise, in which the middle is related to an unreal minor, becomes false. This is illustrated in the inference 'the sky-lotus is fragrant, because it belongs to the class of lotus.' Here, the minor term 'sky-lotus' is unreal, so that the middle 'class of lotus' cannot subsist in it. The

1. *Vide* NSV., 1. 2. 6.
2. *Sādhyāviśiṣṭaḥ sādhyatvāt sādhyasamaḥ*, NS., 1. 2. 8.
3. TS., p. 58; TB., p. 31.

middle term having no *locus standi,* we have a fallacy of the *āśrayāsiddha* or the baseless middle.[1]

The *svarūpāsiddha* is a middle term which cannot be proved to be real in relation to the minor term. It is a middle term which is not found in the minor term.[2] The existence of the middle in the minor being unreal, the minor premise which relates it to the minor term becomes false. Thus if one argues: 'sound is eternal, because it is visible,' he commits this fallacy. Here the middle term 'visible' is wrongly assumed in the minor term 'sound' and is not justified by facts. If the minor term stands for a number of things and the middle is found in some but not all of them, we have the fallacy of *bhāgāsiddha* or *ekadeśāsiddha.* To illustrate: 'the four kinds of atoms of earth, etc., are eternal, because they are fragrant.' Here the middle 'fragrant' is related only to a part of the minor term, namely, the atoms of earth, but not to the other kinds of atoms. Hence the middle term is partly false and so equivalent to the *svarūpāsiddha* middle. The fallacies of *bhāgāsiddha* or *ekadeśāsiddha* are therefore included within the fallacy of *svarūpāsiddha.* It includes also such other fallacies as (*i*) *viśeṣaṇāsiddha,* where the middle term has a false adjunct, as when one argues 'sound is eternal, because *being a substance* it is intangible,' while sound is not a substance but a quality; (*ii*) *viśeṣyāsiddha,* where the middle is an unreal substantive of a real adjective, *e.g.* 'sound is eternal, because it is an intangible *substance*'; (*iii*) *asamarthaviśeṣaṇāsiddha,* where the middle has an unmeaning adjunct, *e.g.* 'sound is eternal, because *being a quality* it has no cause,' in which the adjunct 'being a quality' has no force or sense in the argument; (*iv*) *asamathaviśeṣyāsiddha,* where the middle is an unmeaning substantive of a significant abjective, *e.g.* 'sound is eternal, because it is an uncaused *quality,*'

1. There are two kinds of this fallacy, *viz. asatpakṣa* and *siddhasādhana.* The first is explained above. The second means a middle which seeks to prove a proved or undoubted fact, *e.g.* '*a* body has limbs, because it is so perceived.' *Cf. TM.*, Ch. II.
2. TS. and TB., *ibid.*

in which the adjective 'uncaused' renders the word 'quality' quite superfluous.[1]

The *vyāpyatvāsiddha* is a middle term whose concomitance (*vyāpti*) with the major cannot be proved.[2] A valid middle term must be universally related to the major term. If a middle term is not known to be universally concomitant with the major, it becomes invalid. The result is that the major premise which should express a *vyāpti* or a universal relation between the middle and major terms becomes materially false. The fallacy of the *vyāpyatvāsiddha* may arise in two ways. It may be due to the non-concomitance of the middle term with the major, as in the inference 'all reals are momentary; sound is a real, therefore sound is momentary.' Here the major premise is false, because there is no universal relation between the 'real' and the 'momentary.' Or, it may be due to the presence of an (*upādhi*) or condition, on which the relation between the middle and major terms depends. Here the middle term is not, as it should be, unconditionally related to the major and is, therefore, false. It is illustrated in the inference 'the hill is a case of smoke, because it is a case of fire.' This inference is invalid, because the relation of the middle term 'fire' to the major 'smoke' is conditional on its being 'fire' from wet fuel.[3] This fallacy of the conditional middle is technically called *anyathāsiddha*.[4]

6. The Fallacies of *Kālātīta* and *Bādhita* or the Mistimed and Contradicted Middles

The *kālātīta* literally means a middle term which is vitiated by the lapse of time.[5] In this fallacy the middle term consists of two or more events which succeed one another in time. But on the analogy of the given example, these events must be simultaneous if the

1. *Vide* TB., pp. 34-35.
2. *Vyapyatvāsiddhastu sa eva yatra hetorvyāptirnāvagamyate, ibid.*
3. TB., p. 35.
4. *Vide* NVT., p. 345.
5. *Kālātyayāpadiṣṭaḥ kālātītaḥ*, NS., 1. 2. 9.

middle term, constituted by them, is to prove the conclusion. Since, however, they are successive, the middle term becomes inappropriate in the order of time and is, therefore, called *kālātīla* or the mistimed middle. It is illustrated in the inference 'sound is durable, because it is manifested by conjunction, like colour.' The colour of a thing is manifested when the thing comes in contact with light, although the colour exists before and after the contact. So also, it is argued, sound which is manifested by the contact between two things (*saṁyogavyaṅgya*) must be durable, *i.e,* exist before and after the contact. But the argument is fallacious because its middle term is vitiated by a limitation in time. In the case of colour the manifestation takes place simultaneously with the contact between light and the coloured object. The manifestation of sound, however, is separated by an interval of time from the contact between two things. In fact, we hear the sound when the contact between the two has ceased. Hence it cannot be due to the contact, because when the cause has ceased, the effect also must cease. The middle term being in congruous with the given example fails to prove the conclusion and is therefore fallacious.[1] In this sense the *kālātīta* means a middle term which is subject to different conditions in the two premises of the syllogism. As such, it becomes a kind of fallacy that corresponds to the fallacy of accident in Western logic.

According to a second interpretation, the *kālātīta* is the fallacy of a wrong order of the different members of the syllogism. It is illustrated when there is an inversion of the natural order of the premises and the conclusion, as when we put the premises after the conclusion. On this view, the *kālātīta* corresponds to the fallacy of *hysteron proteron.* But this view of the matter is not accepted by the Naiyāyikas. A change in the order of the members of a syllogism does not really affect its validity nor render it fallacious. Further, such a change does not involve a fallacy of the middle term or an inferential fallacy. It constitutes a defect in the method or procedure

1. *Kālātyena yukto yasyārthasyaikadeśo 'padiśyamānasya sa kālātīta. . . . . . udāharaṇsādharmyasyābyhāvādasādhanamayam,* NB., 1. 2. 9.

and is, therefore, described as the clincher of the inopportune (*aprāptakāla nigrahasthāna*).[1]

Although the fallacy of the *bādhita* has been treated by some writers as another name for that of the *kālātīta,* yet it seems to me better to distinguish between the two in view of the sharp contrast in their meanings. While the *kālātīta* stands for a middle term vitiated by a limitation in time, the *bādhita* means a middle term which is contradicted by some other source of knowledge (*pramāṇāntareṇa*). A middle term is contradicted when it leads to a conclusion, the opposite of which is proved to be true by some other *pramāṇa.* This is illustrated by the argument 'fire is cool, because it is a substance.' Here the middle term 'substance,' which seeks to prove that fire is cool, is contradicted because we know from tactual perception that fire is not cold but hot. The fallacy of *satpratipakṣa,* as explained before, is different from this fallacy of *bādhita* because in the former one inference is contradicted by another inference, while in the latter an inference is contradicted by a non-inferential source of knowledge.[2]

7. The Fallacies of *Cala, Jāti* and *Nigrahasthāna*

Apart from the fallacies of inference, the Naiyāyikas deal with certain other fallacies which occur in connection with the art of debate. These are called *cala, jāti* and *nigrahasthāna.* The fallacy of *cala* consists in using the same word to mean different objects in the course of a debate. It thus corresponds to the fallacy of ambiguity in Western logic. It is of three kinds, namely, *vākcala, sāmānyacala* and *upacāracala.* In *vākchala* or the fallacy of

1. *Ibid.* It should be remarked here that although it be usual in a syllogism to put the premises before the conclusion, yet that is neither logically necessary nor psychologically correct. It is now generally recognised by logicians that a syllogism may take another form in which the conclusion comes first and the premises follow it. Hence, we see that a change in the usual order of the propositions in a syllogism involves neither the fallacy of *hysteron proteron* nor the clincher of the inopportune.
2. *Vide* TB., p. 37; TS., pp. 58-60.

equivocation the same word is used in different senses. This is illustrated when one man says 'the boy is *navakambala*' (possessed of a *new* blanket), and another objects 'he is not *nava-kambala* (possessed of *nine* blankets).[1] In *sāmānyacala* the same word is taken to mean an individual and the class to which it belongs, *e.g.* one man says 'this Brahmin is a learned man,' and another objects 'all Brahmins are not learned men.' In *upacāracala* or the fallacy of figure of speech, a confusion is made between the figurative and literal senses of an expression, *e.g.* when one says 'the scaffolds cry out,' and another objects 'scaffolds cannot cry.'[2]

Jāti is the fallacy of irrelevance. In it a futile argument is based on some irrelevant consideration which does not really prove the conclusion. There are twenty-four kinds of *jāti* or futile arguments. The first is called *sādharmyasama,* where an argument is based on some kind of similarity between two things, *e.g.* 'sound is eternal because it is incorporeal like the sky.' The second is *vaidharmyasama,* where an argument is based on some kind of dissimilarity between two things. The *utkarṣasama, apakarṣasama, varṇyasama, avarṇyasama, vikalpasama* and *sādhyasama* are futile arguments in which the character of the minor term or the example is altered or they are unduly assumed without sufficient reason. The *prāptisama* and *aprāptisama* are futile objections based on the wrong implications of the co-existence between the middle and major terms or their absence. The *prasaṅgasama* and *pratidṛṣṭāntasama* are futile objections based on the ground that the given example has not been proved by a series of arguments, or that there is a counter-example. The *anutpattisama* is an objection based on the ground that the middle term of the given argument cannot exist in the minor term before it comes into existence. The *saṁśayasama* is an objection based on the doubt arising from a middle term with opposite examples. The *prakaraṇasama* is an objection based on the ground of a middle term which is related to both the sides of a controversy. The *ahetusama* is an objection

1. The word 'nava' means both new and nine.
2. *Vide* NS. and NB., 1. 2. 10-14.

which is based on the ground that the middle term is unintelligible in the three orders of time. The *arthāpattisama* is an argument based on mere presumption. The *aviśeṣasama* is an argument to prove the identity of all things on the ground of their having existence in common. The *upapattisama* is an objection based on the ground that there is a counter argument to the given argument. The *upalabdhisama* is the objection to a given argument based on the ground that we can perceive the truth of the conclusion even without the argument. The *anupalabdhisama* is an argument to invalidate a given argument from non-perception, on the ground that non-perception cannot be perceived. The *nityasama* is an argument to prove the eternality of all non-eternal things on the ground that they are eternally non-eternal. The *anityasama* is an argument to prove the non-eternality of all things on the ground of their resembling a non-eternal thing in some respect or other. The *kāryasama* is an argument opposed to a given argument from the nature of an effect, on the ground than an effect may have very different natures, and so cannot be taken to lead to a single conclusion.[1]

The *nigrahasthāna,* which literally means a ground of defeat, is a fallacy which is due either to a misunderstanding or to the want of understanding. It is said to be of twenty-two kinds. These are: *pratijñāhāni* or weakening one's proposition by adducing such examples as run counter to it; *pratijñāntara* or shifting the proposition; *pratijñāvirodha* or contradicting the proposition; *pratijñāsannyāsa* or renouncing the proposition; *hetvantara* or shifting the ground; *arthāntara* or shifting the topic; *nirarthaka* or the meaningless statement like *abracadabra*; *avijñātārtha* or the unintelligible statement; *apārthaka* or the incoherent statement; *aprāptakāla* or the wrong order of the parts of an argument; *nyūna* of the suppression on any part of an argument; *adhika* or the duplication of the middle term or the example; *punarukta* or the meaningless repetition of any part of an argument; *ananubhāṣaṇa* or the refusal to answer a question; *ajñāna* or ignorance of the

1. *Vide* NS., 1. 2. 18; 5. 1. 1 ff.

proposition; *apratibhā* or the inability to give a reply to the argument; *vikṣepa* or evasion of the argument; *matānujñā* or admission of the defect in one's argument; *paryyanuyojyopekṣaṇa* or overlooking a defect in the argument; *niranuyojyānuyoga* or finding fault with the faultless; *apasiddhānta* or the deviation from an accepted position; and *hetvābhāsa* or fallacy of the middle term.[1]

It will appear from the above that some of the fallacies of *chala, jāti* and *nigrahasthāna* come under the inferential fallacies, while others are either semi-logical or non-logical fallacies. These relate either to the meaning of words and propositions, or to the conduct of the parties concerned in any discussion. Hence any elaborate account of these three kind of fallacies with their many subdivisions is not necessary in connection with the Nyāya theory of inference.

1. *Vide* NS., 1. 2. 19; 5. 2. 1 ff.

IV. *UPAMĀNA* OR COMPARISON

Chapter XIV

Nature and Forms of *Upamāna*

1. The Nyāya Definition of *Upamāna*

The word *upamāna* is derived from the words *upa* meaning *sādrśya* or similarity, and *māna* meaning cognition. Hence, *upamāna* derivatively means the knowledge of the similarity between two things. This derivative meaning, however, riquires certain qualifications in order to give a complete definition of *upamāna*. As a *pramāṇa, upamāna* is the source of our knowledge about the relation between a word and its denotation (*saṁjñā-saṁjñisambandha*).[1] We have such knowledge when first we are told by some authoritative person that the word denotes a class of objects of a certain description and, secondly, finding some objects of that description we recognise them as denoted by that word. The description of the unknown objects denoted by the word is generally given in terms of their similarity to some familiar objects of experience. Hence *upamāna* is generally defined as the ground of our knowledge of a thing from its similarity to another thing previously well-known[2] Thus a man, who does not know what a *gevaya* or wild ox, is, may be told by some forester that it is an animal *like* the cow. When next he meets with such an animal in the forest, he knows that it is the *gavaya.* But the description of the unknown objects denoted by a word may also be given in terms of their dissimilarity to certain known object or their peculia properties.[3] Hence, *upamāna* or knowledge by comparison is not always due to the knowledge of similarity or dissimilarity between

1. *Saṁjñāsaṁjñisaṁbandhajñānamupamitiḥ*, etc., TS., p. 62.
2. *Vide* NS. & NB., 1. 1. 6.
3. *Vide* NV & NSV., 1. 1. 6.

things. The knowledge of similarity or dissimilarity is an accidental character of this or that kind of *upamāna.* What, however, is common to all cases of *upamāna* is the knowledge of the denotative relation between a word and a certain class of objects. Hence, the Nayāyikas finally define *upamāna* as the process of reasoning by which we know that a word denotes a certain class of objects on the basis of some authoritative statements.

Analysing the process of reasoning in *upamāna* we get the following steps. First, we have an authoritative statement (*atideśavākya*) that a word denotes object of a certain description, *e.g.* 'the *gavaya* is like the cow.' Secondly, when one observes any such object, he has the knowledge that it answers to the given description (*sādṛśyadhī*). Thirdly, there is a recollection of the descriptive statement received from authority (*vākyārthasmṛti*). Lastly, there is the resulting knowledge that this kind of objects is denoted by the word in question (*upamiti*).[1] Thus a man, who does not know what objects are denoted by the word *gavaya,* may have it from some authority that the word denotes animals resembling the cow. When next he happens to find such animals, he perceives their striking similarity to the cow. Then he remembers the authoritative statement that animals resembling the cow are *gavayas.* With this he comes to the conclusion that the word '*gavaya*' denotes this class of animals.

It may here be asked: Which of the four factors mentioned above is the *karaṇa* or operative cause of the knowledge derived form *upamāna* or comparison? It cannot obviously be the last, since that is the resulting cognition obviously be the last, since that is the resulting cognition, of which we want to know the principal cause. According to the older Naiyāyikas, the first factor, namely, the descriptive statement of some authority is here the *karaṇa* or special cause of the knowledge of denotation of words. The modern Naiyāyikas, however, hole that the perception of similarity, etc., is the special cause whose function (*vyāpāra*) is to revive in memory the authoritative statement and thereby lead to the knowledge in

1. *Vide* BP., 79-80.

question. A man recognises a *gavaya* as such just when he perceives its similarity to the cow and remembers the statement 'the *gavaya* is an animal resembling the cow.'[1]

2. The Jaina, Mīmāṁsā and Vedānta Views of *Upamāna*

According to the Mīmāṁsā and the Vedānta, *upamāna* is the source of our knowledge of the likeness of things. In some cases we may get the knowledge of likeness from perception, as when we perceived a *gavaya* and know it to be like the cow. From the perceived likeness of the *gavaya* to the cow we next know that the cow is like the *gavaya,* although the cow is not now perceived by us. This latter knowledge of the likeness of the unperceived cow to the perceived *gavaya* is due to *upamāna* or comparison. It cannot be due perception, since its locus, namely, the cow is not now perceived, but only remembered. It is no doubt conditioned by the perception of likeness in the *gavaya.* But when from this perceptual knowledge of likeness we pass to the knowledge that the cow, not now perceived, is like the *gavaya,* it is no longer perception. Nor is this second knowledge of likeness due to inference. In inference the *pakṣa* or the minor term is an object of perception and the *liṅga* or the middle term is present in the *pakṣa.* In the alleged inference of the cow's likeness to the *gavaya,* the *pakṣa, i.e.* the cow cannot be an object of perception, and the *linga, i.e.* the likeness of the *gavaya* would be present no in the *pakṣa* 'cow,' but in the *gavaya.* Further, when from the one likeness we know the other, we are not conscious of any inferring, but of comparing. Introspection tells us that the actual process of reasoning involved in the second knowledge of likeness is not inferential.[2] Similarly, when we perceive a horse and know it to be unlike the cow, our knowledge of the unlikeness is perceptual. But when from this we conclude that the cow, not now perceived, is unlike the horse, we depend, not on perception and inference, but on *upamāna* or comparison. Thus, the Mīmāṁsaka and the Vedāntist admit that

1. *Vide* NM., pp. 141-42.
2. *Vide* SD., pp. 74-76; VP., Ch. III.

there is a perceptual element in *upamāna*. But they go further and prove that the reasoning about likeness and unlikeness, based on some perception, cannot be fully explained by perception or inference. It constitutes an independent source of valid knowledge (*pramāṇa*), to which they give the name of *upamāna*.

The Naiyāyikas criticize and reject the above view on the following grounds. First, they point out that it violates the ordinary rule of *upamāna* or comparison. In all cases of *upamāna* we compare the unfamiliar object with something well-known in order to understand it better. In the above view the well-known cow is compared with the strange *gavaya*. But this cannot give us any new knowledge about the cow which is already too well-known to us. Secondly, the knowledge of the cow's likeness may be explained by memory and so does not require a separate source of knowledge like *upamāna*. When we perceive the *gavaya* we are reminded of the cow and not of other things. The reason is that there are certain points of resemblance between the two and that these were previously perceived with the perception of the cow. Hence we have a memory of the cow as that which was previously perceived to have some resemblance with the *gavaya* which is now perceived. Hence there is no need for an independent *pramāṇa* called *upamāna* to explain the knowledge of likeness and unlikeness.[1]

It is to be observed here that Nyāya criticism has so far very little force. It is true that we ordinarily understand an unfamiliar object by comparing it with what is familiar. But this does not prevent us from comparing the familiar with what is new and unfamiliar. Nor does it invalidate our subsequent knowledge of the former as like or unlike the latter. Further, we cannot say that all knowledge of likeness is memory. A man who has seen a *gavaya* may, when perceiving a cow, know its similarity to the *gavaya*. It is possible only for him to remember that a cow was found to be like a *gavaya* at the time when he perceives the *gavaya*. But a man who has never seen a *gavaya* cannot know that a cow is similar to it. When the perception of a *gavaya* suggest to him that the cow is

1. *Vide* NM., pp. 146-47.

like it because the *gavaya* is like the cow, we cannot say that he only remembers the cow's likeness, since there was no previous perception of it.

The Naiyāyika is perhaps conscious of the weakness of his first two arguments and so brings forward a third one to supplement them. He thinks that even if *upamāna* be different from memory, we may very well explain it as a form of inference. From the perception of the *gavaya* we know that it has some points in common with the remembered cow. This leads to the inference that the remembered cow is like the *gavaya,* because it has some points in common with the *gavaya.* The Vedantist's *upamāna* is thus reduced to a mediate syllogistic inference: "Whatever has certain points in common with another thing is like that thing; the remembered cow has some points in common with the perceived *gavaya;* therefore it is like the *gavaya.*"[1]

The Naiyāyika seems to be on strong ground when he reduces the reasoning about likeness and unlikeness to inference. The Vedāntist's *upamāna*, when analytically considered, deals with our knowledge of the relations among correlative terms. Ordinary syllogistic inference is concerned with the relations of subject and predicate among different terms. But there are other relations which furnish grounds of inference. These are the relations among correlative terms. The doctrine of correlation (*pratiyogiva*) and the relations of correlative terms have been much elaborated in the modern Nyāya. There are two kinds of correlation, namely, *abhāvapratiyogitva* or the correlation existing between a term and its contradictory, and *satpatiyogitva* or the correlation existing between relative terms. The relations among contradictory terms like A and not-A, red and not-red, are the grounds of immediate inferences by conversion, obversion, contraposition, etc. The correlations among relative terms are the grounds of both mediate and immediate inferences. There are different types of such correlation. Bradley[2] enumerates four types of these relations. These

1. *Vide* NM., p. 148.
2. Bradley, *Logic,* Vol. I, pp. 264-66.

are: (1) The synthesis of identity, *e.g.* A is the father of B, B is the son of A; or, A is the brother of B, and B of C, then A is the brother of Ç. (2) The synthesis of degree, *e.g.* A is grater than B, B is less than A; or, A is hotter than B, and B than C, therefore A than C. (3) The synthesis of time, *e.g.* A is earlier than B, B is later than A; or, A is a day before B, B contemporary with C, therefore C a day after A. (4) The synthesis of space, *e.g.* A is north of B, B is south of A; or, A is north of B and B west of C, therefore C south-east of A. The Vedāntist's *upamāna* deals with the correlations of likeness and unlikeness which, following Bradley, we may call the synthesis of comparison. It consists in reasoning form the proposition 'A is like B' to the proposition 'B is like A'; or from 'A is unlike B' to 'B is unliked A.' It is really a kind of immediate inference. But there being no such thing as immediate inference in Indian Logic, the Naiyāyika puts it in the form of a syllogism which has the additional advantage of testing the validity of such reasoning.

The Jainas do not recognise *upamāna* as an independent source of knowledge, but include it under *pratyabhijñā* or recognition. They understand *pratyabhijñā* in a very wide sense so as to cover all such cases of knowledge as 'this is that object,' 'this is like that,' 'this is unlike that,' 'this is at a distance fore us,' 'this is a tree,' etc. It is clear from this that *pratyabhijñā* here stands for any knowledge which is conditioned by perception and memory. The reasoning from the proposition 'the *gavaya* is like the cow,' to the proposition the cow is like the *gavaya'* is not a case of *upamāna,* but of *pratyabhijñā,* since it can very well be explained by the perception of likeness in the *gavaya* and memory of the cow. So also the Naiyāyika's *upamāna* is a source of the knowledge of denotation of words is, according to Jainas, a case of *pratyabhijñā* or recognition. The knowledge of the likeness or unlikeness through which we recognise an object is given by perception. The knowledge of the object as a cow or *gavaya* is due to the recollection of their description as supplied to us by some competent person.[1]

1. *Prameyakamalamārtaṇḍa,* pp. 97-100.

It is to be observed here that the Jaina view of *upamāna* as a form of *pratyabhijñā* or recognition rests on a wrong assumption. They seem to think that a knowledge is explained when we explain the constituent parts of it. But to explain the component parts of knowledge is not to explain knowledge itself. To say that it is so is the fundamental error of all associationist theory of knowledge. If it were really so, the Jaina view of *pratyabhijñā* itself as a distinct type of knowledge will have to be discarded, since it is constituted by perception and memory. On this assumption we may reduce all kinds of knowledge to perception, since the constituents of all knowledge ultimately come from perception. That we recognise other kinds of knowledge than perception is due to the fact that the combination of elements derived from perception involves new principles which take us beyond perception. We shall consider hereafter if the Naiyāyika's *upamāna* involves any new principle of combination so as to justify us in treating it as a new kind of knowledge.

3. The Classification of *Upamāna*

Upamāna was at first regarded as only of one kind, namely, as the knowledge of a thing as denoted by a word through its similarity to a well-known object of experience. Later Naiyāyikas, however, distinguished between different kinds of *upamāna,* according as they are based on the knowledge of dissimilarity between things, or on that of their peculiar properties. Thus, the Naiyāyikas generally recognise three kinds of *upamāna* or knowledge by comparison, namely, *sādharmyopamāna, vaidharmyopamāna* and *dharmamātropamāna.*[1]

In *sādharmya-upamāna* we start from the description of an unknown object given in terms of its similarity to a well-known object by some authoritative person. It then we find any object or objects that answer to the given description, *i.e.* are similar to the things they are compared with, we know that they belong to this or that class. Here then we apply a class-concept to certain facts on

1. *Vide* TR. and SS., pp. 86-88.

the basis of some observed similarity between them and other known facts. The concept is given to us and the facts to which it applies are selected by us. This kind of *upamāna* is illustrated in the citizen's application of the name *gavaya* to the wild oxen because they are found to satisfy the description of the *gavaya* as an animal similar to the cow.

In *vaidharmya-upamāna* the objects denoted by a word are described in terms of their contrast or dissimilarity to some well-known objects of experience. This negative description enables a man to recognise certain objects as denoted by a word or as belonging to a certain class in so far as he finds that they fit in with the given description. This is illustrated when a man recognises certain animals as belonging to the class of horses because, unlike the cow, they have no cloven hoofs.

In *dharmamātra-upamāna* the objects denoted by a name are described in terms of their peculiar to them. This description enables us to discriminate the things denoted by the name from all other things and consequently apply the name to just that class of things. This is illustrated when from the description of 'man' as a cooking animal or of the *karabha* as a long-necked animal with projecting lips and feeding on thorns, we recognise the animals denoted by these words. It may be observed here that these three kinds of *upamāna* are illustrated also by medical students when they collect herbs and plants according to the descriptions given of them in the materia medica.

Viśvanātha in his *Nyāya-sūtra-vṛtti* mentions another kind of *upamāna* which is slightly different from the above three. Here *upamāna* consists, not in the knowledge of the denotation of a word, but in that of some unknown property of an object through its similarity to a known thing. Thus if on hearing that a certain herb resembling the *mudgaparṇī* is an antidote and then finding such a herb we conclude that it is an antidote, our knowledge is due to *upamāna* or comparison.[1]

---

1. *Vide Nyāya-sūtra-vṛtti* and *Nyāya-sūtra-vivaraṇa*, 1. 1. 6.

It is sometimes held that the Naiyāyika's *upamāna* is an analogical argument. There are two facts that lend colour to this view. First, the *Nyāya-sūtra* defines *upamāna* as the knowledge of an object (*sādhya*) from some recognised similarity between two things (*prasiddhasādharmyāt*). Secondly the last kind of *upamāna* mentioned by Viśvanātha very closely approximates an analogical reasoning when from the observed resemblances between two things we argue to the presence of some unobserved property in one of them. But from the Nyāya account of *upamāna* as given above it will appear that it does not really correspond to an analogical argument. In analogy we infer one resemblance from other resemblances; *e.g.* when we say A resembles B in having the properties *x* and *y*, therefore it resembles *B* in having the property *z*. But in *upamāna* we argue as much from resemblance as from contrast and peculiarity. Further, *upamāna* leads not to the knowledge of resemblance between things, but to that of the denotation of a word, or to the application of a name to a class of objects. Even the special kind of *upamāna* mentioned by Viśvanātha is not a knowledge of resemblance, but is the identification of an object from a given description.

Chapter XV

Upamāna as an Independent Source of Knowledge (*Pramāṇa*)

1. Can *Upamāna* give us any Valid Knowledge?

With regard to the Nyāya view of *upamāna* it has been urged by the Cārvākas that it cannot gives us any true knowledge about the denotation of words as maintained by the Naiyāyikas. In it we are to know the objects denoted by a word from their similarity or dissimilarity to certain well-known things or from their peculiarities. But mere resemblance or difference without any universal relation cannot be the ground of a certain conclusion. In the stock example of *sādharmyaupamāna,* we are to know that a certain animal must be a *gavaya* because it is similar to the cow. If the similarity between the two be perfect, then they become identical with each other. Hence on the ground of such perfect similarity it is as much true to say that the animal is a cow as to say that it is a *gavaya.* If, on the other hand, the similarity be semi-perfect or considerable, then the word *gavaya* may be taken to denote buffaloes in so far as they are considerably similar to the cow. If, again, the similarity be imperfect or slight, there is nothing to prevent the application of the name *gavaya* to cats and dogs in so far at least as they are *animals* like the cow. Similarly, any description of a class of things in terms of their dissimilarity to certain well-known things or in those of their peculiarities does not always help us to recognise them as such-and-such, or know them as denoted by this or that word. This shows that *upamāna* or mere comparison between things is not a valid source of knowledge.[1]

---

1. *Vide* NS. and NB., 2. 1. 42.

Now, the Naiyāyikas meet the above sceptical argument against the validity of *upamāna* in two ways. First, they point out that the argument rests on a misunderstanding as to the real nature of *upamāna* or comparison as a method of knowledge. It is not the case that when *upamāna* is based on similarity it is committed to one of the three degrees of perfect, semi-perfect or imperfect similarity. Far from this being so, it has been expressly laid down that the similarity must be one that has an accredited bearing on the subject in question (*prasiddha*). The similarity must be essential and requisite, and serve as sufficient ground for the recognition of a class of things as denoted by a word. *Upamāna* or comparison as a source of knowledge operates through such observed similarity or dissimilarity as is rooted in things and limits the denotation of a word to them. As a matter of fact, there is no such rule that the similarity must be of a particular degree as perfect or semi-perfect or imperfect. What particular sort of resemblance is meant by the similarity in question depends on the special circumstances of the case and the context in which an argument through comparison occurs. As such, the given description in terms of similarity, etc., makes a selection of its own objects and brings them under a class-concept or a name in the light of our previous experience. In the stock example, the judgment 'this is a *gavaya*' is brought about, not by the degree of the similarity between the cow and the wild ox, but by the suggestiveness it has acquired in relation to our past and present experiences. It is this suggestive character of the similarity that restricts the denotation of the word *gavaya* to the wild ox and excludes the buffalo and the like. Secondly, the Naiyāyikas do not dent that *upamāna* sometimes leads to wrong judgments, *e.g.* the judgment of a buffalo as a *gavaya*. But then this difficulty is not peculiar to *upamāna*. All of our perceptions and inferences are not *ipso facto* valid. Still we recognise perception and inference as valid sources of knowledge. If so, there is no reason why we should deny that *upamāna* is a valid source of the knowledge of some objects. The wrong judgements of comparison may, like those of perception, be explained as due to the wrong application of a right principle and not to the logical principle itself.[1]

2. Can *Upamāna* be Reduced to any other *Pramāṇa*?

Admitting that *upamāna* is a valid source of knowledge (*pramāṇa*), it may be pertinently asked: Is it an independent source of knowledge, irreducible to any other? This question has been answered in the negative by some systems of Indian philosophy. These systems reject the Naiyāyika view of *upamāna* as an independent method of knowledge. We have already considered the attempt made by the Jainas to reduce it to *pratyabhijñā* or recognition. In some other systems the attempt has been made to reduce it to perception or inference or testimony. Hence, the Naiyāyikas discuss the question of reducing *upamāna* or comparison to some other *pramāṇa*.

According to the Buddhist logicians *upamāna* is a valid but not an independent source of knowledge. It can be explained as a combination of perception and verbal testimony. There are two factors in *upamāna,* namely, the knowledge of the similarity or dissimilarity between two classes of things and the knowledge of the fact that things of a certain class are denoted by a certain word. As to the first factor we see that it is obviously given by perception. When we see two things together we perceive that they are similar or dissimilar to each other. As to the second factor, namely, the knowledge of the denotation of words, it is derived from the statements of authoritative persons, *i.e.* testimony. Hence *upamāna* need not be given the status of an independent source of knowledge. Now, the Naiyāyikas point out that the Buddhist contention rests on a complete misunderstanding of the real nature of an argument by *upamāna* or comparison. The vital point in *upamāna* is neither the perception of similarity nor the verbal knowledge of the denotation of a word, but the recognition of certain objects, not known before, as belonging to a class and denoted by a class-concept. The similarity of those objects to other things may be

1. *Vide* NB. and NVT., 2. 1. 43.

perceived and the class-concept may be given by testimony. But the application of the concept to a particular class of things cannot be due to perception or testimony. Hence, *upamāna* cannot be reduced to perception and tesitmony.[1]

In the Sāṅkhya[2] and Vaiśeṣika[3] systems *upamāna* is explained as a form of inference. It is here admitted that the Naiyāka's *upamāna* is neither the perceptual nor the verbal cognition of the similarity between two objects, *e.g.* the cow and the *gavaya.* On the other hand, *upamāna* really aims at the knowledge of the denotation of a word or class-concept. But this can very well be explained as due to inference. Analysing the Naiyāyika's *upamāna* we get three component factors. First, there is the communication of some knowledge about the denotation of a word by authoritative statements. This is obviously a case of knowledge from testimony and is in the form of the sentence 'the word *gavaya* denotes animals resembling the cow.' Secondly, there is the observation of a certain animal resembling the cow. This gives us a knowledge of the animal's similarity to the cow, which is undoubtedly perceptual in character, since it is due to sense-object contact. Thirdly, there is the knowledge that the word *gavaya* denotes animals of the same class as this particular animal now observed. This last cognition is wrongly supposed by the Naiyāyikas to be due to *upamāna.* But it is really an inferential cognition based on the knowledge of *vyāpti* or a universal relation between the word *gavaya* and animals resembling the cow. The inference may be put in the form of the following syllogism:

> All animals resembling the cow are *gavayas;*
>
> This is an animal resembling the cow;
>
> Therefore this is a *gavaya.*

As against the above attempt to reduce *upamāna* to inference, it has been pointed out by the Naiyāyikas that the knowledge of

---

1. *Vide* NV., 1. 1. 6.
2. *Vide Tattvakaumudī* and *Āvaraṇavāriṇī,* 5.
3. *Vide* PS., p. 109.

the denotation of a word, which *upamāna* aims at, is possible without the knowledge of *vyāpti* or a universal relation between two terms. An argument by *upamāna* or comparison does not consist in an inductive generalisation and its application to a new case. It consists in the application of a class-concept to some objects because they fit in with a given description. *Upamāna* being thus possible without the knowledge of *vyāpti* cannot be reduced to inference which is never possible without a knowledge of *vyāpti* or universal relation between two things. Further, there is an unmistakanble difference between the forms of the cognitions in inference and *upamāna*. In *upamāna* the resulting cognition is always expressed in terms of likeness, etc., while an inferential cognition is expressed in terms of the relation of ground and consequence. In inference the introspective consciousness is a feeling of the 'therefore-relation,' while in *upamāna* it is a feeling of similarity, etc. In *upamāna* we are not conscious of inferring but of comparing. Inference is distinguished from perception because our cognitions are distinctly different in the two cases. Just for the same reason *upamāna* must be distinguished from perception, inference and testimony.[1]

3. Conclusion

The question discussed in the Nyāya theory of *upamāna* is this: How do we know the denotation of a word or a class-name? There are various ways in which we may know it. In the first place, the objects denoted by the word *gavaya* may be pointed out to us by any person who know its denotation and we may be told that these objects are denoted by the word. In this case we know the denotation of the word from direct testimony, because here in the presence of the denoted objects we are told by some authority; 'These are the objects denoted by the word *gavaya.*' But it is not always possible or us to know the denotation of words from direct testimony, for we cannot always be brought to the presence of the

1. *Vide Tarkasaṁgraha-Dīpikā-Prakāśa*, p. 63; *Dinakari* and *Rāmarudrī on Siddhāntamuktāvalī*, pp. 354-55.

denoted objects and told that they are denoted by such and such words. There are, however, other ways open to us to know the denotation of words. We may know the denotation of a word from its accepted definition or from a description of the objects denoted by it. Thus from the definition of the word 'man' as a rational animal we understand what animals are denoted by it. Similarly, from the description of the *gavaya* as an animal resembling the cow, we can recognise the class of animals called *gavaya*. Now the question is: What is the nature of the process of knowledge involved in our understanding the denotation of words in this latter way? Is it perception or inference or testimony or any combination of these? According to the Nyāya, it is a distinct method of knowledge called *upamāna* or comparison. It is no doubt true that the process involves an element of perception and testimony. The definition or the description comes to us as a spoken or written statement of some authority and, as such, is but a form of testimony. Similarly, we know by perception that certain objects possess the attributes or characteristics included in the definition or the description. But from this we cannot conclude that the process involved in the knowledge of those objects as denoted by a word is a combination of perception and testimony. To explain the elements of a knowledge is not to explain the knowledge itself, if it has a distinctive character of its own. Perception does not become ideation because it involves certain ideas and images. So too inference cannot be reduced to perception and testimony even though it includes certain elements derived from them. For the same reason the process of knowing the denotation of a word should not be reduced to perception and testimony, since they explain certain elements of the process but not the process itself. The next question is: Can we not explain the knowledge of denotation by an inference? This can be done if we show that the knowledge of denotation follows as a conclusion from a universal proposition as major premise through the mediation of the minor premise. Now, the knowledge of the denotation of a word can be deduced, at least theoretically, from a universal proposition like 'all animal resembling the cow are *gavayas.*' But to show that the denotation of words *can* be known by inference is not to show that it *is* actually so known. When we know the denotation of a word we do not argue syllogistically from premises to the conclusion, but simply compare certain facts with a given description. To know that these facts fit in with the description one requires a selective activity of the mind which is distinct from perception, inference and testimony. Hence we conclude with the Naiyāyikas that *upamāna* or comparison is an independent source of our knowledge of the denotation of words.

V. *ŚABDA* OR TESTIMONY

Chapter XVI

Nature and Classification of Śabda

1. The Nyāya Definition of *Śabada* and its Different Kinds

Śabda literally means verbal knowledge. It is the knowledge of objects derived from words or sentences. All verbal knowledge, however, is not valid. Hence *śabda,* as a *pramāṇa,* is defined in the Nyāya as valid verbal testimony. It consists in the assertion of a trustworthy person.[1] A verbal statement is valid when it comes from a person who knows the truth and speaks the truth about anything for the guidance of other persons.[2] But it is a matter of common observation that a sentence or statement is not by itself sufficient to give us any knowledge of things. Nor again does the mere perception of the words of a sentence lead to any knowledge about objects. It is only when one perceives the words and understands their meanings that he acquires any knowledge from a verbal statement. Hence, while the validity of verbal knowledge depends on its being based on the statement of trustworthy person, its possibility is conditional on the understanding of the meaning of that statement. Hence, *śabda* or testimony as a source of valid knowledge consists in understanding the meaning of the statement of a trustworthy person.[3]

It will appear from the above definition that the first step in *śabda* or testimony is the perception of the words of a sentence or proposition set forth by some trustworthy person. In the case of a spoken sentence we have an auditory perception, and in that of a written sentence we have a visual perception of the constituent

1. *Āptopadeśaḥ śabdaḥ*, NS., 1. 1. 7.
2. *Vide* TR., pp. 94-95.
3. *Vide* BP. *and* SM., 81. *Cf. Vākyārthajñānam śabdajñānam*, TS., p. 73.

words. Secondly, there must be an understanding of the meaning of the words perceived by us. It is through this understanding of the meaning of words that we come to the final step, namely, the verbal knowledge of objects or the truth about certain objects. Thus the *karaṇa* or the special cause of *śabda* or valid verbal knowledge is the knowledge of words (*padajñāna*) which leads to the knowledge of objects through its function (*vyāpāra*) of recalling to our minds the meanings connected with words or sentences.[1] Thus, *śabda* is distinguished from the preceding *pramāṇas* by the fact that it is due to the knowledge of words of sentences, while perception is due to sense-object contact, inference to the knowledge of *vyāpti* or universal relation, and *upamāna* or comparison to the perception of similarity or dissimilarity.

There are two ways in which all verbal knowledge has been classified in the Nyāya system. According to Vātsyāyana, verbal knowledge is of two kinds, namely, *dṛṣṭārtha* or that relating to perceptible objects and *adṛṣṭārtha* or that relating to imperceptible objects.[2] The first is limited to the ordinary sensible objects of this world, while the second relates to supersensible objects which cannot be known by means of perception. Under the first head we are to include the trustworthy assertions of ordinary persons, the saints and the scriptures in so far as they bear on the perceptible objects of the world. Thus, the evidence given by witnesses in law courts, the knowledge about plants that we get from a reliable farmer, the scriptural injunctions about certain rites and ceremonies for rainfall, birth-control and the like are illustrations of *dṛṣṭārtha śabda*. The second will include all the trustworthy assertions of ordinary persons, saints, prophets and the scriptures in so far as they bear on supersensible realities. Thus the scientist's assertions about atoms, ether, electrons, vitamins, etc., the prophet's instructions about virtue and vice, the scriptural texts on God, heaven, future life and the like are illustrations of *adṛṣṭārtha śabda*.

1. *Padajñānaṁ tu karaṇaṁ dvāraṁ tatra padārthyadhīḥ*, etc., BP. and SM., 81.
2. *Sa dvividho dṛṣṭādṛṣṭārthativāt*, NS. and NB., 1. 1. 8.

According to the later Naiyāyikas, there are two kinds of *śabda* or verbal testimony, namely, *vaidika* or the scripture and *laukika* or the secular. In the firs we have the words of God. The Vedas are created by God and are therefore valid on all points. *Vaidika* or scriptural testimony is thus perfect and infallible by its very nature. As distinguished from this, *laukika* or secular testimony is not all valid. It is the testimony of human beings and may therefore be true or false. Of *laukika* testimony, only that which proceeds from trustworthy persons is valid, but not the rest.[1] It will be observed here that while the first classification of *śabda* depends on the nature of the objects of knowledge, this second classification has reference to the nature of the source of knowledge in testimony. All Naiyāyikas, however, agree in holding that testimony must always be personal, *i.e.* based on the words of some trustworthy person, human or divine. In respect of truth or validity there is no difference between the trustworthy assertions of an ordinary person, a saint, a prophet and the scriptures as revealed by God.

2. Other Systems on the Nature and Forms of *Śabda*

Of the other systems of Indian philosophy, the Cārvāka, Bauddha and Vaiśeṣika do not recognise *śabda* or testimony as a distinct *pramāṇa* or source of knowledge. According to the Cārvākas, there is no logical ground or justification for our believing in anything simply on the statement of another person. If it were so, we shall have to believe in many absurd and fictitious objects about which any fool may tell us. If, however, *śabda* or testimony be constituted by the statement of a trustworthy person, it is only a case of inference from the character of a man to the truth of his assertion. But inference cannot be accepted as a valid source of human knowledge. Hence, *śabda* or testimony should not be recognised as a *pramāṇa* or valid method of knowledge.[2] According to the Buddhist logician, *śabda* is not an independent source of knowledge, but a form of perception or inference. If by *śabda* we

1. *Vākyaṁ dvividham, vaidikam laukikañca*, etc., TS., p. 73
2. *Vide Sarvadarśanasaṁgraha,* Chapter. I.

mean to rove that he person who makes a certain statement is trustworthy, we educe it to inference. If, however, we use it to prove that there are actual facts corresponding to a statement, we reduce it to perception.[1] According to the Vaiśeṣikas, *śabda* as a form of knowledge is to be included in inference, since the ground of our knowledge is the same in both. Just as in inference we know an unperceived objects which are unperceived but related to the words perceived by us.[2]

In the Jaina system *śabda* is recognised as a separate *pramāṇa* or source of knowledge. It consists in the knowledge derived from words which, when properly understood, expressed objects and are not inconsistent with the evidence of perception. It is called *laukika* or secular testimony when the words come from an ordinary reliable person of the world. It is called *śāstraja* or scriptual testimony when it proceeds from a liberated self of extraordinary powers and knowledge, and relates to supersensible realities.[3] Thus while in the Nyāya system scriptural testimony depends on divine revelation, in the Jaina it comes from the perfected and omniscient finite self. In the Sāṅkhya-yoga system too we find a recognition of *śabda* or testimony as a valid method of knowledge.[4] But while in the Sāṅkhya, scriptural testimony is regarded as impersonal and therefore possessing self-evident validity, the Nyāya takes it as neither impersonal nor self-evidently valid. It holds that the scriptures have been created by God and require to be proved by reason as much as any other form of knowledge. According to the Mīmāṁsā system, *śabda* as a *pramāṇa* consists in the true knowledge of objects, derived from the understanding of the meaning of a sentence. It is called *pauruṣeya* or personal when constituted by the words of trustworthy persons, and *apauruṣeya* or impersonal when constituted by the words of the Vedas.[5] The

1. *Vide* S. C. Vidyābhūṣaṇa's *History of Indian Logic*, pp. 287-88.
2. *Vide* PS., pp. 106-8; VS., 9. 2. 3.
3. *Vide Prameyakamala.*, pp. 112-13.
4. *Vide Tattvakaumudī* and *Āvaraṇavāriṇī*, 5; *Yoga-bhāṣya* 1. 7.
5. *Vide* SD., p. 72.

Prābhākara school of the Mīmāṁsā, however, takes *śabda* to mean only *vaidika* or scriptural testimony about the existence of supersensuous realities.[1] According to the Vedāntists, *śabda* or *āgama* as a source of valid knowledge consists in sentences or propositions which assert a certain relation between things, that is not contradicted in any way.[2] It is a verbal knowledge of objects, which is not validly contradicted by any other knowledge. While this is implied in the Nyāya definition of *śabda,* there is some difference between the Nyāya and the Vedānta with regard to the nature of *vaidika* or scriptural testimony. According to the Nyāya, scriptural testimony is personal, since the Vedas have been created by the supreme person or God. For the Vedānta, it is impersonal inasmuch as God does not create but only reveals the contents of the Vedas, which are eternal truths independent of God. So also the Mīmāṁsakas look upon the Vedas as a system of necessary truths or eternal verities which are independent of all persons and therefore purely impersonal in character. For the Naiyāyikas, the Vedas as a system of truths embody the will of God. They expressed eternal reason of the divine being in the order of time.

---

1. *Vide* Jhā's *Prābhākara School of Pūrva-Mīmāṁsā*, p. 52.
2. *Vide* VP., Chapter IV.

Chapter XVII

Words (*Pada*)

1. Sounds and Words

In the last chapter we have seen that *śabda* as a *pramāṇa* consists in sentences or propositions put forth by some trustworthy person. Now a sentence is a group of words (*pada*) arranged in a certain way. To understand a sentence (*vākya*) we have to understand its constituent words. Hence, we propose to consider here the nature and meaning of words, as well as other questions in connection with the understanding of words.

Śabda literally means sound. In linguistics it means also words or sentences. A word is a particular kind of sound. So, also a sentence is a group of sounds arranged in a certain order. How then is a word related to ordinary sounds?

According to the Nyāya, sound is a physical phenomenon. It is the attribute of an intangible and all-pervading substance called *ākāśa* or the ether. Air is not the substratum of the quality of sound, but the medium of its transmission from one place to another. Sound is a product of the conjunction of two bodies or of the disjunction of the parts of one composite body. It is therefore non-eternal or subject to origin and cessation in time.[1] The Mīmāṁsakas here controvert the Nyāya position and hold that sound is eternal, since it is not produced, but only manifested by the contact of two bodies. It is unnecessary for our present purpose to enter upon the long controversy between the Nyāya and the Mīmāṁsā on this point.[2]

---

1. *Vide* TB., pp. 26-27.
2. *Vide* NM., pp. 205-32.

Sound is of two kinds, namely, *dhvani* and *varṇa.*[1] A *dhvani* is an inarticulate sound, *e.g.* the sound of a bell or a drum. It is a confused mass of sound-sensations having no order or arrangement of its parts. It has no fixed nature of its own, nor any fixed relation to other like sounds. *Dhvani* is thus incapable of forming parts of any language. On the other hand, a *varṇa* is a sound produced by the action of the vocal organ of human beings, *e.g.* the alphabet. A *varṇa* is a letter which has a fixed character and a definite place in the alphabet of any language. All *varṇas* or letters are constituents of human speech. They may be either spoken or written. Spoken letters are auditory sensations of significant sounds, while written letters are visual sensations of coloured figures. From the standpoint of linguistics, the cries of birds and beasts, and even of newborn babies are dumb and inarticulate. They are as variable and disorderly as sounds produced by physical things. These do not lend themselves to any use as parts of any language. Hence, they are included within *dhvani* and not made a separate class.

A word is a group of *varṇas* or letters arranged in a certain fixed order. The order of the letters in a word cannot be changed or reversed in any way without altering its meaning. Thus the word 'cow' is a grouping of the letters *c-o-w* in the given order. If we change this order we destroy the word itself. Similarly, the words 'won' and 'own,' which contain the same letters, become different because the fixed order of the letters is different in the two cases. While a letter is a significant sound, a word is a symbolic sound of a higher order. A letter signifies only a part of the alphabet, but a word stands for some thing or some idea. Like letters, words may be either spoken or written. A spoken word is the object of auditory perception and a written word that of visual perception. Thus, words are symbolic sounds constituted by letters arranged in a definite order. A word is not a mere collection of letters but a definite whole of letters or syllables which are its parts and have a fixed order in the whole. It is a unity of the parts in so far as it is the object of a single cognition.[2] The question as to how the constituents

1. *Śabdo dhvaniśca varṇaśca,* etc., BP., 164-65.

2. *Padaṁ ca varṇasamūhaḥ'* etc., p. 14.

of a word are synthesised so as to form one whole, will be considered later on.

2. Words and their Meanings

A word is defined as a group of letters arranged in a fixed order. This definition, however, has in view the existence or the constitution of a word. The essential nature of a word lies in its meaning.[1] Logically a word is a sound that bears a certain meaning. The meaning of a word consists in its relation to the object which it signifies. A word may have different meanings according to the different ways in which it may be related to an object. According to the Naiyāyikas, there are three kinds of meaning of a word, namely, *abhidhā, paribhāṣā* and *lakṣaṇā*.[2] Let us here consider these different kinds of meaning of a word.

By *abhidhā* is meant the primary meaning of a word. It is also called *śakyārtha, vācyārtha* and *mukhyārtha*. The relation between a word and its meaning may be either *saṅketa* or *lakṣaṇā*. *Saṅketa* is the direct relation between a word and its meaning, such that the knowledge of the word leads immediately to the knowledge of its relation to that meaning. Now *saṅketa* or the direct relation between a word and its meaning may be either eternal or non-eternal. When eternal and unchanging, it is called *śakti* or the inherent potency of a word. Thus, the relation between the word *jar* and the object called *jar* is a direct and eternal relation called *śakti*. This *śakti* or potency of a word is due to the will of God which ordains that such and such a word should mean such and such an object. According to the Mīmāṁsakas, the *śakti* of a word is its natural relation to the object which it signifies. Just as fire possesses the power of burning, so words possess a natural potency to mean certain things independently of the will of any person. The Naiyāyikas, however, contend that the relation between a word and its meaning is not a

1. *Cf.* *'padaṁ ca varṇasamūhaḥ'* (*Tarkabhāṣā*, p. 14.), *'śaktaṁ padam'* (*Tarkasaṅgraha*, p. 64).

2. *Vide Śabdaśakti-prakāśikā*, Introduction.

natural but conventional relation. When the relation is established by God it is called *śakti,* and when it is due to the usage of mankind called *paribhāsā.* Now, the meaning called up by the *śakti* or inherent potency of a word is its *abhidhā* or *śakyārtha, i.e.* primary meaning. The word which possesses such a meaning is called a *śakta* or *vācaka* word.[1]

When *saṅketa* or the direct relation between a word and its meaning is non-eternal or changeable, it is called *paribhāṣā.* This is due to the will of the authorities in any science which prescribes that such and such a word should mean such and such an object. The meaning called up by the convention established by authorities is the *paribhāṣita* or technical meaning of a word. Words which bear such meanings are called *pāribhāṣika* or technical words, *e.g.* the words 'article' in grammar, 'premise' in logic, 'court' in law, 'category' in philosophy.[2]

By *lakṣaṇā* is meant the secondary meaning if a word. It is the indirect or implied meaning in which we should understand a word when its direct or primary meaning does not consist with other words or the context. A word indirectly means an object when it is related to it because of its direct relation with something else with which the object is somehow associated. When we are told 'the house is *on* the Ganges,' we take 'the Ganges' not in its primary meaning of 'the current of water,' but in the secondary meaning of 'the bank of the Ganges.' Here the secondary meaning is suggested through its association with the primary meaning. There are three kinds of *lakṣaṇā* or secondary meaning, namely, *jahallakṣaṇā, ajahallakṣaṇā* and *jahadajahallakṣaṅā.* In *jahallakṣaṇā,* no part of the primary meaning is retained, *e.g.* 'the scaffolds cry out.' In *ajahallakṣaṇā,* the primary meaning of a word is also retained in the implied meaning, *e.g.* 'a blue jar' meaning a jar with the attribute of blueness. In *jahadajahallakṣaṇā,* a part of the primary meaning is retained, while another part is discarded, *e.g.* 'this is that man.' meaning the identity of the man leaving out the attributes of 'this'

1. *Vide* TS. and TD., p. 64; *Śabdaśakti-prakāśikā,* pp. 55 f.
2. *Vide Śabdaśakti-prakāśikā,* pp. 54-55.

and 'that.'[1] The Naiyāyikas do not admit with the Vedāntists that not only words but sentences also may have secondary meanings (*lakṣaṇā*).[2]

The *ālaṁkārikas* or rhetoricians recognise another kind of meaning of words, namely, *vyañjanā*. This stands for such meanings of words as are neither directly nor indirectly related to them, but only suggested by them. Thus the sentence, 'the house is on the Ganges,' may be taken to mean that the house is cool and sacred. This meaning is called *vyañjanā* or the suggested meaning. The Naiyāyikas do not recognise *vyañjanā* as a different type of the meaning of words, but include it within *śakti* and *lakṣaṇā* or the primary and secondary meanings. The *vyaṅgyārtha* or suggested meaning of a word is really inferred from its primary and secondary meanings and is not separate from them.[3]

How do we learn the meaning of words? There are different ways in which we may learn them. First, we learn the meanings of the radicals, verbal roots, suffixes, etc., from grammar. Secondly, we know the meanings of certain general names by means of *upamāna* or comparison, as when we know the *gavaya* from its similarity to the cow. Thirdly, we learn the meanings of words from dictionaries. Then we may know the meaning of certain words from authority, as when a connoisseur tells us that such and such objects are denoted by a certain word. Or, we may know it by induction from the different uses of words by authoritative persons, as when we know the meaning of the word *cow* from the different uses made of it by our elders in relation to a particular kind of animal. Or, we may know the meaning of a word from its context, as when the 'chair' means the 'chairman' in a meeting. Or, we may know it from a given explanation, as when we understand a word from any of its synonyms. Finally, we may know the meaning of a word from its application in connection with a familiar word,

---

1. *Vide Śabdaśakti-prakāśikā*, pp. 59 f. *Vide* also *Tattvadīpikā p. 67*.
2. *Vide* VP., Ch. IV; *Śabdaśakti-prakāśikā*, pp. 61 f.
3. *Vide Tattvadīpikā, p. 68; Śabdaśakti-prakāśikā*, pp. 64f.

as when we understand the meaning of the word *pika* from the sentence 'the *pika* is crying cuckoo on this tree.'[1]

That there are so many different ways of knowing the meanings of words proves that the relation between words and their meanings is not a natural but a conventional relation. If there were a fixed natural relation between a word and its meaning as between fire and burning, then the word should have always coexisted with the object signified by it and we should have known their relation simply by perception. But a word does not coexist with the object denoted by it. The word *fire* does not coexist with the object 'fire' and produce any burning sensation in us when we utter the word. Nor do we *perceive* the relation between a word and its meaning in the same way that we perceive the relation between fire and burning. Further, the conventional character of the relation between words and their meanings is evidenced by the different meanings in which the same word is used by different people. The variation in the meanings of words cannot be explained on the hypothesis of a natural relation between words and their meanings. It appears also in the use of different words to mean the same thing, *e.g.* aqua, water, *jala.* The convention (*samaya*) that such and such words should mean such and such objects is established by God where the relation between words and their meanings is a fixed and eternal relation called *śakti* or denotation. It is established by human beings living in a society where the relation between them is a changeable relation called *paribhāṣā* or *lakṣaṇā.*[2]

Words are divided into four kinds according to the different ways in which their meaning is determined. A word is called *yaugika* or etymological when its meaning is solely determined by those of its component parts, *e.g.* the word *dātā* or *giver* meaning one who gives. It is called *rūḍha* or conventional when its meaning is determined by the whole independently of the part meanings, *e.g.* the word go meaning, not one who goes, but the cow. Some

1. *'Śaktigrahaṁ vyākaḍraṇopamāna,'* etc., SM., pp. 359-72. *Cf. Śabdaśaktiprakāśikā,* 20.
2. *Vide* NB., 2. 1. 54 and 55; *Śabdaśakti-prakāśikā, ibid.*

words are called *yogarūḍha* or etymologo-conventional when the meaning determined by the whole agrees with that determined by the parts, *e.g.* the word *paṅkaja* meaning a water-lily which grows in the mud. Lastly, certain words are called *yaugika-rūḍha* or etymological-conventional when their meanings are determined either by the potency of the whole or by those of the parts, *e.g.* the word *udbhid* meaning a germ or the sprouting of a seed or a sacrifice.[1]

3. The Import of Words

What is the primary meaning of a word? Does a word mean an individual (*vyakti*), or a particular form (*ākṛti*) or a universal (*jāti*)? There are different views about the import of words. These have been explained and examined by Vātsyāyana in the *Nyāya-bhāṣya*.

According to some thinkers, including to Sāṅkhyas, a word denotes an individual object (*vyakti*).[2] By an individual is meant a composite material body possessing specific properties. It is a substance which has a limited dimension and may have such qualities as smell, taste, colour, touch, etc. It is manifested and open to sense perception. It follows from this that the principle of individuation is *materia signata* or quantitatively determined matter and the individual must have a manifest body (*mūrti*).[3] That such individual objects are denoted by words is evident from the established usage of mankind. When we use such expressions as 'that cow stands,' 'a herd of cows,' 'he gives a cow to the Brahmin,' etc., we evidently mean the individuals called cows. Such expressions cannot refer to the genus or the universal 'cowness,' since the universal is one and eternal, and so cannot be specified as this or that, or spoken of as a collection of many objects. Further, if words do not by themselves mean individuals, we cannot explain heir reference to individual objects by any process of transference of meaning.

1. *Vide* SM., pp. 381-85.
2. *Vide* NS. and NB., 2. 2. 57; *Vivaraṇaprameyasaṁgraha*, p. 181.
3. *Vyaktirguṇaviśeṣāśrayo mūrtiḥ*, NS., 2. 2. 64. *Vide* also NB., *ibid.*

The Naiyāyikas reject the above view of the import of words. If a word mean an individual as such, then any word could mean any and every individual. A word, however, does not mean any individuals, but the individuals of a certain class. In such expressions as 'that cow stands,' etc., what is meant by the word *cow* is not the mere individual by itself but the individual as distinguished by the generality of cowness. Hence, it is not true to say that words denote individuals only. Although words do not, by themselves, mean individuals, yet they may refer to individual objects by reason of the individuals' association or connection with the primary meaning.[1]

The second view about the import of words, which is accepted by the Jainas and others, is that a word denotes the particular form of configuration of individuals.[2] The form (*ākṛti*) of a thing consists in the particular arrangement of its component parts and the constituent particles of those parts. "The form of a thing is that which indicates the generality and its characteristics." Things are distinguished from one another by their peculiar forms. The cow is differentiated from all other animals by its form which consists in the collocation of the dewlap, etc. Words denote objects only as they express their forms or configurations in space, by which their nature is determined. Hence, a word must primarily mean the form or the structure which determines the individuality of an object. The Naiyāyikas reject this view also on the ground that the form by itself is not sufficient to constitute the nature of a thing. The clay model of a cow is not what we mean by a cow, although it possesses the form of a cow. Hence a word should not be taken to mean only the form or the physical shape of an individual apart from its generality or class-essence.[3]

In view of the above difficulties in the 'individualistic' and the 'configuration' theories, the Mīmāṁsakas and Vedāntists propose a third theory, according to which a word means the genus

1. *Vide* NS. and NB., 2. 2. 58-59.
2. *Vide Vivaraṇaprameyasaṁgraha,* p. 181.
3. *Vide* NS. and NB., 2. 2. 60-61; 2. 2. 65.

or the class-character of individuals. The genus is the basis of similar cognitions with regard to different individuals. It gives us a comprehensive knowledge of many things as similar in essential points. Words primarily mean such universals or genera as distinguish the particulars of experience.[1] If a word were to mean the individual, then it must have as many meanings as there are individuals meant by it. This, however, goes against the law of parsimony which requires that a word should have one primary meaning. Although words primarily mean universals, there is nothing to prevent them from referring to the individuals. We know the individual at the same time that we know the universal, because these are inseparable in respect of both knowledge and existence. Or, it may be said that while the universal is the primary meaning of a word, the individual is its secondary meaning (*lakṣaṇā*). Thus the word *blue* primarily means 'blueness' as a universal, but in the phrase 'the blue pot' it means, by implication, the individual with the attribute of blue colour. In the same way, although the word *cow* means 'cowness,' yet by implication it means the individual possessed of the generic attribute of cowness.[2]

According to the Naiyāyikas, words do not mean universals only, since these cannot be understood apart from the individuals and their particular forms. A genus can be recognised only through the individuals that constitute it and their peculiar configurations. Hence, the true view is that a word means all the three, namely, the individual, the configuration, and the generality.[3] It cannot be said that a word directly means the universal and indirectly the individual, for it has only one primary meaning. The indiversal, the individual and the form enter into the full meaning of a word which does not exclusively mean any of them. All the three factors are present in the meaning of a word in the same way, though with different degrees of prominence. Hence, if in actual usage we do find only one factor to be evident, that is not because the other two

---

1. *Vide* NS. and NB., 2. 2. 61; 2. 2. 66.
2. *Vide* VP., Ch. IV; SD., Ch. I.
3. *Vide* NS. and NB., 2. 2. 62-63.

are absent but because we are not interested in them for the none. When we are interested in the difference or distinction of one thing from others, what we do is to emphasise its individuality in the meaning of the word used for it, *e.g.* when we say 'that cow is standing.' But when we want to stress the unity or similarity of things, we give prominence to the generality as a factor in the meaning of the word used, *e.g.* when we say 'the cow is eternal.' Thus the old Naiyāyikas conclude that every word means the universal, the individual and some particular form, and that one of these is predominant, while the rest are subservient factors in the meaning of a word.[1] Among the modern Naiyāyikas, however, some hold that a word means an individual as characterised by the universal (*jātiviśiṣṭavyakti*),[2] while other maintain that it means an individual as qualified by both the universal and the configuration (*jātyākṛtiviśiṣṭavyakti*).[3] It follows from his that there are three aspects in the meaning of a word, namely, a pictorial, a denotative and a connotative. A word calls up the form, denotes the individual, and connotes the genus or the universal. Every word will therefore be connotative in so far as it means the generic properties of the individuals denoted by it. Indian logic thus leaves no room for the so-called non-connotative terms of Formal logic in the West.

4. The Unity of Words and the Hypothesis of *Sphoṭa*

A word is a group of letters having a certain meaning. The letters composing a word have a definite order of succession among them. We perceive the constituent letters one after the other. But the letters or syllables composing a word cannot mean anything by themselves. Letters and syllables bear a meaning only when they are combined into one whole called a word. To put the same thing

1. *Vide* NB., 2. 2. 63.
2. *Vide Dinakarī* on *Siddhāntamuktāvalī*, 81.
3. *Vide* SM., 81; *Śabdaśakti-prakāśikā*, 19. *Cf.* L. S. Stebbing, *A Modern Introduciton to Logic*, p. 500: "The demonstrative symbol *menas* its denotation, *i.e.*, it stands for the object dneoted; whereas the descriptive phrase *means* the properties and not the obejcts (if any) denoted."

in a different way, a word means an object when it is perceived as the unity of a number of letters or syllables. Thus the word *cow* means a particular kind of animal when the letters *c-o-w,* are perceived and formed into the unity of one word. Hence the question arises: How are the letters in a word combined into one whole? Is the unity of the word due to a synthesis of perception or memory or the intellect or something else?

According to the Naiyāyikas, the letters composing a word cannot be simultaneously perceived. We can perceive only one thing at one instant. Hence the letters of a word must be successively perceived by us. But in the order of succession when one is present, the others are either past or future. How then can there be a synthesis of them all into one word? The Naiyāyikas hold that it is by means of memory. It is true that we perceive the different letters one after the other. But when we come to the last letter, the impressions of the preceding letters are retained in our mind. Hence the perception of the last letter as aided by the impressions of the preceding letters presents the word as a whole of many letters, and its meaning is understood according to convention. Thus the spoken word 'cow' is perceived by the auditory sense all at once when it becomes related to the last letter and is aided by the impressions left by the preceding letters, although they are past.[1] The unity of a word is thus explained by the Naiyāyikas as due to memory and association between the letters composing it. According to the Vedāntist, it is due to the synthetic activity of the intellect. The separate experiences of the constituent letters come to us successively, but they are synthesised into the perception of one word by the intellect that holds together these experiences (*samastapratyavamarśinī buddhi*).[2]

The above explanations of the unity of a word as due to the synthesis of memory or the intellect involve certain difficulties for which the grammarians propose the theory of the *sphoṭa.* When we perceive the last letter of a word, we have no perception of the

1. SM., 82; TB., p. 14.
2. *Vide Śaṅkara-bhāṣya* and *Bhāmatī,* 1. 3. 28.

preceding letters. All that we can have at that moment is a memory of this or that preceding letter, but not of all. Strictly speaking, the Naiyāyikas cannot allow more than one cognition, a perception or an image, to be in the mind at one moment. Even if it were possible for us to have the impressions of all the preceding letters, they will serve to give us a knowledge of those letters by way of memory, but not of the thing signified by a word. Then the Vedāntist simply assumes that the intellect holds together the experiences of all the letters, but does not show how these fleeting and successive experiences can be simultaneously present before the same intellect. In truth, a word is not a unity, but a series of successive sounds called letters. These letters cannot be unified into the experience of one word which, therefore, cannot signify an object. All that the series of letter-sounds does is to manifest one inarticulate sound-essence called *sphoṭa* which is the real unity of a word and brings about the cognition of the object said to be meant by the word. Like the genus, the *sphoṭa* is an eternal essence which is common to all the utterances of word. Corresponding to every word there is such a *sphoṭa* or sound essence which is gradually unfolded by the letters of a word. When a particular word is uttered, its *sphoṭa* or unitary principle is manifested and that directly presents the meaning of the word. Hence the *sphoṭa* is the real word that means an object and there is no such thing as a word of letters meaning things.[1]

The theory of *sphoṭa* has been strongly repudiated by many renowned philosophers. The *sphoṭa* is not only, as Thibaut remarks, a grammatical fiction, but is also useless as an explanation of the unity of words. It has been severely criticised and rejected by Śaṅkara, Kumārila, Vācaspati and others.[2] It cannot be denied that words mean objects and they consist of letters or syllables arranged in a definite order. When a thing is expressed by a word, all that we perceive are letters and no *sphoṭa*. Even if there be such a thing

---

1. *Vide* NVT., 2. 2. 57; *Śaṅkara-bhāṣya,* 1. 3. 28.
2. *Vide Śaṅkara-bhāṣya,* 1. 3. 28; NVT., 2. 2. 57; *Śāstradīpikā,* pp. 95-97; *Ślokavārttika,* pp. 510-44.

as the *sphoṭa,* we do not understand how it can mean an object when it is gradually unfolded by the letters of a word. If a series of successive sounds called letters cannot form a single word, how can the successive stages of the manifestation of the *sphoṭa* or sound-essence be synthesised into a unitary whole? The theory of the *sphoṭa* does not bring us nearer the solution of the problem as to how there can be a simultaneous perception of successive facts as we find it in the perception of a word. Neither the Naiyāyikas nor the Vedāntists give a satisfactory answer to this question. They forget that synthesis of the letters in a word by memory or the intellect is not the direct knowledge that we mean by the perception of a word. The Naiyāyikas were forced to draw this conclusion by their view of the mind as atomic and therefore incapable of having more than one cognition at one instant. Had they fully realised the implication of their view of 'the present' as a block of time comprising several instants, they could have easily solved this problem. As many modern psychologists like James, Titchener, Royce and others have shown, our present consciousness is not like an indivisible mathematical point, but is extended like the saddle-back. It has a span or duration of its own. It extends both backward into the past and forward into the future. Hence in the present consciousness we may have a number of successive facts, although that is very limited in our case. Thus there is a simultaneous perception of all the letters of a word, although these are successively read or heard by us. Hence we conclude that the unity of a word is due to the synthesis of perception and not of memory or anything else.[1]

1. *Vide* James, *The Principles of Psychology,* Vol. I, pp. 608-10; Titchener, *A Text-Book of Psychology,* p. 341; Royce, *The World and the Individual.* II, iii.

Chapter XVIII

Sentences (*Vākya*)

1. The Construction of a Sentence

A sentence (*vākya*) is a combination of words having a certain meaning. Any combination of words, however, does not make a significant sentence. The construction of an intelligible sentence must conform to four conditions. These are *ākāṅkṣā, yogyatā, sannidhi* and *tāparyya.*[1]

By *ākāṅkṣā* or expectancy is meant that quality of the words of a sentence by which they expect or imply one another. A word cannot by itself convey a complete meaning. It must be brought into relation with other words in order to express a full judgement.[2] When one hears the word 'bring' uttered before him, he at once asks 'what?' The verb 'bring' has a need for some other words denoting some object or objects, *e.g.* 'the jar.' In the absence of such words, it has no meaning and falls short of a complete judgment. Similarly, a word in the nominative case requires a verb to convey a complete meaning. Generally speaking, the *ākāṅkṣā* or expectancy of words is the relation between *kriyātya* and *kārakatva,* the verb and the case-endings implied by it.[3] When I say 'dog,' 'horse,' 'cow,' 'man,' etc., I simply utter a string of names which do not imply one another and cannot therefore constitute a sentence. The reason is that there is no *kriyātva* and *kārakatva* between these words in the strictly grammatical sence.[4]

---

1. *Vide* BP., 82.
2. *Padasya padāntaravyatirekaprayuktānanvayānanubhāvakatvamākāṅkṣā*, TS., p. 72.
3. *Vide* SM., pp. 423 f; TC., IV. pp. 218 f.
4. *Vide* TB., p. 13.

In some cases, however, we many have a sentence without the relation of *kriyātva* and *kārakatva* between its constituent words, *e.g.* "so, 'yaṁ Devadatta." In the case of the relation of identity the ordinary conditions of *kriyātva* and *kārakatva* are not necessary. Still, we cannot deny the expectancy of the words in an identity proposition. The words imply each other in so far as one means the same thing as is meant by the other. When we say 'this is the Devadatta,' the 'this' and the 'that' mutually imply each other. According to the Vedāntist, there is *ākāṅkṣā* or expectancy between words, not only when one actually implies the other, but may possibly imply it. Thus, when I say 'bring the cow', one may ask 'what kind of cow?' Hence, the word *cow* may imply adjectives like black, old etc. There cannot be a significant sentence unless its terms are thus capable of implying one another.[1]

The second condition of the combination of words in a sentence is their *yogyatā* or mutual fitness. It consists in the absence of contradiction in the relation of the objects denoted by a sentence. When the meaning of a sentence is not contradicted, there is *yogyatā* or fitness between its constituent words. The sentence 'moisten with fire' (*agninā siñcet*) is wanting in fitness because there is a contradiction between fire and moistening. Hence there must not be any incompatibility between the meanings of the different words so as to render the whole sentence itself meaningless. Some modern Naiyāyikas do not consider the knowledge of fitness to be a necessary condition of verbal knowledge. According to them, what prevents the understanding of a sentence is the knowledge of the incompatibility between its words. As such, we may very well have a verbal cognition only if we are not aware of any inconsistency between the words of a sentence. We do not require a further knowledge of their consistency of fitness with one another.[2]

Sannidhi or *āsatti* is the third condition of verbal knowledge. It consists in the propinquity or proximity between the different words of a sentence. If there is to be an intelligible sentence, then

1. VP., Ch. IV.
2. *Arthābādho yogyatā*, TS., p. 72

its constituent words must be continuous with one another in time or space. Spoken words cannot make a sentence when separated by long intervals of time. Similarly, written words cannot construct one sentence when they are separated by long intervals of space. Thus the words 'bring a cow' will not make a sentence when uttered on three days or written on three pages, even though they possess the first two marks of expectancy and fitness.[1]

Tātparyya as a condition of verbal knowledge stands for the meaning intended to be conveyed by a sentence. A word may mean different things in different cases. Whether it means this or that thing in a particular case depends on the intention of the person who uses the word. To understand the meaning of a sentence we must consider the intention of the writer or the speaker who uses it. Thus when a man is asked to bring *saindhava*, he is at a loss to understand whether he is told to bring salt or a horse, for the word means both. This can be ascertained only if we know the intention of the speaker. Hence the understanding of a sentence depends on the understanding of its *tātparyya* or intended meaning. In the case of ordinary sentences used by human beings, we may ascertain their *tātparyya* from the context (*prakaraṇa*) in which they are used. For the understanding of the Vedic text we are to resort to the logical rules of interpretation systematized by the Mīmāṁsā.[2]

With regard to the importance of *tātpayya* or intention as a condition of verbal knowledge there is much difference of opinion among Indian thinkers. Some hold that a definite knowledge of the *tātparyya* or the intended meaning is an essential condition of verbal knowledge. Others think that an understanding of the *tātparyya* is necessary only in the case of equivocal terms and ambiguous expressions having two or more possible meanings. Others again maintain that while *tātparyya* is a condition of verbal knowledge, it is not to be admitted as a separate condition, but should be included within the first condition of *ākāṅkṣā* or syntactic

1. *Padānāmavilambenoccāraṇaṁ sannidhiḥ, ibid.*
2. *Tatpratītīcchayā uccaritatvaṁ tātparyyajñānaṁ ca vākyārthajñāne hetuḥ* etc., *Tattvadīpikā*, p. 68. *Vide* also BP, & SM., 84

expectancy. By *ākāṅkṣā* we mean the need that one word has for another in order to convey the intended meaning of the speaker. As such, *tātparyya* or the intended meaning is a part of the *ākāṅkṣā* or expectancy of words.[1] The Vedāntists, however, contend that *tātparyya* in the sense of the intended meaning is not a condition of verbal cognition. When the parrot imitates such human expressions as 'who comes,' 'who goes,' etc., we cannot say that there is any intention behind its imitative cries. Yet we have no difficulty in understanding the meaning of these expressions. Or, when one utters the Vedic texts without understanding their meaning, he cannot be said to intend the meaning which his hearers interpret out of them. The Vedāntists, therefore, urge that *tātparyya* as a condition of verbal knowledge is not constituted by the meaning intended to be conveyed by the speaker, but by the fitness of the words of sentence to give a particular meaning (*tatpratītijananayogyatvam*). Thus, the sentence 'the jar is in the room' is fit to denote the relation of the room to the jar, but not to the cloth. In the case of equivocal words, like *saindhava,* etc., which may have more than one meaning, we are to say that the *tātparyya* lies in their fitness to yield a particular meaning in the absence of some other intended meaning. The word *saindhava* is fit to mean salt in the absence of any intention to mean the horse. If, however, it be used to mean both salt and horse, we are to say that it has the fitness to mean both in the absence of any intended meaning other than the two. Thus while the Vedāntists admit that *tātparyya* is a necessary condition in the understanding of words or sentences, they reduce it to the fitness of words themselves to give a particular meaning apart from the intention, if any, of the speaker.[2]

It is to be observed here that the difference between the Nyāya and the Vedānta conception of *tātparyya* is ultimately due to their different notions about the meaning of words. For the Vedāntist and the Mīmāṁsaka, the primary meaning (*śakyārtha*) is a power

1. *Vide* SM., 84. *Vide* also Kuppuswāmī Śāstrī, *A Primer of Indian Logic,* p. 335.
2. *Vide* VP., Ch. IV.

inherent in words, while for the Naiyāyika it is imported into the words by the intention of the person who uses them. Hence the Vedāntist's idea of *tātparyya* is vitiated by the initial assumption that the fitness of a word to mean something is an independent thing by itself, that it is a *śakti* or *power* inherent in the word, but distinct from both the word and the object denoted by it. He is thus led to think that *tātparyya* as a condition of verbal knowledge is constituted by the inherent fitness of words to convey a particular meaning independently of the will or intention of the speaker. A word, however, is a significant sign or symbol. It acquires a meaning or significance in so far as it is 'consciously designed to sand for something.' A newly coined word is such a sign used by some one to signify something. We understand a word when we know what it is that a person using it means to signify, otherwise we misunderstand it. As Dr. Stebbing[1] observes: "A hearer understands a word used by a speaker when he is referred to that which the speaker intended to indicate to him." But for the speaker's intention a word cannot have different meanings in different contexts. Hence, we cannot ignore the aspect of intention in the meaning of a word. It fact the Vedāntists have to recognise it in the case of equivocal words which may have two meanings if it be so intended by the speaker or the writer. It is also indirectly admitted by them when they say that the *tātparyya* of a word depends on the context (*prakaraṇa*) in which it is used.

2. The Meaning of a Sentence

A *vākya* or a sentence is a combination of *padas* or words, which conforms to certain conditions. Just as words mean objects, so sentences man the relations of objects. A sentence bears a certain meaning like the constituent words. Hence the question here arises: How are the meanings of the separate words constituting a sentence related to that of the sentence as a whole? Is the meaning of a sentence merely the sum of the meanings of its words? Or, is it something new, but determined by the meanings of the component

1. *Logic in Practice*, p. 66.

words? Or again, does a sentence convey a meaning of its own independently of the words constituting it?

One theory of the relation between the meaning of a sentence and those of its constituent words is know as *abhihitānvayavāda*. According to it, the meaning of a sentence is merely the synthesis (*anvaya*) of the meanings of the separate words composing it. When we read or hear a sentence we have first an understanding of the separate meanings of the words one after the other. Then by putting together the meanings of all the words, according to their expectancy, proximity, fitness and intention (*ākāṅkṣā, sannidhi, yogyatā, tātparyya*), we arrive at the construed meaning of the whole sentence. On this view, then, the expression of the meanings of words precedes the construction of a sentence, *i.e.* there is a construction of the meanings as expressed in the words (*abhihitānvaya*). As to how the different meanings, which are successively expressed by the words, are put together, we are told that it is by means of memory. We understand the meanings of the words successively; but when we come to the last word of a sentence we remember the meanings of all the preceding words. The meaning to the last word being combined with those of the preceding words by means of memory, we have an understanding of the meaning of the sentence as a whole. The theory of *abhihitānvaya* is advocated in the Nyāya, the Bhāṭṭa Mīmāṁsā and the Vedānta system. It is generally supported by the following reasons. If the words of a sentence have no separate meanings of their own, then the classification of words into nouns, adjectivs, verbs, etc., becomes meaningless. Further, in every case in which we are to understand the meaning of a sentence, we must first understand the meaning of its component words. Without a previous understanding of the words no one can understand the meaning of a sentence. Moreover, if the meaning of a sentence were quite independent of the meaning of its constituent words, then any sentence could convey any meaning. Lastly, when we understand the meaning of a new verse, we do so obviously on the basis of our knowledge of the words and their separate meanings. This cannot be explained by any understanding of the sentences, since they are new and unintelligible to us. So it is concluded that the meaning of a sentence is just the synthesis of the separate meanings of its words.[1] Russell subscribes to this view when he observes that 'a sentence may consist of a single word, or of a wink; but generally it consists of several words. In that case it has a meaning which is a function of the meanings of the separate words and their order.'[2]

Another theory of the relation between the meaning of a sentence and those of its constituent words is known as *anvitādhidhāna-vāda*. According to it, the meaning of a sentence is not merely the aggregate of the separate meanings of its constituent words. The sentence has a unitary meaning of its own which cannot be resolved into the complex meaning of its words. Every sentence means an action (*kriyārtha*). It either commands or forbids us to do something. Hence the *kriyā* or the verb is the central unit of a sentence. All the other words of a sentence develop or particularise the action which is the central meaning of it. The constituent words possess meaning only as they are related to the action meant by the sentence. Thus in the sentence 'bring the cow,' the word *cow* means, not the cow as such , but as the object of the verb *bring*. Hence in a sentence there is first a construction (*anvaya*) of the words with one another and then an expression (*abhidhāna*) of the construed meaning of the whole sentence, *i.e.* there is an expression of the construed meaning (*anvitābhidhāna*). The theory of *anvitābhidhāna* is advocated by the Prābhākara Mīmāṁsakas and the grammarians. There is, however, some difference of opinion between them with regard to the function of the words in the construed meaning of the sentence. According to the grammarians, the constituent words have no separate meanings of their own. They convey only the integral meaning of the sentence in different ways and degrees. Hence, the words lose their individual meanings in the unitary meaning of the sentence. The Prābhākaras, on the other hand, maintain that the words convey both their separate meanings

1. *Vide* TB., 14; NM., pp. 395-96; *Vivaraṇaprameyasaṁgraha*, pp. 257 f. *Vide* aslo VP., Ch. IV; SD., p. 153.
2. *Vide An Outline of Philosophy*, p. 266.

and the construed meaning of the sentence. Just as in a machine the parts perform their respective functions and at the same time contribute to the function of the whole, so the words in a sentence present their individual meanings till these are construed into the unitary meaning of the sentence. Hence the meaning of a sentence is neither the aggregate meaning of the words nor is it quite independent of their separate meanings. Rather, the sentence is a new combination of the individual meanings of the words and, therefore, conveys a new meaning. The Prābhākaras agree with others in holding that the combination of the separate meanings of the words is effected by memory, since the words appear in succession and their meanings are only remembered by us when we come to the end of the sentence.[1]

Of the different views about the meaning of a sentence, that of the Prābhākaras seems to be the best. If the meaning of a sentence be, as the grammarians think, quite independent of the words, then we can have no other way of knowing it than a personal explanation from the speaker or writer of it. If, on the other hand, its meaning be merely the aggregate of the word-meanings, we do not see how any sentence can convey a new meaning to meet a new situation. If the word-meanings are not modified in the meaning of the sentence, according to its context, no sentence can go further than the old meanings of its words. On the other hand, without something of their old meanings persisting in the words, the new meaning of a sentence cannot be understood by us. Hence we are to say that in the meaning of a sentence the separate meanings of the words are so modified as to fit in with the contest in which the sentence is used.[2] That the meaning of the sentence dominates the meanings of its words will appear also from the fact that in the life of the

---

1. *Vide* NM., pp. 387-98; *Vivaraṇaprameyasaṁgraha*, pp. 257-60.
2. *Cf.* Schiller, *Logic for Use*, p. 56; 'A successful transfer of meaning has to satisfy two conditions. (1) It has to presuppose and respect old meaning and to employ old truths; but it has also (2) so to arrange them in their contexts as to develop new meanings out of them, in order to express new truths.'

individual the judgment precedes the separate concepts related in it. The child makes assertions about objects before he understands the separate meanings of words. It is the sentence and not the word that is the staring-point of our thought and speech. Hence, the meaning of a word should follow the meaning of the sentence in which it is used. The meaning of the sentence is not a function of the meanings of the separate words, rather, it functions in and determines the meanings of its words. This appears from the fact that we cannot ascertain the meaning of a word unless we know the sentence in which it is used.

3. The Import of Sentences

For the Naiyāyikas, a sentence is the verbal expression of determinate knowledge (*savikalpakajñāna*). It is only determinate knowledge that can be conveyed by a sentence. Indeterminate knowledge (*nirvikalpakajñāna*) cannot be expressed in words or sentences. Now, determinate knowledge is the knowledge of a thing as qualified by an attribute (*viśeṣaṇa-viśeṣyāvagāhi*). In it we know something to be related to something else as substantive to adjective. Hence a sentence as the verbal expression of determinate knowledge must contain two terms and express a relation between them. Of these two terms one is called *uddeśya* or the subject about which something is asserted. It is also called *viśeṣya* or the substantive which is regarded as the seat or locus of some quality. It may thus be called the determinandum or what is presented to be determined and characterized by thought. In relation to it, the other term is called *vidheya* or that which is asserted about the subject and is therefore a predicate. It is known also as the *viśeṣaṇa* or the adjective which is referred to the subject. It is that which determines the subject and may thus be called the determinants in relation to it. On this analysis of it, a sentence corresponds to a proposition in Western logic. But unlike the propositions of Formal Logic, the sentence has no need for a copula. That there must be a copula or a verb in a sentence is not admitted by the Naiyāyikas and many other Indian thinkers. The analysis of a sentence into the subject, the predicate and the copula is repudiated by the Naiyāyikas as utterly groundless.[1] We can very well express a complete meaning without the copula, as when we say "*parvato vahnimān.*" That the copula, as some form of the very 'to be,' is not an essential part of the proposition is also recognised by modern logicians like Bradley,[2] Bosanquet[3] and Johnson,[4] The Naiyāyikas go further than this and hold that no verb is necessary for a sentence. It may be said that a verb is implied, if not expressly mentioned, in a sentence. When we say 'a fiery hill,' or 'a red colour,' we imply the verb 'exists' or 'is' For the Naiyāyikas, however, such verbs stand for a subjective mode of our assertion, but not for any part of the asserted fact or content.[5] The 'hill as fiery,' or the 'colour as red' is the content of our assertion. The verb is or *exists* stands for no objective content. Hence a sentence does not require a very as an essential part of its content. So also we may have a proposition without the copula or the verb 'to be.' But we should observe that although the sentence as a predicative judgment (*viśeṣyaviśeṣaṇāvagāhai*) corresponds to a proposition, yet it is in itself wider than a proposition. There are sentences which do not express any relation between subject and predicate, or in which there may not be any subject or predicate, *e.g.* 'a dog runs,' 'go there,' etc. These are sentences, but not propositions expressing a relation between two terms. The Naiyāyikas, however, take the sentence as equivalent to a proposition.

It will appear from the above that, according to the Naiyāyikas, the import of a sentence or proposition is the predication of an attribute with regard to some thing or things. It expresses the relation between a substantive and an adjective (*viśeṣyaviśeṣaṇa*). The substantive is some thing or real, while the adjective is some other

---

1. *Kriyārahitaṁ na vākyamastītyādikastu prācāṁ pravādo niryuktikatvādaśraddheyaḥ, Śabdaśakti-prakāśikā,* p. 28.
2. *The Principles of Logic, Vol.* I, p. 21.
3. *Logic, Vol.* I, p. 81.
4. *Logic,* Pt. I, pp. 10-11.
5. *Cf.* S. H. Mellone, *An Introductory Text-Book of Logic,* p. 10; 'There is no separate existnece in thought corresponding to the separate exisence of the copula in the typical proposition, S is P.'

fact or real found in relation to it. Hence we may say that both the subject and the predicate are real facts forming one complete whole. The proposition does not bring the one into relation with the other, but finds them as related. The Naiyāyikas, therefore, cannot agree with Bradley[1] and Bosanquet[2] who hold that proposition is the reference of an ideal content to reality, or that a proposition characterised some part of reality, with which we are in immediate contact, by referring an ideal content to it. For them, the predicate is not an ideal content but a real fact. In the proposition 'the ball is red,' the redness is as much a perceived fact as the ball, and so also their relation is not ideal but an actual fact. They do not accept the subjective view that a proposition expresses a relation between two ideas, or the idealistic view that it is the reference of an ideal content to reality. As radical realists they are in favour of the objective view that the proposition expresses a real relation between two facts or real. This native view of the Naiyāyikas has been ably supported by Mr. Gotshalk[3] who opposes the idealistic view and shows that 'the subject of an ordinary judgment is not Reality itself but merely and simply that limited situation within Reality engaging attention,' *i.e.* a finite and limited reality. So also what is predicated of the subject is some real fact, a thing or quality, etc., and not a mere piece of meaning or an ideal content referred by a judgment to an existent reality.

The above view of the Naiyāyikas that all propositions express the subject-predicate relation between a substantive and an adjective has been opposed by the Mīmāṁsakas, the Vedāntins and other logicians. According to the grammarians and the Prābhākaras,[4] every significant proposition means an action. If a proposition is to give us any new knowledge, it must not relate to matters of fact (*siddhapadārtha*), for there may be known by means of perception and inference. On the other hand, the *kriyā* or the verb is the central

1. *The Principles of Logic,* Vol. I, p. 10.
2. *Logic,* Vol. I, p. 83.
3. *Vide Mind,* Jan., 1933.
4. *Vide Vivaraṇaprameyasaṁgraha,* pp. 257-58.

unit of a sentence or proposition. The subject and the predicate have meaning only as they are related to the verb by the nominative and objective cases. Hence the import of a proposition lies, not in the subject-predicate relation between two terms, but in the action denoted by its verb. Every proposition expresses a command and is, therefore, an imperative proposition. According to the Advaita Vedāntins,[1] all propositions cannot be brought under the subject-predicate form. Identity propositions, like 'this is that man,' cannot be construed according to the subject-predicate relation. These propositions do not express any relation between two things, but the simple identity of a thing with itself. We cannot say here that 'that man' is the predicate or adjective of 'this man.' These are non-relational and therefore non-predicative propositions. Russell[2] also opposes the view that all propositions are reducible to the subject-predicate form. He thinks that the propositions which assign the qualities of things come under this form, *e.g.* "this thing is round, and red and so on." On the other hand, the propositions which express relations cannot be reduced to the subject-predicate form. Thus, in the propositions 'A is like B,' 'B is the brother of C,' 'C is greater than D,' we cannot say that the terminal term is predicated of the initial term. They express respectively a symmetrical, a non-symmetrical and an asymmetrical relation between different terms, of which one cannot be regarded as the quality of the other.

When we consider the different views about the import of propositions, we are led to think that a distinction should be made between predicative and non-predicative propositions.[3] In a predicative proposition a subject is related to a predicate as substantive to adjective. All propositions, however, are not predicative in this sense. There are many propositions which cannot be brought under the subject-predicate form. Thus Russell's relation propositions, 'A is like B,' 'C is greater than D,' do not

1. *Vide* VP., Ch. I.
2. *Cf. Our Knowledge of the External World,* pp. 45-50.
3. The distinction between Subject-predicate and relational propositions is now recognised by all modern logicians.

conform to the subject-predicate form. It may be said that these propositions are predicative because in the one 'likeness to B' is predicated of A, and in the other 'being greater than D' is predicated of C. This will mean that A has the attribute of being like B, and C has the attribute of being greater than D. But 'being like B' is not a quality of A, nor 'being greater than D' of C, in the same way in which the red colour is a quality of the ball. Similarly, the Vedāntin's identity proposition 'this is that man' can hardly be reduced to the subject-predicate form. For the Naiyāyikas, this proposition is predicative in so far as it means that 'this man is characterised by a past existence.' In it a man's existence at some other time and space is predicated as a character of his present existence. Although the proposition may be interpreted in this way, yet it loses its real force when so interpreted. The proposition expresses a judgment of recognition (*pratyabhijñā*). In recognition we are primarily interested in the identity of a man from the past to the present. To recognise a man as 'that Devadata' is to know not only that he was known before, but that he is identical in the past and the present. Hence, the proposition 'this is that man' does not characterise a man by his past existence and is, therefore, non-predicative. Finally, the sentences which mean action cannot be called predicative propositions by any stretch of imagination. The sentence 'a dog runs' is not a predicative proposition, because there is in it no subject-predicate relation between two terms. To make it predicative it may be converted into the logical form 'a dog is a running animal.' But this form of the sentence does not bring out its real sense. It is an altogether different proposition, and a false proposition too, for dogs do not always run. Similarly, sentence expressing commands or imperatives are not predicative propositions in any sense or form. 'Thou shalt not steal,' 'pray to god' are sentences which enjoin certain duties on us, but do not assert any relation, predicative or otherwise, between two ideas or things.

4. *Śabda* as an Independent Source of Knowledge

According to many schools of Indian philosophy, *śabda* or verbal testimony is an indepent *pramāṇa* like perception and inference. As we have already seen, there is some difference of opinion among them as to the nature of *śabda* or verbal testimony. There are two main views with regard to it. On the one hand, the Jainal[1] and the Naiyāyikas take *śabda* as the statement of a perfectly reliable person. In this sense, *śabda* as a *pramāṇa* means a sentence which is spoken or written by a trustworthy person, or the statement of some authority. On the other hand, *śabda* as a *pamāṇa* is taken by the Mīmāṁsakas[2] and the Vedāntins[3] to mean a sentence or proposition whose import is not contradicted in any way. On this view, a sentence as the significant combination of words, according to the four conditions of expectancy, compatibility, proximity and fitness, is *pramāṇa* or a valid source of knowledge.

Let us now consider whether *śabda* can in any sense be regarded as an independent method of knowledge (*pramāṇa*). This question resolves itself into two other questions. The first question is: Can *śabda* give us a true knowledge of objects? If it can, it will have to be regarded as a *pramāṇa* or source of knowledge. Then the second question will be this: Is the way in which *śabda* gives us a knowledge of objects different and distinct from perception, inference and the rest? It does not matter if the same objects can be known by perception or inference. So long as we cannot reduce *śabda* or the verbal knowledge of objects to the conditions of any other kind of knowledge, we must recognise it as an independent method of knowledge.

The first question deserves an affirmative answer. *Śabda* or testimony gives us true knowledge about many things. The Buddhists, however, contend that *śabda* which consists of words cannot give us any knowledge. Words are physical objects and cannot, therefore, take the place of an organ of knowledge like the senses or the reason. Further, there is no part or aspect of reality

---

1. *Āptena praṇītaṁ vacanamāptavacanam, Prameyakamalamārtaṇḍa*, p. 112.
2. *Cf. Padārthābhidhānadvāreṇa yadvākyārthavijñānaṁ tacchābdaṁ nāma pramāṇam*, SD., p. 72.
3. *Vide* VP. Chap. IV.

which cannot be known by perception or inference, and for which we require a different method like *śabda* or testimony. This contention, however, rests on a misunderstanding. Just as the same objects may be known by perception and inference, so they may be known by *śabda* or testimony. Or, we may say that *śabda* has to do with supramundane realities which cannot be known by perception or inference. Further, words as physical sounds or coloured figures do not give us any knowledge of facts.[1] *Śabda* as the understanding of sentences or propositions gives us more knowledge about the world than perception and inference. A man's knowledge would very mearge if he were to depend solely on his own experience and reason. The bulk of our knowledge comes from the testimony of our fellow beings, *e.g.* books and speeches. We accept on trust by far the greater part of what we hold to be true. Hence, it is established that *śabda* does give us true knowledge of facts and is, therefore, a *pramāṅa* or source of true knowledge.

Turning the second question, we ask if *śabda* or verbal testimony can be reduced to any other method or form of knowledge. While standing on the bank of an unknown river I am told by a local gentleman: "This river is fordable." I know the depth of the river from this statement. Can this knowledge be explained by perception, or any other source of knowledge? It cannot be a case of perception, because I cannot directly see the river's depth no measure it before going into its water. It cannot be explained by memory, for there is no previous experience corresponding to my present knowledge of the river's depth. I cannot now member that the river is fordable because I have not perceived it to be such in the past. It cannot be said that my present knowledge of the river as fordable is the result of the synthesis of my ideas of a river and of fordability acquired from the previous experiences of other fordable rivers. Even if I have such ideas or memory-images from previous experience, they will not explain

1. *Vide* NV. and NVT., 2. 1. 49.

my knowledge of *this* river as fordable, because there is no previous experience in relation to it.[1]

Next we are to consider whether *śabda* or verbal testimony can be reduced to inference. It has been held by many thinkers, both Indian and European, that knowledge from testimony is really a form of inference. The Buddhist logicians hold the generally accepted view that testimony is a kind of inference, because in it we infer the truth or falsity of a statement from the character of the person who makes that statement. But this view makes a confusion between two different questions. To determine whether testimony is a separate source of knowledge or not, we are only to see if it gives us a true knowledge of facts, and not how its truth is known or tested by us. We can very well know the meaning of a sentence even before we enquire into its source, or when its source cannot be known. In fact, testimony is the source of the greater parts of our knowledge of the word. Thus, the Buddhist contention falls to the ground.[2] The Vaiśeṣikas try to reduce testimony to inference on more plausible grounds.[3] According to them, knowledge from testimony is governed by the fundamental law of inferential reasoning. Just as in an inference we know an unperceived fact from the perception of a sign that is universally related to it (*vyāptiśāli-liṅga*), so in testimony we have the knowledge of some unperceived facts from the perception of the words by which they are denoted. I hear the sentence 'there are five trees on the river-bank.' With this I have an auditory perception of a number of words. I know that each of these words has a fixed and universal relation with the object meant by it. Hence to know these words is, for me, to know the objects denoted by them, just as to know smoke is, for a man who knows the universal relation between smoke and fire, to know the existence of fire in relation to it. In testimony our

1. So'*Yam niyantritārthatvānna pratyakṣam na cānumā . . . na cāsau smṛtiḥ samānākāra-saṁskārāprabhavatvāt*, *Śabdaśakti-prakāśikā*, pp. 3-4.
2. *Vide* NV., 1.1.7. *Cf.* '*Vākyaśravaṇānantarameva hyāptānāptajñānāna-pekṣaireva padāirthairvākyārtho 'vagamyate*, SD., p. 73.
3. *Śabdopamānayornaiva pṛthakprāmāṇyamiṣyate anumānagatārthat-vāditi vaiśeṣikaṁ matam*, BP., 140-41.

knowledge about facts is brought about by the knowledge of words as signs or middle terms (*liṅga*) and that of their invariable relation (*vyāpti*) with those facts. Hence knowledge from testimony is really inferential in character.[1] But this attempt to reduce testimony to a kind of inference reminds us of the Procrustean method. It violently turns and twists the nature of testimony to make it conformable to the standard on difference and yet it cannot succeed. Inference depends on the knowledge of *vyāpti* which is a natural relation of coexistence between two things, *e.g.* smoke and fire. No knowledge of the meanings of words is necessary to infer the existence of fire from smoke. From the mere perception of smoke in the hill we know that there must be fire in it. If there were such a natural relation of coexistence between words and their meanings, then an illiterate man should have had as good knowledge from words as any man of letters. Further, the relation between the middle and the major term of an inference is such that if the middle is present in a certain locus, the major also must be present in it. If there were such a relation between words and the objects denoted by them, we should expect to find the objects in the body of the person or the book in which the words occur. In truth, the relation between words and their objects is quite different from that which holds between the middle and the major term of an inference. Words mean certain objects, but do not coexist with them. So also, the conditions of verbal knowledge or testimony are specifically different from those of an inference. It is true that both depend on a mental construction of certain given data. But in inference the construction is limited to only three terms and proceeds according to their relations of inclusion and exclusion. In verbal knowledge there is a construction of the meanings of any number of words constituting a sentence, according to their syntactical expectancy, propinquity, mutual fitness and intention.[2] Even if our understanding of the meaning of a word may be said to be

---

1. *Śabdo 'numānam vyāptibalenārthapratipādakatvāddhūmavat*, NK., p. 213.
2. *Yogyatārthagatā 'kāṅkṣā śabdaniṣṭhā 'nubhāvikā, pratyekaṁ vā militvā vā naite liṅgamasiddhitaḥ*, *Śabdaśakti-prakāśikā*, Kār. 4.

conditioned, like inference, by a fixed association between the two, we cannot speak of any fixed relation between a sentence and its meaning. A sentence conveys different meanings according to its different constructions. Its meaning depends on such specific conditions as the expectancy, fitness, proximity and intended meaning of words, which are not to be found in inference or any other kind of knowledge. Finally, the evidence of introspection (*anuvyavasāya*) confirms the result of the logical analysis that testimony is distinct from inference. It clearly shows that we cannot detect any inferential process in the knowledge from testimony. When from the sentence 'the cow exists' I know hat a certain cow does exist, I feel that I do not infer the existence of a cow, but understand it from a sentence.[1] Hence we conclude that testimony is a distinct method of knowledge which cannot be reduced to any other method.

Some Western thinkers now recognise testimony as a separate source of knowledge. Thus Russell[2] frankly admits that 'testimony is essential to science, although it is open to criticism by the sceptic.' So also Montague[3] thinks that 'testimony that is open to free and honest study remains as legitimate a source of knowledge as any other.' He, however, holds that testimony is not a primary but a secondary source of knowledge. For him the weakness of testimony consists first in the fact that authorities conflict. But on his own admission this difficulty is not peculiar to testimony; it is present in each of the other methods. There are conflicting perceptions and inferences, like conflicting testimonies. Hence, this cannot be a ground of distinction between one method as primary and another as secondary. The second and more serious source of weakness in

---

1. *Vastuto....astitivena gāmanuminomītyāderanuvyavasāyasya tatrāsattvāt, pratyuta gaurastīti-vākyādastitvena gauḥ śruto na tvanumita ityevānubhavācca, Śabdaśakti-prakāśikā*, p. 7.
2. *An Outline of Philosophy*, p. 6.
3. *The Ways of Knowing*, Chap. I. It may be noted here that L. S. Stebbing also inclines to the view that while testimony is a source of human knowledge, it is not an independent source, but can be reduced to inference (*vide Logic in Practice*, p. 102).

testimony is, for him, its dependence on some other method for establishing its validity. When questioned as to why we should accept a given authority, the answer must be that the authority knows the truth direct through some other method like experience or intuition. This shows that the truth of testimony ultimately depends on the direct experience, reason or intuition, of some person. In testimony the individual's relation to truth is not direct but indirect, for it depends on the direct knowledge of a second individual, while in sense and reason the individual is in direct relation with the truth of things. Hence, testimony cannot be a primary and an ultimate source of knowledge like the other methods. According to the Naiyāyikas also, the validity of the knowledge derived from testimony depends on the reliability of the person who is its source. So, also the truth of testimony is to be proved or tested by successful activity or verification in direct experience. Still the Naiyāyikas recognise testimony as an independent source of knowledge like perception and inference.

The Mīmāṁsakas and the Vedāntins go further than the Naiyāyikas and hold that the truth of the knowledge from testimony is both constituted and known by itself. By testimony they mean a significant combination of ideas expressed by words, according to their expectancy, compatibility, propinquity and fitness. It is a sentence in which the ideas expressed by the words are consistent with one another and also with the facts denoted by them. The meaning conveyed by a sentence is not only consistent in itself but also with the facts of experience. As such, it naturally leads to a knowledge of the truth. The truth of the knowledge derived from testimony is thus constituted by its own intrinsic conditions. And truth is, wherever it is, known by itself. It is a self-evident character of knowledge and requires no other test than itself in order to be known as true. For example, a true perception is by itself known as true. Similarly, the knowledge derived from a proposition or sentence is true and is known as true, it there be no ground to contradict or doubt it. The truth of testimony is both constituted and established by itself.

Although we do not go so far as to say with the Mīmāṁsakas and the Vedāntins that testimony has self-evident validity, yet we find no reason to deny that it is an independent or ultimate source of knowledge. Whether a certain source of knowledge is independent or not depends on two things: (*i*) whether it gives us a true knowledge of facts, and (*ii*) whether its conditions are distinct from those of any other source. It does not matter if the truth of the knowledge is constituted or ascertained by some other source. Thus the validity of an inference depends on the validity of our perceptions of the middle term and its relation to the major term. So also the truth of its conclusion is tested by verification in direct experience. Still no one denies that inference is a primary and an ultimate source of knowledge. If it be so, why should we not recognise testimony also as an ultimate source of knowledge? We have already seen that it gives us a true knowledge of facts in a way distinct from any other way of knowing them. If testimony depends on perception to prove its validity, perception also depends on inference to prove its own validity when that is doubted or questioned by any one. The dependence of one method on another for its proof or verification is a difficulty, not peculiar to testimony, but common to all the methods of knowledge. Further, there are certain crucial instances in which we cannot go beyond testimony and prove its truth by some other method. If to the question as to why a given authority should be accepted, the almost inevitable answer is, as Montague thinks, that the authority possessed a direct knowledge of the truth, what should be our answer to the next question as to how we know that he had a direct knowledge of the truth. Here we have to depend on the statement of the authority himself. We do not require any other proof of his direct knowledge of the truth. Similarly, we learn that a name denotes a class of things from the testimony of our elders and they from their elders and so on indefinitely without there being any direct knowledge of the word's meaning on the part of any one. Even in the case of the man who first used the name in relation to certain things or one who first found it to be so used, we cannot speak of a direct knowledge of its meaning, for the name could not be perceived like a label attached to those things. Thus we see that, like perception and inference, testimony does not always require to be proved by direct knowledge, although it may be so proved when necessary. We should therefore recognise it as an independent and ultimate source of knowledge like perception and inference.

Chapter XIX

Others Sources of Knowledge

1. Different Views about the Ultimate Sources of Knowledge

There is much difference of opinion among Indian thinkers as to what the ultimate sources of human knowledge are. For the Cārvākas, who are radical empiricists, perception is the only valid source of our knowledge and all true knowledge comes from perception. The Buddhists hold that perception and inference are the two ultimate sources of true knowledge, which include other sources like *upamāna* and *śabda*. According to the Sāṅkhya and the Yoga system, *śabda* or verbal testimony also should be recognised as an independent source of knowledge like perception and inference. The Sāṅkhya includes *upamāna, arthāpatti* and *saṁbhava* under inference, and inference, and *abhāva* under perception.[1] The Naiyāyikas are in favour of the view that there are four independent sources of knowledge, namely perception, inference, testimony and *upamāna* or comparison. According to them, the other sources of knowledge may be included within these four and so need not be taken as ultimate or independent sources of knowledge. According to the Vaiśeṣikas, there are four kinds of *vidyā* or true knowledge, namely, perception, inference, memory and intuitive experience (*ārṣajñāna*). They include *śabda, upamāna, arthāpatti, abhāva, saṁbhava* and *aitihya* within reference.[2] But there is some difference of opinion as to whether all the four kinds of *vidyā* or knowledge are independent sources of knowledge or not. It will follow from the definition of *vidyā* as definite knowledge which is free from doubt and contradiction that

1. TKD., Kār. 5; *Yoga-sūtra,* 1. 7.
2. NK., pp. 213-31.

all kinds of *vidyā* are *pramāṇa* or independent sources of knowledge. Śrīdhara in his *Nyāyakandalī*[1] at first tells us that perception, inference and *smṛti* or memory are treated first because they are *laukika pramāṇa* or ordinary sources of knowledge, and then *ārṣa* because it is an extraordinary source of knowledge. But in the course of the discussion on *smṛti* he observes that it is not a *pramāṇa* because it depends on previous experience to give us knowledge of past objects. The *Nyāyalīlāvatī*,[2] a compendium of the Vaiśeṣika philosophy, establishes the view that *smṛti* or memory is an independent source of knowledge like perception, inference and intuitive knowledge. In the later works of the Nyāya-Vaiśeṣika philosophy, however, it is generally maintained that the Vaiśeṣikas accept only perception and inference as two independent sources of knowledge.[3] According to the Jainas, perception, both ordinary and extraordinary, inference, testimony, *pratyabhijñā* or recognition and *smṛti* or memory are all independent sources of knowledge, although they may be classified under the two heads of *pratyakṣa* and *parokṣa,* immediate and mediate knowledge.[4] The Prābhākaras hold that *arthāpatti* or postulation should be accepted as a separate source of knowledge like perception, inference, testimony and comparison. The Bhāṭṭas and the Vedāntins add *anupalabdhi* or non-perception to these five and maintain that there are six distinct sources of knowledge. The Paurāṇikas go further than this in holding that *saṁbhava* or probability and *aitihya* or tradition also are to be recognised as separate sources of knowledge like the six *pramāṇas* admitted by the Bhāṭṭas and the Vedāntins.[5]

Now, the question is this: How many independent sources of knowledge are we to accept? The Naiyāyikas accept only four sources of knowledge as distinct and independent. These are perception, inference, comparison and testimony as explained and discussed before. What then are they to say with regard to such

1. *Vide* pp. 186, 257.
2. *Smṛtirapi mānāntarameva*, etc., NL., p. 67 (Bombay Edn.).
3. *Vide* TR., p. 56; TK., p. 7.
4. *Vide* TTS., I, 10-13.
5. *Vide* TR., p. 56.

alleged sources of knowledge as *aitihya, saṁbhava, abhāva* or *anupalabdhi, arthāpatti, smṛti, pratyabhijñā* and *ārṣajñāna?* According to them, *ārṣajāña* or intuitive knowledge is a kind of extraordinary (*alaukika*) perception, while *pratyabhijñā* is only a kind of qualified perception.[1] These two come under perception as an ultimate source of knowledge and are not themselves separate sources of knowledge. As regards *artihya* or tradition, the Naiyāyikas hole that it is a kind of testimony, of which the source is not definitely known.[2] Tradition means the continuous communication of a body of ideas and beliefs from one generation to another. It has its origin in no living individual, but is enjoyed by all individuals as the common property of the race. Now the body of ideas and beliefs constituting a particular tradition is accepted as true on the authority of some person or persons, whoever they may be. We believe in tradition because we are pretty confident that it must have originally emanated from some reliable persons. As such, tradition is a form of vague testimony, in which we know certain things on the authority of some unknown persons. Similarly, *saṁbhava* may be included within inference. It may be taken to mean either probable knowledge or the knowledge of numerical inclusion. In the first sense it is illustrated when we expect rain from the appearance of clouds in the sky. Here we think that there will probably be rainfall because we know that clouds are generally followed by rain. But such probable knowledge is not *pramā* or valid knowledge and so requires no *pramāṇa* or source of knowledge to explain it.[3] In the second sense, however, *saṁbhava*[4] means the knowledge of the part from that of the whole within which it is included. Thus we know that there is a hundred within a thousand, a seer within a maund. Such knowledge is really inferential in character, since it depends on the knowledge of *vyāpti*

1. *Vide* Chaps. IX and X *ante*.
2. *Anirdiṣṭapravaktkaṁ pravādapāraṁparyam aitihyam*, NB., 2. 2. 1.
3. *Pracurasāhacaryasaṁvedanāt buddhirabādhitā saṁbhavaḥ*, etc., NL., p. 57.
4. *Saṁbhavo nāma avinābhāvino 'rthasya sattāgrahaṇādanyasya sattāgraha-ṇam...tadapyanumānameva*, NB., 2. 2. 1-2.

or invariable concomitance between the part and the whole. Hence *saṁbhava* need not be taken as a separate source of knowledge other than *anumāna* or inference. The question as to whether *arthāpatti, abhāva* or *anupalabdhi*, and *smṛti* should be recognised as separate sources of knowledge or not will be separately considered in the following sections.

2. *Arthāpatti* or Postulation as a Source of Knowledge

Arthāpatti as a source of knowledge consists in the supposition of some unperceived fact in order to explain a given fact. When a given or perceived fact cannot be explained without some other fact we have to presuppose or postulate the existence of this other fact even though we do not perceive it. A phenomenon is presented to our experience and we find that there is a seeming contradiction involved in it. We try to get over this contradiction by supposing some other fact which explains away the contradiction. The given fact which is to be explained is called the *upapādya,* and that which explains it is called the *upapādaka*. Hence here we proceed from the knowledge of something to be explained to the knowledge of that which explains it, *i.e.* from the consequence to the ground.[1] Thus, when a man who is growing fat says that he fasts, we find an apparent contradiction between his increasing fatness and his fasting. We get out of this contradiction by the supposition that the man eats at night, because a man who fasts at day cannot grow fat unless he takes food at night. Or, a man, who is living, is not found in his house. To explain the absence of the man from his house we suppose that he is somewhere outside his house, because a living man cannot be absent from his house unless he lives outside it.

According to the Advaita Vedānta and the Bhāṭṭa Mīmāṁsā, *arthāpatti* is a separate source of knowledge, because it gives us a knowledge of facts which cannot be otherwise explained. It cannot

1. *Upapādyajñānena upapādakajñānam arthāpattiḥ,* etc., VP., Ch. V. *Arthāpattirapi dṛṣṭaḥ śruto vā 'rtho' nyathā nopapadyata ityarthakalpanā*, SD., p. 76.

be explained by perception, since the fact known through *arthāpatti* is not perceived by us. That the fat man eats at night is not a matter of perception for us. No can we explain this knowledge by inference. According to the Advaitins, *arthāpatti* is not an inference. It cannot be reduced to *anvayi* inference, because there is no *anvaya* or agreement in presence between fatness and eating at night as between smoke and fire. We cannot say that wherever there is fatness there is eating at night, just as we can say that wherever there is smoke there is fire. Nor can *arthāpatti* be reduced to *vyatireki* inference, because there is no such thing as *vyatireki* inference. Further, the direct report of our consciousness is against supposition that *arthāpatti* is an inference. In *anuvyavasāya* or introspection of the knowledge by *arthāpatti* we do not feel to have 'inferred' anything, but simply to have supposed or presumed something in order to explain something else.[1]

The Naiyāyikas, Sāṅkhyas and others object to the above view of *arthāpatti* as a separate source of knowledge. According to the Naiyāyikas, *arthāpatti* may be reduced to an inference of the *vyatireki* type. It is not indeed an *anvayi* inference in which the major premise expresses a positive relation of agreement in presence between the middle and the major term, *e.g.* 'whenever there is fatness, there is eating at night.' On the other hand, it is a *vyatireki* inference in which the major premise expresses a universal relation between the absence of the major and the absence of the middle. Thus the above example of *arthāpati* may be reduced to the following syllogism:

A man who does not eat at night while fasting by day is not fat;

This man who fasts at day is fat;

∴ This man is not a man who does not eat at night, *i.e.* he eats at night.

As *arthāpatti* may thus be reduced to *vyatireki* inference, the Naiyāyikas refuse to acknowledge it as a separate source of

1. VP., Ch. V.

knowledge.[1] So also the Sāṅkhya philosophers explain *athāpatti* as a form of inference. Taking the second example of *arthāpatti* given above, Vācaspati points out that it can be reduced to the following inference:

> If a living individual is absent somewhere, he is present elsewhere;
>
> Devadatta who is living is absent from home;
>
> ∴ He is somewhere outside his home.

Here a man's existence outside his home is inferred from 'his absence from home' as the *liṅga* or the middle term. There is a relation of *vyāpti* or universal concomitance between a man's presence somewhere and his absence elsewhere. Every man finds this to be true in his own case. Hence when we know the one from the other we simply infer it from its *liṅga* or universal concomitant, just as we infer fire from smoke.[2]

The Bhāṭṭa Mīmāṁsakas expose the futility of the attempt to reduce *arthāpatti* to inference. They point out certain fundamental differences between inference and *arthāpatti,* which make it impossible for us to reduce either of them to the other. It may seem at first view that inference and *arthāpatti* involve the same process of reasoning. In *arthāpatti* we pass from the knowledge of an observed phenomenon to that of an unobserved phenomenon without which it cannot be explained. In inference also we pass from the observed smoke to the unobserved fire as that which alone explains the smoke. But a closer view of the matter reveals certain important and unmistakable differences between the two. In inference we proceed from the *gamaka* or the evidentiary fact to the *gamya* or the evidenced fact, while in *arthāpatti* we pass from the *gamya* or the fact to be evidenced and explained to the *gamaka* or that which evidence and explains it. Again, in *arthāpatti* we are

---

1. *Yastu na rātrau bhuṅkte nāsau divābhuñjānatve sati pīno*, etc., TB., p. 15.
2. *Evamarthāpattirapi na pramāṇāntaram...yadā khalvavyāpakaḥ sannekatra nāsti tadānyatrāsti*, etc., *Tattvakaumudī*, p. 46.

confronted with an apparent conflict between two facts, *e.g.* a man's fatness and fasting by day, or, a man being alive and yet absent from home. In order to resolve this conflict we have to presuppose or postulate another fact,· namely, that the man eats at night, or postulate another fact, namely, that the man eats at night, or that the man has gone out. So long as we do not make this supposition we are in doubt as to whether the man really fasts, or whether he really exists or not. Such doubtful facts cannot be the *liṅga* or the middle term of any valid inference. In *arthāpatti* we get over this state of doubt and conflict by supposing something which explains them away. Hence while in inference we pass from man undoubted fact (*niścita gamaka*) to its invariable concomitant, in *arthāpatti* we proceed from a doubtful fact (*saṁdigdha gamaka*) to something which explains it and saves us from the doubt.[1] Finally if *arthāpati* is to be reduced to inference, we must show what the *liṅga* or the middle term of that inference is. When we argue that Devadatta exists outside his house because he is living and yet absent from home, we cannot take mere 'absence from home' as the middle term, for the man may be dead and case to exist at all. Nor can we say that 'living' is the middle term, because a living man may exist inside his house. Nor again can it be said that Devadatta's 'living together with his absence in the house' is the middle term from which we infer his existence outside the house. In an inference we first know the *liṅga* or the middle term and then, through it, the *liṅgī* or the major term. The two are not known together, but one after the other. In the case of Devadatta, however, we cannot connect his living with his absence from the house except through the idea of his existence outside he house. Hence, to know the alleged middle term, namely, 'his living together with his absence from the house. is just to know his existence outside the house, This being known along with the alleged middle term, there remains nothing more to be inferred from it. So *arthāpatti* is not the inference of the major term from the middle term, but the presupposition of one fact in

1. *Syādevam, yadyanupapannaṁ gamakaṁ syāt, iha tu yannopapadyate tadeva gamyam...yathā cānumāne niścitaṁ gamakam, evamarthāpattau saṁdigdhaṁ gamakamiti,* etc., SD., pp. 76-77.

order to explain another, in which is involved a seeming contradiction.[1]

The Bhāṭṭa Mīmāṁsakas next discuss the question of reducing inference of *arthāpatti*. It may be said that if we accept *arthāpatti* as a separate source of knowledge, there is no more any necessity of recognising inference as a different source of knowledge. Inference may be shown to be the same as *arthāpatti* for we can analyse an inference in the following way. When I see smoke in the hill, I think that if there were no fire, this smoke would be unaccounted for. Therefore, either there is no smoke in the hill or the universal proposition, 'wherever there is smoke, there is fire,' is false. But neither of the alternatives can be accepted. The universal proposition has been established with rigorous certainty and the smoke is an object of perception. Hence the apparent contradiction is resolved by the supposition that there is fire. Thus inference becomes identical with *arhāpatti*. To this the Bhāṭṭas reply that inference may be said to be *arthāpatti* only if we admit the universal proposition was not previously known by inference. In certain instances we know that smoke is related to fire. From this we *infer* that all smoke is related to fire. It cannot be said that without the universal proposition our knowledge of the relation between smoke and fire in certain instances involves a contradiction which is resolved by the postulation of it. Hence the knowledge of the universal proposition requires to be explained by inference as a separate source of knowledge.[2]

Now, we are to observe that *arthāpatti* as explained above is an independent *pramāṇa* like perception, inference and the rest. It cannot be reduced to inference as the Naiyāyikas and the Sāṅkhyas endeavour to do. The reason for this, however, is not, as the

---

1. *Na tāvadgṛhābhāvamātraṁ liṅgaṁ mṛte'pi saṁbhavāt, na jīvanamātraṁ gṛhe'pi sadbhāvāt, ato jīvanasaṁsṛṣṭo gṛhābhāvo liṅgamiti vaktavyam, prathamaṁ ca liṅgamavagamya paścālliṅgyanumānena bhavitavyam... atra ca na bahirbhāvagamamantareṇa gṛhābhāvo jīvanaṁ ca saṁsṛṣṭaṁ pratyetuṁ śakyate virodhāt,* etc., SD., p. 78.
2. *Syādevaṁ yadi sarvadhūmavatāmagnimattvamanu-mānādanyenāvagataṁ syāt,* etc., SD., p. 79.

Advaitins suppose, that there is no such thing as *vyatireki* inference, to which *arthāpatti* may possibly be reduced. The Advaita Vedāntins lose their case against those who prove that *vyatireki* is a genuine type of inference, or reduce *arthāpatti* to some other kind of inference like the hypothetical-categorical or the disjunctive-categorical syllogism. The real reason is, as the Bhāṭṭas point out, that *arthāpatti* cannot be reduced to may kind of inference. The fundamental condition of all inference is the relation of *vyāpti* or invariable concomitance between the major and the middle term. In every inference the conclusion *follows* from a universal proposition which is the result of a previous induction. The knowledge of the universal proposition is derived from the uncontradicted experience of agreement in presence or in absence between the middle and the major term. In any inference we apply a universal proposition, which is already known, to a particular case. To reduce *arthāpatti* to inference we must, therefore, show that here our knowledge of the unobserved fact follows from a universal proposition which is already known by induction. The Naiyāyikas and others would say that the knowledge given by *arthāpati* does follow from certain universal propositions. That Devadatta eats at night follows from the universal proposition, "A man who dos not eat at night while fasting by day is not fat." Similarly, the fact that he is out follows from the proposition. "A living man is either at home or out of it." But these propositions are not cases of real *vyāpti* or induction. They are not genealisations from the particular facts of experience. The universal proposition, "Wherever there is smoke there is fire," is derived from the particular instances of their coexistence. So also, the proposition, "Wherever there is no fire there is no smoke," is derived from the particular instances of their agreement in absence. But we have no previous experiences of the agreement in absence between 'eating at night' and fatness. We have pervious experiences of the concomitance between eating and fatness or between their absence. Hence to explain the apparent contradiction between fatness and absence of eating by day we have to suppose that there is eating at night. Our knowledge of the fact that Davadatta eats at night does not follow from any universal proposition which is already known, because there is here no universal proposition at all. It is the result of an attempt to correlate his fatness with the absence of eating by day–a process of reasoning which is different from that involved in inference. Similarly, the proposition, 'A living man is either at home or out of it,' is not a generalisation from particular instances from particular instances of the concomitance between a man's absence from home and presence outside. We cannot say that the one co-exists with the other, just as smoke co-exists with fire. Hence, we cannot deduce our knowledge of the fact that Devadatta is out from any such universal proposition. Rather, it follows in the wake of any attempt to reconcile the facts that Devadatta lives and yet he does not live in the house. In fact, the so-called universal proposition is itself a statement of the conclusion in general terms and cannot really explain it. Hence, *arthāpatti* as not a form of inference, but a separate source of knowledge.

3. *Abhāva* and *Anupalabdhi* as Sources of Knowledge

Abhāva may be taken to mean either contrast or non-cognition. In the first sense it means a relation of contrast or antithesis between two things as between existences and non-existence.[1] When there is such a relation of contrast or contradiction between two things, then from the existence of the one we may know the non-existence of the other and *vice versa*. Thus from the non-existence of rain we know the existence of some contact of the clouds with high winds which prevent rainfall. It is account of the obstruction offered by high winds that rain drops do not fall to the ground, as they otherwise would by the force of gravity. The Naiyāyikas hold that this argument from non-existence to existence is really a form of inference, because it is based on a uniform relation of concomitance between two opposite or contradictory things. Two contradictory objects are so related to one another that the existence of the one implies the non-existence of the other and *vice versa*. Hence *abhāva* or non-existence as a source of knowledge is to be included within

1. *Abhāvo virodhi, abjutaṁ bhūtasya*, etc., NB., 2. 2. 1.

inference.[1] The Vaiśeṣikas also reduce *abhāva* to inference. According to them, the non-existence of the effect indicates the non-existence of the cause, just as its existence indicates the existence of the cause. Hence, *abhāva* or non-existence gives us the knowledge of that which is uniformly related to it, like the *liṅga* or the middle term of an inference. The argument based on *abhāva* or non-existence is thus really a kind of *anumāna* or inference.[2]

Later Naiyāyikas take *abhāva* to mean the absence of cognition and not the relation of contrast or opposition between two things.[3] In this sense *abhāva* concides with *anupalabdhi* or non-cognition. According to the Bhāṭṭa Mīmāṁsā and the Advaita Vedānta, *anupalabdhi* is an independent *pramāṇa* or source of knowledge. It is the unique cause of such presentative knowledge of non-existence as is not due to inference or any other kind of knowledge.[4] Thus, the non-existence of a jar on the table which I see before me is known from the absence of its cognition or its non-perception (*anupalabdhi*). I judge that the jar does not exist on the table because it is not perceived, while I know that it would have been perceived if it existed there. This knowledge of non-existence cannot be explained by inference, since it is not brought about by the knowledge of *vyāpti* or a universal relation between two terms. It cannot be said that the non-existence of the jar is inferred from its non-perception which is known to be universally related to non-existence. The knowledge of a universal relation between non-perception and non-existence requires a previous knowledge of non-existence as such, which cannot be given by any inference.[5] Nor can we explain the knowledge of the jar's non-existence by

1. *Ibid.*
2. NK., p. 225; VS., 9. 2. 1.
3. TB., p. 15; NL., p. 57.
4. *Jñānakaraṇājanyābhāvānubhavāsādhāraṇamanupalabdhirūpaṁ pramāṇam*, VP., Ch. VI.
5. *Nāpyanumeyaḥ, ajñātena tena kasyacilliṅgasya saṁbandhagrahaṇāsaṁbhavāt*, SD., p. 87.

comparison (*upamāna*) or testimony, since it is not due to any knowledge of similarity or of words and sentences. Hence to explain the direct knowledge of the jar's non-existence we have to recognise *anupalabdhi* or non-perception as a separate and independent source of knowledge. All non-perception, however, does not prove the non-existence of what is not perceived. We cannot perceive such supersensible entities as *dharma* and *adharma,* ether and atom. Yet we so not judge them to be non-existent. Non-perception gives us the knowledge of the non-existence of such objects as should have been perceived if they existed. If a thing should be perceived under certain circumstances, then its non-perception under those circumstances is a proof of its non-existence. It is this appropriate (*yogyānupalabdhi*) that is the source of our knowledge of non-existence.[1]

The Naiyāyikas, Sāṅkhyas[2] and others controvert the above view of *anupalabdhi* as an independent source of the knowledge of non-existence. According to them, such knowledge does not require *anupalabdhi* as a separate source of knowledge, but is a special case of perception. Just as we perceive the exisence of objects, so also we can perceive their non-existence under certain conditions. When there is a jar on the table before me I perceive its existence through a direct contact between my senses and the object, jar. Hence, the exisence of the jar is directly perceived by me. But when there is no jar on the same table, I perceive its absence or non-existence as a characteristic of the table. The table is characterised by the absence of the jar. Hence the absence of the jar comes in contact with my senses through being adjectival (*viśeṣaṇa*) to the table which is in direct contact with the senses. So when I directly perceive the table, I indirectly perceive the absence of the jar on it. This perception of the absence or non-exisence of a thing, however, requires two negative conditions, namely, the non-perception (*anupalaṁbha*) of that thing and the hypothetical reasoning (*tarka*) that if it existed it would have been

1. VP. and SD., *ibid.*

2. *Evamabhāvo 'pi pratyakṣameva*, TKD., p. 50.

perceived like the table. Before we come to know the absence of the jar on the table we must be sure of the fact that we do not perceive it there. Further, we must be sure that all the conditions that are necessary for its perception are present at the time when it is not perceived. The absence of the jar is perceived by me when I do not perceive it on the table but know that it would have been perceived if it existed there. The non-existence of the jar is thus known by means of perception when it is combined with the non perception of the jar and the hypothetical reasoning about its existence.[1] That this knowledge of non-existence is a form of perception is directly felt by us. We are immediately aware of the fact that the non-existence of a jar on the table is directly known or perceived by us. *Anupalabdhi* or non-perception of the jar is a negative condition of the perception, and not the source of our knowledge of its non-existence. If non-perception be taken as a source of knowledge, then it must be either cognised by some other non-perception or not cognised at all. On the first alternative we are landed in the fallacy of *argumentum ad infinitum*. On the second, non-perception becomes identical with perception, since, like perception, it is knowledge which is not produced by any other knowledge. Hence, the Naiyāyikas conclude that non-perception is not a separate source of knowledge, but a special case of perception.[2]

We have already seen how the knowledge of non-existence, which is not due to inference or any other kind of reasoning, cannot be explained by perception. A negative fact like the non-existence of a jar is not a sensible fact like the existence of the table. We do not understand how our senses can come in contact with the absence of a thing. A man says at noon that nobody came to his house in the morning. Here we cannot suppose any contact between sense and nobody. It cannot be said that we perceive the non-existence of a thing as a characteristic or quality of the locus in which it is

1. *Tarkasahakāriṇānupalambhasanāthena pratyakṣeṇaivābhā-vagrahaṇāt,* TB., p. 15.
2. *Abhāvapratyakṣasyānubhavikatvādanupalambho'pi na pramāṇāntaram,* etc., SM., p. 502.

non-existent. To know a certain locus as characterised by the absence of an object is to know beforehand what absence or non-existence is. Hence our primary knowledge of non-existence cannot be a perception of it as the quality of any locus, like the red colour of a rose. Nor can it be said that we are immediately aware of he fact that the non-existence of a thing is *perceived*. What we immediately know is that we do *not perceive* a thing in a certain place. This absence of perception gives us the knowledge of its non-existence. The Naiyāyikas practically admit this when they take non-perception as the antecedent condition of the perception of non-existence. If to perceive the non-existence of a thing we are to make sure that we do not perceive it under favourable circumstances, then we are to say that it is the absence of perception that assures us of the thing's non-existence. Hence, we conclude that *anupalabdhi* or non-perception should be recognised as separate source of knowledge to explain our primary cognition of the non-existence of objects.

4. *Smṛti* or Memory as a Distinct Source of Knowledge

We have already given an account of the views of the different schools of Indian philosophy with regard to *smṛti* or memory. It may be recalled here that with the exception of the Jaina, the Vaiśeṣika and the Advaita Vedānta system, all the schools are definitely opposed to *smṛti* being regarded as a form of valid knowledge. All these schools agree in holding that *smṛti* is knowledge which is solely due to the impressions of past experiences. In it there is a revival of the impressions of some old experience and consequently a repetition of the experience itself in the form of images. *Smṛti* as a revival of past experiences has been excluded from the forms of valid knowledge on two main grounds. First, it has been urged by the Mīmāṁsakas that *smṛti* does not give us any new knowledge but is only the revival of some old knowledge. In it we do not know anything new, but only remember that we knew something before. Then the Naiyāyikas, who do not accept this as a conclusive reason, argue hat *smṛti* is not *pramā* or valid knowledge because it is not *anubhava* or presentative knowledge. In it we have the knowledge of what was once given in our experience, but has now ceased to be given and presented to us. It is not the presentation of any objective fact but the representation of what was once presented. The object as remembered is different from the presented object, since the object as presented before has now ceased to exist. Hence, we cannot speak of a true correspondence between memory and its objects (*yāthārthya*).

The Jainas who accept *smṛti* or memory as a source of valid knowledge refute the above grounds urged against it. According to them, *smṛti* is not merely a revival of the impressions of past experience. While the origin of memory is conditioned by the revival of impressions of past experiences, its essence lies in the knowledge of something as 'that,' *i.e.* as past (*tadityākāra*).[1] It is the knowledge of a previously experienced object as past. To put it in the words of Hobhouse, 'memory is an assertion of the past as past.' That memory refers to a previously experienced object, or that it is an assertion of the past, it known from memory itself. Such knowledge of the past by means of memory is valid, since, like perception, it leads to successful activity. We cannot deny the validity of the knowledge by memory simply on the ground that it refers to a previously known object. If memory becomes invalid because its object is previously known, then the perception of the fire which is already known by inference would become invalid. Lastly, if memory be invalid, then all inferences which are based on the remembrance of *vyāpti* between the major and the middle term would become invalid.[2] How can any knowledge be valid when it has its basis in memory which is invalid? The validity of memory is presupposed in the validity of inference as a source of knowledge.

Some Vaiśeṣika writers also are in favour of accepting *smṛti* as a source of our knowledge of the past. Laugākṣi Bhāskara

1. *Tadityākārānubhūtārthaviṣayā hi pratītiḥ smṛtirityucyate*, *Prameya-kamalamārtaṇḍa*, p. 96.
2. *Na cāsāvapramāṇaṁ saṁvādakatvāt.....ko hi smṛtipūrvakamanumāna-mabhyupagmya punbastāṁ nirkuryāt*, etc., *ibid.*, pp. 96-97.

recognises both memory and presentative cognition (*smṛtyanubhava*) as forms of valid knowledge and their instrumental or special causes as sources of knowledge. According to him, *smṛti* or memory arises out of the impressions of past experience and is the knowledge of an individual object as 'that' or as something previously experienced, *e.g.* 'that bathing *ghat*,' 'that city of Benares.'[1] Vallabhācārya proves on strong grounds that *smṛti* or memory also is an independent source of knowledge. *Smṛti* is a separate *pramāṇa* because it gives us a true knowledge of certain facts (*arthaniścayahetutvāt*). The fact that it depends on previous experience is on reason for denying its independence, for that is something common to all the *pramāṇas* or sources of knowledge. It cannot be said that it is merely the repetition of some previous experience. It is something more than the faint repetition of a past experience. If it were not so, we could not at all know that the experience is past. In *smṛti* or memory we know an object as that which is past. The awareness of its 'pastness' is no part of our previous experience of it. It is memory that gives a knowledge of this new element, namely, the 'thatness' or the 'pastness' of an object, and is, therefore, an independent source of knowledge. Hence, the Mīmāṁsaka contention that memory does not give us any new knowledge falls to the ground. Then the Naiyāyikas' objection that *smṛti* or memory does not correspond to its object is also untenable. It is true that in memory an object is thought of as being present at some time in the past (*pūrvavartamānakālā-vacchinna*) and that its once present condition has now been extinct (*nivṛttapūrvāvasthā*). But this is no good ground for denying the correspondence between memory and its object. When we remember an object, we are aware of representing it as no longer present or with its old conditions as now extinct. The object is therefore faithfully represented in memory. It follows from this that memory is the true knowledge of an object.[2] We may add also

1. *Saṁskāramātrajanyaṁ jñānaiṁ smṛtiḥ, yathā sā maṇikarṇikā... smṛtya-nubhavasādhāraṇaṁ pramākaraṇam pramāṇam, Tarkakaumudī.* p. 6.
2. *Smṛtirapi mānāntarameva, arthaniścayahetutvāt, anubhavapāratant-ruānnaivam iti cet, na, utpattipāratantryasya pramāṇāntarasāmyāt.*

that memory is a presentative knowledge (*anubhava*), since it is based on an objective order of things in the world. As we have already seen, *anubhava* or presentative knowledge is the cognition of what is objective (*tattva*) as distinguished from the false or the subjective (*āropita*). In presentative knowledge the object need not be directly given as in perception, for that will exclude inference, comparison and testimony from the field of *anubhava* or presentative knowledge. All these, however, are recognised by the Naiyāyikas as forms of presentative knowledge. What is common to all these recognised forms of presentative knowledge is not that they give us an immediate knowledge of some object, but that they refer, either directly or indirectly, to an objective fact or an objective order of facts. In this sense *smṛti* or memory is as good a presentative knowledge as any other recognised by the Nyāya or any other school of Indian philosophy. The fact that an object is past is as objective as the present existence of another.[1] Hence, memory as the knowledge of the past *as* past is a true presentative knowledge (*yathārthānubhava*). To explain such knowledge of the past we have to accept *smṛti* or memory as a separate source of knowledge (*pramāṇa*).

Among Western thinkers Russell, Hobhouse and others recognise memory as the primary source of all our knowledge concerning the past. They agree in holding that we may know the past in other ways too, for example, by reading history or by inference. But these cannot give us any knowledge of the past unless we have already a direct knowledge of it through memory. Thus, Russell says: "It is obvious that we often remember what we have seen or heard or had otherwise present to our senses, and that in such cases we are still immediately aware of what we remember, in spite of the fact that it appears as past and not as present. This

---

Adhikaparicchede ca pramāṇatvāt, anyathā tadvyavasthānupapatteḥ tatrāvacchinnaṁ hi smṛtirarthamākalayati, sā ca yadi pūrvānbhavasyāpi gocaraḥ, tadā tatrāpi tadityullekhaḥ syāt...na cet, smṛtireva tatrānapekṣeti mānam, Nyāyalīlāvatī, pp. 67-68.

1. *Cf.* H. H. Price, *Perception*, p. 11: "The past is as much a part of the real world as the present, and quite as interesting."

immediate knowledge by memory is the source of all our knowledge concerning the past; without it, there could be no knowledge of the past by inference, since we should never know that there was anything past to be inferred."[1] In another place Russell observes that memory resembles perception in point of immediacy and differs from it mainly by being referred to the past.[2] Similarly, Hobhouse[3] shows that memory is neither the retention of past experience, nor a mere image of past experience, but an assertion of the past *as* past on the basis of such retention and images. Without a direct knowledge of the past by memory we cannot understand retention as an effect of past experience nor an image as an image of the past. It cannot be said that we may know the past by inference from the retention or impression of past experience or from its revival as an image. For, as both Prabhācandra[4] and Hobhouse point out, inference in its turn involves memory. Further, we cannot understand anything as a sign or mark from which to infer the past unless we first know that past as signified or marked by such and such things. Hence, Hobhouse takes memory as a fresh postulate of knowledge. "It is," he says, "a direct or immediate belief about the past, not a belief based on some other truth."[5] A. C. Ewing[6] also thinks that 'the direct view of memory is clearly true if we have any knowledge of the past at all. If we know the past, it is the past we know and not our present ideas.' It is a mistake to suppose, as the Naiyāyikas do, 'that if we are directly aware of the past, the past must be, so to speak, bodily present to our mind or occupy the same position as our present objects of perception.' Thus according to these Western thinkers, memory gives us an immediate knowledge of the present. Hence there can be no objection to memory being regarded as true presentative knowledge

1. *The Problems of Philosophy*, p. 76.
2. *The Analysis of Mind*, p. 173.
3. *The Theory of Knowledge*, Pt. I, Ch. IV.
4. *Vide Prameyakamalamārtaṇḍa*, *ibid.*
5. Hobhouse, *op. cit.*, p. 76.
6. *Mind*, April, 1930, p. 142.

(*yathārthānubhava*). This view of the matter removes the last vestige of the difficulties in the way of taking *smṛti* or memory as a *pramāṇa* or source of valid knowledge. In fact, it stands next to perception in the order of priority among the sources of valid knowledge. All sources of knowledge other than perception involve memory of some kind as one of their conditions. Inference cannot take place without the memory of a universal relation between two things (*vyāpti*). *Upamāna* or comparison depends on memory of the knowledge communicated by a reliable person. In *śabda* or testimony we depend on memory in order to understand the meanings of words and to synthesise the meanings of the separate words into the construed meaning of the sentence. *Arthāpatti* or postulation involves a conflict between the order of our past experience as remembered and that of our present experience. *Anupalabdhi* or non-perception also implies a contrast between the memory of something and the absence of perception with regard to it. Hence, finally, we have to accept seven separate sources of knowledge which may be arranged in order of priority as follows: perception, memory, non-perception, inference, comparison, testimony and postulation.

5. Summary and General Estimate of Nyāya Epistemology

The Nyāya theory of knowledge discusses all the important problems of logic and he relevant problems of metaphysics. It formulates a realistic theory and tries to meet the idealist's objections against realism as a system of philosophy. According to it, knowledge is a quality of the soul, which manifests the objects of the world. All knowledge of objects, however, is not valid. For knowledge, to be valid means to be *given* (*anubhava*) in some way or other, and to have an assurance of truth in it. The truth of knowledge consists in its correspondence to real facts and the test of truth lies in its pragmatic value and the coherence or 'consilience' of its different parts. It follows from this that memory and dream, doubt, error and hypothetical reasoning (*tarka*) cannot be regarded as valid knowledge, since they are either not given or not true cognitions of objects. These are, therefore, brought by the

Naiyāyikas under the class of non-valid knowledge which includes all cognitions which are either not given and true, or are false. The falsity of knowledge is constituted by its non-correspondence to facts and is known through failure of the practical activities inspired by it. It follows that truth and falsity are not intrinsic to knowledge and that these are extrinsic characters determined by external conditions like correspondence and non-correspondence to reality respectively. So also, no knowledge is by itself known to be true or false. That is, truth or falsity is not-self-evident in any knowledge, but must be evidenced by external conditions like the success or failure of practical activity.

There are four kinds of valid knowledge and so four distinct and independent methods of knowledge. These are: perception, inference, comparison and testimony. While the old Naiyāyikas define perception as an unerring cognition produced by sense-object contact, the moderns define it as immediate knowledge or as knowledge not brought about by any antecedent knowledge. There are five external senses and an internal sense called *manas* which is necessary to explain the perception of the soul and its states and processes. The individual soul is an eternal and all-pervading substance which is not essentially conscious, but has the quality of consciousness when it comes into relation with external objects through the senses. Corresponding to the six senses, there are six kinds of ordinary perceptions which give us direct knowledge of all perceptible objects including substances, their qualities and actions, universals, relations and the four kinds of non-existence. There are seven categories of reality, of which six stand for positive, and the last for negative facts. Of positive facts, substance, attribute and action are said to be existents, while generality, particularity, and inherence are called subsistents. Non-existence is a negative but real fact and, according to the Naiyāyika, there may be a direct perception of it along with that of the positive fact which it qualifies. Of ordinary perception, there are three modes, namely, the *nirvikalpala*, the *savikalpaka* and *pratyabhijñā* or recognition. These represent different stages in the development of our perceptual consciousness, but they are equally valid and refer to real contents of the objects of perception. In addition to ordinary perception, the modern Naiyāyikas distinguish three kinds of extraordinary perception called *sāmānyalakṣaṇa, jñānalakṣaṇa* and *yogaja*. The first two are recognised by them as necessary to explain the perception of objects by senses which are not ordinarily competent to perceive them, and the last to explain the supernormal cognition of objects, which cannot be brought about by any sense.

Inference is a type of syllogistic reasoning in which we pass from the apprehension of some mark or sign as related to an object, to something else, by virtue of a relation of invariable concomitance between the two. It is an argument in which some thinker asserts that a certain proposition is true because certain other propositions, which imply it, are asserted to be true. Thus inference is a combined deductive-inductive process which ensures both the validity of the reasoning employed and the truth of the conclusion reached. An inference must have as its constituents three terms and a least three propositions. There are three conditions of valid inference, namely, *vyāpti* or a universal relation between the middle and the major term, *pakṣatā* or the assertion of the minor term, and *liṅgaparāmarśa* or a synthetic view of the middle term as related to the major, on the one hand, and the minor, on the other. *Vyāpti* is the logical ground on which the validity of inference depends. It is an inductive generalisation based ultimately on the direct perception of the universal in the particular. *Pakṣatā* is the psychological ground which conditions the possibility of inference and is defined by the modern Naiyāyikas as the absence of the condition in which there is certainty but no will to infer. *Liṅgaparāmarśa* as the correlation of the major, middle and minor and minor terms is useful for demonstrating the truth of the conclusion. These three steps, together with the initial statement of the object of inference and final conclusion, give us the five-membered form of the syllogism. Since inference is a combined deductive-inductive reasoning in the form of a categorical syllogism, we have not a classification of inferences into deductive-inductive and mediate, syllogistic and non-syllogistic, pure and mixed. Having regard to their purposes, or the nature of *vyāpti,* or the nature of the induction on which it is based, inferences are classified into *svārtha* and *parātha,* or into *pūrvavat, śeṣavat* and *sāmānyatodṛṣṭa*. The fallacies of inference are all material fallacies which affects the truth of the propositions involved in inference. They ultimately arise out of a fallacious reason or middle term. There are six kind of fallacious middle terms which violate one or other of the conditions of a valid middle term. A logically valid inference must be free from all kinds of fallacies.

Comparison is the source of our knowledge of the denotation of a word on the basis of a given description of the objects denoted by it. Thus a man may be told: "A *gavaya* is an animal resembling the cow," If, on subsequently seeing a *gavaya,* he is able to give its name, we are to say that he understands the denotation word through comparison. Comparison is of different kinds, according to the different terms in which the description may be given. It is true that comparison involves an element of perception and of testimony. The description comes to us a the statement of some authority and, as such, is a kind of verbal testimony. So also, we know by perception that certain objects possess the characters mentioned in the given description. Still comparison cannot be reduced to perception and testimony, because these will not reduced to perception and testimony, because these will not explain the application of the name to the relevant objects, which is the essence of comparison. Nor can we explain it by inference, for when we known the denotation of a word from a given description, we do not reason syllogistically, but simply compare certain object with a given description. To understand the denotation of a word in this way requires a selective activity of the mind, which is different form perception, inference and testimony. Therefore, comparison is a distinct method or source of knowledge.

Testimony is the statement of an authoritative person, which serves to give us true knowledge about certain objects. It may come to us in the form of either spoken or written words and may relate to perceptible or imperceptible objects. In any case, there must be a significant combination of the words according to four conditions. They must imply one another and express compatible ideas. There must be adequate proximity among them, and they must convey the intention of the speaker or the writer who uses them. Testimony is the source of the greater part of a man's knowledge of the world. As the verbal knowledge of objects, it is distinct from all other kinds of knowledge. Perception, inference or comparison cannot take the place of testimony, although there may be in it an element of this or that other knowledge. It is true that testimony ultimately depends on perception or inference for its validity or for the proof of its validity. Again, there may sometimes be a conflict of authorities. Since, however, these difficulties are not peculiar to it, but rather common to all the sources of human knowledge, there is no reason why testimony should not be recognised as an independent method of knowledge like perception and inference. If in spite of the conflict of perceptions or of inferences, and the need of their mutual verification, we accept them as independent methods, we must accept testimony and comparison also as equally independent sources of knowledge. All other sources of valid knowledge including non-perception and postulation are brought by the Naiyāyikas under perception, inference, comparison and testimony. Non-perception need not be admitted as a separate source of knowledge to explain our knowledge on non-existence, for it may be perceived by us as adjectival to the existent object which is its locus. So also, postulation my be reduced to *vyatireki* inference and need not be made a separate method of knowledge. For the Naiyāyikas, then, there are four distinct and independent sources of knowledge.

As a realistic theory of knowledge, based on the evidence of direct experience, the Nyāya epistemology has a strong appeal to our common sense. It has also a great value for the orientation of philosophical problems from the common-sense standpoint. But undue reliance on uncriticised experience and common-sense has been the source of certain defects in the Nyāya theory. The Nyāya conception of knowledge as an adventitious quality of the soul substance is true neither to the nature of knowledge nor to that of the soul. To say that knowledge is a quality is to leave unexplained the fact of self-transcendence and ideal reference to objects, which is inherent in knowledge. As we have already observed, knowledge is the most fundamental fact of reality. The distinctions of substance and quality, subject and object, all fall within knowledge and are intelligible only on the ground of knowledge. In this sense knowledge is the *essence* of the ultimate reality which we call the soul or the self. It does not require to be attached as a quality to any other reality, say matter or mind or soul. It is just the self-expression of reality itself. If this be true, then we must give up the Nyāya theory of the individual self as a substance which is not essentially conscious, but is accidentally qualified by consciousness when associated with a body. Such a view of the self is contradicted by the evidence of our introspective consciousness which reveals the self as a conscious subject and not as a thing with the quality of consciousness. Further, on this theory, the disembodied soul will have no consciousness and will, therefore, be indistinguishable from a material substance. So, also, we must give up the idea of an ultimate dualism or opposition between subject and object, mind and matter. To the ordinary understanding, these appear to be two opposed substances which can hardly come into any relation with one another. The Naiyāyika does not go far beyond this common-sense view when he treats the psychological distinction between knowledge and its object as the ground of an ultimate dualism between soul and matter as two realities. In truth, however, the distinction between subject and object, mind and matter is a relative distinction made within knowledge. So, it presupposes the reality of a transcendent self which makes the distinction and is the ground of both the objective and subjective, the material and mental orders of existence. On the purely logical side also the Nyāya theory appears to be inadequate on some points. The view that truth is not self-evident in any knowledge, but requires all cases to be evidenced by independent grounds, logically commits us the fallacy of infinite regress. But, as we have already seen, the self is a self-evident reality which does not require and possibly cannot admit of any other proof, for every proof presupposes the reality of the self as concerned in the act of proving. Some Naiyāyikas practically admit this when they say that the truth of self-consciousness (*anuvyavasāya*) is self-evident. So, also, there seems to be no good ground for the Naiyāyikas's refusal to admit memory, non-perception and postulation as independent ways of knowing. But for memory, we cannot have any knowledge of the past. Memory cannot be explained as a reproduction of past experiences, due solely to the impressions left by them. We could not know certain states as impressions or reproductions of past experiences, it we had not already known the past directly through memory. We may have a direct knowledge of the fact of non-existence, just as we have that of existent facts. But from this we should not conclude that this direct experience is as much a matter of sense perception in the one case as in the other. The truth of the matter is that while the existent is *perceived,* what is not non-existent is *not perceived,* and that directly in both cases. Postulation is not the deduction of a conclusion from given premises, but the necessary supposition of a general principle as the only explanation of some given facts. For Kant the existence of God is a postulate of the moral life, not in the sense that it is deducible from certain ethical propositions, but in the sense that it is the only principle which can explain ethical propositions concerning the moral life. So, we have to admit memory, non-perception and postulation as three distinct ways of knowing in addition to the four recognised by the Naiyāyika.

Nothing that has been said above by way of criticism should give one the impression that the Nyāya epistemology has no value. Such an impression would be entirely wrong. In fact, the contribution of the Nyāya theory of knowledge is not really inferior to that of any other theory, Indian or Western. The method of logical analysis employed by the Nyāya in the study of the problems of logic and metaphysics is a valuable asset for any system of philosophy. The charge is often heard against Indian philosophy that its theories are not based on logical reasoning but on religious authority and, therefore, they are dogmatic, rather than critical. The Nyāya philosophy is a standing repudiation of this charge. The theory of knowledge, formulated by the Nyāya, is made the basis not only of the Nyāya-Vaiśeṣika, but also of other Indian systems, with slight modifications. The Nyāya applies the method of logical criticism to solve the problems of life and reality. It is by means of a sound logic that it tries to ascertain the truth and defend it against hostile criticism. Many of the contributions of this logic are of great value even at the present day. The realistic logic, or more generally, epistemology of the Nyāya will not suffer by compression with the modern realistic theories of the West.

INDEX

R

S